At Home – what the critics thought

'By now, Bryson is certainly famous enough to have got away with a far less bulging compendium. Instead, on our behalf, he's been through those hundreds of books (508 according to the bibliography) . . . He's then extracted their most arresting material and turned the result into a book that, for all its winning randomness, is **not just hugely readable but a genuine page-turner** . . . None of these things, needless to say, are as easy as Bryson in his ever-genial way makes them seem'
Daily Telegraph

'Effortlessly digestible prose, wry self-deprecating humour and lightly-worn erudition . . . **everyone will find something to surprise them**' *Economist*

'Fascinating . . . Join this amiable tour guide as he wanders through his house . . . it takes a very particular kind of thoughtfulness, as well as a bold temperament, to stuff all this research into a mattress that's supportive enough to loll about on while pondering the real subject of this book – the development of the modern world . . . his curiosity is infectious . . . **[his] enthusiasm brightens any dull corner. I recommend that you hand over control and simply enjoy the ride.** You'll be given a delightful smattering of information about everything but, weirdly, the kitchen sink' *New York Times Book Review*

'For blockbuster Bill Bryson, no subject is too vast . . . So he could write a history of the world without leaving home. And very genially and quirkily he does . . . His theme is how nowadays we take home comfort for granted, but how recently we obtained it . . . he is **very good company indeed**' *Daily Mail*

www.billbryson.co.uk

'Exuberant . . . entertaining . . . Bryson is equal to every interesting and curious fact. An unashamed and very good popularizer, **he can sum up complicated motives and remarkable feats by a series of telling anecdotes**' *TLS*

'Delightful . . . Considering our homes means a dash through history, politics, science, sex, and dozens of other fields. **If this book doesn't supply you with five years' worth of dinner conversation, you're not paying attention**' *People* Magazine

'A work of constant delight and discovery. Bryson's wit is both dry and charmingly goofy. **His great skill is to make daily life simultaneously strange and familiar, and in so doing, help us to recognise ourselves.** *At Home* is a treasure: don't leave home without it' Judith Flanders, *Sunday Telegraph*

'Enchanting . . . **a book about reinventing the ordinary, and finding the extraordinary in the humdrum business of living** . . . Bryson tackled science in his brilliant *A Short History of Nearly Everything*. This new book could as easily be categorised as "a short history of nearly everything else" . . . extraordinarily entertaining' *The Times*

'The much-loved writer takes the attention to detail that made *A Short History of Nearly Everything* such a fantastic guide to all things science, and applies it to our homes. Written in his laid-back style, this is **a wonderful celebration of what makes a house a home**' *News of the World*

'Quite as ambitious as his *A Short History of Nearly Everything*, this is **a genuinely compelling book . . . a kind of layman's encyclopaedia** full of "did you know" moments . . . This companionable volume is as dense as a rich fruit cake and, by the same measure, rewarding, too' *Country Life*

'The method is to amass a dazzling number of facts and findings from disparate sources . . . riveting . . . **arguing with Bryson is part of the enjoyment of reading him**, and accompanying him across swathes of layered history'
Victoria Glendinning, *Spectator*

'By rummaging down the back of the nation's sofa, Bryson has come up with a lighthearted and **endlessly fascinating story** . . . What you want from him is his wry humour and ability to raise a quizzical eyebrow at the sheer oddness of the human race'
Mail on Sunday

'Bryson hoards facts. He can't resist a well-turned story . . . **An idiosyncratic sweep through the makings of modernity**'
Observer

'Takes us on a tour not merely of Bryson's house but of the amazingly well-stocked mind of a man who can see a world in a grain of sand. He addresses his readers as if they were welcome visitors to his home whom he is eager both to inform and to entertain; he is **a guide of inexhaustible patience, good humour, and irresistible enthusiasm**'   Susan Hill, *The Lady*

Bill Bryson's opening lines were:

'I come from Des Moines. Someone had to.'

This is what followed:

The Lost Continent

A road trip around the puzzle that is small-town America introduces the world to the adjective 'Brysonesque'

'A very funny performance, littered with wonderful lines and memorable images' LITERARY REVIEW

Neither Here Nor There

Europe never seemed funny until Bill Bryson looked at it.

'Hugely funny (not snigger-snigger funny but great-big-belly-laugh-till-you-cry funny)' DAILY TELEGRAPH

Made in America

A compelling ride along the Route 66 of American language and popular culture gets beneath the skin of the country.

'A tremendous sassy work, full of zip, pizzazz, and all those other great American qualities' INDEPENDENT ON SUNDAY

Notes from a Small Island

A eulogy to Bryson's beloved Britain captures the very essence of the original 'green and pleasant land'.

'Not a book that should be read in public, for fear of emitting loud snorts' THE TIMES

A Walk in the Woods

Bryson's punishing (by his standards) hike across the celebrated Appalachian Trail, the longest footpath in the world.

'This is a seriously funny book' SUNDAY TIMES

Notes from a Big Country

Bryson brings his inimitable wit to bear on that strangest of phenomena – the American way of life.

'Not only hilarious but also insightful and informative'
INDEPENDENT ON SUNDAY

DOWN UNDER

An extraordinary journey to the heart of another big country – Australia.

'Bryson is the perfect travelling companion . . . When it comes to travel's peculiars the man still has no peers'   THE TIMES

A Short History of Nearly Everything

Travels through time and space to explain the world, the universe and everything.

'Truly impressive . . . It's hard to imagine a better rough guide to science'   GUARDIAN

The Life and Times of the Thunderbolt Kid

Quintessential Bryson – a funny, moving and perceptive journey through his childhood.

'He can capture the flavour of the past with the lightest of touches'
SUNDAY TELEGRAPH

At Home

On a tour of his own house, Bill Bryson gives us an instructive and entertaining history of the way we live.

'A work of constant delight and discovery . . . don't leave home without it'   SUNDAY TELEGRAPH

Also by
Bill Bryson

At Home

A SHORT HISTORY OF PRIVATE LIFE

Bill Bryson

BLACK SWAN

TRANSWORLD PUBLISHERS
61–63 Uxbridge Road, London W5 5SA
A Random House Group Company
www.transworldbooks.co.uk

AT HOME
A BLACK SWAN BOOK: 9780552772556

First published in Great Britain
in 2010 by Doubleday
an imprint of Transworld Publishers
Black Swan edition published 2011

Addresses for Random House Group Ltd companies outside the UK
can be found at: www.randomhouse.co.uk
The Random House Group Ltd Reg. No. 954009

The Random House Group Limited supports the Forest Stewardship
Council® (FSC®), the leading international forest-certification
organisation. Our books carrying the FSC label are printed on
FSC®-certified paper. FSC is the only forest-certification scheme
supported by the leading environmental organisations, including
Greenpeace. Our paper procurement policy can be found at
www.randomhouse.co.uk/environment

Typeset in 11/14pt Giovanni Book by Falcon Oast Graphic Art Ltd.
Printed and bound by CPI Group (UK) Ltd, Croydon, CR0 4YY.

10

To Jesse and Wyatt

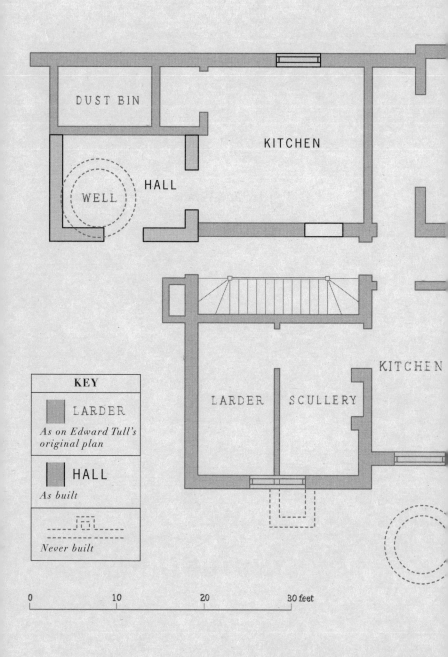

DUST BIN

KITCHEN

HALL

WELL

KITCHEN

LARDER   SCULLERY

KEY

LARDER

As on Edward Tull's original plan

HALL

As built

Never built

0   10   20   30 feet

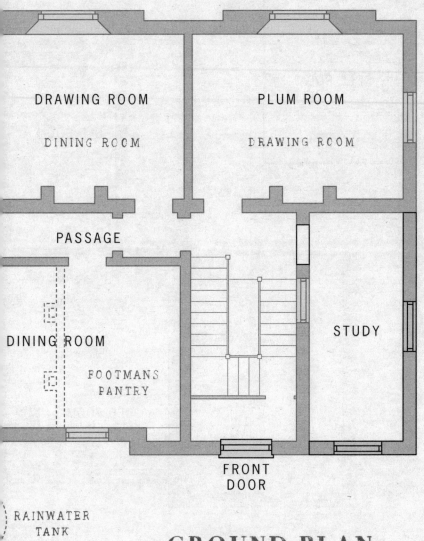

DRAWING ROOM

DINING ROOM

PLUM ROOM

DRAWING ROOM

PASSAGE

DINING ROOM

FOOTMANS
PANTRY

STUDY

FRONT
DOOR

RAINWATER
TANK

GROUND PLAN

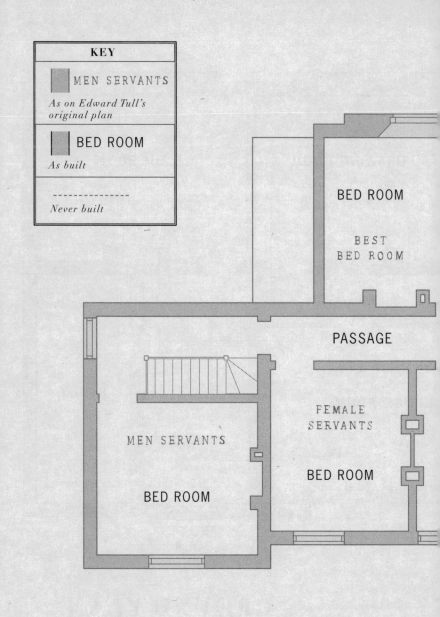

KEY

MEN SERVANTS
As on Edward Tull's original plan

BED ROOM
As built

Never built

BED ROOM

BEST BED ROOM

PASSAGE

MEN SERVANTS

BED ROOM

FEMALE SERVANTS

BED ROOM

0   10   20   30 feet

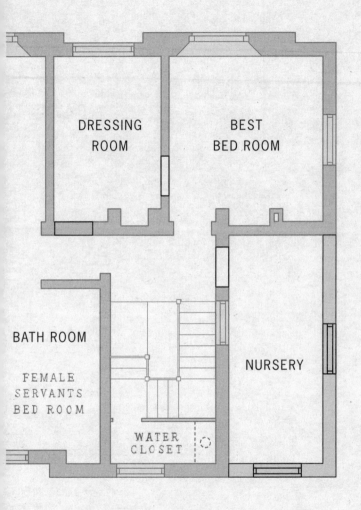

DRESSING
ROOM

BEST
BED ROOM

BATH ROOM

FEMALE
SERVANTS
BED ROOM

NURSERY

WATER
CLOSET

CHAMBER PLAN

Contents

For Notes and Sources please go to
www.billbryson.co.uk/athome

Introduction

SOME TIME AFTER we moved into a former Church of England rectory in a village of tranquil anonymity in Norfolk, I had occasion to go up into the attic to look for the source of a slow but mysterious drip. As there are no stairs to the attic in our house, the process involved a tall stepladder and much unseemly wriggling through a ceiling hatch, which was why I had not been up there before (or have returned with any enthusiasm since).

When I did finally flop into the dusty gloom and clambered to my feet, I was surprised to find a secret door, not visible from anywhere outside the house, in an external wall. The door opened easily and led out on to a tiny rooftop space, not much larger than a tabletop, between the front and back gables of the house. Victorian houses are often a collection of architectural bewilderments, but this one was starkly unfathomable: why an architect had troubled to put in a door to a space so lacking in evident need or purpose was beyond explanation, but it did have the magical and unexpected effect of providing the most wonderful view.

It is always quietly thrilling to find yourself looking at a world you know well but have never seen from such an angle before. I was perhaps fifty feet above the ground, which in mid-Norfolk more or less guarantees a panorama. Immediately in front of me was the ancient flint church to which our house was once an adjunct. Beyond, down a slight incline and slightly separate from church and rectory, was the village to which both belonged. In the distance in the other direction was Wymondham Abbey, a heap of medieval splendour commanding the southern skyline. In a field in the middle distance a tractor rumbled and drew straight lines in the soil. All else in every direction was quiet, agreeable, time-less English countryside.

What gave all this a certain immediacy was that just the day before I had walked across a good part of this view with a friend named Brian Ayers. Brian had just retired as the county archaeologist, and may know more about the history and landscape of Norfolk than anyone alive. He had never been to our village church, and was eager to have a look. It is a handsome and ancient building, older than Notre Dame in Paris and about the same vintage as Chartres and Salisbury cathedrals. But Norfolk is full of medieval churches – it has 659 of them, more per square mile than anywhere else in the world – so any one is easily overlooked.

'Have you ever noticed,' Brian asked as we stepped into the churchyard, 'how country churches nearly always seem to be sinking into the ground?' He pointed out how this one stood in a slight depression, like a weight placed on a cushion. The church foundations were about three feet below the churchyard around it. 'Do you know why that is?'

I allowed, as I often do when following Brian around, that I had no idea.

'Well, it isn't because the church is sinking,' Brian said, smiling. 'It's because the churchyard has risen. How many people do you suppose are buried here?'

I glanced appraisingly at the gravestones and said, 'I don't know. Eighty? A hundred?'

'I think that's probably a *bit* of an underestimate,' Brian replied with an air of kindly equanimity. 'Think about it. A country parish like this has an average of 250 people in it, which translates into roughly a thousand adult deaths per century, plus a few thousand more poor souls that didn't make it to maturity. Multiply that by the number of centuries that the church has been there and you can see that what you have here is not eighty or a hundred burials, but probably something more in the order of, say, twenty thousand.'

This was, bear in mind, just steps from my front door. 'Twenty *thousand*?' I said.

He nodded matter-of-factly. 'That's a lot of mass, needless to say. It's why the ground has risen three feet.' He gave me a moment to absorb this, then went on: 'There are a thousand parishes in Norfolk. Multiply all the centuries of human activity by a thousand parishes and you can see that you are looking at a lot of material culture.' He considered the several steeples that featured in the view. 'From here you can see into perhaps ten or twelve other parishes, so you are probably looking at roughly a quarter of a million burials right here in the immediate landscape – all in a place that has never been anything but quiet and rural, where nothing much has ever happened.'

All this was Brian's way of explaining how a bucolic, lightly populated county like Norfolk could produce 27,000 archaeological finds a year, more than any other county in England. 'People have been dropping things here for a long time – since long before England was England.' He showed me a map of all the known archaeo-logical finds in our parish. Nearly every field had yielded something – Neolithic tools, Roman coins and pottery, Saxon brooches, Bronze Age graves, Viking farmsteads. Just beyond the edge of our property, in 1985 a farmer cross-ing a field found a rare, impossible-to-misconstrue Roman phallic pendant.

To me that was, and remains, an amazement: the idea of a man in a toga, standing on what is now the edge of my land, patting himself all over and realizing with con-sternation that he has lost his treasured keepsake, which then lay in the soil for seventeen or eighteen centuries, through endless generations of human activity, through the comings and goings of Saxons, Vikings and Normans, through the rise of the English language, the birth of the English nation, the development of continuous monarchy and all the rest, before finally being picked up by a late-twentieth-century farmer, presumably with a look of consternation of his own.

Now as I stood on the roof of my house, taking in this unexpected view, it struck me how rather glorious it was that in two thousand years of human activity the only thing that had stirred the notice of the outside world even briefly was the finding of a Roman phallic pendant. The rest was just centuries and centuries of people quietly going about their daily business – eating, sleeping, having sex, endeavouring to be amused – and it occurred to me, with the forcefulness of a thought experienced in 360 degrees, that that's really what history mostly is: masses of people doing ordinary things. Even Einstein will have spent large parts of his life thinking about his holidays or new hammock or how dainty was the ankle on the young lady alighting from the tram across the street. These are the sorts of things that fill our lives and thoughts, and yet we treat them as incidental and hardly worthy of serious consideration. I don't know how many hours of my school years were spent studying the Missouri Compromise or the War of the Roses, but it was vastly more than I was ever encouraged or allowed to give to the history of eating, sleeping, having sex or endeavouring to be amused.

So I thought it might be interesting, for the length of a book, to consider the ordinary things in life, to notice them for once and treat them as if they were important, too. Looking around my house, I was startled and a little appalled to realize how little I knew about the domestic world around me. Sitting at the kitchen table one afternoon, playing idly with the salt and pepper shakers, it occurred to me that I had absolutely no idea why, out of all the spices in the world, we have such an abiding attachment to those two. Why not pepper and cardamom, say, or salt and cinnamon? And why do forks have four tines and not three or five? There must be reasons for these things.

Dressing, I wondered why all my suit jackets have a row of pointless buttons on every sleeve. I heard a reference on the radio to someone paying for room and board, and realized that when people talk about room and board, I have no idea what the board is that they are talking about. Suddenly the house seemed a place of mystery to me.

So I formed the idea to make a journey around it, to wander from room to room and consider how each has featured in the evolution of private life. The bathroom would be a history of hygiene, the kitchen of cooking, the bedroom of sex and death and sleeping, and so on. I would write a history of the world without leaving home.

The idea had a certain appeal, I must say. I had recently done a book in which I tried to understand the universe and how it is put together, which was a bit of an undertaking, as you will appreciate. So the idea of dealing with something as neatly bounded and cosily finite as an old rectory in an English village had obvious attractions. Here was a book I could do in carpet slippers.

In fact it was nothing like that. Houses are amazingly complex repositories. What I found, to my great surprise, is that whatever happens in the world – whatever is discovered or created or bitterly fought over – eventually ends up, in one way or another, in your house. Wars, famines, the Industrial Revolution, the Enlightenment – they are all there in your sofas and chests of drawers, tucked into the folds of your curtains, in the downy softness of your pillows, in the paint on your walls and the water in your pipes. So the history of household life isn't just a history of beds and sofas and kitchen stoves, as I had vaguely supposed it would be, but of scurvy and guano and the Eiffel Tower and bedbugs and body-snatching and just about everything else that has ever happened. Houses aren't refuges from history. They are where history ends up.

I hardly need point out that history of any kind tends to sprawl. In order to fit the story of private life into a single volume, it was obvious from the outset that I would have to be painfully selective. So, although I do venture into the distant past from time to time (you can't talk about baths without talking about Romans, for one thing), what follows mostly concentrates on events of the last 150 years or so, when the modern world was really born – coincidentally just the period that the house we are about to wander through has existed.

We are so used to having a lot of comfort in our lives – to being clean, warm and well fed – that we forget how recent most of that is. In fact, it took us for ever to achieve these things, and then they mostly came in a rush. How that happened when it did, and why it took so long to get it, is what the following pages are all about.

Though I have not identified the village in which the Old Rectory stands, I should note that the house is real, as are (or were) the people mentioned in relation to it. I should also note that the passage referring to the Reverend Thomas Bayes in Chapter One appeared in slightly different form in an introduction I wrote for *Seeing Further: The Story of Science and the Royal Society*.

Interior view of Joseph Paxton's ethereal Crystal Palace at the Great Exhibition of 1851. The gates are still standing in Kensington Gardens.

CHAPTER ONE

The Year

I

IN THE AUTUMN OF 1850, in Hyde Park in London, there arose a most extraordinary structure: a giant iron and glass greenhouse covering nineteen acres of ground and containing within its airy vastness enough room for four St Paul's Cathedrals. For the short time of its existence, it was the biggest building on earth. Known formally as the Palace of the Great Exhibition of the Works of Industry of All Nations, it was incontestably magnificent, but all the more so for being so sudden, so startlingly glassy, so gloriously and unexpectedly *there*. Douglas Jerrold, a columnist for the weekly magazine *Punch*, dubbed it the Crystal Palace, and the name stuck.

It had taken just five months to build. It was a miracle that it was built at all. Less than a year earlier it had not even existed as an idea. The exhibition for which it was conceived was the dream of a civil servant named Henry Cole, whose other principal claim to history's attention is as the inventor of the Christmas card (as a way of encouraging people to use the new penny post). In 1849 Cole visited the Paris Exhibition – a comparatively parochial affair, limited to French manufacturers – and became keen to try something similar in England, but grander. He persuaded many worthies, including Prince Albert, to get excited about the idea of a Great Exhibition, and on 11 January 1850 they held their first meeting with a view to opening on 1 May of the following year. This gave them slightly less than sixteen months to design and erect the largest building ever envisioned, attract and install tens of thousands of displays from every quarter of the globe, fit out restaurants and restrooms, employ staff, arrange insurance and police protection, print up hand-bills, and a million other things, in a country that wasn't at all convinced it wanted such a costly and disruptive production in the first place. It was a patently unachievable ambition, and for the next several months they patently failed to achieve it. In an open competition, 245 designs for the exhibition hall were submitted. All were rejected as unworkable.

Facing disaster, the committee did what committees in desperate circumstances sometimes do: it commissioned another committee with a better title. The Building Committee of the Royal Commission for the Great Exhibition of the Works of Industry of All Nations con-sisted of four men – Matthew Digby Wyatt, Owen Jones, Charles Wild, and the great engineer Isambard Kingdom Brunel – and a single instruction, to come up with a design worthy of the greatest exhibition in history, to begin in ten months, within a constrained and shrunken budget. Of the four committee members, only the youthful Wyatt was a trained architect, and he had not yet actually built anything; at this stage of his career he made his living as a writer. Wild was an engineer whose experience was almost exclusively with boats and bridges. Jones was an interior decorator. Only Brunel had experience of large-scale projects. He was indubitably a genius, but an unnerving one as it nearly always took epic infusions of time and cash to find a point of intersection between his soaring visions and an achievable reality.

The structure the four men came up with now was a thing of unhappy wonder. A vast, low, dark shed of a building, pregnant with gloom, with all the spirit and playfulness of an abattoir, it looked like something designed in a hurry by four people working separately. The cost could scarcely be calculated, but it was almost certainly unbuildable anyway. Construction would require thirty million bricks and there was no guarantee that such a number could be acquired, much less laid, in time. The whole was to be capped off by Brunel's contribution: an iron dome two hundred feet across – a striking feature, without question, but rather an odd one on a one-storey building. No one had ever built such a massive thing of iron before, and Brunel couldn't of course begin to tinker and hoist until there was a building beneath it – and all of this to be undertaken and completed in ten months, for a project intended to stand for less than half a year. Who would take it all down afterwards and what would become of its mighty dome and millions of bricks were questions too uncomfortable to consider.

Into this unfolding crisis stepped the calm figure of Joseph Paxton, head gardener of Chatsworth House, principal seat of the Duke of Devonshire (but located in that peculiar English way in Derbyshire). Paxton was a wonder. Born into a poor farming family in Bedfordshire in 1803, he was sent out to work as an apprentice gardener at the age of fourteen, but so distinguished himself that within six years he was running an experimental arboretum for the new and prestigious Horticultural Society (soon to become the Royal Horticultural Society) in west London – a startlingly responsible job for someone who was really still just a boy. There one day he fell into conversation with the Duke of Devonshire, who owned neighbouring Chiswick House and rather a lot of the rest of the British Isles – some two hundred thousand acres of productive countryside spread beneath seven great stately homes. The duke took an instant shine to Paxton, not so much, it appears, because Paxton showed any particular genius as because he spoke in a strong, clear voice. The duke was hard of hearing and appreciated clarity of speech. Impulsively, he invited Paxton to be head gardener at Chatsworth. Paxton accepted. He was twenty-two years old.

It was the most improbably wise move any aristocrat has ever made. Paxton leapt into the job with levels of energy and application that simply dazzled. He designed and installed the famous Emperor Fountain, which could send a jet of water 290 feet into the air – a feat of hydraulic engineering that has still been exceeded only once in Europe; built the largest rockery in the country; designed a new estate village; became the world's leading expert on the dahlia; won prizes for producing the country's finest melons, figs, peaches and nectarines; and created an enormous tropical hothouse, known as the Great Stove, which covered an acre of ground and was so roomy within that Queen Victoria, on a visit in 1843, was able to tour it in a horse-drawn carriage. Through improved estate management, he eliminated £1 million from the duke's debts. With the duke's blessing, he launched and ran two gardening magazines and a national daily newspaper, the *Daily News*, which was briefly edited by Charles Dickens. He wrote books on gardening, invested so wisely in the shares of railway companies that he was invited on to the boards of three of them, and at Birkenhead, near Liverpool, designed and built the world's first municipal park. This so captivated the American Frederick Law Olmsted that he modelled Central Park in New York on it. In 1849, the head botanist at Kew sent Paxton a rare and ailing lily, wondering if he could save it. Paxton designed a special hothouse and – you won't be surprised to hear – within three months had it flowering.

When he learned that the commissioners of the Great Exhibition were struggling to find a design for their hall, it occurred to him that something like his hothouses might work. While chairing a meeting of a committee of the Midland Railway, he doodled a rough design on a piece of blotting paper and had completed drawings ready for review in two weeks. The design actually broke all the competition rules. It was submitted after the closing date and, for all its glass and iron, it incorporated many combustible materials – acres of wooden flooring, for one thing – which were strictly forbidden. The architectural consultants pointed out, not unreasonably, that Paxton was not a trained architect and had never attempted anything on this scale before. But then, of course, no one had. For that reason, nobody could declare with complete confidence that the scheme would work. Many worried that the building would grow insupportably warm when filled with baking sunshine and jostling crowds. Others feared that the lofty glazing bars would expand in the summer's heat and that giant panes of glass would silently fall out and crash on to the throngs below. The profoundest worry was that the whole frail-looking edifice would simply blow away in a storm.

So the risks were considerable and keenly felt, yet after only a few days of fretful hesitation the commissioners approved Paxton's plan. Nothing – really, absolutely nothing – says more about Victorian Britain and its capacity for brilliance than that the century's most daring and iconic building was entrusted to a gardener. Paxton's Crystal Palace required no bricks at all – indeed, no mortar, no cement, no foundations. It was just bolted together and sat on the ground like a tent. This was not merely an ingenious solution to a monumental challenge, but a radical departure from anything that had ever been tried before.

The central virtue of Paxton's airy palace was that it could be prefabricated from standard parts. At its heart was a single component – a cast-iron truss 3 feet wide and 23 feet 3 inches long – which could be fitted together with matching trusses to make a frame on which to hang the building's glass – nearly a million square feet of it, or a third of all the glass normally produced in Britain in a year. A special mobile platform was designed that moved along the roof supports enabling workmen to install 18,000 panes of glass a week – a rate of productivity that was, and is, a wonder of efficiency. To deal with the enormous amount of guttering required – some twenty miles in all – Paxton designed a machine, manned by a small team, that could attach two thousand feet of guttering a day – a quantity that would previously have represented a day's work for three hundred men. In every sense the project was a marvel.

Paxton was very lucky in his timing, for just at the moment of the Great Exhibition glass suddenly became available in a way it never had before. Glass had always been a tricky material. It was really hard to make well, and not particularly easy to make at all, which is why for so much of its history it was a luxury item. Happily, two recent technological breakthroughs had changed that. First, the French invented plate glass – so called because the molten glass was spread across tables known as plates. This allowed for the first time the creation of really large panes of glass, which made shop windows possible. Plate glass, however, had to be cooled for ten days after being rolled out, which meant that each table was out of action most of the time, and then each sheet required a lot of grinding and polishing. This naturally made it expensive. In 1838, a cheaper refinement was developed – sheet glass. This had most of the virtues of plate glass, but cooled faster and needed less polishing, so could be made much more cheaply. Suddenly glass of a good size could be produced economically in limitless volumes.

Allied with this was the timely abolition of two long-standing taxes: the window tax and glass tax (which, strictly speaking, was an excise duty). The window tax dated from 1696 and was sufficiently punishing that people really did avoid putting windows in buildings where they could. The bricked-up window openings that are such a feature of many period buildings in Britain today were once usually painted to look like windows. (It is sometimes rather a shame that they aren't still.) The tax was sorely resented as 'a tax on air and light', and meant that many servants and others of constrained means were condemned to live in airless rooms.

The second duty, introduced in 1746, was based not on the number of windows but on the weight of the glass within them, so glass was made thin and weak throughout the Georgian period, and window frames had to be compensatingly sturdy. The well-known bull's-eye panes also became a feature at this time. They are a consequence of the type of glass-making that produced what was known as crown glass (so called because it is slightly convex, or crown-shaped). The bull's-eye marked the place on a sheet of glass where the blower's pontil – the blowing tool – had been attached. Because that part of the glass was flawed, it escaped the tax and so developed a certain appeal among the frugal. Bull's-eye panes became popular in cheap inns and businesses and at the backs of private homes where quality was not an issue. The glass levy was abolished in 1845, just shy of its hundredth anniversary, and the abolition of the window tax followed, conveniently and fortuitously, in 1851. Just at the moment when Paxton wanted more glass than anyone ever had before, the price was reduced by more than half. This, along with the technological changes that independently boosted production, was the impetus that made the Crystal Palace possible.

The finished building was precisely 1,851 feet long (in celebration of the year), 408 feet across and almost 110 feet high along its central spine – spacious enough to enclose a much admired avenue of elms that would otherwise have had to be felled. Because of its size, the structure required a lot of inputs: 293,655 panes of glass, 33,000 iron trusses and tens of thousands of feet of wooden flooring, yet thanks to Paxton's methods the final cost came in at an exceedingly agreeable £80,000. From start to finish, the work took just under thirty-five weeks. St Paul's Cathedral had taken thirty-five years.

Two miles away the new Houses of Parliament had been under construction for a decade and still weren't anywhere near complete. A writer for *Punch* suggested, only half in jest, that the government should commission Paxton to design a Crystal Parliament. A catchphrase arose for any problem that proved intractable: 'Ask Paxton.'

The Crystal Palace was at once the world's largest building and its lightest, most ethereal one. Today we are used to encountering glass in volume, but to someone living in 1851 the idea of strolling through cubic acres of airy light *inside* a building was dazzling – indeed, giddying. The arriving visitor's first sight of the Exhibition Hall from afar, glinting and transparent, is really beyond our imagining. It would have seemed as delicate and evanescent, as miraculously improbable, as a soap bubble. To anyone arriving at Hyde Park, the first sight of the Crystal Palace, floating above the trees, sparkling in sunshine, would have been a moment of knee-weakening splendour.

II

As the Crystal Palace rose in London, one hundred and ten miles to the north-east, beside an ancient country church, under the spreading skies of Norfolk, a rather more modest edifice went up in 1851 in a village near the market town of Wymondham: a parsonage of a vague and rambling nature, beneath an irregular rooftop of barge-boarded gables and jaunty chimney stacks in a cautiously

Gothic style – 'a good-sized house, and comfortable enough in a steady, ugly, respectable way', as Margaret Oliphant, a hugely popular and prolific Victorian novelist, described the breed in her novel *The Curate in Charge*.

This is the building to which we shall be attached over the next five hundred pages. It was designed by one Edward Tull of Aylsham, an architect fascinatingly devoid of conventional talent, as we shall see, for a young clergyman of good breeding named Thomas J. G. Marsham. Aged twenty-nine, Marsham was the beneficiary of a system that provided him and others like him with an extremely good living and required little in return.

In 1851, when our story opens, there were 17,621 Anglican clergy, and a country rector, with only 250 or so souls in his care, enjoyed an average income of £500 – as much as a senior civil servant like Henry Cole, the man behind the Great Exhibition. Going into the church became one of the two default activities for the younger sons of peers and gentry (a career in the military was the other) so they often brought family wealth to the position as well. Many livings also carried substantial income through rents of glebe lands, or farmland, that came with the appointment. Even the least privileged incumbents were generally well off. Jane Austen grew up in what she considered to be an embarrassingly deficient rectory at Steventon in Hampshire, but it had a drawing room, kitchen, parlour, study and library, and seven bedrooms – scarcely a hardship posting. The richest living of all was at Doddington in Cambridgeshire, which had 38,000 acres of land and produced an annual income of £7,300 – perhaps as much as £5 million in today's money – for the lucky parson until the estate was broken up in 1865.*

Clergymen in the Church of England were of two types: vicars and rectors. The difference was a narrow one ecclesiastically but a broad one economically. Historically, vicars were stand-ins for rectors (the word is related to *vicarious*, indicating a surrogate role), but by Mr Marsham's day that distinction had largely faded away and whether a parson (from *persona ecclesiae*) was called vicar or rector was largely a matter of local tradition. There was, however, a lingering difference in income.

A clergyman's pay came not from the Church but from rents and tithes. Tithes were of two kinds: great tithes, which came from main crops like wheat and barley, and small tithes, from vegetable gardens, mast and other incidental provender. Rectors got the great tithes and vicars the small ones, which meant that rectors tended to be the wealthier of the two, sometimes very considerably so. Tithes were a chronic source of tension between Church and farmer, and in 1836, the year before Queen Victoria ascended the throne, it was decided to simplify matters. Henceforth instead of giving the local clergyman an agreed portion of his crop, the farmer would pay him a fixed

* Comparing values of 1851 with those of today is not straightforward because those values can be calculated using many different measures, and items that might be expensive now (farmland, live-in servants) were often comparatively cheap then and vice versa. So, depending on which method of comparison is used, Mr Marsham's £500 of 1851 would today be worth anything from £40,000 (using retail price indices as the basis for calculation), to well over £1 million (using a measure of gross domestic product). An average of the six most common measures give a figure of about £200,000. Per capita income in Britain in 1851 was just slightly over £20.

annual sum based on the general worth of his land. This meant that the clergy were entitled to their allotted share even when the farmers had bad years, which in turn meant that clergymen had nothing but good ones.

The role of country clergy was a remarkably loose one. Piety was not necessarily a requirement, or even an expectation. Ordination in the Church of England required a university degree, but most ministers read classics and didn't study divinity at all, and so had no training in how to preach, provide inspiration or solace or otherwise offer meaningful Christian support. Many didn't even bother composing sermons but just bought a big book of prepared sermons and read one out once a week.

Though no one intended it, the effect was to create a class of well-educated, wealthy people who had immense amounts of time on their hands. In consequence many of them began, quite spontaneously, to do remarkable things. Never in history have a group of people engaged in a broader range of creditable activities for which they were not in any sense actually employed.

Consider a few:

George Bayldon, a vicar in a remote corner of Yorkshire, had such poor attendances at his services that he converted half his church into a henhouse, but became a self-taught authority in linguistics and compiled the world's first dictionary of Icelandic. Not far away, Laurence Sterne, vicar of a parish near York, wrote popular novels, of which *The Life and Opinions of Tristram Shandy, Gentleman*, is much the best remembered. Edmund Cartwright, rector of a rural parish in Leicestershire, invented the power loom, which in effect made the Industrial Revolution truly industrial; by the time of the Great Exhibition, over

250,000 of his looms were in use in England alone.

In Devon, the Reverend Jack Russell bred the terrier that shares his name, while in Oxford the Reverend William Buckland wrote the first scientific description of dinosaurs and, not incidentally, became the world's leading authority on coprolites – fossilized faeces. Thomas Robert Malthus, in Surrey, wrote *An Essay on the Principle of Population* (which, as you will recall from your schooldays, suggested that increases in food supply could never keep up with population growth for mathematical reasons), and so started the discipline of political economy. The Reverend William Greenwell of Durham was a founding father of modern archaeology, though he is better remembered among anglers as the inventor of 'Greenwell's glory', the most beloved of trout flies.

In Dorset, the perkily named Octavius Pickard-Cambridge became the world's leading authority on spiders while his contemporary the Reverend William Shepherd wrote a history of dirty jokes. John Clayton of Yorkshire gave the first practical demonstration of gas lighting. The Reverend George Garrett, of Manchester, invented the submarine.* Adam Buddle, a botanist vicar in Essex, was the eponymous inspiration for the flowering buddleia. The Reverend John Mackenzie Bacon of

---

* The ship was called the *Resurgam*, meaning 'I shall rise again,' which proved to be a slightly unfortunate name as it sank in a storm in the Irish Sea three months after it was launched in 1878, and never did rise again. Neither, come to that, did Garrett. Discouraged by his experiences, he gave up preaching and inventing, and moved to Florida where he took up farming. That, too, proved a disaster, and he finished his disappointing and relentlessly downhill life as a foot soldier in the American army during the Spanish–American War before dying of tuberculosis in New York City in 1902.

Berkshire was a pioneering hot-air balloonist and the father of aerial photography. Sabine Baring-Gould wrote the hymn 'Onward, Christian Soldiers' and, more unexpectedly, the first novel to feature a werewolf. The Reverend Robert Stephen Hawker of Cornwall wrote poetry of distinction and was much admired by Longfellow and Tennyson, though he slightly alarmed his parishioners by wearing a pink fez and passing much of his life under the powerfully serene influence of opium.

Gilbert White, in the Western Weald of Hampshire, became the most esteemed naturalist of his day and wrote the luminous and still much loved *Natural History of Selborne*. In Northamptonshire the Reverend M. J. Berkeley became the foremost authority on fungi and plant diseases. John Michell, a rector in Derbyshire, taught William Herschel how to build a telescope, which Herschel then used to discover Uranus. Michell also devised a method for weighing the Earth, which was arguably the most ingenious practical scientific experiment in the whole of the eighteenth century. He died before it could be carried out and the experiment was eventually completed in London by Henry Cavendish, a brilliant kinsman of Paxton's employer the Duke of Devonshire.

Perhaps the most extraordinary clergyman of all was the Reverend Thomas Bayes, from Tunbridge Wells in Kent, who lived from about 1701 to 1761. He was by all accounts a shy and hopeless preacher, but a singularly gifted mathematician. He devised the mathematical equation that has come to be known as the Bayes theorem and that looks like this:

$$p(\theta|y) \;=\; \frac{p(\theta)p(y|\theta)}{\int p(\eta)p(y|\eta)d\eta}$$

People who understand Bayes's theorem can use it to work out complex problems involving probability distributions – or inverse probabilities, as they are sometimes called. It is a way of arriving at statistically reliable probabilities based on partial information. The most remarkable feature of Bayes's theorem is that it had no practical applications without computers to do the necessary calculations, so in his own day it was an interesting but fundamentally pointless exercise. Bayes evidently thought so little of his theorem that he didn't bother to make it public. A friend sent it to the Royal Society in London in 1763, two years after Bayes's death, where it was published in the society's *Philosophical Transactions* with the modest title of 'An Essay Towards Solving a Problem in the Doctrine of Chances'. In fact, it was a milestone in the history of mathematics. Today Bayes's theorem is used in modelling climate change, predicting the behaviour of stock markets, fixing radiocarbon dates, interpreting cosmological events and much else where the interpretation of probabilities is an issue – and all because of the thoughtful jottings of an eighteenth-century English clergyman.

A great many other clergymen didn't produce great works but rather great children. John Dryden, Christopher Wren, Robert Hooke, Thomas Hobbes, Oliver Goldsmith, Jane Austen, Joshua Reynolds, Samuel Taylor Coleridge, Horatio Nelson, the Brontë sisters, Alfred Lord Tennyson, Cecil Rhodes and Lewis Carroll (who was himself ordained, though he never practised) were all the offspring of parsons. Something of the disproportionate influence of the clergy can be found by doing a word search of the electronic version of the *Dictionary of National Biography*. Enter 'rector' and you get nearly 4,600 promptings; 'vicar' yields 3,300 more. This compares with a decidedly more modest 338 for 'physicist', 492 for 'economist', 639 for 'inventor' and 741 for 'scientist'. (Interestingly, these are not greatly larger than the number of entries called forth by entering the words 'philanderer', 'murderer' or 'insane', and are considerably outdistanced by 'eccentric' with 1,010 entries.)

There was so much distinction among clergymen that it is easy to forget that such people were in fact unusual, and that most were more like our own Mr Marsham, who if he had any achievements at all, or indeed any ambitions, left no trace of them. His closest link to fame was that his great-grandfather, Robert Marsham, was the inventor of phenology, the science (if it is not too much to call it that) of keeping track of seasonal changes – the first buds on trees, the first cuckoo of spring, and so on. You might think that that was something people would do spontaneously anyway, but in fact no one had, at least not systematically, and under Marsham's influence it became a wildly popular and highly regarded pastime around the world. In America, Thomas Jefferson was a devoted follower. Even as president he found time to note the first and last appearances of thirty-seven types of fruit and vegetable in Washington markets, and had his agent at Monticello make similar observations there to see if the dates betrayed any significant variations between the two places. When modern climatologists say that apple blossoms of spring are appearing three weeks earlier than formerly, and that sort of thing, often it is Robert Marsham's records they are using as source material. This Marsham was also one of the wealthiest landowners in East Anglia, with a big estate in the curiously named village of Stratton Strawless, near Norwich, where Thomas John Gordon Marsham was born in 1821 and passed most of his life before travelling the twelve miles or so to take up the post of rector in our village.

We know almost nothing about Thomas Marsham's life there, but by chance we do know a great deal about the daily life of country parsons in the great age of country parsons thanks to the writings of one who lived in the nearby parish of Weston Longville, five miles across the fields to the north (and just visible from the roof of our rectory). His name was the Reverend James Woodforde and he preceded Marsham by fifty years, but life won't have changed that much. Woodforde was not notably devoted or learned or gifted, but he enjoyed life and kept a lively diary for forty-five years, which provides an unusually detailed insight into the life of a country clergyman. Forgotten for over a hundred years, the diary was rediscovered and published in condensed form in 1924 as *The Diary of a Country Parson*. It became an international bestseller, even though it was, as one critic noted, 'little more than a chronicle of gluttony'.

The amount of food placed on eighteenth-century tables was staggering, and Woodforde scarcely ever had a meal that he didn't record lovingly and in full. Here are the items he sat down to at a typical dinner in 1784: Dover sole in lobster sauce, spring chicken, ox tongue, roast beef, soup, fillet of veal with morels and truffles, pigeon pie, sweetbreads, green goose and peas, apricot jam, cheese-cakes, stewed mushrooms and trifle. At another meal he could choose from a platter of tench, a ham, three fowls, two roasted ducks, a neck of pork, plum pudding and plum tart, apple tart, and miscellaneous fruit and nuts, all washed down with red and white wines, beer and cider. Nothing got in the way of a good meal. When Woodforde's sister died, he recorded his sincere grief in his diary, but also found space to note: 'Dinner today a fine turkey rosted [sic]'. Nor did anything much from the outside world intrude. The American War of Independence is hardly mentioned. When the Bastille fell in 1789, he noted the fact, but gave more space to what he had for breakfast. Fittingly, the final entry of his diary recorded a meal.

Woodforde was a decent enough human being – he sent food to the poor from time to time and led a life of blameless virtue – but in all the years of his diaries there isn't any indication that he ever gave a moment's thought to the composition of a sermon or felt any particular attachment to his parishioners beyond a gladness to join them for dinner whenever the offer was extended. If he didn't represent what was typical, he certainly represented what was possible.

As for where Mr Marsham fitted into all this, there's simply no telling. If it was his goal in life to make as little impression as possible upon history, he achieved it gloriously. In 1851, he was twenty-nine years old and unmarried – a condition he kept for life. His housekeeper, a woman with the interestingly unusual name of Elizabeth Worm, stayed with him for some fifty years until her death in 1899, so at least she seemed to find him agreeable enough company, but whether anyone else did, or didn't, cannot be known.

There is, however, one small, encouraging clue. On the last Sunday of March 1851, the Church of England conducted a national survey to see how many people actually attended church that day. The results were a shock. More than half the people of England and Wales had not gone to church at all, and only 20 per cent had gone to an Anglican service. However ingenious they may have been at creating mathematical theorems or compiling Icelandic dictionaries, clearly clergymen were no longer anything like as important to their communities as they once had been. Happily, there didn't seem to be any sign of that yet in Mr Marsham's parish. The census records show that 79 worshippers attended his morning service that Sunday and 86 came in the afternoon. That was almost 70 per cent of the parishioners in his benefice – a result much, much better than the national average. Assuming that that was a typical turnout for him, then our Mr Marsham, it appears, was a well-regarded man.

III

In the same month that the Church of England conducted its attendance survey, Britain also had its ten-yearly national census, which put the national population at a confidently precise 20,959,477. This was just 1.6 per cent of the world total, but it is safe to say that nowhere was there a more rich and productive fraction. The 1.6 per cent of people who were British produced half the world's coal and iron, controlled nearly two-thirds of its shipping and engaged in one-third of all trade. Virtually all the finished cotton in the world was produced in British mills on machines invented and built in Britain. London's banks had more money on deposit than all the other financial centres of the world combined. London was at the heart of a huge and growing empire that would at its peak cover 11.5 million square miles and make 'God Save the Queen' the national anthem for a quarter of the world's people. Britain led the world in virtually every measurable category. It was the richest, most innovative, most accomplished nation of the age – a nation where even gardeners rose to greatness.

Suddenly, for the first time in history, there was in most people's lives a lot of everything. Karl Marx, living in London, noted in a tone of wonder, and just a hint of helpless admiration, that it was possible to buy five hundred kinds of hammer in Britain. Everywhere was activity. Modern Londoners live in a great Victorian city; the Victorians lived through it, so to speak. In twelve years eight railway termini opened in London. The scale of disruption – the trenches, the tunnels, the muddy excavations, the congestion of wagons and other vehicles, the smoke, the din, the clutter – that came from filling the city with railways, bridges, sewers, pumping stations, power stations, underground lines and all the rest meant that Victorian London was not just the biggest city in the world but the noisiest, foulest, muddiest, busiest, most choked and dug-over place the world had ever seen.

The 1851 census also showed that more people in Britain now lived in cities than in the countryside – the first time that this had happened anywhere in the world – and the most visible consequence of this was crowds on a scale never before experienced. People now worked en masse, travelled en masse, were schooled, imprisoned and hospitalized en masse. When they went out to enjoy themselves, they did that en masse, and nowhere did they go with greater enthusiasm and rapture than to the Crystal Palace.

If the building itself was a marvel, the wonders within were no less so. Almost 100,000 objects were on display, spread among some 14,000 exhibits. Among the novelties were a knife with 1,851 blades, furniture carved from furniture-sized blocks of coal (for no reason other than to show that it could be done), a four-sided piano for homey quartets, a bed that became a life raft and another that automatically tipped its startled occupant into a freshly drawn bath, flying contraptions of every type (except working), instruments for bleeding, the world's largest mirror, an enormous lump of guano from Peru, the famous Hope and Koh-i-Noor diamonds,* a model of a proposed suspension bridge linking Britain with France, and endless displays of machinery, textiles and manufactures of every type from all over the world. *The Times* calculated that it would take two hundred hours to see it all.

---

* The Koh-i-Noor had become one of the Crown Jewels two years earlier, after being liberated (or looted, depending on your perspective) by the British army during its conquest of the Punjab in India. Most people found the Koh-i-Noor a letdown. Although huge at nearly 200 carats, it had been poorly cut and was disappointingly deficient in lustre. After the exhibition, it was boldly trimmed to a more sparkly 109 carats and set into the royal crown.

Not all displays were equally scintillating. Newfoundland devoted the whole of its exhibition area to the history and manufacture of cod-liver oil, and so became an oasis of tranquillity, much appreciated by those who sought relief from the pressing throngs. The United States section almost didn't get filled at all. Congress, in a mood of parsimony, refused to extend funds, so the money had to be raised privately. Unfortunately when the American products arrived in London it was discovered that the organizers had paid only enough to get the goods to the docks and not onward to Hyde Park. Nor evidently had any money been set aside to erect the displays and man them for five months. Fortunately, the American philanthropist George Peabody, living in London, stepped in and provided $15,000 in emergency funding, rescuing the American delegation from its self-generated crisis. All this reinforced the more or less universal conviction that Americans were little more than amiable backwoodsmen not yet ready for unsupervised outings on the world stage.

So it came as something of a surprise when the displays were erected to discover that the American section was an outpost of wizardry and wonder. Nearly all the American machines did things that the world earnestly wished machines to do – stamp out nails, cut stone, mould candles – but with a neatness, dispatch and tireless reliability that left other nations blinking. Elias Howe's sewing machine dazzled the ladies and held out the impossible promise that one of the great drudge pastimes of domestic life could actually be made exciting and fun. Cyrus McCormick displayed a reaper that could do the work of forty men – a claim so improbably bold that almost no one believed it until the reaper was taken out to a farm in the Home Counties and shown to do all that it promised it could. Most exciting of all was Samuel Colt's repeat-action revolver, which was not only marvellously lethal but made from interchangeable parts, a method of manufacture so distinctive that it became known as 'the American system'. Only one home-grown creation could match these virtuoso qualities of novelty, utility and machine-age precision – Paxton's great hall itself, and that was to disappear when the show was over. For many Europeans this was the first unsettling hint that those tobacco-chewing rustics across the water were quietly creating the next industrial colossus – a transformation so improbable that most wouldn't believe it even as it was happening.

The most popular feature at the Great Exhibition was not an exhibition at all, but rather the elegant 'retiring rooms', where visitors could relieve themselves in comfort, an offer taken up with gratitude and enthusiasm by 827,000 people – 11,000 of them on a single day. Public facilities in London were woefully lacking in 1851. At the British Museum, up to 30,000 daily visitors had to share just two outside privies. At the Crystal Palace the toilets actually flushed, enchanting visitors so much that it started a vogue for installing flushing toilets at home – a development that would quickly have catastrophic consequences for London, as we shall see.

The Great Exhibition offered a social breakthrough as well as a sanitary one, for it was the first time that people of all classes were brought together and allowed to mingle in intimate proximity. Many feared that the common people – 'the Great Unwashed', as William Makepeace Thackeray had dubbed them the previous year in his novel

The History of Pendennis – would prove unworthy of this trust and spoil things for their superiors. There might even be sabotage. This was, after all, just three years after the popular uprisings of 1848, which had convulsed Europe and brought down governments in Paris, Berlin, Kraków, Budapest, Vienna, Naples, Bucharest and Zagreb.

The particular fear was that the exhibition would attract Chartists and their fellow travellers. Chartism was a popular movement named for the People's Charter of 1837, which sought a range of political reforms – all fairly modest in retrospect – from the abolition of rotten and pocket boroughs to the adoption of universal male suffrage.* Over the space of a decade or so, Chartists presented a series of petitions to Parliament, one of them over six miles long and said to be signed by 5.7 million people. Parliament was impressed but rejected them all anyway, for the people's own good. Universal suffrage, it was commonly agreed, was a dangerous notion – 'utterly incompatible with the existence of civilization' as the historian and MP Thomas Babington Macaulay put it.

In London, matters came to a head in 1848 when the Chartists announced a mass rally on Kennington

---

* Rotten boroughs were those where a member of Parliament could be elected by a small number of people, as at Bute in Scotland where just one resident out of fourteen thousand had the right to vote and so obviously could elect himself. Pocket boroughs were constituencies with no inhabitants at all but that retained a seat in Parliament, which could be sold or given away (to an unemployable son, say) by the person who controlled it. The most celebrated pocket borough was Dunwich, a coastal town in Suffolk which had once been a great port – the third biggest in England – but was washed into the sea during a storm in 1286. Despite its conspicuous nonexistence, it was represented in Parliament until 1832 by a succession of privileged nonentities.

Common, south of the Thames. The fear was that they would work themselves into a froth of indignation, swarm over Westminster Bridge and seize Parliament. Government buildings throughout the city were fortified in readiness. At the Foreign Office Lord Palmerston, the foreign secretary, blocked the windows with bound volumes of *The Times*. At the British Museum men were stationed on the roof with a supply of bricks to rain down on the heads of anyone who tried to take the building. Cannons were placed outside the Bank of England and employees at a range of state institutions were issued with swords and ancient, doubtfully maintained muskets, many of them at least as dangerous to their users as to anyone bold enough to step in front of them. One hundred and seventy thousand special constables – mostly rich men and their servants – stood by, under the command of the doddering Duke of Wellington, now eighty-two years old and deaf to anything less noisy than an extremely robust shout.

In the event, the rally fizzled out, partly because the Chartists' leader, Feargus O'Connor, was beginning to behave bizarrely from an as-yet-undiagnosed case of syphilitic dementia (for which he would be committed to an asylum the following year), partly because most of the participants weren't really revolutionaries at heart and didn't wish to cause or be part of a lot of bloodshed, and partly because a timely downpour made retiring to a pub suddenly seem a more attractive option than storming Parliament. *The Times* decided that the 'London mob, though neither heroic, nor poetical, nor patriotic, nor enlightened, nor clean, is a comparatively good-natured body', and, however patronizing, that was about right.

Despite this reprieve, feelings in some quarters continued to run strong in 1851. Henry Mayhew, in his influential *London Labour and the London Poor*, published that year, noted that working people 'almost to a man' were 'red-hot proletarians, entertaining violent opinions'.

But even the most hot-headed proletarian, it seems, loved the Great Exhibition. It opened on 1 May 1851 without incident – a 'beautiful and imposing and touching spectacle', in the words of a radiant Queen Victoria, who called opening day 'the greatest day in our history' and sincerely meant it. People came from every corner of the country. A woman named Mary Callinack, aged eighty-five, walked more than 250 miles from Cornwall, and so made herself famous. Altogether six million people attended in the five and a half months that the Great Exhibition was open. On the busiest day, 7 October, almost 110,000 people were admitted. At one point, 92,000 were in the building at the same time – the largest number of people ever to be indoors in a single location.

Not every visitor was enchanted. William Morris, the future designer and aesthete, then aged seventeen, was so appalled by what he saw as the exhibition's lack of taste and veneration of excess that he staggered from the building and was sick in the bushes. But most people adored it, and nearly all behaved themselves. During the whole of the Great Exhibition just twenty-five people were charged with offences – fifteen for picking pockets and ten for petty larceny. The absence of crime was even more remarkable than it sounds for by the 1850s Hyde Park had become notoriously dangerous, particularly from dusk onwards when the risk of robbery was so great that the practice arose of crossing it only after forming a convoy. Thanks to the crowds, for just under half a year it was one of the safest places in London.

The Great Exhibition cleared a profit of £186,000, enough to buy thirty acres of land south of Hyde Park, in an area informally called Albertopolis, where were built the great museums and institutions that still dominate the neighbourhood today – the Royal Albert Hall, the Victoria & Albert Museum, the Natural History Museum, the Royal College of Art and the Royal College of Music, among others.

Paxton's mighty Crystal Palace remained standing in Hyde Park until the summer of 1852, while people decided what to do with it. Almost no one wanted it to go altogether, but few could agree on what should become of it. One slightly over-excited proposal was to convert it into a glass tower a thousand feet high. Eventually it was agreed to move it to a new park – to be called the Crystal Palace Park – at Sydenham in south London. Somehow in the process it became even larger; the new Crystal Palace was half as big again and employed twice the volume of glass. Because it was sited on a slope, its re-erection was much more of a challenge. Four times it collapsed. Some 6,400 workers were needed to put the new building up and it took them more than two years to do so. Seventeen of them lost their lives. Everything about the Crystal Palace that had seemed magical and blessed had oddly leaked away. It never regained its central place in the nation's affections. In 1936, the whole thing burned down.

Ten years after the Great Exhibition, Prince Albert died, and the great Gothic spaceship known as the Albert Memorial was built just west of where the Crystal Palace had stood, at a whopping cost of £120,000, or about half as much again as the Crystal Palace itself had cost. There today, Albert sits enthroned under an enormous gilded canopy. On his lap he holds a book: the catalogue of the Great Exhibition. All that remains of the original Crystal Palace itself are a pair of large decorative wrought-iron gates that once guarded the ticket checkpoint at the entrance to Paxton's exhibition hall, and now, unnoticed, mark a small stretch of boundary between Hyde Park and Kensington Gardens.

The golden age of the country clergy ended abruptly, too. The 1870s saw the onset of a savage agricultural depression, which hit landowners and all on whom their prosperity depended. In six years, one hundred thousand farmers and farm workers left the land. In our parish the population fell by almost half in fifteen years. By the mid-1880s the rateable value of the entire parish was just £1,713 – barely £100 more than it had cost Thomas Marsham to build his rectory three decades earlier.

By the end of the century the average English clergyman's income was less than half what it had been fifty years before. Adjusted for purchasing power it was an even more miserable pittance. A country parish ceased being an attractive sinecure. Many clergymen could no longer afford to marry. Those who had brains and opportunity took their talents elsewhere. By the turn of the century, writes David Cannadine, 'the best minds of a generation were outside the Church rather than within'.

In 1899, the Marsham family estate was broken up and sold, and that ended the family's benign and dominant relationship with the county. Curiously it was something unexpected that happened in the kitchen that was in large part responsible for the devastating agricultural depression of the 1870s and beyond. We'll get to that story presently, but before we enter the house and begin our tour, we might perhaps take a few pages to consider the unexpectedly pertinent question of why people live in houses at all.

CHAPTER TWO

The Setting

I

IF WE WERE SOMEHOW to bring the Reverend Thomas Marsham back to life and restore him to his rectory, what would probably most surprise him – apart from being here at all, of course – would be to find that the house has become, as it were, invisible. Today it stands in a dense, private woodland that gives it an emphatically secluded air, but in 1851, when it was brand new, it would have stood starkly, even startlingly, in open countryside, a pile of red bricks in a bare field.

In most other respects, however, and allowing for a little ageing and the introduction of some electrical wires and a television aerial, it remains largely unchanged from 1851. It is now, as it was then, manifestly a house. It looks the way a house should look. It has a homely air.

So it is perhaps slightly surprising to reflect that nothing about this house, or any house, is inevitable. Everything had to be thought of – doors, windows, chimneys, stairs – and a good deal of that, as we are about to see, took far more time and experimentation than you might ever have thought.

Houses are really quite odd things. They have almost no universally defining qualities: they can be of practically any shape, incorporate virtually any material, be of almost any size. Yet wherever we go in the world we know houses and recognize domesticity the moment we see them. This aura of homeliness is, it turns out, extremely ancient, and the first hint of that remarkable fact was uncovered by chance just at the time the Old Rectory was being built, in the winter of 1850, when a mighty storm blew into Britain.

It was one of the worst storms in decades and it caused widespread devastation. At the Goodwin Sands, off the Kent coast, five ships were dashed to pieces with the loss of all hands. Off Worthing, in Sussex, eleven men in a lifeboat, going to the aid of a distressed ship, drowned when their boat was upended by a giant wave. At a place called Kilkee, an Irish sailing ship named *Edmund*, bound for America, lost its steering, and passengers and crew watched helplessly as the ship drifted on to rocks and was smashed to splinters. Ninety-six people drowned, though a few managed to struggle ashore, including one elderly lady clinging to the back of the brave captain, whose name was Wilson and who was, the *Illustrated London News* noted with grim satisfaction, English. Altogether more than two hundred people lost their lives in waters around the British Isles that night.

In London at the half-built Crystal Palace, rising in Hyde Park, newly installed glass panes lifted and banged, but stayed in place, and the building itself withstood the battering winds with barely a groan, much to the relief of

Joseph Paxton, who had promised that it was storm-proof but appreciated the confirmation. Seven hundred miles to the north, on the Orkney Islands of Scotland, the storm raged for two days. At a place called the Bay o' Skaill the gale stripped the grassy covering off a large, irregular knoll, of a type known locally as a howie, which had stood as a landmark for as long as anyone had known it.

When at last the storm cleared and the islanders came upon their newly reconfigured beach, they were astounded to find that where the howie had stood were now revealed the remains of a compact, ancient stone village, roofless but otherwise marvellously intact. Consisting of nine houses, all still holding many of their original contents, the village dates from five thousand years ago. It is older than Stonehenge and the Great Pyramids, older than all but a handful of built structures on Earth. It is immensely rare and important. It is known as Skara Brae.

Thanks to its completeness and preservation, Skara Brae offers a scene of intimate, almost eerie domesticity. Nowhere is it possible to get a more potent sense of household life in the stone age. As everyone remarks, it is as if the inhabitants have only just left. What never fails to astonish at Skara Brae is the sophistication. These were the dwellings of Neolithic people, but the houses had locking doors, a system of drainage and even, it seems, elemental plumbing with slots in the walls to sluice away wastes. The interiors were capacious. The walls, still standing, were up to ten feet high, so there was plenty of headroom, and the floors were paved. Each house has built-in stone dressers, storage alcoves, boxed enclosures presumed to be beds, water tanks, and damp courses that would have kept the interiors snug and dry. The houses are all of one size and built to the same plan, suggesting a kind of genial commune rather than a conventional tribal hierarchy. Covered passageways ran between the houses and led to a paved open area – dubbed 'the marketplace' by early archae-ologists – where tasks could be done in a social setting.

Life appears to have been pretty good for the Skara Brae residents. They had jewellery and pottery. They grew wheat and barley, and enjoyed bounteous harvests of shellfish and fish, including a codfish that weighed seventy-five pounds. They kept cattle, sheep, pigs and dogs. The one thing they lacked was wood. They burned seaweed for warmth, and seaweed makes a most reluctant fuel, but that chronic challenge for them was good news for us. Had they been able to build their houses of wood, nothing would remain of them and Skara Brae would have gone forever unimagined.

It is impossible to overstate Skara Brae's rarity and value. Prehistoric Europe was a largely empty place. The number of people in the whole of the British Isles fifteen thousand years ago may have been as little as two thousand. By the time of Skara Brae, the number had risen to perhaps twenty thousand, but that is still just one person per three thousand acres, so to come across any sign of Neolithic life is always an excitement. It would have been pretty exciting even then.

Skara Brae offered some oddities too. One dwelling, standing slightly apart from the others, could be bolted only from the outside, indicating that anyone within was being confined, which rather mars the impression of a society of universal serenity. Why it was necessary to detain someone in such a small community is obviously a question that cannot be answered over such a distance of time. Also slightly mystifying are the watertight storage containers found in each dwelling. The common explanation is that these were used to hold limpets, a hard-shelled mollusc that abounds in the vicinity, but why anyone would want a stock of fresh limpets near at hand is a question not easy to answer even with the luxury of conjecture, for limpets are a terrible food, providing only about one calorie apiece and so rubbery as to be practically inedible anyway; they actually take more energy to chew than they return in the form of nutrition.

We don't know anything at all about these people – where they came from, what language they spoke, what led them to settle on such a lonesome outpost on the tree-less edge of Europe – but from all the evidence it appears that Skara Brae enjoyed six hundred years of uninterrupted comfort and tranquillity. Then one day in about 2500 BC the occupants vanished – quite suddenly, it seems. In the passageway outside one dwelling ornamental beads, almost certainly precious to the owner, were found scattered, suggesting that a necklace had broken and the owner had been too panicked or harried to retrieve them. Why Skara Brae's happy idyll came to a sudden end is, like so much else, impossible to say.

Remarkably, after Skara Brae's discovery more than three-quarters of a century passed before anyone got around to having a good look at it. William Watt, from nearby Skaill House, salvaged a few items, and, more horrifyingly, a later house party, armed with spades and other implements, emerged from Skaill House and cheerfully plundered the site one weekend in 1913, taking away goodness knows what as souvenirs, but that was about all the attention Skara Brae attracted. Then in 1924 in another storm a section of one of the houses was swept into the sea, and it was decided that it was necessary for the site to be formally examined and made secure. The job fell to an interestingly odd but brilliant Australian-born Marxist professor from the University of Edinburgh who loathed fieldwork and didn't really like going outside at all if he could possibly help it. His name was Vere Gordon Childe.

Childe wasn't a trained archaeologist. Few people in the early 1920s were. He had read classics and philology at the University of Sydney, where he had also developed a deep and abiding attachment to Communism, a passion that blinded him to the excesses of Joseph Stalin but coloured his archaeology in surprisingly productive ways. In 1914, he came to the University of Oxford as a graduate student, and there he began the reading and thinking that led to his becoming the foremost authority of his day on the lives and movements of early peoples. In 1927, the University of Edinburgh appointed him to the brand-new post of Abercrombie Professor of Prehistoric Archaeology. This made him the only academic archaeologist in Scotland, so when something like Skara Brae needed investigating the call went out to him. Thus it was in the summer of 1927 that he travelled north by train and boat to Orkney.

Nearly every written description of Childe dwells almost lovingly on his oddness of manner and peculiar looks. His colleague Max Mallowan (now best remembered, when remembered at all, as the second husband of Agatha Christie) said he had a face 'so ugly that it was painful to look at'. Another colleague recalled Childe as

Vere Gordon Childe at Skara Brae, 1930.

'tall, ungainly and ugly, eccentric in dress and often abrupt in manner [with a] curious and often alarming persona'. The few surviving photographs of Childe certainly confirm that he was no beauty – he was skinny and chinless, with squinting eyes behind owlish spectacles, and a moustache that looked as if it might at any moment stir to life and crawl away – but whatever unkind things people might say about the outside of his head, the inside was a place of golden splendour. Childe had a magnificent, retentive mind and an exceptional facility for languages. He could read at least a dozen, living and dead, which allowed him to scour texts both ancient and modern on any subject that interested him, and there was hardly a subject that didn't. The combination of weird looks, mumbling diffidence, physical awkwardness and intensely overpowering intellect was more than many people could take. One student recalled how in a single ostensibly sociable evening Childe had addressed those present in half a dozen languages, demonstrated how to do long division in Roman numerals, expounded critically upon the chemical basis of Bronze Age datings, and quoted lengthily from memory and in the original languages from a range of literary classics. Most people simply found him exhausting.

He wasn't a born excavator, to put it mildly. A colleague, Stuart Piggott, noted almost with awe Childe's 'inability to appreciate the nature of archaeological evidence in the field, and the processes involved in its recovery, recognition and interpretation'. Nearly all his many books were based on reading rather than personal experience. Even his command of languages was only partial. Although he could read them flawlessly, he used his own made-up pronunciations, which no one who spoke the languages could actually understand. In Norway, hoping to impress colleagues, he once tried to order a dish of raspberries and was brought twelve beers.

Whatever his shortcomings of appearance and manner, he was unquestionably a force for good in archaeology. Over the course of three and a half decades he produced six hundred articles and books, popular as well as academic, including the bestsellers *Man Makes Himself* (1936) and *What Happened in History* (1942), which many later archaeologists said inspired them to take up the profession. Above all he was an original thinker, and at just the time that he was excavating at Skara Brae he had what was perhaps the single biggest and most original idea of twentieth-century archaeology.

The human past is traditionally divided into three very unequal epochs – the Palaeolithic (or 'old stone age'), which ran from 2.5 million years ago to about 10,000 years ago; the Mesolithic ('middle stone age'), covering the period of transition from hunter-gathering lifestyles to the widespread emergence of agriculture, from 10,000 to 6,000 years ago; and the Neolithic ('new stone age') which covers the closing but extremely productive two thousand years or so of prehistory, up to the Bronze Age. Within each of these periods are many further sub-periods – Olduwan, Mousterian, Gravettian and so on – that are mostly of concern to specialists and needn't distract us here.

The important thought to hold on to is that for the first 99 per cent of our history as human beings we didn't do much of anything but procreate and survive, but then people all over the world discovered farming, irrigation,

writing, architecture, government and the other refinements of existence that collectively add up to what we
fondly call civilization. This has been many times
described as the most momentous event in human history,
and the first person who fully recognized and conceptual-
ized the whole complex process was Vere Gordon Childe.
He called it the Neolithic Revolution.

It remains one of the great mysteries of human
development. Even now scientists can tell you where it
happened and when, but not why. Almost certainly (well,
we think almost certainly) it had something to do with
some big changes in the weather. About 12,000 years ago,
Earth began to warm quite rapidly, then for reasons
unknown it plunged back into frigidity for a thousand
years or so – a kind of last gasp of the ice ages. This period
is known to scientists as the Younger Dryas. (It was named
for an arctic plant, the dryas, which is one of the first to
recolonize land after an ice sheet withdraws. There was an
Older Dryas period, too, but it wasn't important for
human development.) After ten further centuries of cold,
the world warmed rapidly again and has stayed comparatively warm ever since. Almost everything we have done
as advanced beings has been done in this brief spell of
climatological glory.

The interesting thing about the Neolithic Revolution is
that it happened all over the Earth, among people who
could have no idea that others in distant places were doing
precisely the same things. Farming was independently
invented at least seven times – in China, the Middle East,
New Guinea, the Andes, the Amazon basin, Mexico and
west Africa. Cities likewise emerged in six places – China,
Egypt, India, Mesopotamia, Central America and the

Andes. That all of these things happened all over, often without any possibility of shared contact, is on the face of it really quite uncanny. As one historian has put it: 'When Cortés landed in Mexico he found roads, canals, cities, palaces, schools, law courts, markets, irrigation works, kings, priests, temples, peasants, artisans, armies, astronomers, merchants, sports, theatre, art, music, and books' – all invented quite independently of similar developments on other continents. And some of it is, to be sure, a little uncanny. Dogs, for instance, were domesticated at much the same time in places as far apart as England, Siberia and North America.

It is tempting to think of this as a kind of global light-bulb moment, but that is really stretching things. Most of the developments actually involved vast periods of trial, error and adjustment, often over the course of thousands of years. Agriculture started 11,500 years ago in the Levant, but 8,000 years ago in China and only a little over 5,000 years ago in most of the Americas. People had been living with domesticated animals for 4,000 years before it occurred to anyone to put the bigger of them to work pulling ploughs; Westerners used a clumsy, heavy, exceedingly inefficient straight-bladed plough for a further 2,000 years before someone introduced them to the simple curved plough the Chinese had been using since time immemorial. Mesopotamians invented and used the wheel, but neighbouring Egypt waited 2,000 years before adopting it. In Central America, the Maya also independently invented the wheel but couldn't think of any practical applications for it and so reserved it exclusively for children's toys. The Incas didn't have wheels at all, or money or iron or writing. The march of progress, in short, has been anything but predictable and rhythmic.

For a long time it was thought that settling down – sedentism, as it is known – and farming went hand in hand. People, it was assumed, abandoned nomadism and took up farming in order to guarantee their food supplies. Killing wild game is difficult and chancy, and hunters must often have come home empty-handed. Much better to control your food sources and have them permanently and conveniently at hand. In fact, researchers realized quite early on that sedentism was not nearly as straightforward as that. At about the time that Childe was excavating at Skara Brae, a Cambridge University archaeologist named Dorothy Garrod, working in Palestine at a place called Shuqba, discovered an ancient culture that she dubbed the Natufian, after a wadi, or dried riverbed, that lay nearby. The Natufians built the first villages and founded Jericho, which became the world's first true city. So they were very settled people. But they didn't farm. This was most unexpected. However, other excavations across the Middle East showed that it was not uncommon for people to settle in permanent communities long before they took up farming – sometimes by as much as 8,000 years.

So, if people didn't settle down to take up farming, why then did they embark on this entirely new way of living? We have no idea – or actually, we have lots of ideas, but we don't know if any of them are right. According to Felipe Fernández-Armesto, at least thirty-eight theories have been put forward to explain why people took to living in communities: that they were driven to it by climatic change, or by a wish to stay near their dead, or by a powerful desire to brew and drink beer, which could only be indulged by staying in one place. One theory, evidently seriously suggested (Jane Jacobs cites it in her landmark work of 1969, *The Economy of Cities*), was that 'fortuitous showers' of cosmic rays caused mutations in grasses that made them suddenly attractive as a food source. The short answer is that no one knows why agriculture developed as it did.

Making food out of plants is hard work. The conversion of wheat, rice, corn, millet, barley and other grasses into staple foodstuffs is one of the great achievements of human history, but also one of the more unexpected ones. You have only to consider the lawn outside your window to realize that grass in its natural state is not an obvious foodstuff for non-ruminants such as ourselves. For us, making grass edible is a challenge that can be solved only with a lot of careful manipulation and protracted ingenuity. Take wheat. Wheat is useless as a food until made into something much more complex and ambitious like bread, and that takes a great deal of effort. Somebody must first separate out the grain and grind it into meal, then convert the meal into flour, then mix that with other components like yeast and salt to make dough. Then the dough must be kneaded to a particular consistency, and finally the resulting lump must be baked with precision and care. The scope for failure in the last step alone is so great that in every society in which bread has featured baking has been turned over to professionals from the earliest stages.

It is not as if farming brought a great improvement in living standards either. A typical hunter-gatherer enjoyed a more varied diet and consumed more protein and calories than settled people, and took in five times as much vitamin C as the average person today. Even in the bitterest depths of the ice ages, we now know, nomadic people ate surprisingly well – and surprisingly healthily. Settled people, by contrast, became reliant on a much smaller range of foods, which all but ensured dietary insufficiencies. The three great domesticated crops of pre-history were rice, wheat and maize, but all had significant drawbacks as staples. As John Lanchester explains: 'Rice inhibits the activity of Vitamin A; wheat has a chemical that impedes the action of zinc and can lead to stunted growth; maize is deficient in essential amino acids and contains phytates, which prevent the absorption of iron.' The average height of people actually fell by almost six inches in the early days of farming in the Near East. Even on Orkney, where prehistoric life was probably as good as it could get, an analysis of 340 ancient skeletons showed that hardly any people lived beyond their twenties.

What killed the Orcadians was not dietary deficiency but disease. People living together are vastly more likely to spread illness from household to household, and the close exposure to animals through domestication meant that flu (from pigs or fowl), smallpox and measles (from cows and sheep), and anthrax (from horses and goats, among others) could become part of the human condition, too. As far as we can tell, virtually all of the infectious diseases have become endemic only since people took to living together. Settling down also brought a huge increase in 'human commensals' – mice, rats and other creatures that live with and off us – and these all too often acted as disease vectors, too.

So sedentism meant poorer diets, more illness, lots of toothache and gum disease, and earlier deaths. What is truly extraordinary is that these are all still factors in our lives today. Out of the thirty thousand types of edible plant thought to exist on earth, just eleven – corn, rice, wheat, potatoes, cassava, sorghum, millet, beans, barley, rye and oats – account for 93 per cent of all that humans eat, and every one of them was first cultivated by our Neolithic ancestors. Exactly the same is true of husbandry. The animals we raise for food today are not eaten because they are notably delectable or nutritious or a pleasure to be around, but because they were the ones first domesticated in the stone age.

We are, in the most fundamental way, stone age people ourselves. From a dietary point of view, the Neolithic age is still with us. We may sprinkle our dishes with bay leaves and chopped fennel, but underneath it all is stone age food. And when we get sick, it is stone age diseases we suffer.

II

If, ten thousand years ago, you had been asked to guess which would be the seat of the greatest future civilizations, you would probably have settled on some part of Central or South America on the basis of the amazing things they were doing with food there. Academics call this portion of the New World Mesoamerica, an accommodatingly vague term which could fairly be defined as Central America plus as much or as little of North and South America as are needed to support a hypothesis.

Mesoamericans were the greatest cultivators in history,

but of all their many horticultural innovations none was more lastingly important or unexpected than the creation of maize, or corn as it is known where I come from.* We still don't have any idea how they did it. If you look at primitive forms of barley, rice or wheat set beside their modern counterparts you can see the affinities at once. But nothing in the wild remotely resembles modern corn. Genetically its nearest relative is a wispy grass called teosinte, but beyond the level of chromosomes there is no discernible kinship. Corn grows into a hefty cob on a single stalk and its grains are encased in a stiff, protective husk. An ear of teosinte, in comparison, is less than an inch long, huskless and grows on a multiplicity of stems. It is almost valueless as a food; one kernel of corn is more nutritious than a whole ear of teosinte.

It is beyond us to divine how any people could have bred cobs of corn from such a thin and unpropitious plant – or even thought to try. Hoping to settle the matter once and for all, in 1969 food scientists from all over the world convened at 'An Origin of Corn Conference' at the University of Illinois, but the debates grew so vituperative and bitter, and at times personal, that the conference broke up in confusion, and no papers from it were ever published. Nothing like it has been attempted since. Scientists are now pretty sure, however, that corn was first domesticated on the plains of western Mexico and are in

---

* In Britain 'corn' has meant any grain since the time of the Anglo-Saxons. It also came to signify any small round object, which explains the corns on your feet. Corned beef is so called because originally it was cured in kernels of salt. Because of the importance of maize in America, the term became attached to maize exclusively in the early eighteenth century.

no doubt, thanks to the persuasive wonders of genetics, that somehow it was coaxed into being from teosinte, but how it was done remains as much a mystery as it ever did.

However they did it, they created the world's first fully engineered plant – a plant so thoroughly manipulated that it is now wholly dependent on us for its survival. Corn kernels do not spontaneously disengage from their cobs, so unless they are deliberately stripped and planted, no corn will grow. Had people not been tending it continuously for these thousands of years, corn would be extinct. The inventors of corn not only created a new kind of plant, they also created – conceived from nothing really – a new type of ecosystem that existed nowhere in their world. In Mesopotamia natural meadows grew everywhere already, so cultivation was largely a matter of transforming natural grain fields into superior managed ones. In the arid scrubs of Central America, however, fields were unknown. They had to be created from scratch by people who had never seen such a thing before. It was like someone in a desert imagining lawns.

Today corn is far more indispensable than most people realize. Cornstarch is used in the manufacture of fizzy drinks, chewing gum, ice cream, peanut butter, ketchup, automobile paint, embalming fluid, gunpowder, insecticides, deodorants, soap, potato crisps, surgical dressings, nail polish, foot powder, salad dressing and several hundred things more. To borrow from Michael Pollan, it is not so much as if we have domesticated corn as it has domesticated us.

The worry is that as crops are engineered to a state of uniform genetic perfection they will lose their protective variability. When you drive past a field of corn today, every stalk in it is identical to every other – not just extremely similar, but eerily, molecularly identical. Replicants live in perfect harmony since none can out-compete any others. But they also have matching vulnerabilities. In 1970, the corn world suffered a real fright when a disease called southern corn-leaf blight started killing corn all over America and it was realized that practically the entire national crop was planted from seeds with genetically identical cytoplasm. Had the cytoplasm been directly affected or the disease proved more virulent, food scientists all over the world might now be scratching their heads over ears of teosinte and we would all be eating potato crisps and ice creams that didn't taste quite right.

Potatoes, the other great food crop of the New World, present an almost equally intriguing batch of mysteries. Potatoes are from the nightshade family, which is of course notoriously toxic, and in their wild state they are full of poisonous glycoalkaloids – the same stuff, at lower doses, that puts the zip in caffeine and nicotine. Making any wild potatoes safe to eat required reducing the glycoalkaloid content to between one-fifteenth and one-twentieth of its normal level. This raises a lot of questions, beginning most obviously with: how did they do it? And while they were doing it how did they *know* they were doing it? How do you tell that the poison content has been reduced by, say, 20 per cent or 35 per cent or some other intermediate figure? How do you assess progress in such a process? Above all, how did they know that the whole exercise was worth the effort and that they would get a safe and nutritious foodstuff in the end?

Of course, a non-toxic potato might equally have mutated spontaneously, saving them generations of experimental selective breeding. But if so, how did they know that it had mutated and that out of all the poisonous wild potatoes around them here at last was one that was safe to eat?

The fact is, people in the ancient world were often doing things that are not just surprising but unfathomable.

III

While Mesoamericans were harvesting corn and potatoes (and avocados and tomatoes and beans and about a hundred other plants we would be desolate to be without now), people on the other side of the planet were building the first cities. These are no less mysterious and surprising.

Just how surprising was brought home by a discovery in Turkey in 1958. One day towards the end of that year, a young British archaeologist named James Mellaart was driving through an empty corner of central Anatolia with two colleagues when he noticed an unnatural-looking earthen mound – a 'thistle-covered hump' – stretching across the arid plain. It was fifty or sixty feet high and two thousand feet long. Altogether it covered about thirty-three acres – a mysteriously immense area. Returning the next year, Mellaart did some experimental digging and, to his astonishment, discovered that the mound contained the remains of an ancient city.

This wasn't supposed to happen. Ancient cities, as even laymen knew, were phenomena of Mesopotamia and the Levant. They were not supposed to exist in Anatolia. Yet here was one of the very oldest – possibly *the* very oldest – bang in the middle of Turkey and of a size that was astoundingly unprecedented. Çatalhöyük (the name means 'forked mound') was nine thousand years old. It had been lived in continuously for well over a thousand years and at its peak had a population of eight thousand.

Mellaart called Çatalhöyük the world's first city, a conclusion given additional weight and publicity by Jane Jacobs in her influential work *The Economy of Cities*, but that is incorrect on two counts. First, it wasn't a city but really just a very large village. (The distinction to archaeologists is that cities have not just size but a discernible administrative structure.) Even more pertinently, other communities – Jericho in Palestine, Mallaha in Israel, Abu Hureyra in Syria – are now known to be considerably older. None, however, would prove stranger than Çatalhöyük.

Vere Gordon Childe, father of the Neolithic Revolution, didn't quite live long enough to learn about Çatalhöyük. Shortly before its discovery, he made his first visit home to Australia in thirty-five years. He had been away for well over half his lifetime. While walking in the Blue Mountains he either fell to his death or jumped. In either case, he was found at the bottom of an eminence called Govett's Leap. A thousand feet above, a passer-by found his jacket carefully folded, with his glasses, compass and pipe neatly arranged on top.

He would almost certainly have been fascinated with Çatalhöyük because hardly anything about the place made sense. The town was built without streets or lanes. The houses huddled together in a more or less solid mass. Those in the middle of the mass could only be reached by

clambering over the roofs of many other houses, all of
differing heights, and entering through roof hatches – a
staggeringly inconvenient arrangement. There were no
squares or marketplaces, no municipal or administrative
buildings – no signs of social organization at all. Each
builder put up four new walls, even when building against
existing walls. It was as if they hadn't got the hang of
collective living yet. It may well be that they hadn't. It is
certainly a vivid reminder that the nature of communities
and the buildings within them is not pre-ordained. It may
seem to us natural to have doors at ground level and
houses separated from one another by streets and lanes,
but the people of Çatalhöyük clearly saw it another way
altogether.

No roads or tracks led to or from the community
either. It was built on marshy ground, on a flood plain. For
miles around there was nothing but space, and yet the
people packed themselves densely together as if pressed by
incoming tides on all sides. Nothing at all indicates why
people should have congregated there in their thousands
when they might have spread out across the surrounding
countryside.

The people farmed – but on farms that were at least
seven miles away. The land around the village provided
poor grazing, and offered nothing at all in the way of
fruits, nuts or other natural sources of nutrition. There was
no wood for fuel either. In short there wasn't any very
obvious reason for people to settle there at all, and yet
clearly they did in large numbers.

Çatalhöyük was not a primitive place by any means. It
was strikingly advanced and sophisticated for its time –
full of weavers, basketmakers, carpenters, joiners,

beadmakers, bowmakers and many others with specialized skills. The inhabitants practised art of a high order and not only had fabrics but a variety of stylish weaves. They could even produce stripes – not evidently an easy thing to do. Looking good was important to them. It is remarkable to think that people thought of striped fabrics before they thought of doors and windows.

All this is just another reminder of how little we know, or can even begin to guess, about the lifestyles and habits of people from the ancient past. And with that thought in mind let's go into the house at last and begin to see how little we know about it too.

CHAPTER THREE

The Hall

I

NO ROOM HAS FALLEN further in history than the hall. Now a place to wipe feet and hang hats, once it was the most important room in the house. Indeed, for a long time it *was* the house. How it came to this curious pass is a story that goes back to the very beginnings of England and a time, 1,600 years ago, when boatloads of people from mainland Europe came ashore and began, in an entirely mysterious way, to take over. We know remarkably little about who these people were, and the little we do know often makes no sense, but it was with them that the history of England and the modern house begins.

As conventionally related, events were straightforward: in AD 410, their empire collapsing, the Romans withdrew from Britain in haste and confusion, and Germanic tribes – the Angles, Saxons and Jutes of a thousand schoolbooks – swarmed in to take their place. It seems, however, that much of that may not be so.

First, the invaders didn't necessarily swarm. By one

estimate, perhaps as few as ten thousand outsiders moved into Britain in the century after the Romans left – an average of only one hundred people a year. Most historians think that is much too small a figure, though none can put a more certain number in its place. Nor, come to that, can anyone say how many native Britons were there to receive or oppose the invaders. The number is variously put at between 1.5 million and 5 million – in itself a vivid demonstration of just how comprehensively vague a period we are dealing with here – but what seems nearly certain is that the invaders were very considerably outnumbered by those they conquered.

Why the vanquished Britons couldn't find the means or spirit to resist more effectively is a deep mystery. They were, after all, giving up a great deal. For almost four centuries they had been part of the mightiest civilization on earth and had enjoyed benefits – running water, central heating, good communications, orderly governments, hot baths – with which their rough conquerors were un- comfortable or unacquainted. It is difficult to conceive the sense of indignity that the natives must have felt at finding themselves overrun by illiterate, unwashed pagans from the wooded fringes of Europe. Under the new regime they would give up nearly all their material advantages and not return to many of them for a thousand years.

This was a period of *Völkerwanderung*, 'the wandering of peoples', when groups all across the ancient world – Huns, Vandals, Goths, Visigoths, Ostrogoths, Magyars, Franks, Angles, Saxons, Danes, Alamanni and more – developed a strange, seemingly unquenchable restlessness, and Britain's invaders were clearly part of that. The only written account we have of what happened is that left by the monk known as the Venerable Bede, who was writing three centuries after the fact. It is Bede who tells us that the invading force was made up of Angles, Saxons and Jutes, but who they were exactly and what their relationship with each other was is unknown.

The Jutes are completely mysterious. They are usually presumed to have come from Denmark because of the presence there of the province called Jutland. But a problem pointed out by the historian F. M. Stenton is that Jutland got its name long after any Jutes had departed, and naming a territory after people who are no longer there would be an act unusual to the point of uniqueness. In any case, *Jótar*, the Scandinavian word from which Jutland is derived, doesn't necessarily, or even plausibly, have anything to do with any group or race. Bede's reference is in fact the only mention of Jutes anywhere, and he never cites them again. Some scholars think that the reference is an interlineation added by a later hand anyway and has nothing to do with Bede at all.

The Angles are only a little less obscure. They do get mentioned from time to time in European texts, so at least we can be confident that they really existed, but nothing about them suggests any importance. If they were feared or admired, it was within very small circles. So it is more than slightly ironic that it was their name that came, more or less accidentally, to be attached to a country that they may only lightly have helped to form.

That leaves only the Saxons, who were unquestionably a presence on the continent – the existence in modern Germany of various Saxonys, Saxe-Coburgs and the like attests to that – though not a particularly mighty one either, it seems. The best Stenton can say for them is that they were 'the least obscure' of the three. Compared with the Goths sacking Rome or the Vandals sweeping over Spain, these were pretty marginal people. Britain, it seems, was conquered by farmers, not warriors.

They brought almost nothing that was new – just a language and their own DNA. No aspect of their technology or mode of living offered even a moderate improvement over what existed already. They can't have been well liked. They don't seem to have been very impressive. Yet somehow they made such a profound impact that their culture remains with us, more than a millennium and a half later, in the most extraordinary and fundamental ways. We may know nothing of their beliefs, but we still pay homage to three of their gods – Tiw, Woden and Thor – in the names of our three middle weekdays, and eternally commemorate Woden's wife, Frig, every Friday. That's quite a line of attachment.

They simply obliterated the existing culture. The Romans had been in Britain for 367 years and the Celts for at least a thousand, yet now it was as if they had never been. Nothing like this happened elsewhere. When the Romans left Gaul and Spain, life went on much as before. The inhabitants continued to speak their own versions of Latin, which were already evolving into modern French and Spanish. Government continued. Business thrived. Coins circulated. Society's structures were maintained. In Britain, however, the Romans left barely five words and the Celts no more than twenty, mostly geographical terms to describe features specific to the British landscape. 'Crag', for instance, is a Celtic word, and so too is 'tor', meaning a rocky outcrop.

After the Romans withdrew, some Celts fled to France

and founded Brittany. Some no doubt fought and were slain or enslaved. But the greater number seem simply to have accepted the invasion as an unhappy fact and adjusted their lives accordingly. 'It didn't have to involve a lot of slaughter or bloodshed,' my friend Brian Ayers, the former county archaeologist for Norfolk, told me one time as we stood looking at the field beyond my house. 'Probably one day you would just look out in your field and see there were twenty people camped there, and gradually it would dawn on you that they weren't about to go away, that they were taking your land from you. There were no doubt *some* bloody clashes here and there, but on the whole I think it was just a matter of the existing people learning to adjust to dramatically changed circumstances.'

There are various accounts of battles – one at Crecgan Ford (a place of uncertain location) was said to have left four thousand Britons dead – and legend has of course left us tales of the valiant resistance of King Arthur and his men, but legend is all there is. Nothing in the archaeo-logical record indicates wholesale slaughter or populations fleeing as if before a storm. Not only were the invaders not mighty warriors, they weren't even very good hunters, as far as can be told. All the archaeological evidence shows that from the moment of arrival they lived off domesticated animals and did virtually no hunting. Farming appears to have continued without interruption, too. From what the record shows, the transition seems to have been as smooth as a change of shift in a factory. That can't have been the case surely, but what really happened we will probably never know. This became a time without history. Britain was no longer just at the end of the known world; now it was beyond it.

Even what we can know, from archaeology, is often hard to fathom. For one thing, the newcomers declined to live in Roman houses even though the Roman houses were soundly built, superior to anything they had had at home, and there for the taking. Instead they erected far more basic structures, often right alongside abandoned Roman villas. They didn't use Roman towns either. For three hundred years, London stood mostly empty.

On the continent the Germanic peoples had commonly lived in longhouses – the 'classic' peasant dwelling in which humans live at one end and livestock at the other – but the incomers abandoned those too for the next six hundred years. No one knows why. Instead they dotted the landscape with strange little structures known as *grubenhäuser* – literally 'pit houses' – though there are sound reasons to doubt that they were houses at all. A *grubenhaus* consisted simply of a sloping pit, about a foot and a half deep, over which a small building was erected. For the first two centuries of Anglo-Saxon occupation, these were the most numerous and seemingly important new structures in the country. Many archaeologists think that a floor was laid across the pit, making it into a shallow cellar, though for what purpose is hard to say. The two most common theories are that the pits were for storage, the thought being that the cool air below would better preserve perishables, or that they were designed to improve air circulation and keep the floorboards from rotting. But the effort of excavating the holes – some were hewn straight out of bedrock – seems patently disproportionate to any possible benefits to air flow, and anyway it's thought exceedingly unlikely that better air circulation would have brought either of the theorized results.

The first *grubenhaus* wasn't found until 1921 – remarkably late considering how numerous these structures are now known to be – during an excavation at Sutton Courtenay (now in Oxfordshire, then in Berkshire). The discoverer was Edward Thurlow Leeds of the Ashmolean Museum in Oxford and frankly he didn't like what he saw at all. People who lived in them had led 'a semitroglodytic existence' so squalid that 'it inspires disbelief in modern minds', Professor Leeds all but sputtered in a monograph of 1936. The occupants, he continued, lived 'amid a filthy litter of broken bones, of food and shattered pottery . . . in almost as primitive a condition as can be imagined. They had no regard for cleanliness, and were content to throw the remains of a meal into the furthest corner of the hut and leave it there.' Leeds seems to have seen *grubenhäuser* almost as a betrayal of civilization.

For nearly thirty years this view held sway, but gradually authorities began to question whether people really had lived in these odd little structures. For one thing, they were awfully small – only about seven feet by ten typically – which would make a very snug house even for the meanest peasants, particularly with a fire burning. One *grubenhaus* had a floor area that was nine feet across, of which just over seven feet was occupied by a hearth, leaving no room at all for people. So perhaps they weren't habitations at all, but workshops or storage sheds, though why they required a subterranean aspect may well permanently remain a mystery.

Fortunately the newcomers – the English, as we may as well call them from now on – brought a second kind of building with them, much less numerous but ultimately far more important. These buildings were much larger than *grubenhäuser*, but that was about as much as could be said for them. They were simply large, barnlike spaces with an open hearth in the middle. Their word for this kind of structure was already old in 410, and it now became one of the first words in English. They called them *halls*.

Practically all living, awake or asleep, was done in this single large, mostly bare, always smoky chamber. Servants and family ate, dressed and slept together – 'a custom which conduced neither to comfort nor the observance of the proprieties', as J. Alfred Gotch noted with a certain clear absence of comfort himself in his classic *The Growth of the English House* in 1909. Through the whole of the medieval period, till well into the fifteenth century, the hall effectively *was* the house, so much so that it became the convention to give its name to the entire dwelling, as in Hardwick Hall or Toad Hall.

Every member of the household, including servants, retainers, dowager widows and anyone else with a continuing attachment, was considered family – they were literally 'familiar', to use the word in its original sense. In the most commanding (and usually least draughty) position in the hall was a raised platform called a dais, where the owner and his family ate – a practice recalled by the high tables still found in colleges and boarding schools that have (or sometimes simply wish to project) a sense of long tradition. The head of the household was the 'husband' – a compound term meaning literally 'householder' or 'house owner'. His role as manager and provider was so central that the practice of land management became known as husbandry. Only much later did 'husband' come to signify a marriage partner.

Even the very grandest homes had only three or four

interior spaces – the hall itself, a kitchen and perhaps one or two side chambers, known variously as bowers, parlours or chambers, where the head of the house could retire to conduct private business. By the ninth or tenth century, there was often a chapel, too, though this tended to be used as much for business as worship. Sometimes these private rooms were built in two storeys, with the upper – called a 'solar' – reached by a ladder or very basic stairway. 'Solar' sounds sunny and light, but in fact the name was merely an adaptation of *solive*, the French word for floor joist or beam. Solars were simply rooms perched on joists, and for a long time they were the only upstairs room that most houses afforded. Often they were little more than storerooms. So little did people think of rooms in the modern sense that the word 'room' with the meaning of an enclosed chamber or distinct space isn't recorded in English until the time of the Tudors.

Society consisted principally of freemen, serfs and slaves. Upon the death of a serf the lord was entitled to take a small personal possession, such as an article of clothing, as a kind of death duty. Often peasants only owned one main item of apparel, a type of loose gown known as a *cotta* (which eventually evolved into the modern 'coat'). The fact that that was the best that a peasant had to offer, and that the lord of the manor would want it, tells you about all you need to know about the quality of medieval life at many levels. Serfdom was a form of permanent bondage to a particular lord, and often it was offered as a religious declaration – an act that must have dismayed more than a few offspring, for serfdom, once declared, extended in perpetuity to all the declaring party's descendants. The principal effect of serfdom was to remove the holder's freedom to move elsewhere or marry outside the estate. But serfs could still become prosperous. In the late medieval period, one in twenty owned fifty acres or more – substantial holdings for the time. By contrast, freemen, known as *ceorls*, had freedom in principle, but often were too poor to exercise it.

Slaves, often rivals captured in wartime, were pretty numerous from the ninth to eleventh centuries – one estate listed in the Domesday Book had more than seventy of them – but it was not quite the kind of dehumanizing bondage we think of from more modern times, as in the American South, for instance. Although slaves were property and could be sold – and for quite a lot: a healthy male slave was worth eight oxen – slaves were able to own property, marry and move about freely within the community. The Old English word for a slave was *thrall*, which is why when we are enslaved by an emotion we are enthralled.

Medieval estates were often highly fragmented. One eleventh-century thegn named Wulfric had seventy-two properties all over England, and even smaller estates tended to be scattered. Medieval households were, in consequence, forever on the move. They were also often very large. Royal households could easily have five hundred servants and retainers, and important peers and prelates were unlikely to have fewer than one hundred. With numbers so substantial, it was as easy to take the household to food as it was to bring food to the household, so motion was more or less constant, and everything was designed to be mobile (which is why, not incidentally, the French and Italian words for furniture are *meubles* and *mobili*). So furniture tended to be sparing, portable and starkly utilitarian, 'treated more as equipment than as prized personal possessions', to quote Witold Rybczynski.

Portability also explains why many old chests and trunks had domed lids – to throw off water during travel. The great drawback of trunks, of course, is that everything has to be lifted out to get at things at the bottom. It took a remarkably long time – till the 1600s – before it occurred to anyone to put drawers in and thus convert trunks into chests of drawers.

In even the best houses, floors were generally just bare earth strewn with rushes, harbouring 'spittle and vomit and urine of dogs and men, beer that hath been cast forth and remnants of fishes and other filth unmentionable', as the Dutch theologian and traveller Desiderius Erasmus rather crisply summarized in 1524. New layers of rushes were laid down twice a year normally, but the old accretions were seldom removed, so that, Erasmus added glumly, 'the substratum may be unmolested for twenty years'. The floors were in effect a very large nest, much appreciated by insects and furtive rodents, and a perfect incubator for plague. Yet a deep pile of flooring was generally a sign of prestige. It was common among the French to say of a rich man that he was 'waist deep in straw'.

Bare earth floors remained the norm in much of rural Britain and Ireland until the twentieth century. 'The "ground floor" was justly named,' as the historian James Ayres has put it. Even after wood or tile floors began to grow common in superior homes, at about the time of William Shakespeare, carpets were too precious to be placed underfoot. They were hung on the walls or laid over tables. Often, however, they were kept in chests and brought out only to impress special visitors.

Dining tables were simply boards laid across trestles, and cupboards were just what the name says – plain boards on which cups and other vessels could be arrayed. But there weren't many of those. Glass vessels were rare and diners were generally expected to share with a neighbour. Eventually cupboards were incorporated into rather more ornate dressers, which have nothing to do with clothing but rather with the preparation, or dressing, of food.

In humbler dwellings, matters were generally about as simple as they could be. The dining table was a plain board called by that name. It was hung on the wall when not in use, and was perched on the diners' knees when food was served. Over time, 'board' came to signify not just the dining surface but the meal itself, which is where the 'board' comes from in 'room and board'. It also explains why lodgers are called 'boarders' and why an honest person – someone who keeps his hands visible at all times – is said to be above board.

Seating was on plain benches – in French, *bancs*, from which comes 'banquet'. Until the 1600s chairs were rare – the word itself dates only from about 1300 – and were designed not to be comfortable but to impute authority. Even now, of course, the person in charge of a meeting chairs it, and a person in charge of a company is the chairman of the board – a term that additionally, and a little oddly, recalls the dining habits of medieval peasants.

Medieval banquets show people eating all kinds of exotic foods that are no longer eaten. Birds especially featured. Eagles, herons, peacocks, sparrows, larks, finches, swans and much else that flew were all widely consumed. This wasn't so much because swans and other exotic birds

A medieval banquet.

were fantastically delicious – they weren't; that's why we don't eat them now – but rather because other, better meats weren't available. Beef, mutton and lamb were hardly eaten at all for a thousand years because the animals they came from were needed for their fleeces, manure or muscle power and thus were much too valuable to kill. For much of the medieval period the largest source of animal protein for most people was smoked herring.

Even had meat been freely available, it was forbidden much of the time. Medieval diners had to accommodate three fish days a week, plus forty days of Lent and many other religious days when land-based flesh was forbidden. The total number of days of dietary restriction varied over time, but at its peak nearly half the days of the year were 'lean' days, as they were known. There was hardly a fish or other swimming thing that wasn't consumed. The kitchen accounts for the Bishop of Hereford show his household eating herring, cod, haddock, salmon, pike, bream, mackerel, ling, hake, roach, eels, lampreys, stockfish, tench, trout, minnows, gudgeon, gurnet and a few others – more than two dozen types altogether. Also widely eaten were barbel, dace and even porpoise. Until the time of Henry VIII, failing to observe fish days was punishable by death, at least in theory. Fish days were abandoned after the break with Rome, but were restored by Elizabeth in the interests of supporting the British fishing fleet. The Church was keen to keep the fish days too, not so much because of any religious conviction as because it had developed a lucrative sideline in selling dispensations.

Sleeping arrangements tended to be informal. We 'make a bed' today because in the Middle Ages that is essentially what you did – you rolled out a cloth sleeping pallet or heaped a pile of straw, found a cloak or blanket and fashioned whatever comfort you could. Sleeping arrangements appear to have remained relaxed for a long time. The plot of one of the *Canterbury Tales* hinges on the miller's wife getting into the wrong bed in her own home, something she could hardly do if she slept in the same place every night. Until well into the seventeenth century, 'bed' meant only the mattress and what it was stuffed with, not the frame and its contents. For that there was the separate word 'bedstead'.

Household inventories into the Elizabethan period show that people placed great attachment on beds and bedding, with kitchen equipment following behind. Only then did general household furniture make it on to inventories, and then generally in vague terms like 'a few tables and some benches'. People, it seems, simply were not that attached to their furniture, in much the way that we are not emotionally attached to our appliances. We wouldn't want to be without them, of course, but they are not treasured heirlooms. One other thing people recorded with care was, somewhat surprisingly, window glass. Other than in churches and a few wealthy homes, window glass was a rarity well into the 1600s. Eleanor Godfrey, in her history of glass-making, notes how in 1590 an alderman in Doncaster left his house to his wife but the windows to his son. The owners of Alnwick Castle from the same period always had their windows taken out and stored when they were away to minimize the risk of breakage.

Even in the largest houses generally only the windows in the most important rooms had glass in them. All the others were covered with shutters. Lower down the economic scale, windows remained rare until quite late. Even glaziers rarely had glass windows in their own homes at the time William Shakespeare was born, in 1564; by the time of his death half a century later, that had changed somewhat, though not completely. Most middle-class homes had glass in about half the rooms by then.

The one thing that is certain is that there wasn't a great deal of comfort in even the best homes. It really is extra-ordinary how long it took people to achieve even the most elemental levels of comfort. There was one good reason for it: life was tough. Throughout the Middle Ages, a good deal of every life was devoted simply to surviving. Famine was common. The medieval world was a world without reserves and when harvests were poor, as they were about one year in four on average, hunger was immediate. When crops failed altogether, starvation inevitably followed. England suffered especially catastrophic harvests in 1272, 1277, 1283, 1292 and 1311, and then an unrelievedly murderous stretch from 1315 to 1319. And this was of course on top of plagues and other illnesses that swept away millions. People condemned to short lives and chronic hard-ship are perhaps somewhat less likely to worry about decor. But even allowing for all that, there was just a great, strange slowness to strive for even modest levels of comfort. Roof holes, for instance, let smoke escape, but they also let in rain and draughts until somebody finally, belatedly, invented a lantern structure with louvred slats that allowed smoke to escape but kept out rain, birds and wind. It was a marvellous invention, but by the time it was thought of, in the four-teenth century, chimneys were already coming in and louvred caps were not needed.

Beyond that, we know practically nothing about household interiors before the middle of the Middle Ages. In fact, according to the furniture historian Edward Lucie-Smith, we know more about how ancient Greeks and Romans sat or reclined than we do about the English of eight hundred years ago. Almost no furniture survives from before 1300 or so, and illustrations in manuscripts or paintings are scarce and contradictory. Furniture historians are so starved of fact that they must even trawl through nursery rhymes. It is often written that a kind of medieval footstool was called a *tuffet* – a presumption based entirely on the venerable line 'Little Miss Muffet sat on a tuffet.' In fact, the only place the word appears in historic English is in the nursery rhyme itself. If tuffets ever actually existed, they are not otherwise recorded.

All this applies to the homes of the comparatively well-to-do, but two things need to be borne in mind: superior homes were not necessarily all that superior and inferior homes were not necessarily all that bad. Grander homes, on the whole, weren't more complex structures, they just had bigger halls.

About the houses themselves we often know even less because hardly anything survives above ground from the earlier periods of settlement. Anglo-Saxons were extremely attached to timber as a construction material, so much so that *timbran* was their generic term for a building, but unfortunately it is in the nature of wood to rot and almost none of it remains. In the whole of Britain, as far as can be told, just one door survives from the Anglo-Saxon period – a battered oak door in an outer vestibule at Westminster Abbey, which escaped attention until the summer of 2005 when it was realized that it was 950 years old and thus the oldest known door in the country.

A question worth considering is how you can tell how old a door is anyway. The answer lies in dendrochronology – the scientific counting of tree rings. Tree rings give a very precise guide, each marking a year, and so all together form a kind of woody fingerprint. If you have a piece of timber whose age is certain, you can use the patterns of rings on it to match and date other pieces of wood from the same period. To get back centuries you simply find overlapping patterns. If you have a tree that lived from 1850 to 1910 and another that lived from 1890 to 1970, say, they should show overlapping patterns from 1890 to 1910, the period when they were both alive. By building up a library of ring sequences, you can go back a long way.

In Britain, it is lucky that so much was built from oak because that is the only British tree that provides clear, usable evidence. But even the best woods present problems. No two trees will ever have quite the same pattern. One may have narrower rings than another because it grew in shade or had more competition at ground level or a poorer water supply. In practice you need a huge supply of tree-ring sequences to provide a reliable database and you must make many ingenious statistical adjustments to get an accurate reading – and for this you need the magical theorem of the Reverend Thomas Bayes, which we mentioned in the first chapter.

By taking a sample of wood about the thickness of a pencil and applying all the aforementioned tests, scientists worked out that the door at Westminster Abbey was made from the wood of a tree that was felled between 1032 and 1064, just before the Norman Conquest, so at the very end of the Anglo-Saxon period. And that solitary door is very nearly all that remains.*

With so little to go on, there is plenty of room for argument. Jane Grenville in her scholarly and definitive work *Medieval Housing* provides an arresting pair of illustrations showing how two archaeological teams, using the same information, envisioned the appearance of a longhouse at Wharram Percy, a lost medieval village in Yorkshire. One illustration shows a strikingly plain, basic dwelling, with walls made of mud or clunch (a composite of mud and dung) and a roof of grass or sod. The other shows a much sturdier and more sophisticated cruck-framed construction in which hefty beams have been fitted together with skill and care. The simple fact is that archaeological evidence shows mostly how buildings met the ground, not how they looked.

For a very long time it was believed that medieval peasant houses were little more than primitive huts – the kind of frail, twiggy structures that get blown down by wolves in fairy tales. The feeling was that they were unlikely to have lasted more than a single generation. Grenville quotes one scholar who felt confident enough to assert that the houses of common people were 'of uniformly poor quality throughout the whole of England' right up to the time of the Tudors – quite a sweeping statement, and a wrong one, it appears. The evidence now

*The low doors of so many old European houses, on which those of us who are absent-minded tend to crack our heads, are low not because people were shorter and required less headroom in former times, as is commonly supposed. People in the distant past were not in fact all that small. Doors were small for the same reason windows were small: they were expensive.

increasingly indicates that common people of the Middle Ages, and probably long before, could have good houses if they wanted them. One clue is the growth of specialized trades, such as thatching, carpentry, daubing and the like, in the late Middle Ages. Doors increasingly had locks, too – a clear indication that buildings and their contents were valued. Above all, cottages were evolving into a multiplicity of types – 'full Wealden', 'half Wealden', 'double pile', 'rear outshut', 'H-shape', 'open hall', 'cross-passage with cow house', 'cross-passage without cow house' and so on. The distinctions are unimportant, but to the people who lived in them they are what gave their houses character and distinction. Pride, almost certainly, developed early on in the ownership of houses, even quite simple ones.

One thing that did not escape notice in medieval times was that nearly all the space above head height was unusable because it was so generally filled with smoke. An open hearth had certain clear advantages – it radiated heat in all directions and allowed people to sit around it on all four sides – but it was also like having a permanent bonfire in the middle of one's living room. Smoke and sparks went wherever passing draughts directed them – and with many people coming and going and all the windows glassless, every passing gust must have brought somebody a faceful of smoke – or otherwise rose up to the ceiling and hung thickly until it leaked out of a hole in the roof.

What was needed was something that would seem, on the face of it, uncomplicatedly straightforward: a practical chimney. This took a long time to happen, however, not because of a lack of will but because of the technical challenges. A roaring fire in a large fireplace generates a lot of heat and needs a sound flue and backstop (or *reredos*, to use the architectural term), and no one knew how to make good ones before about 1330 (when 'chimney' is first recorded in English). Fireplaces already existed – they had been brought to England by the Normans – but they weren't impressive. They were made simply by scooping out part of the thick walls of Norman castles and poking a hole through the outer wall to let smoke escape. They drew air poorly, so didn't make good fires or generate much heat, and so weren't often used outside castles. They couldn't be safely used at all in timber houses, which is what most houses were.

What made the difference eventually was the development of good bricks, which can deal with heat better over the long term than almost any rock can. Chimneys also permitted a change in fuel to coal – which was timely because Britain's wood supplies were rapidly dwindling. Because coal smoke was acrid and poisonous, it needed to be contained within a fireplace, or chimneypiece as they were first known (to distinguish them from open hearths, also known as fireplaces), where fumes and smoke could be directed up a flue. This made for a cleaner house but a filthier world outside, and that, as we shall see, had very significant consequences for the look and design of homes.

Meanwhile, not everyone was happy with the loss of open hearths. Many people missed the drifting smoke and were convinced they had been healthier when kept 'well kippered in wood smoke', as one observer put it. As late as 1577 a William Harrison insisted that in the days of open fires 'our heads did never ake'. Smoke in the roof space discouraged nesting birds and was believed to strengthen timbers. Above all, people complained that they weren't nearly as warm as before, which was true. Because fireplaces were so inefficient, they were constantly enlarged. Some became so enormous that they were built with benches in them, letting people sit inside the fireplace, almost the only place in the house where they could be really warm.

Whatever the losses in warmth and comfort, the gains in space proved irresistible. So the development of the fireplace became one of the great breakthrough moments in domestic history. Suddenly it was possible to lay boards across the beams and create a whole new world upstairs.

II

The upward expansion of houses changed everything. Rooms began to proliferate as wealthy householders discovered the satisfactions of having space to themselves. The first step, generally, was to build a grand new room upstairs called the great chamber, where the lord and his family did all the things they had done in the hall before – eat, sleep, loll and play – but without so many other people about, returning to the great hall below only for banquets and other special occasions. Servants stopped being part of the family and became, well, servants.

The idea of personal space, which seems so natural to us now, was a revelation. People couldn't get enough of it. Soon it wasn't merely sufficient to live apart from one's inferiors, it was necessary to have time apart from one's equals, too.

As houses sprouted wings and spread, and domestic arrangements grew more complex, words were created or adapted to describe all the new room types: study, bed-chamber, privy chamber, closet, oratory (for a place of prayer), parlour, withdrawing chamber and library (in a domestic as opposed to institutional sense) all date from the fourteenth century or a little earlier. Others followed soon after: gallery, long gallery, presence chamber, tiring (for attiring) chamber, salon or saloon, apartment, lodg-ings and suite. 'How widely different is all this from the ancient custom of the whole household living by day and night in the great hall!' wrote Gotch in a moment of rare exuberance. One new type not mentioned by Gotch was boudoir, literally 'a room to sulk in', which from its earliest days was associated with sexual intrigue.

Even with the growth of comparative privacy, life remained much more communal and exposed than today. Toilets often had multiple seats, for ease of conversation, and paintings regularly showed couples in bed or a bath in an attitude of casual friskiness while attendants waited on them and their friends sat amiably nearby, playing cards or conversing but comfortably within sight and earshot.

The uses to which all the new rooms in the house were put were not for a long time so rigorously segregated as now. All rooms were in some sense living rooms. Italian blueprints from the time of the Renaissance, and beyond, didn't label rooms for type at all because they didn't have set purposes. People moved around the house looking for shade or sunlight and often took their furniture with them, so rooms, when they were labelled at all, were generally marked '*mattina*' (for morning use) or '*sera*' (for afternoon). Much the same sort of informality obtained in England. A bedchamber was used not just for sleeping but for private meals and entertaining favoured visitors. In fact, the bedroom became so much a place of general resort that it was necessary to devise more private spaces beyond. ('Bedroom' was first used by Shakespeare in *A Midsummer Night's Dream* in about 1590, though he meant it only in the sense of space within a bed. As a word to describe a dedicated sleeping chamber, it didn't become common until the following century.)

The small rooms off the bedchamber were used for every sort of private purpose, from defecation to assignation, and so the words for these rooms have come down to us in a curiously fractured fashion. 'Closet', Mark Girouard tells us, had 'a long and honourable history before descending to final ignominy as a large cupboard or a room for the housemaid's sink and mops'. Originally it was more like a study than a storeroom. 'Cabinet', originally a diminutive form of cabin, by the mid-1500s had come to signify a case where valuables were kept. Very soon after that – in only a decade or so – it had come to mean the room itself. The French, as so often, refined the original concept into a variety of room types, so that by the eighteenth century a large French chateau might have a *cabinet de compagnie, a cabinet d'assemblée, a cabinet de propriété and a cabinet de toilette* in addition to a plain *cabinet.*

In English the cabinet became the most exclusive and private of all chambers – the innermost sanctum where the most private meetings could take place. Then it made one of those bizarre leaps that words sometimes make and came to describe (by 1605) not just where the king met with his ministers but the collective term for the ministers themselves. This explains why this one word now describes both the most intimate and exalted group of advisers in government and the shelved recess in the bathroom where we keep Ex-Lax and the like.

Often this private room had a small cell or alcove off it, generally known as the privy, but also called a jakes, latrine, draughts, place of easement, necessarium, garderobe, house of office or gong, among other names, containing a bench with a hole in it, which was strategically positioned over a long drop into a moat or deep shaft. It is often supposed and sometimes written that 'privy' gave its name to the appurtenances of government in England, notably the Privy Seal and Privy Council. In fact, those terms came to England with the Normans nearly two centuries before 'privy' took on its lavatorial sense. It is true, however, that the person in charge of the royal privy was known as the groom of the stool, or stole, and over time advanced from being a cleaner of toilets to being the monarch's trusted adviser.

The same process occurred with many other words. 'Wardrobe' originally signified a room for storing apparel. Then it became successively a dressing room, a sleeping room, a privy and finally a piece of furniture. Along the way it also collected the meaning of one's full set of clothes.

To accommodate all the new room types, houses grew outwards as well as upwards. An entirely new type of house, known as the prodigy house, began to sprout and proliferate all over the countryside. Such houses were almost never less than three storeys high and sometimes four, and they were often staggeringly immense. The most enormous of all was Knole in Kent, which grew and grew until it covered nearly four acres and incorporated seven courtyards (one for each day of the week), fifty-two stair-cases (one for each week of the year) and three hundred and sixty-five rooms (one for each day of the year), or so it has long been said.

Looking at these houses now you can sometimes see, in the most startling way, how the builders were learning as they went. A striking example is Hardwick Hall in Derbyshire, which was built for the Countess of Shrewsbury – Bess of Hardwick, as she is always called – in 1591. Hardwick Hall was the marvel of its age and instantly became famous for its great expanses of windows, prompting the much quoted epigram 'Hardwick Hall, more glass than wall.' To modern eyes, the windows are of a size and distribution that seems pretty close to normal, but it was such a dazzling novelty in 1591 that the architect (who is thought to have been Robert Smythson) didn't actually know how to fit them all in. Some of the windows are in fact blanks hiding chimneys. Others are shared by rooms on separate floors. Some big rooms don't have nearly enough windows and some tiny rooms have little else. Only intermittently do the windows and the spaces they light actually match.

Bess filled the house with the finest array of silver, tapestries, paintings and the like of any private house in England, yet the most striking thing to modern eyes is how bare and modest is the overall effect. The floors were covered in simple rush mats. The great long gallery was 166 feet long but contained only three tables, a few straight-backed chairs and benches, and two mirrors (which in Elizabethan England were exceedingly precious treasures, more valuable than any paintings).

People didn't just build enormous houses, they built lots of enormous houses. Part of what makes Hardwick Hall so remarkable is that there was already a perfectly good existing Hardwick Hall (now to become known as Hardwick *Old* Hall) just across the grounds. Today it is a ruin, but it remained in use in Bess's day and for another hundred and fifty years beyond.

Traditionally, the great house builders (and house accumulators) were monarchs. At the time of his death Henry VIII had no fewer than forty-two palaces. But his daughter Elizabeth cannily saw that it was much cheaper to visit others and let them absorb the costs of her travels, and so she resurrected in a big way the venerable practice of making annual royal progresses. The queen was not in truth a great traveller – she never left England or even ventured very far within it – but she was a terrific visitor. Her annual progresses lasted eight to twelve weeks and took in about two dozen homes.

Royal progresses were nearly always greeted with a mixture of excitement and dread by those on whom the monarch called. On the one hand, they provided un-rivalled opportunities for preferment and social advancement, but on the other they were stupefyingly expensive. The royal household numbered up to about fifteen hundred people, and a good many of these – a hundred and fifty or so in the case of Elizabeth I – travelled with the royal personage on her annual pilgrimages. Hosts had not only the towering expenditure of feeding, housing and entertaining an army of spoiled and privileged people, but could expect to experience quite a lot of pilfering and property damage too, as well as some less salubrious surprises. After the court of Charles II departed from Oxford in about 1660, one of those left behind remarked in an understandably appalled tone how the royal visitors had left 'their excrements in every corner, in chimneys, studies, coal-houses, cellars'.

Since a successful royal visit could pay big dividends, most hosts laboured in the most inventive and painstaking manner to please the royal guest. Owners learned to provide elaborate masques and pageants as a very minimum, but many built boating lakes, added wings, reconstructed whole landscapes in the hope of eliciting a small cry of pleasure from the royal lips. Gifts were lavished freely. A hapless courtier named Sir John Puckering gave Elizabeth a silk fan festooned with diamonds, several loose jewels, a gown of rare splendour and a pair of exceptionally fine virginals, then watched at their first dinner as Her Majesty admired the silver cutlery and a salt cellar and, without a word, dropped them into the royal handbag.

Even her most longstanding ministers learned to be hypersensitive to the queen's pleasures. When Elizabeth complained of the distance to Lord Burghley's country house in Lincolnshire, he bought and extended another at Waltham Cross, now in the north-east London suburbs, because it was nearer. Christopher Hatton, Elizabeth's lord chancellor, built a mighty edifice called Holdenby House expressly for receiving the queen. In the event, she never came, and he died £18,000 in debt – a crushing burden, equivalent to about £9 million today.

Sometimes the builders of these houses didn't have a

great deal of choice. James I ordered the loyal but in-
consequential Sir Francis Fane to rebuild Apethorpe Hall
in Northamptonshire on a colossal scale so that he and the
Duke of Buckingham, his lover, would have some rooms
of suitable grandeur to saunter through en route to the
bedroom.

The worst imposition of all was to be instructed to take
on some longstanding, costly obligation to the crown.
Such was the fate of Bess of Hardwick's husband, the sixth
Lord Shrewsbury. For sixteen years he was required to act
as jailer to Mary, Queen of Scots, which in effect meant
maintaining the court of a small, fantastically disloyal
state in his own home. We can only imagine his sinking
heart as he saw a line of eighty horse-drawn wagons –
enough to make a procession a third of a mile long
– coming up his drive bearing the Scottish queen, fifty
servants and secretaries and all their possessions. In
addition to housing and feeding this force of people,
Shrewsbury had to maintain a private army to provide
security. The costs and emotional strain ensured that his
marriage to Bess was never a happy one – though it was
probably never going to be a happy one anyway. Bess
rather devoured men; Shrewsbury was her fourth husband
and her marriage to him was more of a business merger
than a twining of hearts. Eventually she accused him of
conducting an affair with the Scottish queen – a dangerous
charge whether or not a true one – and they separated. It
was then that Bess began building one of the great houses
of the age.

As life withdrew deeper and deeper into ever-larger
houses, the hall lost its original purpose and became a
mere entrance lobby with a staircase – a room to be

received in and pass through on the way to more important spaces. Such was the case at Hardwick Hall, its name notwithstanding. There all the important rooms were upstairs. Never again would the hall be a room of any real significance. As early as 1663, the word was being used to describe any modest space, particularly an entrance or associated passageway. Perversely, at the same time its original sense was preserved and indeed extended to describe large, important spaces, particularly public ones: Carnegie Hall, Royal Albert Hall, town hall and hall of fame, among many others.

Domestically, however, it became and remains the most semantically demoted room in the home. At the Old Rectory, as in most homes these days, it is a shrunken vestibule, a small utilitarian square with cupboards and hooks, where we take off boots and hang jackets – a clear preliminary to the house itself. Most of us unconsciously acknowledge this fact by inviting arriving guests into our houses twice: once at the door when they are brought in from outside, and then again, after they have been divested of coats and hats, into the house proper with a hearty, more emphatic double cry of 'Come in! Come in!'

And on that note, we can drop our outerwear here and at last step into the room where the house truly begins.

CHAPTER FOUR

The Kitchen

I

IN THE SUMMER OF 1662, Samuel Pepys, then a rising young figure in the British Navy Office, invited his boss, Naval Commissioner Peter Pett, to dinner at his home on Seething Lane, near the Tower of London. Pepys was twenty-nine years old and presumably hoped to impress his superior. Instead, to his horror and dismay, he discovered when his plate of sturgeon was set before him that it had within it 'many little worms creeping'.

Finding one's food in an advanced state of animation was not a commonplace event even in Pepys's day – he was truly mortified – but being at least a little uncertain about the freshness and integrity of food was a fairly usual condition. If it wasn't rapidly decomposing from inadequate preservation, there was every chance that it was coloured or bulked out with some dangerous and unappealing substances.

Almost nothing, it seems, escaped the devious wiles of food adulterers. Sugar and other expensive ingredients were often stretched with gypsum, plaster of Paris, sand, dust and other forms of 'daft', as such additives were collectively known. Butter reportedly was bulked out with tallow and lard. A tea drinker, according to various authorities, might unwittingly take in anything from saw-dust to powdered sheep's dung. One closely inspected shipment, Judith Flanders reports, proved to be only slightly more than half tea; the rest was made up of sand and dirt. Sulphuric acid was added to vinegar for extra sharpness, chalk to milk, turpentine to gin. Arsenite of copper was used to make vegetables greener or to make jellies glisten. Lead chromate gave bakery products a golden glow and brought radiance to mustard. Lead acetate was added to drinks as a sweetener, and red lead somehow made Gloucester cheese lovelier to behold, if not safer to eat.

There was hardly a foodstuff, it seems, that couldn't be improved or made more economical to the retailer through a little deceptive manipulation. Even cherries, Tobias Smollett reported, could be made to glisten afresh by being gently rolled around in the vendor's mouth before being put on display. How many unsuspecting ladies of quality, he wondered, had enjoyed a plate of luscious cherries that had been 'rolled and moistened between the filthy and, perhaps, ulcerated chops of a St Giles's huckster'?

Bread seems to have been particularly a target. In his popular novel *The Expedition of Humphry Clinker* (1771), Smollett characterized London bread as a poisonous com-pound of 'chalk, alum and bone-ashes, insipid to the taste and destructive to the constitution', but such charges were in fact already a commonplace by then, and probably had been for a very long time, as evidenced by the line in the tale of Jack and the Beanstalk, 'I'll crush his bones to make my bread.' The earliest formal allegation of widespread bread adulteration yet found came in a book called *Poison Detected: Or Frightful Truths* written anonymously in 1757 by 'My Friend, a Physician', who revealed on 'very credible authority' that 'sacks of old bones are not infrequently used by some of the Bakers' and that 'the charnel houses of the dead are raked to add filthiness to the food of the living'. Almost at the same time another, very similar book came out: *The Nature of Bread, Honestly and Dishonestly Made*, by Joseph Manning, MD, who reported that it was common for bakers to add bean meal, chalk, white lead, slaked lime and bone ash to every loaf they made.

Even now these assertions are routinely reported as fact even though it was demonstrated pretty conclusively over seventy years ago by Frederick A. Filby in his classic work *Food Adulteration* that the claims could not possibly be true. Filby took the interesting and obvious step of baking loaves of bread using the accused adulterants in the manner and proportions described. In every case but one the bread was either as hard as concrete or failed to set at all, and nearly all the loaves smelled or tasted disgusting. Several needed more baking time than conventional loaves, and so were actually more expensive to produce. Not one of the adulterated loaves was edible.

The fact of the matter is that bread is sensitive stuff and if you put foreign products into it in almost any quantity it is bound to become apparent. But then this could be said about most foodstuffs. It is hard to believe that anyone could drink a cup of tea and not notice that it was 50 per cent iron filings. Although some adulteration doubtless did happen, particularly when it enhanced colour or lent an appearance of freshness, most cases of claimed adulteration are likely to be either exceptional or untrue, and this is certainly the case with all the things said to be put into bread (with the single notable exception of alum, about which more in a moment).

It is hard to overemphasize just how important bread was to the English diet through the nineteenth century. For many people bread wasn't just an important accompaniment to a meal, it *was* the meal. Up to 80 per cent of all household expenditure, according to the bread historian Christian Petersen, was spent on food, and up to 80 per cent of that went on bread. Even middle-class people spent as much as two-thirds of their income on food (compared with about one-quarter today), of which a fairly high and sensitive proportion was bread. For a poorer family, nearly every history tells us, the daily diet was likely to consist of a few ounces of tea and sugar, some vegetables, a slice or two of cheese and, just occasionally, a very little meat. All the rest was bread.

Because bread was so important, the laws governing its purity were strict and the punishments severe. A baker who cheated his customers could be fined £10 per loaf sold, or made to do a month's hard labour in prison. For a time, transportation to Australia was seriously considered for malfeasant bakers. This was a matter of real concern for bakers because every loaf of bread loses weight in baking through evaporation, so it is easy to blunder accidentally. For that reason, bakers sometimes provided a little extra – the famous baker's dozen.

Alum, however, is another matter. Alum is a chemical compound – technically a double sulphate – used as a fixative for dyes. (The formal term is a mordant.) It was also used as a clarifying agent in all kinds of industrial processes and for dressing leather. It provides excellent whitening for flour, but that isn't necessarily a bad thing. For a start, a very little alum goes a long way. Just three or four spoonfuls can whiten a 280-pound sack of flour, and such a dilute amount would harm no one. In fact, alum is added to foods and medicines even now. It is a regular constituent in baking powder and vaccines, and some-times it is added to drinking water because of its clarifying properties. It actually made inferior grades of flour – flour that was perfectly good nutritionally but just not very attractive – acceptable to the masses and therefore allowed bakers to make more efficient use of their wheat. It was also added to flour for perfectly legitimate reasons as a drying agent.

It wasn't always that foreign substances were intro-duced with the intention of bulking things up. Sometimes they just fell in. A parliamentary investigation of bakeries in 1862 found many of them filled 'with masses of cob-webs, weighed down with flour dust that had accumulated upon them, and hanging in strips' ready to drop into any passing pot or tray. Insects and vermin scurried along walls and countertops. A sample of ice cream sold in London in 1881, according to Adam Hart-Davis, was found to con-tain human hair, cat hair, insects, cotton fibres and several other insalubrious constituents, but this probably reflected a lack of hygiene rather than the fraudulent addition of bulking agents. In the same period, a London confectioner was fined 'for colouring his sweets yellow with surplus pigment left over from painting his cart'. But it is the very fact that these things attracted the interest of newspapers that indicates that they were exceptional events rather than routine ones.

Humphry Clinker, a sprawling novel written in the form of a series of letters, paints such a vivid picture of life in eighteenth-century England that it is much quoted even now and almost certainly therefore has a lot to answer for. In one of its more colourful passages Smollett describes how milk was carried through the streets of London in open pails, into which plopped 'spittle, snot and tobacco-quids from foot passengers, over-flowings from mud-carts, spatterings from coach-wheels, dirt and trash chucked into it by roguish boys for the joke's-sake, the spewings of infants . . . and, finally, the vermin that drops from the rags of the nasty drab that vends this precious mixture . . .' What is easily overlooked is that the book was intended as satire, not as documentary. Smollett wasn't even in England when he wrote it, but slowly dying in Italy. (He died three months after its publication.)

All this isn't to say that there wasn't bad food about. There most certainly was. Infected and rotten meat was a particular problem. The filth of London's Smithfield Market, the city's principal meat exchange, was celebrated. One witness to a parliamentary investigation of 1828 said he saw 'a cow's carcass that was so rancid, the fat was no more than dripping yellow slime'. Animals driven in on the hoof from distant parts often arrived exhausted and sick, and didn't get any better while there. Sheep reportedly were sometimes skinned while still alive. Many animals were covered with sores. Smithfield sold so much bad meat that it had a private name for it: *cag-mag*, which was an abbreviation of two slang words meaning literally 'cheap crap'.

Even when the producers' intentions were pure, the food itself wasn't always. Getting food to distant markets in an edible condition was a constant challenge. People dreamed of being able to eat foods from far away or out of season. In January 1859, much of America followed eagerly as a ship laden with three hundred thousand juicy oranges raced under full sail from Puerto Rico to New England to show that it could be done. By the time it arrived, however, more than two-thirds of the cargo had rotted to a fragrant mush. Producers in more distant lands could not hope to achieve even that much. Argentinians raised massive herds of cattle on their endless and accommodating pampas, but had no way to ship the meat, so most of their cows were boiled down for their bones and tallow and the meat was simply wasted. Seeking ways to help them, the German chemist Justus Liebig devised a formula for a meat extract, which came to be known as Oxo, but clearly that could never make more than a marginal difference.

What was desperately needed was a way of keeping foods safe and fresh for longer periods than nature allowed. In the late eighteenth century a Frenchman named François Appert (or possibly Nicolas Appert – sources vary confusingly) produced a book called *The Art of Preserving All Kinds of Animal and Vegetable Substances for Several Years*, which represented a real breakthrough. Appert's system consisted essentially of sealing food in glass jars and then heating them slowly. The method generally worked pretty well, but the seals were not entirely foolproof and sometimes air and contaminants got in, to the gastro-intestinal distress of those who partook of the contents. Since it wasn't possible to have total confidence in Appert's jars, no one did.

In short, a lot of things could go wrong with food on its way to the table. So when in the early 1840s a miracle product came along that promised to transform matters, there was a great deal of excitement. The product was an unexpectedly familiar one: ice.

II

In the summer of 1844, the Wenham Lake Ice Company – named for a lake in Massachusetts – took premises in the Strand in London, and there each day placed a fresh block of ice in the window. No one in England had ever seen a block of ice that big before – certainly not in summer, not in the middle of London – or one that was so wondrously glassy and clear. You could actually read a newspaper through it: one was regularly propped behind the block so that passers-by could see this amazing fact for themselves. The shop window became a sensation, and was regularly crowded with gawkers.

Thackeray mentioned Wenham ice by name in a novel. Queen Victoria and Prince Albert insisted on its use at Buckingham Palace and awarded the company a royal warrant. Many people supposed Wenham to be a massive body of water, on the scale of one of the Great Lakes. Charles Lyell, the English geologist, was so intrigued that he made a special trip to the lake from Boston – not a particularly easy thing to do – while on a speaking tour. He was fascinated by how slowly Wenham ice melted, and assumed it had something to do with its celebrated purity. In fact, Wenham ice melted at the same speed as any other ice. Except that it had travelled far, it wasn't actually special in any way at all.

Lake ice was a marvellous product. It created itself at no cost to the producer, was clean, renewable and infinite in supply. The only drawbacks were that there was no infrastructure to produce and store it, and no market to sell it to. In order to make the ice industry exist, it was necessary to work out ways to cut and lift ice on a large scale, build storehouses, secure trading rights, engage a reliable chain of shippers and agents and, above all, create a demand for ice in places where ice had seldom or never been seen, and was most assuredly not something anyone was predisposed to pay for. The man who did all this was a Bostonian of good birth and challenging disposition named Frederic Tudor. Making ice a commercial proposition became his overweening obsession.

The notion of shipping ice from New England to distant ports was considered completely mad – 'the vagary of a disordered brain', in the words of one of his contemporaries. The first shipment of ice to Britain so puzzled customs officials as to how to classify it that all 300 tons of it melted away before it could be moved off the docks. Shipowners were highly reluctant to accept it as cargo. They didn't relish the humiliation of arriving in a port with a holdful of useless water, but they were also wary of the very real danger of tons of shifting ice and sloshing meltwater making their ships unstable. These were men, after all, whose nautical instincts were based entirely on the idea of keeping water *outside* the ship, so they were loath to take on such an eccentric risk when there wasn't even a certain market at the end of it all.

Tudor was a strange and difficult man – 'imperious, vain, contemptuous of competitors and implacable to enemies', in the estimation of Daniel J. Boorstin. He alienated all his closest friends and betrayed the trust of colleagues, almost as if that were his life's ambition. Nearly all the technological innovations that made the ice trade possible were actually the work of his retiring, compliant, long-suffering associate Nathaniel Wyeth. It cost Tudor years of frustrated endeavour, and all of his family fortune, to get the ice business up and running, but gradually it caught on and eventually it made him and many others rich. For several decades, ice was America's second biggest crop, measured by weight. If securely insulated, ice could last a surprisingly long while. It could even survive the 16,000-mile, 130-day trip from Boston to Bombay – or at least about two-thirds of it could, enough to make the long trip profitable. Ice went to the furthest corners of South America and from New England to California via Cape Horn. Sawdust, a product previously without any value at all, proved to be an excellent insulator, providing useful extra income for Maine lumber mills.

Lake Wenham was actually completely incidental to the ice business in America. It never produced more than about ten thousand tons of ice in a year, compared with almost a million tons lifted annually just from the Kennebec River in Maine. In England, Wenham ice was more talked about than used. A few businesses took regular deliveries, but hardly any households (other than the royal one) did. By the 1850s not only was most ice sold in Britain not from Wenham, it wasn't from America at all. The Norwegians – not a people one normally associates with sharp practices – changed the name of Lake Oppegaard, near Oslo, to Lake Wenham so that they could tap into the lucrative market. By the 1850s most ice sold in Britain was in fact Norwegian, though it has to be said that ice never really caught on with the British. Even now, it is still often dispensed in the UK as if it were on prescription. The real market, it turned out, was in America itself.

As Gavin Weightman notes in his history of the business, *The Frozen Water Trade*, Americans appreciated ice as no people had before. They used it to chill beer and wine, to make delectable icy cocktails, to soothe fevers and to create a vast range of frozen treats. Ice creams became popular – and startlingly inventive, too. At Delmonico's, the celebrated New York restaurant, customers could order pumpernickel rye ice cream and asparagus ice cream, among many other unexpected flavours. New York City alone consumed nearly a million tons of ice a year. Brooklyn sucked down 334,000 tons, Boston 380,000, Philadelphia 377,000. Americans grew immensely proud of the civilizing conveniences of ice. 'Whenever you hear America abused,' one American told Sarah Maury, a visiting Briton, 'remember the ice.'

Where ice really came into its own was in the refrigeration of railway cars, which allowed the transport of meat and other perishables from coast to coast. Chicago became the epicentre of the railway industry in part because it could generate and keep huge quantities of ice. Individual ice houses in Chicago held up to 250,000 tons of ice. Before ice, in hot weather milk (which came out of the cow warm, of course) could only be kept for an hour or two before it began to spoil. Chicken had to be eaten on the day of plucking. Fresh meat was seldom safe for more than a day. Now food could be kept longer locally, but it could also be sold in distant markets. Chicago got its first lobster in 1842, brought in from the east coast in a refrigerated railway car. Chicagoans came to stare at it as if it had arrived from a distant planet. For the first time in history food didn't have to be consumed close to where it was produced. Farmers on the boundless plains of the American Midwest could not only produce food more cheaply and abundantly than anywhere else, but they could now sell it almost anywhere.

Meanwhile, other developments increased the range of food storage possibilities enormously. In 1859 an American named John Landis Mason solved the challenge that the Frenchman François (or Nicolas) Appert had not quite mastered the better part of a century before. Mason patented the threaded glass jar with a metal screw-on lid. This provided a perfect seal and made it possible to preserve all kinds of foods that would previously spoil. The Mason jar became a huge hit everywhere, though Mason himself scarcely benefited from it. He sold the rights in it for a modest sum, then turned his attention to other inventions – a folding life raft, a case for keeping cigars fresh, a self-draining soap dish – that he assumed would make him rich, but his other inventions not only weren't successful, they weren't even very good. As one after another failed, Mason withdrew into a semi-demented poverty. He died alone and forgotten in a New York City tenement house in 1902.

An alternative and ultimately even more successful method for preserving food, namely canning, was perfected in England by a man named Bryan Donkin working between 1810 and 1820. Donkin's invention preserved foods beautifully, though the early cans, made of wrought iron, were heavy and practically impossible to get into. One brand bore instructions to open them with a hammer and chisel. Soldiers usually attacked them with bayonets or fired bullets into them. The real breakthrough awaited the development of lighter materials, which in turn enabled mass production. At the beginning of the 1800s, one man, working hard, could produce about sixty cans a day. By 1880 machines could pump out fifteen hundred in a day. Surprisingly, getting them open remained a serious impediment much longer. Various cutting devices were patented, but all were difficult to use or nearly lethal if they slipped. The safe modern manual can opener – the sort with two rolling wheels and a twisting key – dates only from 1925.

Developments in food preservation were part of a much wider revolution in food production that changed the dynamics of agriculture everywhere. The McCormick reaper permitted the mass production of grain, which in turn allowed America to produce livestock on an industrial scale. This in its turn led to the development of large meat-packing centres and improved methods of refrigeration – and ice remained at the heart of that well into the modern era. As late as 1930 America had 181,000 refrigerated railway cars and they were all cooled with ice.

The sudden ability to transport food over great distances and to keep it fresh enough to reach far-off markets transformed agriculture in many distant lands. Kansas wheat, Argentinian beef, New Zealand lamb and other foodstuffs from around the world began to turn up on dinner tables thousands of miles away. The repercussions in traditional farming areas were enormous. You don't have to venture far into any New England forest to find the ghostly house foundations and old field walls that denote a farm abandoned in the nineteenth century. Farmers throughout the region left their farms in droves, either to work in factories or to try their hand at farming on better land further west. In a single generation Vermont lost nearly half its population. Europe suffered equally. 'British agriculture virtually collapsed in the last generation of the nineteenth century,' says Felipe Fernández-Armesto, and with it went all the things it had previously supported – farm labourers, villages, country churches and parsonages, a landed aristocracy. Ultimately, it put our rectory, and thousands of others like it, into private hands.

In the autumn of 2007, during a visit to New England, I drove out from Boston to Lake Wenham to see this lake that was once briefly the most famous in the world. Today Wenham stands along a quiet highway in attractive countryside some fifteen miles north of Boston, and provides a picturesque glimpse of water for anyone driving between the towns of Wenham and Ipswich. Lake Wenham now serves as a reservoir for Boston, so it is surrounded by a high chain-link fence and is closed to the public. A historical marker beside the road celebrates the town of Wenham's tercentenary in 1935, but makes no mention of the ice trade that once made it famous.

III

If we were to step into the kitchen of the rectory in 1851, a number of differences would strike us immediately. For one thing, there would have been no sink. Kitchens in the mid-nineteenth century were for cooking only (at least in middle-class homes); washing-up was done in a separate scullery – the room we will visit next – which meant that every dish and pot had to be carried to a room across the corridor to be scrubbed, dried and put away, then brought back to the kitchen the next time it was needed. That could entail many trips, for the Victorians did a lot of cooking and provided an awesome array of dishes. A popular book of 1851 by a Lady Maria Clutterbuck (who was actually Mrs Charles Dickens) gives a good impression of the kind of cooking that went on in those days. One suggested menu – for a dinner for six people – comprises 'carrot soup, turbot with shrimp sauce, lobster patties, stewed kidneys, roast saddle of lamb, boiled turkey, knuckle of ham, mashed and brown potatoes, stewed onions, cabinet pudding, blancmange and cream, and macaroni'. Such a meal, it has been calculated, could generate 450 pieces of washing-up. The swing door leading from the kitchen to the scullery must have swung a lot.

Had you arrived at a time when the housekeeper, Miss Worm, and her assistant, a nineteen-year-old village girl named Martha Seely, were baking or cooking, you might well have found them doing something that until recently had not been done at all – carefully measuring out ingredients. Until almost the middle of the century instructions in cookery books were always wonderfully

Plate 1st

FARMER GILES'S ESTABLISHMENT — Christmas day 1800

The golden age of gluttony.

imprecise, calling merely for 'some flour' or 'enough milk'. What changed all that was a revolutionary book by a shy and by all accounts sweet-natured poet in Kent named Eliza Acton. Because her poems weren't selling, her publisher gently suggested she might try something more commercial, and in 1845 Miss Acton produced *Modern Cookery for Private Families*. It was the first book to give exact measurements and cooking times, and it became the work on which all cookery books since have been, almost always unwittingly, modelled.

The book enjoyed considerable success, but then was abruptly shouldered aside by a brasher work – the vastly, lastingly, powerfully, mystifyingly influential *Book of Household Management* by Isabella Beeton. There has never been another book quite like it, for both influence and content. It was an instant success and would remain a success well into the following century.

Mrs Beeton made clear from the first line that running a household was a grave and cheerless business. 'As with the commander of an Army, or the leader of any enterprise, so it is with the mistress of a house,' she declared. Only a moment earlier she had saluted her own selfless heroism: 'I must frankly own, that if I had known, beforehand, that this book would cost me the labour which it has, I should never have been courageous enough to commence it,' she declared, leaving the reader with a sense of mild gloom and guilty indebtedness.

Its title notwithstanding, *The Book of Household Management* whips through its professed subject in just twenty-three pages, then turns to cooking for nearly the whole of the next nine hundred. Despite this bias towards the kitchen, however, Mrs Beeton didn't actually like cooking and didn't go near her own kitchen if she could possibly help it. You don't have to read far into the recipes to begin to suspect as much – when she suggests, for instance, boiling pasta for an hour and three-quarters before serving. Like many of her nation and generation, she had an innate suspicion of anything exotic. Mangoes, she said, were liked only 'by those who have not a prejudice against turpentine'. Lobsters she found 'rather indigestible' and 'not so nutritive as they are generally supposed to be'. Garlic was 'offensive'. Potatoes were 'suspicious; a great many are narcotic, and many are deleterious'. Cheese she thought fit only for sedentary people – she didn't say why – and then only 'in very small quantities.' Especially to be avoided were cheeses with veins, since these were fungal growths. 'Generally speaking,' she added, just a touch ambiguously, 'decomposing bodies are not wholesome eating, and the line must be drawn somewhere.' Worst of all was the tomato: 'The whole plant has a disagreeable odour, and its juice, subjected to the action of the fire, emits a vapour so powerful as to cause vertigo and vomiting.'

Mrs Beeton appears to have been unacquainted with ice as a preservative, but we may safely assume that she wouldn't have liked it, for she didn't like chilled things generally. 'The aged, the delicate and children should abstain from ices or cold beverages,' she wrote. 'It is also necessary to abstain from them when persons are very warm, or immediately after taking violent exercise, as in some cases they have produced illnesses which have ended fatally.' A great many foods and activities had fatal consequences in Mrs Beeton's book.

For all her matronly airs, Mrs Beeton was just

twenty-three when she began the book. She wrote it for her husband's publishing company, where it was issued as a partwork in thirty-three monthly instalments beginning in 1859 (the year that also saw the publication of Charles Darwin's *On the Origin of Species*) and produced as a single volume in 1861. Samuel Beeton had already made quite a lot of money from publishing *Uncle Tom's Cabin*, which was as much of a sensation in Britain as in America. He also started some popular magazines, including the *Englishwoman's Domestic Magazine* (1852), which had many innovations – a problem page, medical column, dress patterns – still often found in women's magazines today.

Nearly everything about *Household Management* suggested it was done in carelessness and haste. The recipes were mostly contributed by readers, and nearly all the rest was plagiarized. Mrs Beeton stole shamelessly from the most obvious and traceable sources. Whole passages are lifted verbatim from the autobiography of Florence Nightingale. Others are taken straight from Eliza Acton. Remarkably, Mrs Beeton didn't even trouble to adjust gender, so that one or two of her stories are related in a voice that, disconcertingly and bewilderingly, can only be male. Organizationally the whole is a mess. She devotes more space to the making of turtle soup than to breakfast, lunch and supper combined, and never mentions after-noon tea at all. The inconsistencies are little short of spectacular. On the very page on which she lengthily explicates the tomato's dangerous failings ('it has been found to contain a particular acid, a volatile oil, a brown, very fragrant extracto-resinous matter, a vegeto-mineral matter, muco-saccharine, some salts, and, in all probability, an alkaloid'), she gives a recipe for stewed tomatoes, which she calls a 'delicious accompaniment', and notes, 'It is a wholesome fruit and digests easily. Its flavour stimulates the appetite and it is almost universally approved.'

Despite its manifold peculiarities, Mrs Beeton's book was a huge and lasting success. Its two unimpeachable virtues were its supreme confidence and its comprehensiveness. The Victorian era was an age of anxiety, and Mrs Beeton's plump tome promised to guide the worried homemaker through every one of life's foamy shoals. Flicking through the pages, the homemaker could learn how to fold napkins, dismiss a servant, eradicate freckles, compose a menu, apply leeches, make a Battenberg cake and restore to life someone struck by lightning. Mrs Beeton elucidated in precise steps how to make hot buttered toast. She gave cures for stammering and for thrush, discussed the history of lambs as a sacrifice, provided an exhaustive list of the many brushes (stove brush, cornice brush, banister broom, whisk broom, carpet broom, crumb brush – some forty in all) that were needed in any house that aspired to hygienic respectability, discussed the dangers of making friendships in haste and the precautions to be taken before entering a sickroom. It was an instruction manual that could be followed religiously and that was exactly what people wanted. Mrs Beeton was decisive on every manner of topic – the domestic equivalent of a drill sergeant.

She was just twenty-eight years old when she died, of puerperal fever, eight days after giving birth for the fourth time, but her book lived on and on. It sold more than two million copies in its first decade alone and continued to sell steadily well into the twentieth century.

*   *   *

Looking back now, it is nearly impossible to get a fix on Victorians and their diet. For a start, the range of foods was dazzling. People, it seems, ate practically anything that stirred in the undergrowth or could be hauled from water. Ptarmigan, sturgeon, larks, hare, woodcock, gurnet, barbel, smelts, plover, snipe, gudgeon, dace, eels, tench, sprats, turkey poults and many more largely forgotten delicacies featured in Mrs Beeton's many recipes. Fruits and vegetables seemed almost infinite in number. Of apples alone there were, almost unbelievably, more than 2,000 varieties to choose from – Worcester pearmain, Beauty of Bath, Cox's orange pippin and so on in long and poetic vein. At Monticello in the early nineteenth century Thomas Jefferson grew twenty-three different types of peas and more than 250 kinds of fruit and vegetable. (Unusually for his day, Jefferson was practically a vegetarian and ate only small portions of meat as a kind of 'condiment'.) As well as gooseberries, strawberries, plums, figs and other produce well known to us today, Jefferson and his contemporaries also enjoyed tayberries, tansy, purslane, Japanese wine berries, damsons, medlars, seakale, screwpine, rounceval peas, skirrets (a kind of sweet root), cardoons (a thistle), scorzonera (a type of salsify), lovage, turnip-cabbage, and scores more that nowadays are encountered rarely or not at all. Jefferson, incidentally, was also a great adventurer with foods. Among his many other accomplishments, he was the first person in America to slice potatoes lengthwise and fry them. So as well as being the author of the Declaration of Independence, he was also the father of the American French fry.

Part of the reason people could eat so well was that many foods that we now think of as delicacies were plenteous then. Lobsters bred in such abundance around Britain's coastline that they were fed to prisoners and orphans or ground up for fertilizer; servants sought written agreements from their employers that they would not be served lobster more than twice a week. Americans enjoyed even greater abundance. New York Harbor alone held half the world's oysters and yielded so much sturgeon that caviar was set out as a bar snack. (The idea was that salty food would lead people to drink more beer.) The size and variety of dishes and condiments on offer was almost breathtaking. One hotel in New York in 1867 had 145 dishes on the menu. A popular American recipe book of 1853, *Home Cookery*, casually mentions adding one hundred oysters to a pot of gumbo soup to 'enhance' it. Mrs Beeton provided no fewer than 135 recipes just for sauces.

Remarkably, Victorian appetites were really comparatively restrained. The golden age of gluttony was actually the eighteenth century. This was the age of John Bull, the most red-faced, overfed, coronary-ready icon ever created by any nation in the hope of impressing other nations. It is perhaps no coincidence that two of the fattest monarchs in British history did a great deal of their eating in the 1700s. The first was Queen Anne. Although paintings of Anne always tactfully make her look no more than a little fleshy, like one of Rubens's plump beauties, she was in fact jumbo-sized – 'exceedingly gross and corpulent' in the candid words of her former best friend the Duchess of Marlborough. Eventually Anne grew so stout that she could not go up and down stairs. A trapdoor had to be cut in the floor of her rooms at Windsor Castle through which she was lowered, jerkily and inelegantly, by means of pulleys and a hoist to the state rooms below. It must have been a most remarkable sight to behold. When she died, she was buried in a coffin that was 'almost square'. Even more famously enormous was the Prince Regent, the future George IV, whose stomach when let out of its corset reportedly spilled to his knees. By the age of forty his waist was more than four feet around.

Even slenderer people routinely sat down to quantities of food that seem impossibly munificent, if not positively destabilizing. A breakfast recorded by the Duke of Wellington consisted of 'two pigeons and three beef-steaks, three parts of a bottle of Mozelle, a glass of champagne, two glasses of port and a glass of brandy' – and this was when he was feeling a little under the weather. The Reverend Sydney Smith, though a man of the cloth, caught the spirit of the age by declining to say grace. 'With the ravenous orgasm upon you, it seems impertinent to interpose a religious sentiment,' he explained. 'It is a confusion of purpose to mutter out praises from a mouth that waters.'

By the middle of the nineteenth century, gargantuan portions had become institutionalized and routine. Mrs Beeton gives the following as a menu for a small dinner party: mock turtle soup, fillets of turbot in cream, fried sole with anchovy sauce, rabbits, veal, stewed rump of beef, roasted fowls, boiled ham, a platter of roasted pigeons or larks, and, to finish, rhubarb tartlets, meringues, clear jelly, cream, ice pudding and soufflé. This was, in Mrs Beeton's book, food for six people.

The ironic aspect was that the more attention the

Victorians devoted to food, the less comfortable with it they seemed to be. Mrs Beeton didn't actually appear to like food at all and treated it, as she treated most things, as a kind of grim necessity to be dealt with swiftly and decisively. She was especially suspicious of anything that added zest to food. Garlic she abhorred. Chillies were barely worth mentioning. Even black pepper was only for the foolhardy. 'It should never be forgotten,' she warned her readers, 'that, even in small quantities, it produces detrimental effects on inflammatory constitutions.' These alarmed sentiments were echoed endlessly in books and periodicals throughout the age.

Eventually many Victorian households gave up on flavour altogether and just concentrated on trying to get food to the table hot. In larger homes that was ambition enough because kitchens could be wondrously distant from dining rooms. Audley End in Essex set something of a record in this respect by having the kitchen and dining room more than two hundred yards apart. At Tatton Park in Cheshire, to try to speed things up an internal railway line was laid down so that trolleys could be rushed from the kitchen to a distant dumbwaiter, there to be hastily dispatched onwards. Sir Arthur Middleton of Belsay Hall near Newcastle became so obsessed with the temperature of the food sent to his table that he plunged a thermometer into each arriving dish, and sent back for a further blast of heat, sometimes repeatedly, any that failed to register to his expected standards, so that many of his dinners were taken very late and in a more or less carbonized condition. Auguste Escoffier, the great French chef at the Savoy Hotel in London, earned the esteem of British diners not just by producing very good food, but by employing a brigade

system in the kitchens with different cooks concentrating
on different foods – one for meats, one for vegetables and
so on – so that everything could be deposited on the plate
at once and brought to the table in unaccustomedly
steamy glory.

All this is of course at striking variance with what was said
earlier about the poverty of the average person's diet in the
nineteenth century. The fact is there is such a confusion of
evidence that it is impossible to know how well or not
people ate.

If *average* consumption is any guide, then people ate
quite a lot of healthy food: almost eight pounds of pears
per person in 1851, compared with just three pounds now;
almost nine pounds of grapes and other soft fruits,
roughly double the amount eaten now; and just under
eighteen pounds of dried fruit, as against three and a half
pounds today. For vegetables the figures are even more
striking. The average Londoner in 1851 ate 31.8 pounds of
onions, as against 13.2 pounds today; consumed over
forty pounds of turnips and swedes, compared with 2.3
pounds today; and packed away almost seventy pounds of
cabbages per year, as against twenty-one pounds now. Sugar
consumption was about thirty pounds a head – less than a
third the amount consumed today. So on the whole it seems
that people ate pretty healthily.

Yet most anecdotal accounts, written then and sub-
sequently, indicate the very opposite. Henry Mayhew, in
his classic *London Labour and the London Poor*, published
in the year our rectory was built, suggested that a piece of
bread and an onion constituted a typical dinner for a
labourer, while a much more recent (and deservedly much

praised) history, *Consuming Passions* by Judith Flanders, states that 'the staple diet of the working classes and much of the lower middle classes in the mid nineteenth century consisted of bread or potatoes, a little bit of butter, cheese or bacon, tea with sugar.'

What is certainly true is that people who had no control of their diets often ate very poorly indeed. A magistrate's report of conditions at a factory in northern England in 1810 revealed that apprentices were kept at their machines from 5.50 in the morning to 9.10 or 9.15 at night, with a single short break for dinner. 'They have Water Porridge for Breakfast and Supper' – taken at their machines – 'and generally Oatcake and Treacle, or Oatcake and poor Broth, for Dinner,' he wrote. That was, almost certainly, pretty typical fare for anyone stuck in a factory, prison, orphanage or other powerless situation.

It is also true that for many poorer people diets were remarkably unvaried. In Scotland, farm labourers in the early 1800s received an average ration of 17.5 pounds of oatmeal a week, plus a little milk, and almost nothing else, though they generally considered themselves lucky because at least they didn't have to eat potatoes. These were widely disdained for the first hundred and fifty years or so after their introduction to Europe. Many people considered the potato an unwholesome vegetable because its edible parts grew below ground rather than reaching nobly for the sun. Clergymen sometimes preached against the potato on the grounds that it nowhere appears in the Bible.

Only the Irish couldn't afford to be so particular. For them the potato was a godsend because of its very high yields. A single acre of stony soil could support a family of six if they were prepared to eat a lot of potatoes, and the Irish, of necessity, were. By 1780, 90 per cent of people there were dependent for their survival exclusively or almost exclusively on potatoes. Unfortunately, the potato is also one of the most vulnerable of vegetables, susceptible to more than 260 types of blight or infestation. From the moment of the potato's introduction to Europe, failed harvests became regular. In the 120 years leading up to the great famine, the potato crop failed no fewer than twenty-four times. Three hundred thousand people died in a single failure in 1739. But that appalling total was made to seem insignificant by the scale of death and suffering in 1845–6.

It happened very quickly. The crops looked fine until August and then suddenly they drooped and shrivelled. The tubers when dug up were spongy and already putrefying. That year half the Irish crop was lost. The following year virtually all of it was wiped out. The culprit was a fungus called *Phytophthora infestans*, but people didn't know that. Instead they blamed almost anything else they could think of – steam from steam trains, the electricity from telegraph signals, the new guano fertilizers which were just becoming popular. It wasn't only in Ireland the crops failed. They failed across Europe. It was just that the Irish were especially dependent on them.

Relief was famously slow to come. Months after the starvation had started, Sir Robert Peel, the British prime minister, was still urging caution. 'There is such a tendency to exaggeration and inaccuracy in Irish reports that delay in acting on them is always desirable,' he wrote. In the worst year of the potato famine, London's fish market, Billingsgate, sold 500 million oysters, one billion fresh herrings, almost 100 million soles, 498 million shrimps, 304 million periwinkles, 33 million plaice, 23 million mackerel and other similarly massive amounts, and not one morsel of any of it made its way to Ireland to relieve the starving people there.

The greatest part of the tragedy is that there was actually plenty of food in Ireland itself. The country produced great quantities of eggs, cereals and meats of every type, and brought in large hauls of food from the sea, but almost all went for export. So 1.5 million people needlessly starved. It was the greatest loss of life anywhere in Europe since the Black Death.

CHAPTER FIVE

The Scullery and Larder

A MONG THE MANY small puzzles of the Old Rectory as it would have been originally is that there wasn't anywhere much for the servants to put themselves when they weren't working. The kitchen was barely big enough for a table and a couple of chairs, and the conjoined scullery and larder, where I have brought you now, were smaller still.*

As with the kitchen, these were rooms that Mr Marsham almost certainly entered diffidently, if at all, for this was very much the servants' realm – though it wasn't much of a realm. By the standards of the day, the servants' area was curiously deficient for a rectory. At Barham Rectory in Kent, built at about the same time, the architect

---

* The scullery, from *escullier*, an Old French word for dishes, was where dishes were washed and stacked, and it was here that you found a big, deep sink. Larder isn't, as one might suppose, directly related to lard; it is from the French *lardon*, for bacon – a place where meat was kept. The terms are the ones used on the original plans, but the servants themselves might well have called the second room a pantry, from Latin *panna* or 'bread room', which by the mid-nineteenth century had come to signify a place of general food storage.

gave the servants not only a kitchen, larder and scullery but also a pantry, storeroom, coal store, miscellaneous cupboards and, crucially, housekeeper's room, which was clearly meant for retreat and relaxation.

What makes all this rather hard to figure is that the house as built doesn't always match up with the house that Edward Tull designed. Mr Marsham evidently suggested (or perhaps even insisted upon) some substantial revisions, and not altogether surprisingly, for the house that Tull designed for him contained a number of arresting peculiarities. Tull stuck the front entrance on the side of the house, for no logical or deducible reason. He put a water closet on the main staircase landing – a truly odd and irregular spot – leaving the stairs without windows so that they would have been as dark as a cellar even in daytime. He designed a dressing room to go with the master bedroom, but failed to include a connecting door. He built an attic that had no stairs to it, but did have an excellent door to nowhere.

Most of the more wayward of these ideas were revised out of the house at some unknown point before or during construction. In the end, the principal entrance was placed more conventionally on the front of the house, not the side. The water closet was never built. The staircase was provided with a large window that still pleasantly bathes the stairs in sunlight when there is sunlight to be had, and provides a lovely view of the church beyond. Two extra rooms – a study downstairs and additional bedroom or nursery above – were added. Altogether, the house as built is quite different from the house that Tull designed.

Out of all the changes, one is particularly intriguing. In Tull's original plans, the area now occupied by the dining room was much smaller and included space for a 'Footman's Pantry' – what clearly would have been a room for the servants to eat and rest in. That was never built. Instead the dining room was roughly doubled in size to fill the entire space. Why the bachelor rector decided to deprive his employees of a place to sit and instead give himself a large dining room is of course impossible to say across such a distance of time. The upshot is that the servants had nowhere comfortable to sit when they weren't working. It may be that they hardly sat at all. Servants often didn't.

Mr Marsham kept three servants: the housekeeper Miss Worm, the village girl Martha Seely who worked as an underservant, and a groom and gardener named James Baker. Like their master, all were unmarried. Three servants to look after one bachelor clergyman might seem excessive to us, but it wouldn't have seemed so to anyone in Marsham's day. Most rectors kept at least four servants and some had ten or more. It was an age of servants. Households had servants the way modern people have appliances. Common labourers had servants. Sometimes servants had servants.

Servants were more than a help and convenience, they were a vital indicator of status. Guests at dinner parties might find that they had been seated according to the number of servants they kept. People held on to their servants almost for dear life. Even on the American frontier and even after she had lost almost everything in a doomed business venture, Frances Trollope, mother of the novelist Anthony Trollope, kept a liveried footman. Karl Marx, living in chronic indebtedness in Soho and often barely able to put food on the table, employed a housekeeper *and* a personal secretary. The household was so crowded that the secretary – a man named Pieper – had to share a bed with Marx. (Somehow, even so, Marx managed to put together enough private moments to seduce and impregnate the housekeeper, who bore him a son in the year of the Great Exhibition.)

So servitude was a big part of life for a great many people. By 1851, one-third of all the young women in London – those aged from about fifteen to twenty-five – were servants. Another one in three was a prostitute. For many, that was about all the choice there was. The total number of servants in London, male and female, was greater than the total populations of all but the six largest English cities. It was very much a female world. Females in service in 1851 outnumbered males by ten to one. For women, however, seldom was it a job for life. Most left the profession by the age of thirty-five, usually to get married, and very few stayed in any one job for more than a year or so. That is little wonder, as we shall see. Being a servant was generally hard and thankless work.

Staff sizes, as you would expect, varied enormously, but at the upper end of the scale they were usually substantial. A large country house typically had forty indoor staff. The bachelor Earl of Lonsdale lived alone, but had forty-nine people to look after him. Lord Derby had two dozen just to wait at dinner. The first Duke of Chandos kept a private orchestra for his mealtimes, though he managed to get extra value out of some of his musicians by making them do servants' work as well; a violinist, for instance, was required to give his son his daily shave.

Outdoor staff swelled the ranks further, particularly if the owners did a lot of riding or shooting. At Elveden, the

Guinness family estate in Suffolk, the household employed sixteen gamekeepers, nine underkeepers, twenty-eight warreners (for culling rabbits) and two dozen miscellaneous hands – seventy-seven people in all – just to make sure they and their guests always had plenty of flustered birds to blow to smithereens. Visitors to Elveden managed to slaughter over one hundred thousand birds every year. The sixth Baron Walsingham once single-handedly shot 1,070 grouse in a day, a toll that has not been bettered and we may reasonably hope never is. (Walsingham would have had a team of loaders providing him with a steady supply of loaded guns, so managing to fire the requisite number of shots was easy. The real challenge would have been in keeping up a steady flow of targets. The grouse were almost certainly released a few at a time from cages. For all the sport in it, Walsingham might just as well have fired straight into the cages and given himself more time for tea.)

Guests brought their own servants, too, so at weekends it was not unusual for the number of people within a country house to swell by as many as 150. Amid such a mass of bodies, confusion was inevitable. On one occasion in the 1890s Lord Charles Beresford, a well-known rake, let himself into what he believed was his mistress's bedroom and with a lusty cry of 'Cock-a-doodle-doo!' leapt into the bed, only to discover that it was occupied by the Bishop of Chester and his wife. To avoid such confusions, guests at Wentworth Woodhouse, a stately pile in Yorkshire, were given silver boxes containing personalized confetti, which they could sprinkle through the corridors to help them find their way back to, or between, rooms.

Everything tended to be on a grand scale. The kitchen at Saltram, a house in Devon, had 600 copper pots and pans, and that was pretty typical. The average country house might have as many as 600 towels, and similarly vast quantities of sheets and linens. Just keeping everything marked, recorded and correctly shelved was a monumental task. But even at a more modest level – at that of a parsonage, for instance – a dinner for ten people could easily require the use and washing of over 400 separate dishes, glasses, pieces of cutlery and so on.

Servants at all levels put in long hours and worked hard. Writing in 1925, one retired servant recalled how early in his career he had had to light a fire, polish twenty pairs of boots and clean and trim thirty-five lamps, all by the time the rest of the household began to stir. As the novelist George Moore wrote from experience in his memoir *Confessions of a Young Man*, the lot of the servant was to spend seventeen hours a day 'drudging in and out of the kitchen, running upstairs with coals and breakfasts and cans of hot water, or down on your knees before a grate . . . The lodgers sometimes threw you a kind word, but never one that recognized you as one of our kin; only the pity that might be extended to a dog.'

Before the advent of indoor plumbing, water had to be carried to each bedroom and then taken away again once used. As a rule each active bedroom had to be visited and refreshed five times between breakfast and bedtime. And each visit required a complicated array of receptacles and cloths so that, for instance, fresh water didn't ever come up in the same receptacle that waste water went down in. The maid had to carry three cloths – one for wiping drinking glasses, one for commodes and one for washbasins – and remember (or be sufficiently unpeeved with her mistress) to use the right ones on the right objects. And that of course was just for general light washing. If a guest or family member wished for a bath the workload rose dramatically. A gallon of water weighs ten pounds and a typical bath held 45 gallons, all of which had to be heated in the kitchen and brought up in special cans – and there might be two dozen or more baths to fill of an evening. Cooking likewise often required enormous strength and reserves of energy. A full cooking kettle could weigh 60 pounds.

Furniture, fire grates, curtains, mirrors, windows, marble, brass, glass and silver – all had to be cleaned and polished regularly, usually with the household's own particular brand of home-made polish. To keep steel knives and forks gleaming, it wasn't enough to wash and polish them; they had to be vigorously stropped against a piece of leather on which had been smeared a paste of emery powder, chalk, brick dust, crocus or hartshorn liberally mixed with lard. Before being put away, knives were greased with mutton fat (to defeat rusting) and wrapped in brown paper, and so had to be unwrapped, washed and dried before they could be used again. Knife cleaning was such a tedious and heavy process that a knife-cleaning machine – essentially a box with a handle to turn a stiff brush – became one of the very first labour-saving appliances. One was marketed as 'The Servant's Friend'. Doubtless it was.

It wasn't just a question of doing the work, either, but often of doing it to the kind of exacting standards that generally only occur to people who don't have to do the work themselves. At Manderston, in Scotland, a team of workers had to devote three full days twice a year to dismantling, polishing and then reassembling a grand staircase. Some of the extra work was as demeaning as it was pointless. The historian Elisabeth Garrett notes one household where the butler and his staff were required to put down spare stair carpet around the dining-room table before setting it so as not to tread on good carpet. One maid in London complained that her employers made her change out of her work clothes and into something more presentable before being sent out into the street to hail a cab for them.

The provisioning of households was an enormous preoccupation. Often groceries were bought in just two or three times a year, and stored in bulk. Tea was purchased by the chest, flour by the barrel. Sugar came in large cones called loaves. Servants became adept at preserving and storing items for long periods. Self-sufficiency was both a desire and a necessity. It wasn't just a question of doing the work, but of making the materials with which the work could be done. If you needed to starch a collar or polish shoes, you had to concoct your own ingredients. Commercial boot polishes didn't become available until the 1890s. Before that it was necessary to boil up a supply of polish at home from a mixture of ingredients, a process that not only stained boots but also pots, stirring spoons, hands and anything else it came into contact with. Starch had to be laboriously made from rice or potatoes. Even linens didn't come in a finished state. One bought bolts of cloth and had them made up into tablecloths, sheets, shirts, towels and so on.

Most large households had a still-room for distilling spirits and here were brewed an exhaustive repertoire of items – inks, weedkillers, soap, toothpaste, candles, waxes, vinegars and pickles, cold creams and cosmetics, rat poisons, flea powders, shampoos, medicines, solutions for removing stains from marble, for taking the shine off trousers, for stiffening collars, even for removing freckles. (A combination of borax, lemon juice and sugar was said to do the trick.) These treasured concoctions could involve any number of ingredients – beeswax, bullock's gall, alum, vinegar, turpentine and others even more startling. The author of one mid-nineteenth-century manual recommended that paintings be cleaned annually with a mixture of 'salt and stale urine', though whose urine and how stale was left to the reader to determine.

Many houses were so filled with pantries, storerooms and other service areas that the greater part of the house actually belonged to the servants. In *The Gentleman's House* of 1864, Robert Kerr stated that the typical stately home had two hundred rooms (counting all storage spaces) of which almost exactly half were household offices, which is to say rooms devoted to servants and their tasks, or their bedrooms. When stables and other outbuildings were added in, the property was overwhelmingly in the servants' control.

The division of labour behind the scenes could be enormously complicated. Kerr divided the suites of offices into nine categories: kitchen, bakery and brewery, upper servants' hall, lower servants' hall, cellars and outhouses, laundry, private rooms, 'supplementaries' and thoroughfares. Other homes used different reckonings. Florence Court in Ireland had more than sixty departments, while Eaton Hall, the Cheshire seat of the Duke of Westminster, got by with just sixteen – quite a modest number bearing in mind that he had more than three hundred servants. It all depended on the organizational predispositions of master, mistress, butler and housekeeper.

A large country house was likely to have a gun room, lamp room, still-room, pastry room, butler's pantry, fish store, bakehouse, coal store, game larder, brewery, knife room, brush room, shoe room and at least a dozen more. Lanhydrock House in Cornwall had a room exclusively for dealing with bedpans. Another in Wales, according to Juliet Gardiner, had a room set aside for ironing newspapers. The grandest or oldest homes might also have a saucery, spicery, poultery, buttery and others of more exotic provenance, such as a ewery (a room for keeping water jugs; the word is somehow derived from *aquaria*), chandry (for candles), avenery (for game beasts), napery (for linen) and more.

Some of the workroom names are not quite as straightforward as they might seem. 'Buttery' has nothing to do with butter. It refers to 'butts', as in butts of ale. (It is a corruption of *boutellerie*, the same word from which butler and bottle are derived; looking after the wine bottles is what butlers originally did.) Curiously the one service room not named for the products it contains is 'dairy'. The name derives from an Old French term, *dey*, meaning maiden. A dairy, in other words, was the room where the milkmaids were to be found, from which we might reasonably deduce that an Old Frenchman was more interested in finding the maid than the milk.

In all but the most modest households owners rarely set foot in the kitchen or servants' area and, as Juliet Gardiner puts it, 'knew only by report the conditions in which their servants lived'. It was not uncommon for the head of the household to know nothing about his servants beyond their names. Most would have had little idea how to find their way through the darker recesses of the servants' areas.

Every aspect of life was rigorously stratified, and these anxious distinctions existed for houseguests and family as much as for servants. Strict protocol dictated into which parts of the house each might venture – which corridors and staircases they might use, which doors they might open – depending on whether they were a guest or close relative, governess or tutor, child or adult, aristocrat or commoner, male or female, upper house servant or lower house servant. Such were the rigidities, Mark Girouard observes, that afternoon tea in one stately home was served in eleven different places to eleven different castes of people. In her history of country house servants, Pamela Sambrook notes how two sisters worked in the same house, one as a housemaid, one as a nursemaid, but were not allowed to speak or indicate acquaintance when they met because they inhabited different social realms.

Servants were given little time for personal grooming, and then were constantly accused of being dirty, which was decidedly unfair since a typical servant's day ran from 6.30 in the morning to 10 o'clock at night – later if an evening social event was involved. The author of one household manual noted wistfully how she would have loved to provide her servants with nice rooms, but sadly they always grew untidy. 'The simpler, therefore, a servant's room is furnished, the better,' she decided. By the Edwardian period servants got half a day off per week and one full day per month – hardly munificent when you consider that that was all the time they had to shop for personal items, get their hair cut, visit family, court, relax or otherwise enjoy a few hours of precious liberty.

Perhaps the hardest part of the job was simply being attached to and dependent upon people who didn't think much of you. Virginia Woolf's diaries are almost obsessively preoccupied with her servants and the challenge of maintaining patience with them. Of one, she writes: 'She is in a state of nature: untrained; uneducated . . . so that one sees a human mind wriggling undressed.' As a class they were as irritating as 'kitchen flies'. Woolf's contemporary Edna St Vincent Millay was rather more blunt. 'The only people I really hate are servants,' she wrote. 'They are not really human beings at all.'

It was unquestionably a strange world. Servants constituted a class of humans whose existences were fundamentally devoted to making certain that another class of humans would find everything they desired within arm's reach more or less the moment it occurred to them to desire it. The recipients of this attention became spoiled almost beyond imagining. Visiting his daughter in the 1920s, in a house too small to keep his servants with him, the tenth Duke of Marlborough emerged from the bathroom in a state of helpless bewilderment because his toothbrush wasn't foaming properly. It turned out that his valet had always put the toothpaste on the brush for him and the duke was unaware that toothbrushes didn't recharge automatically.

The servants' payoff for all this was often to be treated appallingly. It was common for mistresses to test the honesty of servants by leaving some temptation where they were bound to find it – a coin on the floor, say – and then punishing them if they pocketed it. The effect was to instil in servants a slightly paranoid sense that they were in the presence of a superior omniscience. Servants were also suspected of abetting burglars, by providing inside information and leaving doors unlocked. It was a perfect recipe for unhappiness on both sides. Servants, especially in smaller households, tended to think of their masters as unreasonable and demanding. Masters saw servants as slothful and untrustworthy.

Casual humiliation was a regular feature of life in service. Servants were sometimes required, for instance, to adopt a new name, so that the second footman in a household would always be called 'Johnson', say, thus sparing the family the tedium of having to learn a new name each time a footman retired or fell under the wheels of a carriage. Butlers were an especially delicate issue. They were expected to have the bearing and comportment of a gentleman, and to dress accordingly, but often the butler was required to engage in some intentional sartorial gaucherie – wearing trousers that didn't match his jacket, for instance – to ensure that his inferiority was instantly manifest.*

One handbook actually gave instructions – in fact, provided a working script – for how to humiliate a servant in front of a child, for the good of both child and servant. In this model scenario, the child is summoned to the study, where he finds his mother standing with the shamed servant, who is weeping quietly.

---

* Incidentally, our standard image of servants in black uniforms with frilly caps, starched aprons and the like actually reflects a fairly short-lived reality. Servants' uniforms didn't become routine until the rise of cotton imports in the 1850s. Before then the quality of clothes worn by the upper classes was so instantly and visibly superior to that of the working classes that it wasn't necessary to distinguish servants with uniforms.

'Nurse Mary,' the mother begins, 'is going to tell you that there are no black men who creep into little boys' rooms in the dark and carry them off when they are naughty. I want you to listen while Nurse Mary tells you this, for she is going away to-day, and you will probably never see her again.'

The nurse is then confronted with each of her foolish tales, and made to recant them one by one.

The boy listens carefully, then offers his hand to the departing employee. 'Thank you, nurse,' he says crisply. 'I ought not to have been afraid, but I believed you, you know.' Then he turns to his mother. 'I shall not be afraid, now, Mother,' he reassures her in an appropriately manly fashion, and all return to their normal lives – except of course the nurse who will probably never find respectable work again.

Dismissal, especially for females, was the most dreaded calamity, for it meant loss of employment, loss of shelter, loss of prospects, loss of everything. Mrs Beeton was at particular pains to warn her readers not to allow sentiment or Christian charity or any other consideration of compassion to lead them to write a false or misleading recommendation for a dismissed employee. 'In giving a character, it is scarcely necessary to say that the mistress should be guided by a sense of strict justice. It is not fair for one lady to recommend to another a servant she would not keep herself,' Mrs Beeton wrote, and that was all the reflection anyone needed to give to the matter.

As the Victorian era progressed servants increasingly were required not just to be honest, clean, hard-working, sober, dutiful and circumspect, but to become, as near as

possible, invisible. Jenny Uglow, in her history of gardening, mentions one estate where, when the family was in
residence, the gardeners were required to detour a mile
when emptying their wheelbarrows in order not to
become an irksome presence in the owner's field of view.
At one home in Suffolk, meanwhile, servants were
required to press their faces to the wall when members of
the family passed by.

Houses were increasingly designed to keep staff out of
sight and separate from the household except to the point
of absolute necessity. The architectural refinement that
most added to segregation was the back staircase. 'The
gentry walking up the stairs no longer met their last night's
faeces coming down them' is how Mark Girouard neatly
put it. 'On both sides this privacy is highly valued,' wrote
Robert Kerr in *The Gentleman's House* of 1864, though we
may safely assume that Mr Kerr had a closer acquaintanceship with the feelings of those who filled the chamber pots
than those who emptied them.

At the highest level it was not just servants but guests
and permanent members of the household who were
required to be minimally visible. When Queen Victoria
went on her afternoon walks through the grounds of
Osborne House on the Isle of Wight, no one at all, from
any level of society, was permitted to encounter her. It was
said that you could fix her location anywhere on the estate
by the sight of panicked people fleeing before her. On one
occasion the chancellor of the exchequer, Sir William
Harcourt, found himself out on open ground with
nothing to hide behind but a dwarf shrub. As Harcourt
was six feet four inches tall and very stout, his hiding could
be no more than a token gesture. Her Majesty affected not

to see him, but then she was very accomplished at not seeing things. In the house, where encounters in the corridors were unavoidable, it was her practice to gaze fixedly ahead and, with an imperious glint, dematerialize anyone encountered en route. Servants, unless extremely well trusted, were not allowed to look directly at her.

'The division of classes is the one thing which is most dangerous and reprehensible and never intended by the law of nature and which the Queen is always labouring to alter,' the queen once wrote, conveniently ignoring that the one place this noble principle didn't apply was in her own regal presence.

The senior servant within the household was the butler. His female counterpart was the housekeeper. Below them came the clerk of the kitchen and chef and an array of housemaids, parlourmaids, valets, houseboys and footmen. Footmen were originally just that – men who trotted on foot beside their master or mistress's sedan chair or carriage, to look glorious and perform any necessary services en route. By the seventeenth century, they were prized like racehorses, and sometimes their masters raced them against each other for high stakes. Footmen did most of the public jobs in the household – answered the door, served at table, delivered messages – and so were often chosen for their height, bearing and general dishiness, much to the disgust of Mrs Beeton. 'When the lady of fashion chooses her footman without any other consideration than his height, shape and tournure of his calf, it is not surprising that she should find a domestic who has no attachment for the family,' she sniffed.

Liaisons between footmen and mistresses were popularly supposed to be a feature of some of the more relaxed of the nation's households. In one well-known case Viscount Ligonier of Clonmell discovered that his wife had been consorting with an Italian nobleman, Count Vittorio Amadeo Alfieri. Ligonier offered a challenge, as honour required, and the two men had a duel of sorts in Green Park, using swords borrowed from a nearby shop. They tapped weapons for a few minutes, but their hearts didn't really appear to be in it, possibly because they knew the capricious Lady Ligonier wasn't worth spilling blood over, a suspicion she confirmed almost immediately by running off with her footman. This prompted a good deal of appreciative ribaldry throughout the nation and some happy versifying of which I can offer this couplet:

> But see the luscious Ligonier
> Prefers her post boy to her Peer.

Life for servants wasn't all bad by any means. The big country houses generally were lived in for only two or three months a year, so for some servants life was long periods of comparative ease punctuated by seasons of hard work and very long hours. For town servants, the opposite was generally the case.

They were warm, well fed, decently attired and had a place to sleep every night at a time when those things meant a good deal. When all the comforts are factored in, it has been calculated, a senior servant enjoyed a salary equivalent to £50,000 in today's money. Additional perks were generally also available for those ingenious or daring enough to seize them. At Chatsworth, for instance, beer was sent from the brewhouse to the house in a pipe that ran through Joseph Paxton's great conservatory. At some point during routine maintenance it was discovered that an enterprising member of the household had, equally routinely, been tapping into it.

Servants often made pretty good money from tips, too. It was usual when departing from a dinner party to have to pass a line of five or six footmen, each expecting his shilling, making a dinner out a very expensive business for everyone but the servants. Weekend guests were expected to be lavish in their tips, too. Servants also made money from showing visitors around. A custom arose in the eighteenth century of providing tours to callers if they were respectably dressed, and it became common for middle-class people to visit stately homes in much the same way they do today. In 1776, a visitor to Wilton House noted that she was visitor number 3,025 that year, and it was still only August. Some properties received so many sightseers that arrangements had to be formalized to keep things under control. Chatsworth was open on two designated days a week, and Woburn, Blenheim, Castle Howard, Hardwick Hall and Hampton Court similarly introduced opening hours to try to limit the throngs. Horace Walpole was so plagued with visitors to his house, Strawberry Hill in Twickenham, that he issued tickets and printed a long, rather peevish list of rules about what would be permitted and what not. If, for example, an applicant applied for four tickets but five people then turned up, none would be admitted. Other houses were more accommodating. Rokeby Hall, in Yorkshire, opened a tearoom.

Often the hardest work was in smaller households, where one servant might have to do the work of two or three elsewhere. Mrs Beeton, predictably, had a great deal

to say about how many servants one should have depending on financial position and breeding. Someone of noble
birth, she decreed, would require at least twenty-five
servants. A person earning £1,000 a year needed five – a
cook, two housemaids, a nursemaid and a footman. The
minimum for a middle-class, professional household was
three: parlourmaid, housemaid and cook. Even someone
on as little as £150 a year was deemed wealthy enough to
employ a maid-of-all-work (a job title that truly said it all).
Mrs Beeton herself had four servants. In practice, however,
it appears that most people didn't employ nearly as many
people as Mrs Beeton thought they should.

A much more typical household was that of Thomas
and Jane Carlyle, the historian and his wife, who
employed a single maid at 5 Great Cheyne Row in Chelsea.
This under-appreciated soul had not only to cook, clean,
clear away dishes, tend fires, haul ash, deal with callers,
manage supplies and all the rest, but each time the
Carlyles wanted a bath – and they wanted many – she had
to draw, heat and carry eight or ten gallons of hot water up
three flights of stairs, and afterwards repeat the process in
reverse.

In the Carlyles' house, the maid didn't have a room of
her own, but lived and slept in the kitchen – a surprisingly
common arrangement in smaller households, even refined
ones such as the Carlyles'. The kitchen at Great Cheyne
Row was in the basement, and was warm and snug, if a
touch dark, but even this elemental space was not hers to
control. Thomas Carlyle liked its cosiness, too, and often
chose to read there in the evenings, banishing the maid to
the 'back kitchen', which doesn't sound too dire but in fact
was just an unheated storeroom. There the maid perched

among sacks of potatoes and other provisions until she heard the scrape of Carlyle's chair, the tap of his pipe on the grate and the sounds of his retiring, which was often very late, and could at last claim her spartan bed.

In thirty-two years at Great Cheyne Row, the Carlyles employed thirty-four maids – and the Carlyles were comparatively easy people to work for since they had no children and were reasonably patient and compassionate by nature. But it was nearly impossible to find employees who could meet their exacting standards. Sometimes the servants failed spectacularly, as when Mrs Carlyle came home one afternoon in 1843 to find her housekeeper dead drunk on the kitchen floor, 'with a chair upset beside her and in the midst of a perfect chaos of dirty dishes and fragments of broken crockery'. On another occasion Mrs Carlyle learned to her horror that a maid had given birth to an illegitimate child in the downstairs parlour while she was away. She was particularly exercised that the woman had used 'all my fine napkins'. Most maids, however, left or were asked to leave because they declined to work as hard as the Carlyles expected them to.

The inevitable fact was that servants were only human, and only rarely possessed the acuity, skills, endurance and patience necessary to satisfy the ceaseless whims of employers. Anyone in command of the many talents necessary to be an outstanding servant was unlikely to want to be one.

The greatest vulnerability of servants was powerlessness. They could be blamed for almost anything. There have never been more convenient scapegoats, as the Carlyles themselves discovered in a famous incident on the evening of 6 March 1835. At that time, the Carlyles had

only recently moved to London from their native
Scotland, with the hope that Thomas would there fashion
a career as a writer. He was thirty-eight years old and had
already established a slight reputation – a very slight one,
it has to be said – with a work of dense personal
philosophy called *Sartor Resartus*, but he had yet to write
his magnum opus. He intended to correct that deficiency
with a multi-volume history of the French Revolution. In
the winter of 1835, after much exhausting labour, he had
finished the first volume and given the manuscript to his
friend and mentor John Stuart Mill for his valued opinion.

This was the background against which Mill turned up
at Carlyle's door on that chilly evening in early March,
looking ashen. Behind him, waiting in a carriage, was
Harriet Taylor, Mill's mistress. Taylor was the wife of a
businessman of such relaxed disposition that he
essentially shared her with Mill, and even provided them
with a cottage west of London, in Walton-on-Thames,
where they could go to tryst. I'll let Carlyle himself take up
the story at this point:

> Mill's rap was heard at the door: he entered pale, unable
> to speak; gasped out to my wife to go down and speak
> with Mrs Taylor; and came forward (led by my hand,
> and astonished looks) the very picture of desperation.
> After various inarticulate and articulate utterances to
> merely the same effect, he informs me that my First
> Volume (left out by him in too careless a manner, after
> or while reading it) was, except for four or five bits of
> leaves, irrevocably ANNIHILATED! I remember and still
> can remember less of it than anything I ever wrote with
> such toil: it is gone, the whole world and myself backed

by it could not bring that back: nay the old spirit too is
fled . . . It is gone, and will not return.

A servant, Mill explained, had seen it lying by the
fender and had used it to light a fire. Now, you don't have
to consider the matter too carefully to realize that this
explanation has some problems. First, a handwritten
manuscript, however disposed, does not look incon-
sequential; any maid who worked in the Mill household
would be used to seeing manuscripts and could not fail to
have had impressed upon her their importance and value.
In any case, it hardly takes an entire manuscript to light a
fire. Burning the whole would require patiently feeding
the pages in a few at a time – the action you would take if
you wished to be rid of the manuscript, but not if all you
wanted was to start a blaze. In short, it is impossible to
conceive circumstances in which a maid, however dim and
deficient, could accidentally but plausibly destroy such a
piece of work in its entirety.

An alternative possibility was that Mill himself had
burned the manuscript in a fit of jealousy or anger. Mill
was an authority on the French Revolution and had told
Carlyle that he had it in mind to write a book on the
subject himself one day, so jealousy was certainly a
possible motive. Also Mill at this time was going through
a personal crisis: Mrs Taylor had just told him that she
would not leave her husband, but insisted on maintaining
their peculiar tripartite relationship. So we might allow
that the balance of his mind was disturbed. Still, such a
wanton and destructive act simply didn't fit with either
Mill's previous good character or his seemingly genuine
horror and pain over the loss. The only possibility that

remained then was that Mrs Taylor, whom the staid Carlyles didn't much like, was in some unspecified way responsible. Mill had told them that he had read large parts of the work to her at Walton, so the suspicion arose that she had been in charge of the manuscript at the time of the disaster and somehow was at the dark, unhappy root of the matter.

The one thing the Carlyles could not do was question any of this, even in a despairing, rhetorical sort of way. The rules of decorum decreed that Carlyle had to accept the facts as Mill delivered them, and was not permitted any supplementary questions about how this terrible, amazing, inexplicable catastrophe had happened. An unspecified servant had carelessly destroyed Carlyle's manuscript in its entirety, and that was an end to it.

Carlyle had no option but to sit down and recompose the book as best he could – a task made all the more challenging by the fact that he no longer had notes to call on, for it had been his bizarre and patently misguided practice to burn his notes as he had finished each chapter, as a kind of celebration of work done. Mill insisted on giving Carlyle compensation of £100, enough to live on for a year while he redid the book, but their friendship, not surprisingly, never really recovered. Three weeks later, in a letter to his brother, Carlyle complained that Mill had not even had the courtesy to let them sorrow in private but had 'remained injudiciously enough to almost midnight, and my poor Dame and I had to sit talking of indifferent matters; and could not till then get our lament freely uttered'.

It is impossible to know how the reworked version differed from the original. What can be said is that the volume we now have is one of the most unreadable books ever to attract the esteem of its age. It is written entirely in the present tense in strange, overwrought language that seems always to be tiptoeing around on the brink of incoherence. Here is Carlyle discussing the man behind the guillotine:

> And worthy *Doctor Guillotin*, whom we hoped to behold one other time? If not here, the Doctor should be here, and we see him with the eye of prophecy: for indeed the Parisian Deputies are all a little late. Singular Guillotin, respectable practitioner; doomed by a satiric destiny to the strangest immortal glory that ever kept obscure mortal from the resting-place, the bosom of oblivion! . . . Unfortunate doctor! For two-and-twenty years, unguillotined, shall hear nothing but guillotine; then dying, shall through long centuries wander, as it were, a disconsolate ghost, on the wrong side of Styx and Lethe; his name like to outlive Caesar's.

Readers had never encountered such perky intimacy in a book and found it thrilling. Dickens claimed to have read the work five hundred times and credited it as the inspiration behind *A Tale of Two Cities*. Oscar Wilde venerated Carlyle. 'He made history a song for the first time in our language,' he wrote. 'He was our English Tacitus.' For half a century, Carlyle was, for literary folk, a god.

He died in 1881. His written histories barely outlived him, but his personal history goes on and on, thanks in very large part to the exceptionally voluminous correspondence that he and his wife left behind – enough to fill thirty volumes of close-printed text. Thomas Carlyle would no doubt be astonished and dismayed today to learn that his histories are largely unread, but that he is known now for the minutiae of his daily life, including decades of petty moans about servants. The irony, of course, is that employing a succession of thankless servants is what gave him and his wife the leisure to write all those letters.

Much of this had always been thus. Like the Carlyles but nearly two centuries earlier, Samuel Pepys and his wife, Elizabeth, had a seemingly endless string of servants during the eight and a half years of his diary, and perhaps little wonder since Samuel spent a good deal of his time pawing the females and beating the boys – though, come to that, he beat the girls quite a lot, too. Once he took a broom to a servant named Jane 'and basted her till she cried extremely'. Her crime was that she was untidy. Pepys kept a boy whose principal function seems to have been to give him something convenient to hit – 'with a cane or a birch or a whip or a rope's end, or even a salted eel', as Liza Picard puts it.

Pepys was also a great one for dismissing servants. One was sacked for uttering 'some sawcy words', another for being a gossip. One was given new clothes upon arrival, but ran off that night; when caught, Pepys retrieved the clothes and insisted that she be severely whipped. Others were dismissed for drinking or pilfering food. Some almost certainly went because they spurned his amorous fumblings. An amazing number, however, submitted. During the eight and a half years of his diary Pepys had sex with at least ten women other than his wife and sexual encounters with forty more. Many were servants. Of one maid, Mary Mercer, the *Dictionary of National Biography* calmly notes: 'Samuel seems to have made a habit of fondling Mercer's breasts while she dressed him in the morning.' (It is interesting that it is 'Samuel' for our rakish hero and 'Mercer' for the drudge.) When they weren't dressing him, absorbing his blows or providing roosts for his gropes, Pepys expected his servants to comb his hair and wash his ears. This was on top of a normal day's cooking, cleaning, fetching, carrying and all the rest. Not altogether surprisingly, the Pepyses had great difficulty finding and keeping servants.

Pepys's experience also demonstrated that servants could betray. In 1679, Pepys dismissed his butler for sleeping with the housekeeper (who, interestingly, remained in his employ). The butler sought revenge by claiming to Pepys's political enemies that Pepys was a papist. This was during a period of religious hysteria and Pepys was imprisoned in the Tower. It was only because the butler was seized by conscience and admitted that he had made the whole thing up that Pepys was allowed to go free, but it was a painfully vivid reminder that masters could be as much at the mercy of servants as servants were of masters.

As for the servants themselves, we generally don't know much about them because their existences went mostly unrecorded. One interesting exception was Hannah Cullwick, who kept an unusually thorough diary for nearly forty years. Cullwick was born in 1833 in Shropshire and entered household service full time as a pot girl – a kitchen skivvy – at the age of eight. In the course of a long career she was an undermaid, kitchen-maid, cook, scullion and general housekeeper. In all capacities, the work was hard and the hours long. She

*Hannah Cullwick photographed by her husband at various servants'
tasks, and dressed as a chimney sweep (bottom right). Note the
locked chain round her neck.*

began the diary in 1859 at the age of twenty-five and kept it up until just shy of her sixty-fifth birthday. Thanks to its span, it constitutes the most complete record of the daily life of an underservant during the great age of servitude. Like most house servants, she worked from before seven in the morning till nine or ten at night, sometimes later. The diaries are an endless, largely emotionless catalogue of tasks performed. Here is a typical entry, for 14 July 1860:

> Opened the shutters & lighted the kitchen fire. Shook my sooty thing in the dusthole & emptied the soot there. Swept & dusted the rooms & the hall. Laid the hearth & got breakfast up. Clean'd 2 pairs of boots. Made the beds & emptied the slops. Clean'd & washed the breakfast things up. Clean'd the plate; clean'd the knives & got dinner up. Clean'd away. Clean'd the kitchen up; unpack'd a hamper. Took two chickens to Mrs Brewer's & brought the message back. Made a tart & pick'd & gutted two ducks & roasted them. Clean'd the steps & flags on my knees. Blackleaded the scraper in front of the house; clean'd the street flags too on my knees. Wash'd up in the scullery. Clean'd the pantry on my knees & scour'd the tables. Scrubbed the flags around the house & clean'd the window sills. Got tea for the Master & Mrs Warwick . . . Clean'd the privy & Passage & scullery floor on my knees. Wash'd the dog & clean'd the sinks down. Put the supper ready for Ann to take up, for I was too dirty & tired to go upstairs. Wash'd in a bath & to bed.

This is a numbingly typical day. All that is unusual here is that she managed a bath. On most days she concludes her entries with a weary, fatalistic 'Slept in my dirt.'

Beyond her spare account of duties, there was something even more extraordinary about Hannah Cullwick's life, for she spent thirty-six years of it, from 1873 to her death in 1909, secretly married to her employer, a civil servant and minor poet named Arthur Munby, who never disclosed the relationship to family or friends. When alone, they lived as man and wife, but when visitors called, Cullwick stepped back into the role of maid. If overnight guests were present, Cullwick withdrew from the marital bed and slept in the kitchen. Munby was a man of some standing. He numbered among his friends Ruskin, Rossetti and Browning, and they were frequent visitors to his home, but none had any idea that the woman who called him 'sir' was actually his wife. Even in private their relationship was a touch unorthodox, to say the least. At his bidding, she called him 'massa' and blacked her skin to make herself look like a slave. The diaries, it transpires, were kept largely so that he could read about her getting dirty.

It was only in 1910, after he died and his will was made public, that the news came out, causing a minor sensation. It was her odd marriage rather than her poignant diaries that made Hannah Cullwick famous.

At the bottom of the servant heap were laundrymaids, who were so lowly that often they were kept almost entirely out of sight. Washing was taken to them rather than them collecting the washing. Laundry duty was so despised that in larger households servants were sometimes sent to the laundry as a punishment. It was an exhausting job. In a good-sized country house laundry staff could easily deal with six or seven hundred separate items of clothing, towels and bedlinen every week. Because there were no detergents before the 1850s, most laundry loads had to be soaked in soapy water or lye for hours, then pounded and scrubbed with vigour, boiled for an hour or more, rinsed repeatedly, wrung out by hand or (after about 1850) fed through a roller, and carried outside to be draped over a hedge or spread on a lawn to dry. (One of the commonest of crimes in the countryside was the theft of drying clothes, so someone often had to stay with the laundry until it was dry.) Altogether, according to Judith Flanders in *The Victorian House*, a straightforward load – one involving sheets and other household linens, say – was likely to incorporate at least eight separate processes. But many loads were far from straightforward. Difficult or delicate fabrics had to be treated with the greatest care and items of clothing made of different types of fabric – of velvet and lace, say – often had to be carefully taken apart, washed separately, then sewn back together again.

Because most dyes were impermanent and finicky, it was necessary to add precise doses of chemical compounds to the water of every load either to preserve the colour or to restore it: alum and vinegar for greens, baking soda for purples, oil of vitriol for reds. Every accomplished laundress had a catalogue of recipes for removing different kinds of stains. Linen was often steeped in stale urine, or a dilute solution of poultry dung, as this had a bleaching effect, but since these stank (not surprisingly) they required additional vigorous rinsing, usually in some kind of herbal extract, to sweeten their smell.

Starching was such a big job that it was often left to a

following day. Ironing was another massive and dauntingly separate task. Irons cooled quickly, so they had to be used with speed and then exchanged with a freshly heated one. Generally there would be one on the go and two being heated. The irons were heavy in themselves and it was necessary to press down with great force to get the desired results. But they also required delicacy and care because there were no controls, so it was easy to scorch fabrics. Heating irons over a fire often made them sooty, too, so they had to be constantly wiped down. If starch was involved, it stuck to the bottom of the iron, which then had to be rubbed with sandpaper or an emery board.

On laundry day it was often necessary for somebody to get up as early as 3 a.m. to get the hot water going. In many houses with only one servant it was necessary to hire in an outside laundress for the day. Some houses sent their laundry out, but until the invention of carbolic acid and other potent disinfectants, this was always attended with the fear that the laundry would come back infected with some dread disease like scarlet fever. There was also the squeamish uncertainty of not knowing whose clothes were being washed with one's own. Whiteley's, a large London department store, offered a laundry service beginning in 1892 but it didn't do well until a store manager thought to post a large notice saying that servants' clothing and customers' clothing were always washed separately. Until well into the twentieth century, many of the wealthiest London residents chose to send their weekly laundry to their country estates by train and have it done by people they felt they could trust.

In America the servant situation was very different in almost every way. Americans, it is often written, didn't have nearly as many servants as Europeans, but that is true only up to a point. In one area in particular some Americans had lots of servants: slavery. Thomas Jefferson had more than two hundred slaves, including twenty-five for his household alone. As one of his biographers has noted, 'When Jefferson wrote that he planted olive trees and pomegranates, one must be reminded that he wielded no shovel, but simply directed his slaves.'

Slavery and race were not automatic in the early days. Some blacks were treated as indentured servants, and freed like anyone else when their time was up. A seventeenth-century black man in Virginia named Anthony Johnson acquired a 250-acre tobacco plantation and grew prosperous enough to be a slave owner himself. Nor was it a southern institution at first. Slavery was legal in New York until 1827. In Pennsylvania, William Penn owned slaves. When Benjamin Franklin moved to London in 1757, he brought with him two slaves, named King and Peter.

What America didn't have a lot of were free servants. Even at its peak, fewer than half of American households employed a servant, and many servants didn't see themselves as servants at all. Most refused to wear livery and many expected to sit down to meals with the family – to be treated, in short, as something much closer to equals.

As one historian has put it, rather than try to reform the servants it was easier to reform the house, so from an early period America became besotted with convenience and labour-saving devices, though nineteenth-century appliances often added nearly as much labour as they saved. In 1899, the Boston School of Housekeeping calculated that a coal stove required fifty-four minutes of heavy maintenance a day – emptying ash, replenishing coal, blacking and polishing and so on – before the harried homemaker so much as boiled a pot of water. The rise of gas actually made matters even worse. A book called *The Cost of Cleanness* calculated that a typical eight-room house with gas fittings required fourteen hundred hours a year of special heavy cleaning, including ten hours a month of washing windows.

In any case, many of the new conveniences mostly eliminated work previously done by men – chopping wood, for instance – and so were of little benefit to women. In fact, changing lifestyles and improved technologies mostly just brought more work to women through bigger houses, more complicated meals, more copious and frequent laundry, and ever higher expectations of cleanliness.

But a potent and invisible presence was about to change all that for everyone, and for the story of that we need to proceed not to another room but to a small box that hangs on the wall.

CHAPTER SIX

The Fusebox

IN THE AUTUMN OF 1939, during the slightly hysterical confusion that comes with the outbreak of war, Great
Britain introduced stringent blackout regulations to thwart
any murderous ambitions by the Luftwaffe. For three months
it was essentially illegal to show any light at night, however
faint. Rule-breakers could be arrested for lighting a cigarette
in a doorway or holding a match up to read a road sign. One
man was fined for not covering the glow of the heater light
from his tropical fish tank. Hotels and offices spent hours
every day putting up and taking down special blackout
covers. Drivers had to drive around in almost perfect in-
visibility – even dashboard lights were not allowed – so they
had to guess not only where the road was but at what speed
they were moving.

Not since the Middle Ages had Britain been so dark,
and the consequences were noisy and profound. To avoid
striking the kerb or anything parked along it, cars took to
straddling the middle white lines, which was fine until
they encountered another vehicle doing likewise from the
opposite direction. Pedestrians found themselves in
constant peril as every pavement became an obstacle

Reading by candlelight.

course of unseen lampposts, trees and street furniture. Trams, known with respect as 'the silent peril', were especially unnerving. 'During the first four months of the war,' Juliet Gardiner relates in *Wartime*, 'a total of 4,133 people were killed on Britain's roads' – a 100 per cent increase over the year before. Nearly three-quarters of the victims were pedestrians. Without dropping a single bomb, the Luftwaffe was already killing six hundred people a month, as the *British Medical Journal* drily observed.

Fortunately, matters soon calmed down and a little illumination was allowed into people's lives – just enough to stop most of the carnage – but it was a salutary reminder of how used to abundant illumination the world had grown.

We forget just how painfully dim the world was before electricity. A candle – a good candle – provides barely a hundredth of the illumination of a single 100-watt light bulb. Open your refrigerator door and you summon forth more light than the total amount enjoyed by most households in the eighteenth century. The world at night for much of history was a very dark place indeed.

Occasionally we can see into the dimness, as it were, when we find descriptions of what was considered sumptuous, as when a guest at a Virginia plantation, Nomini Hall, marvelled in his diary how 'luminous and splendid' the dining room was during a banquet because seven candles were burning – four on the table and three elsewhere in the room. To him this was a blaze of light. At about the same time, across the ocean in England, a gifted amateur artist named John Harden left a charming set of drawings showing family life at his home, Brathay Hall in Westmorland. What is striking is how little illumination the family expected or required. A typical drawing shows four members sitting companionably at a table sewing, reading and conversing by the light of a single candle, and there is no sense of hardship or deprivation, and certainly no sign of the desperate postures of people trying to get a tiny bit of light to fall more productively on a page or piece of embroidery. A Rembrandt drawing, 'Student at a Table by Candlelight', is actually much closer to the reality. It shows a youth sitting at a table, all but lost in a depth of shadow and gloom that a single candle on the wall beside him cannot begin to penetrate. Yet he has a newspaper. The fact is that people put up with dim evenings because they knew no other kind.*

The widespread belief that people in the pre-electrical world went to bed at nightfall seems to be based entirely on the presumption that anyone deprived of robust illumination would be driven by frustration to retire. In fact, it appears that most people didn't retire terribly early – nine or ten o'clock seems to have been standard for most people in the days before electricity, and for some, particularly in cities, it was even later. For those who could control their working hours bedtimes and rising times were at least as variable then as now, and appear to have had little to do with the amount of light available. Samuel Pepys, in his diary, records rising at 4 a.m. in one place, but going to bed at 4 a.m. in another. Samuel Johnson famously stayed abed till noon if he could; generally he could. The writer Joseph Addison routinely rose at 3 a.m. in summer (and sometimes even earlier), but not till 11 in

* The French, according to Roger Ekirch, had a curious expression, which I pass on without comment: 'By candle-light a goat is ladylike.'

winter. There certainly seems to have been no rush to bring the day to a close. Visitors to eighteenth-century London often noted that the shops were open till 10 at night, and clearly there would be no shops without shoppers. When guests were present it was usual to serve supper at 10 and for company to stay till midnight or so. Including conversation beforehand and music after, a dinner gathering could last for seven hours or more. Balls often went on until two or three in the morning, at which time a supper would be served. People were so keen to go out and stay up that they didn't let much get in their way. In 1785 a Louisa Stewart wrote to her sister that the French ambassador suffered 'a stroke of the palsy yesterday', yet guests turned up at his house that night anyway 'and played at faro, etc., as if he had not been dying in the next room. We are a curious people.'

Getting around was a good deal harder because it was so dark outside. On the darkest nights it was not uncommon for the stumbling pedestrian to 'run his Head against a Post' or suffer some other painful surprise. People had to grope their way through the darkness, although in some cases they simply groped *in* the darkness. Lighting in London was still so poor in 1763 that James Boswell was able to have sex with a prostitute on Westminster Bridge – hardly the most private of trysting places. Darkness also meant danger. Thieves were at large everywhere, and as one London authority noted in 1718, people were often reluctant to go out at night for fear that 'they may be blinded, knocked down, cut or stabbed'. To avoid smacking into the unyielding, or being waylaid by brigands, people often secured the services of linkboys – so called because they carried torches known as links made from stout lengths of rope soaked in resin or some other combustible material – to see them home. Unfortunately, the linkboys themselves couldn't always be trusted and sometimes led their customers into back alleys where they or their confederates relieved the hapless customer of money and silken items.

Even after gas street lighting became widely available in the mid-nineteenth century, by modern standards it was still a pretty murky world after nightfall. The very brightest gas street lamps provided less light than a modern 25-watt bulb. Moreover they were distantly spaced. Generally at least thirty yards of darkness lay between each, but on some roads – the King's Road through London's Chelsea, for instance – they were seventy yards apart, so that they didn't so much light the way as provide distant points of brightness to aim for. Yet gas lamps held out for a surprisingly long time in some quarters. As late as the 1930s, almost half of London streets were still lit by gas.

If anything drove people to bed early in the pre-electrified world, it was not boredom but exhaustion. Many people worked immensely long hours. An Elizabethan Statute of Artificers of 1563 laid down that all artificers (which is to say, artisans and craftsmen) and labourers 'must be and continue at their work, at or before five of the clock in the morning, and continue at work, and not depart, until between seven and eight of the clock at night' – giving an eighty-four-hour working week. At the same time, it is worth bearing in mind that a typical London theatre like Shakespeare's Globe could hold two thousand people – about 1 per cent of London's population – of whom a great part were working people, and that there were, moreover, several theatres in operation at any time, as well as alternative entertainments like bear-baiting and cockfighting. So, whatever the statutes may have decreed, it is apparent that on any given day several thousand working Londoners patently were not at their workbenches but were out having a good time.

What unquestionably consolidated long working hours was the Industrial Revolution and the rise of the factory system. In factories, workers were expected to be at their places from 7 a.m. to 7 p.m. on weekdays and from seven to two on Saturdays, but during the busiest periods of the year – what were known as 'brisk times' – they could be kept at their machines from 3 a.m. to 10 p.m. – a nineteen-hour day. Until the introduction of the Factory Act of 1833, children as young as seven were required to work as long. In such circumstances, not surprisingly, people ate and slept when they could.

The rich kept gentler hours. Writing of country life in 1768, Fanny Burney noted: 'We breakfast always at ten, and rise as much before as we please; we dine precisely at two, drink tea about six and sup exactly at nine.' Her routine is echoed in countless diaries and letters from others of her class. 'I will give an account of one day and then you will see every day,' a young correspondent wrote to Edward Gibbon in about 1780. Her day, she wrote, began at nine, and breakfast was at ten. 'And then about 11 I play on the harpsichord, or I draw; at 1 I translate and 2 walk out again, 3 I generally read, and 4 we go to dine, after dinner we play at backgammon, we drink tea at 7, and I work or play on the piano till 10, when we have our little bit of supper and 11, we go to bed.'

Lighting was of many types, all pretty unsatisfactory by modern standards. The most basic form was rushlights, which were made by cutting meadow rushes into strips about a foot and a half in length and coating them in animal fat, usually mutton. These were then placed in a metal holder and burned like a taper. A rushlight typically lasted fifteen to twenty minutes, so a good supply of rushes and patience was required to get through a long evening. Rushes were gathered once a year, in springtime, so it was necessary to work out with some care how much illumination was needed over the coming twelve months.

For the better off, the usual form of lighting was candles. These were of two types – tallow and wax. Tallow, made from rendered animal fat, had the great advantage that it could be made at home from the fat of any slaughtered animal and so it was cheap – or at least it was until 1709, when Parliament, under pressure from the chandlers' guilds, enacted a law making it illegal to make candles at home. This became a source of great resentment in the countryside, and probably was widely flouted, but at some risk. People were still permitted to make rushlights, though this was sometimes a largely notional freedom. During times of hardship peasants didn't have animals to slaughter and rushlights required a supply of animal fat, so they had to pass their evenings not only hungry but in the dark.

Tallow was an exasperating material. Because it melted so swiftly, the candle was constantly guttering, and needed trimming up to forty times an hour. Tallow also burned with an uneven light, and stank. And because tallow was really just a shaft of decomposing organic matter, the older a tallow candle got the more malodorous it grew. Far superior were candles made of beeswax. These gave a steadier light and needed less trimming, but they cost about four times as much and so tended only to be used for best. The amount of illumination one gave oneself was a telling indicator of status. Elizabeth Gaskell in one of her novels had a character, a Miss Jenkyns, who kept two candles out but burned only one at a time, and constantly, fussily switched between the two to keep them at exactly equal lengths. That way if guests came they wouldn't find candles of unequal sizes and deduce her embarrassing frugality.

Where conventional fuels were scarce, people used what they could – gorse, ferns, seaweed, dried dung, whatever would burn. In the Shetland Islands, according to James Boswell, stormy petrels were so naturally oily that people sometimes just stuck a wick down their throats and lit it, but I suspect Boswell was being a touch gullible. Elsewhere in Scotland dung was gathered and dried out to be used as an illuminant and fuel. The loss of fertilizing dung from fields left a lot of land impoverished and is said to have accelerated the agricultural decline there. Some people were luckier than others. In Dorset, around Kimmeridge Bay, the oil-rich shales on the beach burned like coal, could be gathered for free, and actually provided a better light. For those who could afford it, oil lamps were the most efficient option, but oil was expensive and oil lamps were dirty and needed cleaning daily. Even over the course of an evening, a lamp might lose 40 per cent of its illuminating power as its chimney accumulated soot. If not properly attended to, they could be terribly filthy. Elisabeth Garrett records how one girl who had attended a party in New England where the lamps smoked reported afterwards: 'Our noses were all black, & our clothes were perfectly gray and . . . quite ruined.' For that reason, many people stuck with candles even after other options became available. Catherine Beecher and her sister Harriet Beecher Stowe in *The American Woman's Home*, a sort of American answer to Mrs Beeton's *Book of Household Management*, continued providing instructions for making candles at home until 1869.

Until the late eighteenth century the quality of lighting had remained unchanged for some three thousand years. But in 1783 a Swiss physicist named Ami Argand invented a lamp that increased lighting levels dramatically by the simple expedient of getting more oxygen to the flame. Argand's lamps also came with a knob that allowed the user to adjust the flame's level of brightness – a novelty that left many users almost speechless with gratitude. Thomas Jefferson was an early enthusiast and remarked in frank admiration how a single Argand lamp could provide illumination equal to half a dozen candles. He was so impressed that he brought back several Argand lamps from Paris in 1790.

Argand himself never got the riches he deserved. His patents were not respected in France, so he relocated to England, but they weren't respected there either or indeed anywhere else, and Argand made almost nothing from his devoted ingenuity.

The best light of all came from whale oil, and the best type of whale oil was spermaceti from the head of the sperm whale. Sperm whales are mysterious and elusive animals that are even now little understood. They produce and store great reserves of spermaceti – up to three tons of it – in a cavernous chamber in their skulls. Despite its name spermaceti is not sperm and has no reproductive function, but when exposed to air it turns from a translucent watery liquid to a milky white cream and it is obvious at once why sailors gave the sperm whale its name. No one has ever worked out what spermaceti is for. It may somehow assist with buoyancy, or it may help with the processing of nitrogen in the whale's blood. Sperm whales dive with great speed to enormous depths – up to a mile – without evident ill effects and it is thought that the spermaceti may in some unfathomed way explain why they don't get the bends. Another theory is that the spermaceti provides shock absorption for males when they fight for mating rights. This would help to explain the sperm whale's infamous predilection for headbutting whaling ships, often lethally, when angered. But it isn't actually known whether sperm whales headbutt each other. No less mysterious for centuries was the very valuable commodity they produce known as ambergris (from French words meaning 'grey amber', though in fact ambergris is as likely to be black as grey). Ambergris is formed in the digestive system of sperm whales – only recently has it been determined that it is made from the beaks of squid, the one part of that animal that they cannot digest – and excreted at irregular intervals. For centuries it was found floating in the sea or washed up on beaches, and so no one knew where it came from. It made a peerless fixative for perfumes, which gave it great value, although people who could afford it ate it as well. Charles II thought ambergris and eggs the finest dish in existence. (The taste of ambergris is said to recall vanilla.) In any case, the presence of ambergris alongside all that precious spermaceti made sperm whales hugely attractive as prey.

In common with other types of whales, the oil of sperm whales was also craved by industry as an emollient in the manufacture of soaps and paints and as lubrication for machinery. Whales also yielded gratifying quantities of baleen, a bone-like material taken from the upper jaw, which provided a sturdy but flexible material for corset stays, buggy whips and other items that needed a measure of natural springiness.

Whale oil was an American speciality, both to produce and to consume. It was whaling that brought so much early wealth to New England ports like Nantucket and Salem. In 1846, America had more than 650 whaling ships, roughly three times as many as all the rest of the world put together. Whale oil was taxed heavily throughout Europe, so people there tended to use colza, which was made from the oil of cole-seeds (a member of the cabbage family), or camphene, a derivative of turpentine, which made an excellent light, though it was highly unstable and tended, unnervingly, to explode.

Nobody knows how many whales were killed during the great age of whaling, but one estimate suggests that about 300,000 were slaughtered in the four decades or so to 1870. That may not seem an especially vast number, but then whale numbers were not vast to begin with. In any case, the hunting was enough to drive many species to the edge of extinction. As whale numbers dwindled, whaling voyages grew longer and longer – up to four years became common and five years not unknown – and whalers were driven to search the loneliest corners of the most distant seas. All this translated into greatly increased costs. By the 1850s a gallon of whale oil sold for $2.50 – half an average worker's weekly wage – yet still the remorseless hunt continued. Many species of whale – possibly all – would have vanished for ever but for a sequence of unlikely events that began in Nova Scotia in 1846 when a man named Abraham Gesner invented what for some time would be the most valuable product on Earth.

Gesner was a physician by profession but he had an odd passion for coal geology, and while experimenting with coal tar – a useless, sticky residue left over from the processing of coal into gas – he devised a way to distil it into a combustible liquid that he called (for uncertain reasons) kerosene. Kerosene burned beautifully and gave a light as strong and steady as that of whale oil, but with the potential to be produced much more cheaply. The problem was that production in volume seemed impossible. Gesner made enough to light the streets of Halifax and eventually started a plant in New York City, which made him prosperously secure, but kerosene squeezed from coal was never going to be more than a marginal product in the world at large. By the late 1850s, total American output was just six hundred barrels a day. (Coal tar itself, on the other hand, soon found applications in a vast range of products – paints, dyes, pesticides, medicines and more. Coal tar became the basis of the modern chemical industry.)

Into this quandary strode another unexpected hero – a bright young man named George Bissell, who had just stepped down as superintendent of schools in New Orleans after a brief but distinguished career in public education. In 1853, on a visit to his home town of Hanover, New Hampshire, Bissell called on a professor at his alma mater, Dartmouth College, and there he noticed a bottle of rock oil on the professor's shelf. The professor told him that rock oil – what we would now call petroleum – seeped to the surface in western Pennsylvania. If you soaked a rag in it, the rag would burn, but nobody had found any use for rock oil other than as a constituent of patent medicines. Bissell conducted some experiments with rock oil and saw that it would make an outstanding illuminant if only it could be extracted on an industrial scale.

He formed a company called the Pennsylvania Rock Oil Company and bought mineral leases along a sluggish waterway called Oil Creek, near Titusville in western Pennsylvania. Bissell's novel idea was to drill for oil, as you would for water. Everyone before had dug for it. To get things going he dispatched a man named Edwin Drake – always referred to in history books as 'Colonel' Edwin Drake – to Titusville with instructions to drill. Drake had no expertise in drilling and was not a colonel. He was a railway ticket collector. He had lately been forced to retire through ill health. His sole advantage to the enterprise was that he still possessed a railway pass and could travel to Pennsylvania for free. To enhance his stature, Bissell and his associates sent correspondence to Drake addressed to 'Colonel E. L. Drake'.

With a wad of borrowed money, Drake commissioned a team of drillers to begin the search for oil. Although the drillers thought Drake was an amiable fool, they gladly accepted the work and began to drill to his instructions. Almost at once the project ran into technical difficulties. To the astonishment of all, Drake showed an unexpected knack for solving mechanical problems and was able to keep the project moving. For more than a year and a half they drilled, but no oil came. By the summer of 1859, Bissell and his partners were out of funds. Reluctantly they dispatched a letter to Drake instructing him to shut down operations. Before the letter got there, however, on 27 August 1859, at a depth of just under seventy feet, Drake and his men hit oil. It wasn't the towering gusher that we traditionally associate with oil strikes – this oil had to be laboriously pumped to the surface – but it produced a steady volume of thick, viscous, blue-green liquid.

Although no one remotely appreciated it at the time, they had just changed the world completely and for ever.

The first problem for the company was where to store all the oil they were producing. There weren't barrels enough locally, so for the first few weeks they stored oil in bath-tubs, washbasins, buckets and whatever else they could find. Eventually, they started making purpose-built barrels with a capacity of forty-two gallons, and these remain today the standard measure for oil. Then there was the even more pressing question of exploiting it commercially. In its natural state, oil was really just horrible gunk. Bissell set to work distilling it into something purer. In so doing he discovered that once purified it not only made an excellent lubricant, but produced as a side effect very con-siderable quantities of gasoline and kerosene.* The gasoline had no use at all – it was way too volatile – and so was poured away, but the kerosene made a brilliant

* Both gasoline and kerosene were variously spelled in the beginning. Gesner actually termed his product 'Kerocene' in his patent application of 1854. Scientists hate inconsistency, and petroleum geologists have from time to time tried to make the spelling of the terminal syllables match, but obviously without success. They have been equally unsuccessful with the terminal pronunciations of hydrocarbons, as evidenced by turpen*tine*. The British resolved part of the problem by calling kerosene paraffin.

light, as Bissell had hoped, but at a much lower cost than Gesner's coal-squeezed product. At last the world had a cheap illuminant to rival whale oil.

Once others saw how easy it was to extract oil and turn it into kerosene, a land rush was on. Soon hundreds of derricks crowded the landscape around Oil Creek. 'In three months,' John McPhee notes in *In Suspect Terrain*, 'the endearingly named Pithole City went from a population of zero to 15,000, and other towns throughout the region sprang up – Oil City, Petroleum Center, Red Hot. John Wilkes Booth came and lost his savings, then went off to kill a president.'

In the year of Drake's discovery America produced two thousand barrels of oil; within ten years it was well over four million and in forty years it was sixty million. Unfortunately, Bissell, Drake and the other investors in his company (now renamed the Seneca Oil Company) didn't prosper to quite the degree that they had hoped. Other wells produced far greater volumes – one called Pool Well pumped out three thousand barrels a day – and the sheer number of producing wells provided such a glut for the market that the price of oil plunged catastrophically, from $10 a barrel in January 1861 to just 10 cents a barrel by the end of the year. This was good news for consumers and whales, but not so good for oilmen. As the boom turned to bust, prices of land collapsed. In 1878, a plot of land in Pithole City sold for $4.37. Thirteen years earlier it had fetched $2 million.

While others were failing and desperately trying to get out of the oil business, a small firm in Cleveland called Clark and Rockefeller, which normally dealt in pork and other farm commodities, decided to move in. It began buying up failed leases. By 1877, less than twenty years after the discovery of oil in Pennsylvania, Clark had vanished from the scene and John D. Rockefeller controlled some 90 per cent of America's oil business. Oil not only provided the raw material for an exceedingly lucrative form of illumination, but answered a desperate need for lubrication for all the engines and machinery of the new industrial age. Rockefeller's virtual monopoly allowed him to keep prices stable and to grow fantastically rich in the process. By the closing years of the century, his personal wealth was increasing by about $1 billion a year, measured in today's money – and this in an age without income taxes. No human being in modern times has been richer.

Bissell and his partners had more mixed fortunes, and at a decidedly more modest level. The Seneca Oil Company made money for a while, but in 1864, just five years after Drake's drilling breakthrough, it could no longer compete and went out of business. Drake squandered the money he made and died soon after, penniless and crippled by neuralgia. Bissell did much better. He invested his earnings in a bank and other businesses, and accrued a small fortune – enough to build Dartmouth a handsome gymnasium, which still stands.

While kerosene was establishing itself as the illuminant of choice in millions of homes, particularly in small towns and rural areas, it was challenged in many larger communities by another wonder of the age: gas. For the well-to-do in many large cities, gas was an additional option from about 1820. Mostly, however, it was used in factories and shops and for street lighting, and didn't become common in homes till closer to the middle of the century.

Gas had many drawbacks. Those who worked in gas-supplied offices or visited gas-lit theatres often complained of headaches and nausea. To minimize that problem, gas lights were sometimes erected outside factory windows. Indoors it blackened ceilings, discoloured fabrics, corroded metal and left a greasy layer of soot on every horizontal surface. Flowers wilted swiftly in its presence and most plants turned yellow unless isolated in a terrarium. Only the aspidistra seemed immune to its ill effects, which accounts for its presence in nearly every Victorian parlour photograph. Gas also needed some care in use. Most gas-supply companies reduced gas flow through their pipes during the day when demand was low. So anyone lighting a gas jet during the day had to open the tap wide to get a decent light. But later in the day as the pressure was stepped up, the light could flare danger-ously, scorching ceilings or even starting fires, wherever someone had forgotten to turn down the tap. So gas was dangerous as well as dirty.

Gas had one irresistible advantage, however. It was bright – at least compared with anything else the pre-electric world knew. The average room with gas was twenty times brighter than it had been before. It wasn't an intimate light – you couldn't move it nearer your book or sewing, as you could a table lamp – but it provided wonderful overall illumination. It made reading, card-playing and even conversation more agreeable. Diners could see the condition of their food; they could find their way around delicate fishbones and know how much salt came out the hole. One could drop a needle and find it before daylight. Book titles became discernible on their shelves. People read more and stayed up later. It is no coincidence that the mid-nineteenth century saw a sudden and lasting boom in newspapers, magazines, books and sheet music. The number of newspapers and periodicals in Britain leapt from fewer than 150 at the start of the century to almost 5,000 by the end of it.

Gas was particularly popular in America and Britain. By 1850 it was available in most large cities in both countries. Gas remained, however, a middle-class indulgence. The poor couldn't afford it and the rich tended to disdain it, partly because of the cost and disruption of installing it and partly because of the damage it did to paintings and precious fabrics, and partly because when you have servants to do everything for you already there isn't the same urgency to invest in further conveniences. The ironic upshot, as Mark Girouard has noted, is that not only middle-class homes but institutions like lunatic asylums and prisons tended to be better lit – and, come to that, better warmed – long before England's stateliest homes were.

Keeping warm remained a challenge for most people right through the nineteenth century. Mr Marsham had a fireplace in virtually every room of his rectory, even the dressing room, in addition to a hefty kitchen stove. Cleaning, laying and stoking such a number must have been an enormous amount of work, yet for several months of the year the house was almost certainly uncomfortably cold. (It still is.) Fireplaces simply aren't efficient enough to keep any but the smallest spaces warm. This could just about be overlooked in a temperate place like England, but in the frigid winters of much of North America the fireplace's inadequacies at projecting warmth into a room became numbingly apparent. Thomas Jefferson complained that he had to stop writing one evening because the ink had frozen in his inkwell. A diarist named George Templeton Strong recorded in the winter of 1866 that even with two furnaces alight and all the fireplaces blazing, he couldn't get the temperature of his Boston home above thirty-eight degrees.

It was Benjamin Franklin, predictably enough, who turned his attention to the matter and invented what became known as the Franklin (or Pennsylvania) stove. Franklin's stove was an undoubted improvement – though more on paper than in practice. Essentially it was a metal stove inserted into a fireplace, but with additional flues and vents that ingeniously redirected air flow and wafted more heat back into the room. But it was also complex and expensive and brought great – and often intolerable – disruption to every room in which it was installed. The heart of the system was a second, rear flue, which proved to be impossible to sweep unless it was fully dismantled. The stove also required an underfloor cool air vent, which in practical terms meant the stove couldn't be installed in upstairs rooms or where there was a basement below – which disqualified it from many houses altogether. Franklin's design was improved upon in America by David Rittenhouse and in Europe by Benjamin Thompson, Count Rumford, but real comfort only came when people sealed off their fireplaces and brought a stove fully into the room. This kind of stove, known as a Dutch stove, smelled of hot iron and dried out the atmosphere, but at least it kept the occupants warm.

As Americans moved west into the prairies and

beyond, an absence of wood for fuel caused problems. Corn cobs were widely used as fuel, as were dried cowpats – known euphemistically and rather charmingly as 'surface coal'. In wilderness areas, Americans also burned all kinds of fat – hog fat, deer fat, bear fat, even the fat of passenger pigeons – and fish oils, though all these were smoky and stank.

Stoves became something of an American obsession. By the early twentieth century more than seven thousand types had been registered with the US Patent Office. The one quality all had in common was that they took quite a lot of work to keep going. A typical stove in 1899, according to a study in Boston, burned some three hundred pounds of coal in a week, produced twenty-seven pounds of ash, and required three hours and eleven minutes of attention. If one had stoves in both kitchen and living room, as well perhaps as open fires elsewhere, that represented a lot of extra work. One other significant drawback of enclosed stoves was that they robbed the room of a good deal of light.

The combination of open flames and combustible materials brought an element of alarm and excitement to every aspect of daily life in the pre-electrical world. Samuel Pepys recorded in his diary how he bent over a candle while working at his desk, and soon afterwards became aware of a horrible, pungent smell, as of burning wool; only then did he realize that his new and very expensive wig was impressively aflame. Such small fires were a common occurrence. Nearly every room of every house had open flames at least some of the time, and nearly every house was fabulously combustible since almost everything within or on it, from straw beds to thatched roofs, was a fuel in waiting. To reduce dangers at night, fires were covered with a kind of domed lid called a *couvre-feu* (from which comes the term 'curfew'), but danger could never be entirely avoided.

Technological refinements sometimes improved the quality of light, but just as often increased the risk of fire. Argand lamps were top-heavy, and easily knocked over, because their fuel reservoirs had to be elevated to assist the flow of fuel to the wick. Kerosene, if tipped or spilled, was almost impossible to put out if it caught fire. By the 1870s as many as six thousand people a year were dying in kerosene fires in America alone.

Fires in public places became a great worry, too, especially after the development of a now-forgotten but lively form of illumination known as the Drummond light, named for a Thomas Drummond of Britain's Royal Engineers who was popularly but wrongly credited with its invention in the early 1820s. It was in fact invented by Sir Goldsworthy Gurney, a fellow engineer and an inventor of considerable talent. Drummond merely popularized the light and never claimed to have invented it, but somehow the credit became attached to him and has remained there ever since. The Drummond light, or calcium light as it was also called, was based on a phenomenon that had been known about for a long time – that if you took a lump of lime or magnesia and burned it in a really hot flame, it would glow with an intense white light. Using a flame made from a rich blend of oxygen and alcohol, Gurney could heat a ball of lime no bigger than a child's marble so efficiently that its light could be seen sixty miles away. The device was successfully put to use in lighthouses, but it was also taken up by theatres. Not only was the light perfect and steady, but it could be focused into a beam and cast on to selected performers – which is where the term 'in the limelight' comes from. The downside was that the intense heat of limelight caused a lot of fires. In one decade in America more than four hundred theatres burned down. Over the nineteenth century as a whole, nearly ten thousand people were killed in theatre fires in Britain, according to a report published in 1899 by William Paul Gerhard, the leading fire authority of the day.

Fire was even a danger on the move – indeed, often more so since means of escape were constrained or impossible. In 1858, the immigrant ship *Austria* caught fire at sea en route for the United States and nearly five hundred people perished horribly as the ship was consumed beneath them. Trains were dangerous too. From about 1840 passenger carriages came with wood- or coal-burning stoves in the winter and oil lamps to read by, and the scope for catastrophes on a lurching train is easily imagined. As late as 1921, twenty-seven people perished in a stove fire on a train near Philadelphia.

On solid land, the greatest fear with fires was that they would get out of control and spread, destroying whole districts. The most famous urban fire in history is almost certainly the Great Fire of London of 1666, which began as a small fire in a bakery near London Bridge but quickly spread until it was half a mile across. As far away as Oxford the smoke was visible and the fire could be heard as a small, eerie whisper. Altogether it consumed 13,200 houses and 140 churches. But the fire of 1666 was actually the second Great Fire of London. A fire in 1212 was far more devastating. Though smaller in extent than the one of 1666, it was swifter and more frenzied, and leapt from

street to street with such dreadful rapidity that many fleeing citizens were overtaken or left without escape routes.
Altogether it claimed 12,000 lives. By contrast the fire of
1666 killed only five people, as far as is known. For 454
years, the fire of 1212 was known as the Great Fire of
London. It really still ought to be.

Most cities suffered devastating fires from time to time,
some repeatedly. Boston had them in 1653, 1676, 1679,
1711 and 1761. Then it had a lull until the winter of 1834
when a fire in the night burned down 700 buildings –
most of the downtown – and grew so fierce that it spread
to ships in the harbour. But all city fires pale when compared with the fire that swept through Chicago on a windy
night in October 1871, when a Mrs Patrick O'Leary's cow
reputedly kicked over a kerosene lantern in a milking shed
on DeKoven Street, and all kinds of dreadful mayhem
swiftly followed. The fire destroyed eighteen thousand
buildings and made one hundred and fifty thousand
people homeless. Damages topped $200 million and put
fifty-one insurance companies out of business.

Where houses were packed close together, as in
European cities, there wasn't a great deal anyone could do,
though housebuilders did come up with one useful
remedy. Originally the joists in English terraced houses ran
from side to side and sat on the partition walls between
houses. This essentially created a linear run of joists along
a street, heightening the risk of fires spreading from house
to house. So from the Georgian period on, joists were run
front to back in houses, making the partition walls into
firebreaks. However, having joists run from the front
of the house to the back meant they needed supporting
walls, which dictated room sizes, which in turn

determined how rooms were used and houses lived in.

One natural phenomenon had the promise to eliminate all the foregoing dangers and shortcomings: electricity. Electricity was exciting stuff, but it was hard to devise practical applications for it. Using the legs of frogs and electricity from simple batteries, Luigi Galvani showed how electricity could make muscles twitch. His nephew, Giovanni Aldini, realizing that money could be made from this, devised a stage show in which he applied electricity to animate the bodies of recently executed murderers and the heads of guillotine victims, causing their eyes to open and their mouths to make noiseless shapes. The logical assumption was that if electricity could stir the dead, imagine how it might help the living. In small doses (at least we may hope they were small) it was used for all kinds of maladies, from treating constipation to stopping young men having illicit erections (or at least enjoying them). Charles Darwin, driven to desperation by a mysterious lifelong malady that left him chronically lethargic, routinely draped himself with electrified zinc chains, doused his body with vinegar and glumly underwent hours of pointless tingling in the hope that it would effect some improvement. It never did. President James Garfield, though slowly dying from an assassin's bullet, expressed weak but palpable alarm when he found Alexander Graham Bell draping him with electrified wires in an attempt to locate the bullet.

The real need was for a practical electric light. In 1846, rather out of the blue, a man named Frederick Hale Holmes patented an electric arc lamp. Holmes's light was made by generating a strong electric current and forcing it to jump between two carbon rods – a trick that Humphry

Davy had demonstrated but not capitalized upon more than forty years earlier. In Holmes's hands the result was a blindingly bright light. Almost nothing is known about Holmes – where he came from, what his educational background was, how he learned to master electricity. All that is known is that he worked at the Ecole Militaire in Brussels, where he developed the concept with a Professor Floris Nollet, then returned to England and brought his invention to the great Michael Faraday, who saw at once that it could provide a perfect light for lighthouses.

The first one was installed at the South Foreland Lighthouse, just outside Dover, and powered up on 8 December 1858.* It ran for thirteen years, and others were installed elsewhere, but arc lighting was never a huge success because it was complicated and expensive. It required an electromagnetic motor and a steam engine together weighing two tons, and needed constant attention to run smoothly.

The one thing to be said for arc lamps was that they were amazingly bright. St Enoch's Railway Station in Glasgow was lit with six Crompton lamps – named for R. E. Crompton, their manufacturer – that each boasted 6,000 candlepower. In Paris, a Russian-born inventor named Paul Jablochkoff developed a form of arc lights that came to be known as Jablochkoff candles. They were used to light many Parisian streets and monuments in the 1870s and became a sensation. Unfortunately the system

---

* South Foreland light, now in the hands of the National Trust and very much worth a visit, became famous again in 1899 when Guglielmo Marconi transmitted the first international radio signal from there to Wimereux in France.

was expensive and didn't work very well. The lights operated in sequence and if one failed they all failed, like Christmas tree lights. Failing was something they did a lot. After just five years the Jablochkoff company fell into bankruptcy.

Arc lights were way too bright for domestic use. What was needed was a practical domestic filament that would burn with a steady light for long periods. The principle of incandescent lighting had been understood, and in fact conquered, for a surprisingly long time. As early as 1840, seven years before Thomas Edison was even born, Sir William Grove, a lawyer and judge who was also a brilliant amateur scientist with a particular interest in electricity, demonstrated an incandescent lamp which worked for several hours, but nobody wanted a light bulb that cost a lot to make and only worked for a few hours, so Grove didn't pursue its development. In Newcastle, a young pharmacist and keen inventor named Joseph Swan saw a demonstration of Grove's light and made some successful experiments of his own, but the technology was lacking to get a really good vacuum in a bulb. Without that vacuum any filament would burn out quickly, making a bulb a costly, short-lived indulgence. Besides, Swan was interested in other matters, in particular photography, where he made many important contributions. He invented silver bromide photographic paper, which allowed the first high-quality photographic prints to be made, perfected the collodion process and also made several refinements to photographic chemicals. Meanwhile, his pharmaceutical business, which involved manufacturing as well as retailing, was booming. In 1867, his business partner and brother-in-law John Mawson died in a freak accident while disposing of nitroglycerine on a moor outside the city. It was, in short, a complicated and distracted time for Swan, and his interests moved away from illumination for thirty years.

Then in the early 1870s Hermann Sprengel, a German chemist working in London, invented a device that came to be called the Sprengel mercury pump. This was the crucial invention that actually made household illumination possible. Unfortunately, only one person in history thought Hermann Sprengel deserved to be better known: Hermann Sprengel. Sprengel's pump could reduce the amount of air in a glass chamber to one-millionth of its normal volume, which would enable a filament to glow for hundreds of hours. All that was necessary now was to find a suitable material for the filament.

The most determined and well-promoted search was undertaken by Thomas Edison, America's premier inventor. By 1877, when he started his quest to make a commercially successful light, Edison was already well on his way to becoming known as 'the Wizard of Menlo Park'. Edison was not a wholly attractive human being. He didn't scruple to cheat or lie, and was prepared to steal patents or bribe journalists for favourable coverage. In the words of one of his contemporaries, he had 'a vacuum where his conscience ought to be'. But he was enterprising and hardworking and a peerless organizer.

Edison dispatched men to the far corners of the world to search for potential filaments, and had teams of men working on up to 250 materials at a time in the hope of finding one that had the necessary characteristics of permanence and resistance. They tried everything, including even hair from the luxuriant red beard of a family friend. Just before Thanksgiving 1879 Edison's workmen developed a piece of carbonized cardboard, twisted thin and carefully folded, that would burn for as much as thirteen hours – still not nearly long enough to be practical. On the last day of 1879, Edison invited a select audience to come and witness a demonstration of his new incandescent lights. As they arrived at his estate at Menlo Park, New Jersey, they were wowed by the sight of two buildings warmly aglow. What they didn't realize was that the light was mostly non-electrical. Edison's overworked glassblowers had been able to prepare only thirty-four bulbs, so the bulk of the illumination actually came from carefully positioned oil lamps.

Swan didn't get back into electric lighting until 1877, but, working on his own, he independently came up with a more or less identical lighting system. In January or February 1879, Swan gave a public display of his new electric incandescent lamp in Newcastle. The vagueness of date is because it isn't certain whether he demonstrated his lamp at a public lecture in January or merely talked about it; but the following month he most certainly fired it up to an appreciative audience. In either case, his demonstration was at least eight months ahead of anything Edison could manage. That same year Swan installed lights in his own home and by 1881 had wired up the house of the great scientist Lord Kelvin in Glasgow – again well ahead of any-thing Edison was able to achieve.

However, when Edison's first practical installation did come it was far more prominent and therefore more last-ingly significant. Edison wired a whole district of lower Manhattan, around Wall Street, to be powered by a plant installed in two semi-derelict buildings on Pearl Street.

Through the winter, spring and summer of 1881-2 Edison laid fifteen miles of cable and fanatically tested and retested his system. Not all went smoothly. Horses behaved skittishly in the vicinity until it was realized that leaking electricity was making their horseshoes tingle. Back at his workshops, several of his men lost teeth from mercury poisoning from over-exposure to Sprengel's mercury pump. But finally all the problems were resolved, and on the afternoon of 4 September 1882, Edison, standing in the office of the financier J. P. Morgan, threw a switch that illuminated eight hundred electric bulbs in the eighty-five businesses that had signed up to his scheme.

Where Edison truly excelled was as an organizer of systems. The invention of the light bulb was a wondrous thing but of not much practical use when no one had a socket to plug it into. Edison and his tireless workers had to design and build the entire system from scratch, from power stations to cheap and reliable wiring, to lamp-stands and switches. Within months Edison had set up no fewer than 334 small electrical plants all over the world and within a year or so his plants were powering thirteen thousand light bulbs. Cannily he put them in places where they would be sure to make maximum impact: on the New York Stock Exchange, in the Palmer House Hotel in Chicago, La Scala opera house in Milan, the dining room of the House of Commons in London. Swan, meanwhile, was still doing much of his manufacturing in his own home. He didn't, in short, have a lot of vision. Indeed, he didn't even file for a patent. Edison took out patents everywhere, including in Britain in November 1879, and so secured his pre-eminence.

By modern standards those first lights were pretty feeble, but to people of the time an electric light was a blazing miracle – 'a little globe of sunshine, a veritable Aladdin's lamp', as a journalist for the *New York Herald* breathlessly reported. It is hard to imagine now how bright and clean and eerily steady this new phenomenon was. When the lights of Fulton Street were switched on in September 1882, the awed *Herald* reporter described for his readers the scene as the customary 'dim flicker of gas' suddenly yielded to a brilliant 'steady glare . . . fixed and unwavering'. It was exciting, but clearly it was also going to take some getting used to.

And of course electricity had applications way beyond simply providing lighting. As early as 1893, the Columbian Exposition in Chicago displayed a 'model electric kitchen'. It was exciting, too, though not yet very practical. For one thing, since electricity distribution was not yet general, it was necessary for most owners to build their own 'electric plant' on the property to provide the necessary power. Even if they were lucky enough to be wired up to the outside world, utilities couldn't supply sufficient power to make appliances work really well. It took an hour just to preheat an oven. Even then it could produce no more than a very modest six hundred watts of heating and you couldn't use the stovetop at the same time as the oven. There were certain design deficiencies too. The knobs to regulate the heat were just above floor level. To modern eyes, these new electric stoves looked odd because they were built of wood, generally oak, lined with zinc or some other protective material. White porcelain models didn't come in until the 1920s – and they were considered very odd when they did. Many people thought they looked as if they should be in a hospital or factory, not in a private home.

As electricity became more freely available, many people found it unnerving to be relying for comfort on an invisible force that could swiftly and silently kill. Most electricians were hastily trained and all were necessarily inexperienced, so it quickly became a profession for daredevils. Newspapers gave full and vivid accounts whenever one electrocuted himself, as happened pretty routinely. In England Hilaire Belloc offered a snatch of doggerel that caught the public mood:

> Some random touch – a hand's imprudent slip –
> The Terminals – flash – a sound like 'Zip!'
> A smell of burning fills the startled Air –
> The Electrician is no longer there!

In 1896, Edison's former partner Franklin Pope electrocuted himself while working on the wiring in his own house, proving to many people's satisfaction that electricity was too dangerous even for experts. Fires due to electrical faults were not uncommon. Light bulbs sometimes exploded, always startlingly, sometimes disastrously. The new Dreamland Park at Coney Island burned down in 1911 because of a fire caused by a bursting light bulb. Errant sparks from faulty connections caused more than a few gas mains to explode, which meant that one didn't even have to be connected to the electricity supply to be at risk.

Something of the prevailing ambivalence was demonstrated by Mrs Cornelius Vanderbilt, who went to a costume ball dressed as an electric light to celebrate the installation of electricity in her Fifth Avenue home in New York, but then had the whole system taken out when it was suspected of being the source of a small fire. Others detected more insidious threats. One authority named S. F. Murphy identified a whole host of electrically induced maladies – eyestrain, headaches, general unhealthiness and possibly even 'the premature exhaustion of life'. One architect was certain electric light caused freckles.

For the first few years, no one thought of the idea of plugs and sockets, so any electrical household appliances had to be wired directly into the system. When sockets did finally come in, around the turn of the century, they were available only as part of overhead light fittings, which meant having to stand on a chair or stepladder to plug in any early appliance. Wall sockets soon followed, but weren't always terribly reliable. Early ones reportedly tended to crackle and smoke and sometimes shot out sparks. At Manderston, a stately home in Scotland, until well into Edwardian times it was the practice to throw cushions at one particularly lively wall outlet, according to Juliet Gardiner.

Consumer growth was also held back by the fact that the 1890s was a period of depression. But electric lighting was ultimately irresistible. It was clean, steady, easy to maintain, and available instantaneously and in infinite amounts at the flick of a switch. Gas lighting had taken half a century to establish itself, but electric lighting happened much more quickly. By 1900, in cities anyway, electric lighting was increasingly the norm – and electrical appliances ineluctably followed: the electric fan in 1891, the vacuum cleaner in 1901, the washing machine and iron in 1909, the toaster in 1910, the refrigerator and dishwasher in 1918. By that time, some fifty types of household appliance were reasonably common, and electrical gadgets were so fashionable that manufacturers were producing every possible kind they could think of, from curling tongs to an electrical potato peeler. The use of electricity in the United States went from 79 kilowatt hours per capita in 1902 to 960 in 1929 to well over 13,000 today.

It is right to give Thomas Edison the credit for much of this so long as we remember that his genius was not in creating electric light but in creating methods of producing and supplying it on a grand commercial scale, which was actually a much larger and far more challenging ambition. But it was also a vastly more lucrative one. Thanks to Thomas Edison, electric lighting became the wonder of the age. Interestingly, as we shall see a little further on, electric lighting turned out to be one of the remarkably few Edison inventions that actually did what he hoped it would do.

Joseph Swan was so thoroughly eclipsed that few have heard of him outside England, and he isn't terribly much celebrated there. Britain's *Dictionary of National Biography* gives him a modest three pages, less than it gives to the courtesan Kitty Fisher or any number of talentless aristocrats. But then that's much more than Frederick Hale Holmes, who doesn't get mentioned at all. History is often like that.

CHAPTER SEVEN

The Drawing Room

I

IF YOU HAD TO summarize it in a sentence, you could say that the history of private life is a history of getting comfortable slowly. Until the eighteenth century the idea of having comfort at home was so unfamiliar that there wasn't even a word for the condition. 'Comfortable' meant merely 'capable of being consoled'. Comfort was something you gave to the wounded or distressed. The first person to use the word in its modern sense was the writer Horace Walpole, who remarked in a letter to a friend in 1770 that a certain Mrs White was looking after him well and making him 'as comfortable as is possible'. By the early nineteenth century, everyone was talking about having a comfortable home or enjoying a comfortable living, but before Walpole's day no one did.

Nowhere in the house is the spirit (if not always the actuality) of comfort better captured than in the curiously named room in which we find ourselves now, the drawing room. The term is a shortening of the much older 'withdrawing room', meaning a space where the family could withdraw from the rest of the household for greater privacy, and it has never settled altogether comfortably into widespread English usage. For a time in the seventeenth and eighteenth centuries, 'drawing room' was challenged in more refined circles by the French *salon*, which was sometimes anglicized to 'saloon', but both those words gradually became associated with spaces outside the home, so that 'saloon' came first to signify a room for socializing in a hotel or on a ship, then a place for dedicated drinking, and finally, and a little unexpectedly, a type of automobile. *Salon*, meanwhile, became indelibly attached to places associated with artistic endeavours before being appropriated (from about 1910) by providers of hair care and beauty treatments. 'Parlour', the word long favoured by Americans for the main room of the home, has a kind of nineteenth-century frontier feel to it, but in fact is the oldest of all. It is first recorded as a room where monks could go to talk (it is from the French *parler*, 'to speak') in 1225 and was extended to secular contexts by the last quarter of the following century. 'Drawing room' is the term used by Edward Tull on his floor plan of the rectory, and almost certainly is the term used by the well-bred Mr Marsham, though he was probably in a minority even then. By mid-century it was being supplanted in all but the most genteel circles by 'sitting room', a term first appearing in English in 1806. A later challenger was 'lounge', which originally signified a type of chair or sofa, then a jacket for relaxing in, and finally, from 1881, a room.

Assuming he was a conventional sort of fellow, Mr Marsham will have strived to make this the most comfortable room in the house, with the softest and finest furnishings. In practice, however, it was probably anything but comfortable for much of the year since it has just one fireplace, which could do no more than warm a small, central part of the room. Even with a good fire going, I can attest, it is possible in the depths of winter to stand across the room and see your breath.

Though the drawing room became the focus of comfort in the home, the story doesn't actually start there; it doesn't start in the house at all. It starts outdoors, a century or so before Mr Marsham's birth, with a simple discovery that would make landed families like his very rich and allow him one day to build himself a handsome rectory. The discovery was merely this: land didn't have to be rested regularly to retain its fertility. It was not the most scintillating of insights, but it changed the world.

Traditionally, most English farmland was divided into long strips called furlongs and each furlong was left fallow for one season in every three – sometimes one season in two – to recover its ability to produce healthy crops.* This meant that in any year at least one-third of farmland stood idle. In consequence, there wasn't sufficient feed to keep large numbers of animals alive through the winter, so landowners had no choice but to slaughter most of their stock each autumn and face a long, lean period till spring.

Then English farmers discovered something that Dutch farmers had known for a long time: if turnips, clover or one or two other suitable crops were sown on the idle fields, they miraculously refreshed the soil and

---

* A furlong in horse racing is 220 yards, or one-eighth of a mile, but farming furlongs originally were of no particular length. The word means simply 'long furrow'.

produced a bounty of winter fodder into the bargain. It was the infusion of nitrogen that did it, though no one would understand that for nearly two hundred years. What *was* understood, and very much appreciated, was that it transformed agricultural fortunes dramatically. Moreover, because more animals lived through the winter, they produced heaps of additional manure, and these glorious, gratis ploppings enriched the soil even further.

It is hard to exaggerate what a miracle all this seemed. Before the eighteenth century, agriculture in Britain lurched from crisis to crisis. An academic named W. G. Hoskins calculated (in 1964) that between 1480 and 1700, one harvest in four was bad, and almost one in five was catastrophically bad. Now, thanks to the simple expedient of crop rotation, agriculture was able to settle into a continuous, more or less reliable prosperity. It was this long golden age that gave so much of the countryside the air of prosperous comeliness it enjoys still today, and allowed the likes of Mr Marsham to embrace that gratifying new commodity: comfort.

Farmers also benefited from a new wheeled contraption invented in about 1700 by Jethro Tull, a farmer and agricultural thinker in Berkshire. Called a seed drill, it allowed seeds to be planted directly into the soil rather than broadcast by hand. Seed was expensive, and Tull's new drill reduced the amount needed from three or four bushels per acre to under one; and because the seeds were planted at even depths in neat rows, more of them sprouted successfully, so yields improved significantly too, from between twenty and forty bushels an acre to as much as eighty.

The new vitality was also reflected in breeding pro-
grammes. Nearly all the great cattle breeds – Jersey,
Guernsey, Hereford, Aberdeen Angus, Ayrshire* – were
eighteenth-century creations. Sheep likewise were successfully manipulated to become the bundles of unnatural
fleeciness we see today. A medieval sheep gave about one
and a half pounds of wool; re-engineered eighteenth-
century sheep gave up to nine pounds. Underneath all that
lovely fleece, sheep were gratifyingly plumper too. Between
1700 and 1800 the average weight of sheep sold at
Smithfield Market in London more than doubled, from
thirty-eight pounds to eighty. Beef cattle expanded similarly.
Dairy yields went up too.

All this was not without cost, however. To make the
new systems of production work, it was necessary to
amalgamate small fields into large ones and move the
peasant farmers off the land. This enclosure movement, in
which small fields that had formerly supported many were
converted into much larger enclosed fields that enriched a
few, made farming immensely lucrative for those with
large holdings – and soon in many areas that was almost
the only kind of holding there was. Enclosure had been
going on slowly for centuries, but it gathered pace between
1750 and 1830, when some six million acres of British
farmland were enclosed. Enclosure was hard on the

---

* Ayrshires were the creation of Bruce Campbell, inventive second
cousin of James Boswell, who was put in charge of the family estate in
Scotland only after Boswell himself declined the responsibility,
preferring a life of conversation and refined debauchery in London to
dairy farming in lowland Scotland. Had Boswell been more dutiful, we
would have lost not only his great life of Samuel Johnson but also one
of the world's best breeds of dairy cattle.

displaced peasant farmers, but it did leave them and their descendants conveniently available to move to towns and become the toiling masses of the new Industrial Revolution – which was also just beginning and was funded to a very large extent by the surplus wealth enjoyed by the ever-richer landowners.

Many landowners also discovered that they sat on great seams of coal just at a time when coal was suddenly needed for industry. This didn't always represent a great advance in beauty – at one time in the eighteenth century, eighty-five open-cast coal mines could be seen from Chatsworth House, or so it has been written – but it did translate into gratifying heaps of lucre. Still others made money from leasing land to railways or building canals and controlling rights of way. The Duke of Bridgewater earned annual returns of 40 per cent per year – and really returns don't get much better than that – from a canal monopoly in the north of England. All of this was in an age in which there was no income tax, no capital gains tax, no tax on dividends or interest – almost nothing to disturb the steady flow of money being banked. Many people were born into a world in which they had to do virtually nothing with their wealth but stack it. The third Earl of Burlington, to take one example of many, owned vast estates in Ireland – some 42,000 acres in all – and never visited the country. Eventually he was made Lord Treasurer of Ireland and still never visited it.

This wealthy elite and their offspring covered the British countryside with stout and rambling expressions of this new *joie de richesse*. By one count, at least 840 large country houses were built in England between 1710 and the end of the century – 'dispersed like great rarity plums in a vast pudding of a country', in the exuberant words of Horace Walpole.

Extraordinary houses need extraordinary people to design and build them, and perhaps none was more extraordinary – or at least more unexpected – than Sir John Vanbrugh. Vanbrugh (1664–1726) came from a large family – he was one of nineteen children – that was well-to-do and of Dutch extraction, though they had been settled in England for nearly half a century by the time Vanbrugh himself was born.* 'A most sweet-natur'd gentleman, and pleasant,' in the words of the poet Nicholas Rowe, Vanbrugh seems to have been well liked by everyone who met him (with the notable exception of the Duchess of Marlborough, as we shall see). A portrait of him by Sir Godfrey Kneller in the National Portrait Gallery in London, made when he was about forty, shows an agreeable man with a pink, well-fed, rather ordinary face framed – indeed, all but overwhelmed – by a periwig of baroque magnificence, as was the fashion of the day.

For the first three decades of his life he showed no particular sense of direction. He worked in a family wine business, went to India as an agent for the East India Company – then still a fairly new and undistinguished enterprise – and finally took up soldiering, though without much distinction there either. Sent to France, he was arrested as a spy almost as soon as he stepped ashore and spent nearly five years in prison, albeit in reasonable, gentlemanly comfort.

* Though the name is now pronounced 'Van-bruh' or 'Van-burra' (like the terminal diphthong of 'Edinburgh' or 'Barbara'), it appears to have been pronounced 'Vanbrook' in his own lifetime. It was frequently so spelled.

Prison appears to have had a galvanizing effect on him, for upon his return to England he became with remarkable swiftness a celebrated playwright, producing in rapid succession two of the most popular comedies of his day, *The Relapse* and *The Provok'd Wife*. Featuring characters with names like Fondlewife, Lord Foppington, Sir Tunbelly Clumsey and Sir John Brute, they may seem just a touch heavy-handed to us, but were the height of drollery in that overdone and highly fragranced age. It was pretty risqué stuff. One scandalized member of the Society for the Reformation of Manners said Vanbrugh 'had debauch'd the stage beyond the looseness of all former times'. Others loved his plays for exactly the same reasons. The poet Samuel Rogers thought him 'almost as great a genius as ever lived'.

Altogether Vanbrugh would write or adapt ten works for the stage, but meanwhile, and with no less startling abruptness, he also turned his talents to architecture. Where *this* impulse came from was as much a mystery to his contemporaries as it is to us. All that is known is that in 1701, at the age of thirty-five, he began work on one of the grandest houses ever built in England, Castle Howard in Yorkshire. How he persuaded his friend Charles Howard, third Earl of Carlisle – described by one architectural historian as 'rather nondescript but obviously uncontrollably wealthy' – to underwrite this seemingly insane ambition is no less uncertain. This was not just a big house, it was a place that was positively and determinedly palatial, built 'on a scale previously the prerogative of royalty', in the words of Vanbrugh's biographer Kerry Downes. Clearly Carlisle saw something in Vanbrugh's rough sketches, and Vanbrugh, it must be said, did have the back-up of a real architect of undoubted gifts, Nicholas Hawksmoor, who had twenty years of experience but was oddly content to work as Vanbrugh's assistant. It seems also that Vanbrugh may have worked for free. (No indication of money changing hands has ever been found – and on both sides these were men who kept track of such things.) In any case, Carlisle dismissed the distinguished architect he had been planning to use, William Talman, and gave the novice Vanbrugh free rein.

Vanbrugh and Carlisle were both members of a secretive society known as the Kit-Cat Club, an organization of Whiggish disposition that had been founded more or less exclusively to ensure the Hanoverian succession – the dynastic change that guaranteed that all future British monarchs would be Protestant even if, in the short term, they were not notably British.* That the Kit-Cats achieved this aim was no small accomplishment since their candidate, George I, spoke no English, had almost no admirable qualities, and was by one count no better than fifty-eighth in line to the throne. Beyond this one piece of political manoeuvring, the club operated with such discretion that almost nothing is known about it. One of its founding members was a pastry chef named Christopher – or 'Kit' – Cat. Kit-cat was also the name of his famous mutton pies, so whether the club was named

* 'Whig' is a shortening of 'Whiggamore', the name for a group of seventeenth-century Scottish insurgents. Where Whiggamore itself came from is uncertain, as is the question of how it then suggested itself as a suitable name for a group of powerful English aristocrats. It was first applied derisively by the Tories, but embraced with pride by the target group. Exactly the same thing happened with the term 'Tory'.

for him or his pies has been a matter of debate in certain very small circles for three hundred years. The club lasted from only about 1696 to 1720 – specific details are unknown – and total membership was only about fifty, of whom two-thirds were peers of the realm. Five members – Lords Carlisle, Halifax and Scarborough and the Dukes of Manchester and Marlborough – commissioned work from Vanbrugh. Membership also included the prime minister Robert Walpole (father of Horace), the journalists Joseph Addison and Richard Steele, and the playwright William Congreve.

At Castle Howard, Vanbrugh didn't exactly ignore the classical proprieties, he just buried them under a kind of kudzu of baroque ornamentation. A Vanbrugh structure is always like no other, but Castle Howard is, as it were, unusually unusual. It had a large number of formal rooms – thirteen on one floor – but few bedrooms: nothing like the amount that would normally be expected. Many rooms were oddly shaped or poorly lit. Much of the external detailing is unusual, if not actually erratic. The columns on one side of the house are simple Doric, but are a more ornate Corinthian on the other. (Vanbrugh argued, with some logic, that no one could see the two sides at the same time.) The most striking characteristic of all, at least for its first twenty-five years, was that the house was built without its west wing – though this was not in fact Vanbrugh's fault. Carlisle got distracted and neglected to put up the west wing, leaving the house conspicuously unfinished. When the wing was finally built, twenty-five years later by another party, it was in an entirely different style, so that the visitor today is met with a baroque east wing as Vanbrugh intended and an inescapably unmatching Palladian west wing that pleased a later owner and hardly anyone else.

Castle Howard's most famous feature, its domed crown (formally a lantern, from a Greek word meaning to admit light) over the entrance hall, was a late addition, and is strikingly out of scale with the building beneath it. It is too tall and too thin. It looks as if it were designed for another structure altogether. As one architectural critic has noted diplomatically, 'at close quarters it does not fit very logically on to the building below'. It was at least novel. The only other domed structure in England at the time was Christopher Wren's new St Paul's Cathedral. No house anywhere had ever had anything like it.

Castle Howard is in short a very fine property, but fine in a way that is entirely its own. The dome may be slightly odd, but Castle Howard would be nothing without it. We can say that with unusual confidence because for twenty years Castle Howard actually *was* without it. Late on the night of 9 November 1940, a fire was discovered in the east wing. In those days the house had just one telephone, and the phone melted like chocolate before anyone could get to it. So someone had to run to the gatehouse, a mile away, and call the fire brigade from there. By the time the fire crew arrived from Malton, six miles distant, two hours had passed and much of the house was lost. The dome had crumpled in the heat and fallen into the house. Castle Howard was domeless for the next twenty years, and it looked all right – it was still stately, still imposing, still stolidly grand – but it had lost its perk. When the dome was finally restored in the early 1960s, it became instantly and peculiarly endearing once again.

Despite his limited experience, Vanbrugh now landed

the commission for one of the most important houses ever built in Great Britain, Blenheim Palace, that colossal explosion of magnificence at Woodstock in Oxfordshire. Blenheim was intended to be a gift from the nation to the Duke of Marlborough for his victory over the French in the Battle of Blindheim (which the English somehow managed to anglicize into Blenheim), in Bavaria, in 1704. The estate came with 22,000 acres of prime land, which brought an income of £6,000 a year, a hale sum for the time, but not, alas, nearly enough to pay for a house on the scale of Blenheim – and Blenheim was so big as to be effectively off any scale.

It contained three hundred rooms and sprawled over seven acres.* A frontage of 250 feet for a stately home was enormous; at Blenheim the frontage was to be 856 feet. It was the greatest monument to vanity Britain had ever seen. Every inch of it was covered in decorative stony sumptuousness. It was grander than any royal palace, and so, not surprisingly, very, very expensive. The duke, a fellow member of the Kit-Cat Club, seems to have got along with Vanbrugh well enough, but, after agreeing the general principles of the thing, he went off to fight more wars, leaving domestic arrangements in the hands of his wife, Sarah, Duchess of Marlborough. She thus oversaw most of the work, and from the start she and Vanbrugh did not get along. At all.

Work began in the summer of 1705 and there was trouble from the start. Many costly adjustments had to be

* In a large house, room numbers are generally notional. It depends on the extent to which you count storerooms, closets and the like as separate rooms (and also, no doubt, how carefully you count). The published numbers for the total rooms at Blenheim range from 187 to 320 – quite a disparity.

made along the way. The principal entrance had to be changed when a cottage owner refused to move, so the main gate had to be located in an odd place at the back of Woodstock, requiring visitors to pass along the high street, turn a corner and enter the grounds through what even today feels oddly like a tradesman's entrance (albeit rather a grand one).

Blenheim was budgeted to cost £40,000. Ultimately it cost about £300,000. This was unfortunate as the Marlboroughs were notoriously parsimonious. The duke was so cheap that he refused to dot his i's when he wrote, to save on ink. It was never clear who was to pay for the work – Queen Anne, the Treasury or the Marlboroughs themselves. The duchess and Queen Anne had a close, rather strange and just possibly intimate relationship. When alone they gave each other odd pet names – 'Mrs Morley' and 'Mrs Freeman' – to avoid any awkwardness arising from the fact that one of them was regal and the other was not. Unfortunately the building of Blenheim coincided with a cooling of their affections, which added to the uncertainty of financial responsibility. Things grew more complicated still after the queen died in 1714 and was replaced by a king who felt no particular affection for, or debt to, the Marlboroughs. Many of the builders went unpaid for years as the disputes dragged on, and most eventually got only a fraction of what they were owed. Building work ceased altogether for four years, from 1712 to 1716, and many of the unpaid workers were understandably loath to return when work resumed. Vanbrugh himself didn't get paid until 1725 – almost exactly twenty years after work started.

Even when things were moving along, Vanbrugh and

the duchess squabbled endlessly. She thought the palace 'too big, too dark and too martial'. She accused Vanbrugh of extravagance and insubordination, and became implacably convinced that he was a bad thing. In 1716, she dismissed him altogether – though at the same time instructing the workmen to stay faithful to his plans. When Vanbrugh came with his wife in 1725 to see the finished building – a building on which he had lavished some two-thirds of his architectural career and one-third of his life – he was informed at the gate that the duchess had left standing instructions that he was not to be admitted to the grounds. So he never saw his finished masterwork except as a shimmer in the distance. Eight months later he was dead.

Like Castle Howard, Blenheim is in a baroque style, but even more so. Its roofline is a festive eruption of orbs and urns and other upright embellishments. Many people hated its monumental scale and ostentation. The Earl of Ailesbury dismissed it as 'one mass of stone without taste or relish'. Alexander Pope, after exhaustively enumerating its failings, concluded: 'In a word, it is a most expensive absurdity'. The Duke of Shrewsbury dismissed it as 'a great quarry of stones above ground'. A wag named Abel Evans wrote a mock epitaph for Vanbrugh:

> Lie heavy on him, earth, for he
> Laid many a heavy load on thee.

Blenheim is a gloriously overwrought piece of work without question, but transfixing nonetheless, and the scale is so off the chart that it can hardly fail to awe the first-time visitor. It is hard to believe that anyone would want to live in such an oppressive vastness, and in fact the Marlboroughs barely did. They didn't move in until 1719 and the duke died just two years later.

Whatever one thought of Vanbrugh and his creations, the age of the celebrity architect had begun.*

Before Vanbrugh's day architects weren't much celebrated. Generally fame went to those who paid for the houses, not those who designed them. Hardwick Hall, which we encountered in the hall chapter earlier, was one of the great buildings of its age, yet it is merely supposed that Robert Smythson was the architect. It is a pretty good

---

*It was also, come to that, the age of the celebrity craftsman. One such was the great carver Grinling Gibbons, who lived from 1648 to 1723. His interesting Christian name was his mother's maiden name. He grew up in Holland, of English parents, and came to England in about 1667, after the restoration of Charles II as king. He settled in Deptford, in south-east London, where he made a very basic living carving figure-heads for ships, but one day in 1671, John Evelyn, the diarist, chanced to pass his workshop and was immediately taken with Gibbons's skill, personable manner and possibly good looks. (Gibbons was by all accounts stunningly good-looking.) He encouraged the young man to take on more challenging commissions and introduced him to people of influence, such as Christopher Wren.

Thanks to Evelyn's support, Gibbons became very successful, but most of his wealth actually came from running a workshop that produced statuary and other stonework. It was Gibbons, it appears, who came up with the idea of depicting British heroes as Roman statesmen, in togas and sandals, and this made his work in stone extremely fashionable. Though he is now widely thought of as the greatest wood-carver in modern times, he was not especially famous for it in his own lifetime. For Blenheim Palace, Gibbons produced £4,000-worth of decorative stonework but only £36-worth of woodcarving. Part of the reason his sumptuous woodcarvings are so valued today is that there aren't very many of them.

supposition, for all kinds of reasons, but there is no actual proof of it. Smythson was in fact the first man to be called an architect – or nearly to be called an architect – on a monument of about 1588 in which he is described as 'architector and survayor'. But as with so many others of his era, very little is known about his early life, including where he was born and when. He makes his first appearance in the records at Longleat House in Wiltshire in 1568, when he was already in his thirties and a master mason. Where he was before that is completely unknown.

Even after architecture became a recognized profession, most practitioners came from other backgrounds. Inigo Jones was a designer of theatrical productions, Christopher Wren an astronomer, Robert Hooke a scientist, Vanbrugh a soldier and playwright, William Kent a painter and interior designer. As a formal profession, architecture was actually very late developing. Compulsory examinations were not introduced until 1882 in Britain and architecture wasn't offered anywhere as a full-time academic discipline until 1895.

By the mid-eighteenth century, however, domestic architecture was getting a lot of respect and attention, and for a time no one had more of both than Robert Adam. If Vanbrugh was the first celebrity architect, Adam was the greatest. Born in 1728 in Scotland, the son of an architect, he was one of a quartet of brothers who all became successful architects, though Robert was the undoubted genius of the family and the one remembered by history. The period from 1755 to 1785 is sometimes called the Age of Adam.

A painting of Adam in the National Portrait Gallery in London, made in about 1770 when he was in his early forties, shows a kindly looking man in a powdered grey wig, but in fact Adam was not a particularly adorable fellow. He was arrogant and egotistical and treated his employees poorly, paying them little and keeping them in a kind of perpetual servitude. He fined them severely if they were caught doing any work other than for him, even a sketch for their own amusement. Adam's clients, however, venerated his abilities and for thirty years simply couldn't give him enough work. The Adam brothers became a kind of architectural industry. They owned quarries, a timber business, brickworks, a company for making stucco and much else. At one point they employed two thousand people. They designed not just houses but every object within them – furniture, fireplaces, carpets, beds, lamps and everything else down to incidental objects like doorknobs, bell pulls and inkstands.

Adam's designs were intense – sometimes overwhelming – and gradually he fell out of favour. He had an inescapable weakness for over-decoration. To walk into an Adam room is rather like walking into a large, over-frosted cake. Indeed one of his contemporary critics called him 'a Pastry Cook'. By the late 1780s, Adam was being denounced as 'sugary and effeminate' and had fallen so far out of fashion that he retreated to his native Scotland, where he died in 1792. By 1831, he was so thoroughly forgotten that the influential *Lives of the Most Eminent British Architects* didn't mention him at all. The banishment didn't last terribly long, however. By the 1860s his reputation was undergoing a revival, which continues now, though these days he is remembered more for his rich interiors than for his architecture.

The one thing all buildings had in common during

Adam's day was a rigorous devotion to symmetry. Vanbrugh, to be sure, didn't entirely achieve symmetry at Castle Howard, but that was largely accidental. Elsewhere, however, symmetry was adhered to as an immutable law of design. Every wing had to have a matching wing, whether it was needed or not, and every window and pediment to one side of the main entrance had to be exactly mirrored by windows and pediments on the other side regardless of what went on behind them. The result often was the building of wings that no one really wanted. Not until the nineteenth century did this absurdity begin to end, and it was a remarkable property in Wiltshire – one of the most extraordinary ever built – that started the process.

It was called Fonthill Abbey, and it was the creation of two strange and fascinating men: William Beckford and the architect James Wyatt. Beckford was fabulously rich. His family owned plantations all across Jamaica and had dominated the West Indian sugar trade for a hundred years. Beckford's doting mother made sure her son enjoyed every advantage in his upbringing. The eight-year-old Wolfgang Mozart was brought in to give him piano lessons. Sir William Chambers, the king's architect, taught him to draw. Beckford's wealth was so inexhaustibly great that when he came into his inheritance on his twenty-first birthday, he spent £40,000 – an obscenely colossal sum – on the party. Byron in a poem called him 'England's wealthiest son', probably rightly.

In 1784, Beckford became the centrepiece of the most spectacularly juicy scandal of his age when it emerged that he was involved in a pair of tempestuous, wildly dangerous dalliances. One was with Louisa Beckford, the wife of his first cousin. At the same time, he also fell for a slim and delicate youth named William Courtenay, the future ninth Earl of Devon, who was generally agreed to be the most beautiful boy in England. For a few torrid and presumably exhausting years, Beckford maintained both relationships, often under the same roof. But the autumn of 1784 saw a sudden rupture. Beckford received or discovered a note in Courtenay's hand that threw him into a fit of jealous rage. No record exists of what the note said, but it provoked Beckford into intemperate action. He went to Courtenay's room and, in the slightly confused words of one of the other houseguests, 'horsewhipped him, which created a noise, and the door being opened, Courtenay was discovered in his shirt, and Beckford in some posture or other – Strange story'.

Indeed.

The particular misfortune here was that Courtenay was the darling of his family – he was the only boy among fourteen siblings – and shockingly youthful. He was sixteen at the time of the incident, but may have been as young as ten when he fell under Beckford's unwholesome sway. This was not a matter that Courtenay's family would ever let drop, and we may take it for granted that Beckford's cuckolded cousin was less than jubilant, too. Disgraced beyond any hope of redemption, Beckford fled to the continent. There he travelled widely and wrote, in French, a gothic novel called *Vathek: An Arabian Tale*, which is virtually unreadable now but was much admired in its day.

Then in 1796, his disgrace nowhere near over, Beckford did a wholly unexpected thing. He returned to England and announced a plan to tear down the family mansion in Wiltshire, Fonthill Splendens, which was only about forty years old, and build a new house in its place – and not just any house but the largest house in England since Blenheim. It was a strange thing to do for he had no prospect of ever filling it with company. The architect he selected for this slightly demented exercise was James Wyatt.

Wyatt is a curiously neglected figure. His only substantial biography, by Antony Dale, was published over half a century ago. He would perhaps be more famous but for the fact that so many of his buildings no longer exist. Today he is remembered more for what he destroyed than what he built.

Born in Staffordshire, the son of a farmer, Wyatt was drawn to architecture as a young man and spent six years in Italy studying architectural drawing. In 1770, aged just twenty-four, he designed the Pantheon, an exhibition hall and assembly room on Oxford Street in London, which was loosely modelled on the ancient building of the same name in Rome. Horace Walpole thought it 'the most beautiful edifice in England.' In 1931, the building, still beautiful though much altered, was torn down to make way for a Marks & Spencer department store.

Wyatt was an architect of talent and distinction – under George III he was appointed Surveyor of the Office of Works, in effect official architect to the nation – but a perennial shambles as a human being. He was disorganized, forgetful and perpetually dissolute. He was famously bibulous, and sometimes went on tremendous benders. One year he missed fifty straight weekly meetings at the Office of Works. His supervision of the office was so poor that one man was discovered to have been on holiday for three years. When sober, however, he was much liked and widely praised for his charm, good nature and architectural vision. A bust of him in the National Portrait Gallery in London shows him clean-shaven (and indeed clean, a slightly unusual condition for him), with a very full head of hair and a face that seems curiously mournful or perhaps just slightly hung over.

Despite his shortcomings, he became the most sought-after architect of his day, but took on more commissions than he could manage and seldom gave satisfactory attention to any one, to the endless exasperation of his clients. 'If he can get with a large fire and have a bottle by him, he cares for nothing else,' wrote one of his many frustrated customers.

'There is an overwhelming consensus of opinion,' wrote his biographer Dale, 'that Wyatt had three outstand-ing faults: an entire lack of business capability, the complete incapacity for constant or intensive application . . . and utter improvidence.' And these were the words of a sympathetic observer. Wyatt was, in short, feckless and impossible. A client named William Windham stuck it out for eleven years on a job that should have taken a fraction of the time. 'A person has some right to feel impatient,' Windham wearily wrote to his absent architect at one point, 'finding the principal rooms of his house near un-inhabitable because he has not been able to obtain from you what would not be the work of a couple of hours.' To be a Wyatt client was to be long-suffering.

Yet his career was both successful and remarkably pro-ductive. Over a span of forty years he built or refashioned a hundred country houses, extravagantly reworked five cathedrals and did much to change the face of British architecture – not always, it must be said, for the good. His treatment of cathedrals was particularly rash and sweeping. A critic named John Carter was so exercised by Wyatt's predilection for ripping out ancient interiors that he dubbed him 'the Destroyer' and devoted 212 essays in the *Gentleman's Magazine* – essentially his whole career – to attacking Wyatt's style and character.

At Durham Cathedral, Wyatt had plans to surmount the building with a mighty spire. This never came to pass, which is perhaps no bad thing for at Fonthill Wyatt would soon show that there were few places more dangerous to be than under a Wyatt tower. He also wished to sweep away the ancient Galilee Chapel, the last resting place of the Venerable Bede and one of the great achievements of English Norman architecture. Happily that plan was rejected too.

Beckford was enthralled by Wyatt's dashing genius, but driven to sputtering distraction by his dissolute habits and utter unreliability. Still, he somehow managed to keep him focused enough to draw a plan, and work started shortly before the turn of the century.

Everything at Fonthill was designed on a fantastic scale. Windows stood fifty feet high. Staircases were as wide as they were long. The front door rose to a height of thirty feet, but was made to seem even taller by Beckford's practice of employing dwarf doormen. Eighty-foot curtains hung from the four arches in the Octagon, a central chamber from which radiated four long arms. The view down the central corridor stretched for over three hundred feet. The dining-room table – Beckford its only occupant night after night – was fifty feet long. Every ceiling was lost in a distant gloom of hammerbeams.

Fonthill was very possibly the most exhausting residence ever built – and all for a man who lived alone and was known everywhere as 'the man on whom no neighbour would call'. To preserve his privacy Beckford built a formidable wall, known as The Barrier, around the estate. It was twelve feet high, twelve miles long, and surmounted by iron spikes.

Among the additional, incidental planned structures was a mighty tomb, one hundred and twenty-five feet long, in which his coffin would be placed on a dais twenty-five feet above the ground, so that, he believed, no worms could ever get to him.

Fonthill was deliberately and riotously asymmetrical – 'architectural anarchy' in the words of the historian Simon Thurley – and rendered in an ornate Gothic style that made it look like a cross between a medieval cathedral and Dracula's castle. Wyatt didn't invent neo-Gothicism. That distinction goes to Horace Walpole for his house Strawberry Hill in outer London. Gothick, as it was some-times spelled to distinguish it from the genuine medieval stuff, originally signalled not an architectural style but a type of gloomy, overwrought novel, and Walpole invented that too with *The Castle of Otranto* in 1764. Strawberry Hill, however, was a fairly cautious, picturesque sort of thing – a more or less conventional house with some Gothic tracery and other embellishments attached. Wyatt's Gothic creations were vastly darker and heavier. They had looming towers and romantic spires and jumbled rooflines that were studiously asymmetrical, so that they looked as if the whole structure had grown organically over centuries. It was a kind of Hollywood imagining of the past, long before there was a

The Great Western Hall, leading to the Grand Saloon or Octagon, at Fonthill Abbey.

Hollywood. Walpole invented a term, 'gloomth', to convey the ambience of Gothick; Wyatt's houses were the very quintessence of gloomth.* They dripped it.

In his obsession to get the project completed Beckford kept up to five hundred men working round the clock, but things constantly went wrong. Fonthill's tower, rising to a height of 280 feet, was the tallest ever put on a private house, and it was a nightmare. Rashly, Wyatt used a new kind of rendering called Parker's Roman cement, invented by a Reverend James Parker of Gravesend, yet another of that inquisitive breed of clergymen whom we encountered at the outset of the book. What impulse brought the Reverend Mr Parker to the world of building materials is unknown, but his idea was to produce a quick-drying cement of the type once used by the Romans, from a recipe since lost. Unfortunately, his cement had little inherent strength and, if not mixed exactly correctly, tended to fall apart in chunks – as it did now at Fonthill. Appalled, Beckford found his mighty abbey coming to pieces even as it went up. Twice it collapsed during construction. Even when fully erect it creaked and groaned ominously.

To Beckford's boundless exasperation, Wyatt was often away either drunk or working on other projects. Just as

---

*Although he is hardly read now, Walpole was immensely popular in his day for his histories and romances. He was a particularly adept coiner of words. The *Oxford English Dictionary* credits him with no fewer than 233 coinages. Many, like 'gloomth', 'greenth', 'fluctuable' and 'betweenity', didn't take, but a great many others did. Among the terms he invented or otherwise brought into English are 'airsickness', 'ante-room', 'bask', 'beefy', 'boulevard', 'café', 'cause célèbre', 'caricature', 'fairy tale', 'falsetto', 'frisson', 'impresario', 'malaria', 'mudbath', 'nuance', 'serendipity', 'sombre', 'souvenir' and, as mentioned a few pages back, 'comfortable' in its modern sense.

things were literally falling apart at Fonthill and the five hundred workers were either running for their lives or twiddling their thumbs awaiting instructions, Wyatt was engaged in a massive, abortive project to build George III a new palace at Kew. Why George III wanted a new palace at Kew is a reasonable question as he had a very good one there already, but Wyatt went ahead and designed a formidable edifice (nicknamed the Bastille because of its forbidding looks), one of the first buildings anywhere to use cast iron as a structural material. We don't know what the new palace looked like because no reproduction of it exists, but it must have been quite a sight for it was made completely of cast iron except for doors and floorboards. Presumably, it would have been rather like living inside a cauldron. Unfortunately, as the building rose on the banks of the Thames the king began to lose his sight and his interest in things he couldn't see, and anyway he never liked Wyatt much to begin with. So, with the structure half built and more than £100,000 spent on it, work abruptly ceased. The house remained an unfinished shell for some twenty years until a new king, George IV, finally had it pulled down.

Beckford bombarded Wyatt with outraged letters. 'What putrid inn, what stinking tavern or pox ridden brothel hides your hoary and glutinous limbs?' ran one typical enquiry. His pet name for Wyatt was 'Bagasse' or pimp. Every letter was a screed of rage and inventive insult. Wyatt was, to be sure, maddening. Once he left Fonthill to go to London, ostensibly on urgent business, but got only three miles, to another property owned by Beckford, where he fell in with another boozy guest. Beckford discovered them there together, surrounded by empty bottles and insensate, a week later.

The final cost of Fonthill Abbey is unknown but in
1801 an informed observer suggested that Beckford had
already spent £242,000 – enough to build two Crystal
Palaces – and it was less than half done. Beckford moved
into the abbey in the summer of 1807 even though it was
uncompleted. There was no comfort in it at all. 'Sixty fires
had to be kept continually burning winter and summer to
keep the house dry, let alone warm,' Simon Thurley
records. Most of the bedrooms were as bare as monastic
cells; thirteen had no windows. Beckford's own bedchamber was strikingly austere, and contained a single
narrow bed.

Wyatt continued to attend intermittently and to drive
Beckford to fury with his absences. In early September
1813, just after his sixty-seventh birthday, Wyatt was riding
back to London from Gloucestershire with a client when
his carriage overturned and he was dashed against the
wall, striking his head a fatal blow. He died more or less
instantly, and left his widow penniless.

Just at this time, sugar prices went into a depression
and Beckford ended up uncomfortably exposed to the
downside of capitalism. By 1823, he was so strapped for
funds that he was forced to sell Fonthill. It was bought
for £300,000 by an eccentric character, John Farquhar,
who had been born in rural Scotland but went to India as
a young man and made a fortune manufacturing gunpowder. Returning to England in 1814, he settled in
London in a fine house on Portman Square, which he conspicuously neglected. He conspicuously neglected himself
too – to such an extent that on his walks through the
neighbourhood he was sometimes stopped and
questioned as a suspicious vagrant. After buying Fonthill,

he hardly ever visited it. He was, however, in residence on the most spectacular day in Fonthill's brief existence, just before Christmas 1825, when the tower emitted a sustained groan, then collapsed for a third and final time. A servant was blown thirty feet down a corridor by the rush of air, but miraculously neither he nor anyone else was injured. About a third of the house lay under the heaped wreckage of the tower, and would never be habitable again. Farquhar was remarkably equable about his misfortune and merely remarked that this greatly simplified the care of the place. He died the following year, immensely rich but intestate, and none of his bickering relatives would take on the house. What remained of it was torn down and cleared away not long after.

Beckford, meanwhile, took his £300,000 and retired to Bath, where he built a 154-foot tower in a restrained classical style. Called the Lansdown Tower, it was erected with good materials and prudent care, and still stands.

II

Fonthill marked the summit not only of ambition and folly in the domestic realm but also of discomfort. A curious inverse relationship had arisen, it seems, between the amount of effort and expense that went into a house and the extent to which it was actually habitable. The great age of housebuilding brought new levels of elegance and grandeur to private life in Britain, but almost nothing in the way of softness, warmth and convenience.

Those homely attributes would be the creation of a new type of person who had scarcely existed a generation or so before: the middle-class professional. There had always been people of middling rank, of course, but as a distinct entity and force to be reckoned with the middle class was an eighteenth-century phenomenon. The term 'middle class' wasn't coined until 1745 (in a book on the Irish wool trade, of all things), but from that point onwards the streets and coffee houses of Britain abounded with confident, voluble, well-to-do people who answered to that description: bankers, lawyers, artists, publishers, designers, merchants, property developers and others of generally creative spirit and ambition. This new and swelling middle class served not only the very wealthy but also, even more lucratively, each other. This was the change that made the modern world.

The invention of the middle class injected new levels of demand into society. Suddenly there were swarms of people with splendid townhouses that all needed furnishing, and just as suddenly the world was full of desirable objects with which to fill them. Carpets, mirrors, curtains, upholstered and embroidered furniture and a hundred things more that were rarely found in homes before 1750 now became commonplace.

The growth of empire and of overseas business interests had a dramatic effect, too, often in unexpected ways. Take wood. When Britain was an isolated island nation, it had essentially just one wood for furniture-making: oak. Oak is a noble material, solid, long-lasting, literally hard as iron, but it is really only suitable for dense, blocky furniture – trunks, beds, heavy tables and the like. But the development of the British navy and the spread of

Britain's commercial interests meant that woods of many types – walnut from Virginia, tulipwood from the Carolinas, teak from Asia – became available, and these changed everything within the home, including how people sat and conversed and entertained.

The most prized wood of all was mahogany from the Caribbean. Mahogany was lustrous, warp-resistant and sublimely accommodating. It could be carved and fretted into the delicate shapes that perfectly suited the exuberance of rococo, yet was strong enough to be a piece of furniture. No wood had had these characteristics before: suddenly furniture had a sculptural quality. The central uprights of the chairs – the splats – could be worked in a way that was wondrous to a people who had never seen anything less clunky than a Windsor chair. The legs had flowing curves and luscious feet; the arms swept their way to terminal scrolls and volutes that were a pleasure to grasp and a delight to behold. Every chair – indeed, every built thing in the house – seemed suddenly to have elegance and style and fluidity.

Mahogany would have been nothing like as esteemed a wood as it was had it not been for one other magical new material, from the other side of the Earth, that gave it the most splendid finish: shellac. Shellac is a hard, resinous secretion from the Indian lac beetle. Lac beetles emerge in swarms in parts of India at certain times of the year and their secretions make varnish that is odourless, non-toxic, brilliantly shiny and highly resistant to scratches and fading. It doesn't attract dust while wet and dries in minutes. Even now, in an age of chemistry, shellac has scores of applications against which synthetic products cannot compete. When you go bowling, it is shellac that gives the alleys their peerless sheen, for instance.

New woods and varnishes transformed the forms that furniture could take, but something else was needed – a new system of manufacture – to produce the volumes of quality furniture necessary to satisfy the endless demand. Where traditional designers like Robert Adam made a new design for each commission, furniture makers now realized that it was far more cost-effective to make lots of furniture from a single design. They began to operate a factory system on a large scale, cranking out pieces that were cut from templates, then assembled and finished by teams of specialists. The age of mass manufacture had been born.

There is a certain irony in the thought that the people who did most to establish mass manufacturing techniques were the ones we now most revere for their craftsmanship, and of no one is that more true than a shadowy furniture maker from the north of England named Thomas Chippendale. His influence was enormous. He was the first commoner for whom a furniture style was named; before him the names faithfully recalled monarchies: Tudor, Elizabethan, Louis XIV, Queen Anne. Yet we know remarkably little about him. We have no idea, for instance, what he looked like. Except that he was born and grew up in the market town of Otley, on the edge of the Yorkshire Dales, nothing at all is known of his early life. His first appearance in the written record is in 1748, when he arrives in London, already aged thirty, and sets up as a new type of maker and purveyor of household furnishings known as an upholder.

That was an ambitious thing to do, for upholders' businesses tended to be complicated and extensive. One of the most successful, George Seddon, employed four hundred workmen – carvers, gilders, joiners, makers of mirrors and brass, and so on. Chippendale did not operate on quite that scale, but he employed forty or fifty men, and his premises covered two frontages at 60–62 St Martin's Lane, just around the corner from the modern Trafalgar Square (though that wouldn't exist for another eighty years). He also provided an extremely complete service, making and selling chairs, occasional tables, dressing tables, writing tables, card tables, bookcases, bureaus, mirrors, clock cases, candelabra, candle stands, music stands, sconces, commodes and an exotic new contrivance that he called a 'sopha'. Sofas were daring, even titillating, because they resembled beds and so hinted at salacious repose. The firm also stocked wallpaper and carpets, and undertook repairs, furniture removals and even funerals.

Thomas Chippendale made indisputably fine furniture, but so did lots of others. St Martin's Lane alone had thirty furniture makers in the eighteenth century, and hundreds more were scattered across London and throughout the country. The reason we all know Chippendale's name today is that in 1754 he did something quite audacious. He issued a book of designs called *The Gentleman and Cabinet-Maker's Director*, containing 160 plates. Architects had been doing this sort of thing for nearly two hundred years, but nobody had thought to do it for furniture. The drawings were unexpectedly beguiling. Instead of being flat, two-dimensional templates, as was standard, they were perspective drawings, full of shadow and sheen. The prospective purchaser could immediately visualize how these handsome and desirable objects would look in his own home. It would be misleading to call Chippendale's book a sensation because only 308 copies were sold, but the purchasers included forty-nine members of the aristocracy, which made it disproportionately influential. It was also snapped up by other furniture makers and craftsmen, raising another point of oddness – that Chippendale was openly inviting his competitors to make use of his designs for their own commercial purposes. This helped to ensure Chippendale's posterity, but didn't do much for his immediate fortunes since potential clients could now get Chippendale furniture made more cheaply by any reasonably skilled joiner. It also meant two centuries of difficulty for furniture historians in determining which pieces of furniture are genuine Chippendales and which are copies made using his book. Even if a piece is a 'genuine' Chippendale, it doesn't mean that Thomas Chippendale ever touched it or was even aware of its existence. It doesn't even necessarily mean that he designed it. No one knows how much talent he bought in, or whether the designs in his books are in fact from his own hand. A genuine Chippendale simply means that it came from his workshop.

Such is the Chippendale aura, however, that it needn't even have been as close to him as that. In 1756 in colonial Boston, a furniture maker named John Welch, using a Chippendale pattern as a guide, made a mahogany desk, which he sold to a man named Dublois. The desk stayed in the Dublois family for 250 years. In 2007 they put it up for auction with Sotheby's in New York. Though Thomas Chippendale had no direct connection to it, it sold for just under $3.3 million.

Inspired by Chippendale's success, other English furniture makers issued pattern books of their own.

George Hepplewhite's *Cabinet-Maker and Upholsterer's Guide* was published in 1788 and Thomas Sheraton followed with the *Cabinet-Maker and Upholsterer's Drawing-Book*, issued in instalments between 1791 and 1794. Sheraton's book had more than twice as many subscribers as Chippendale's and was translated into German, a distinction not accorded Chippendale's own volume. Hepplewhite and Sheraton became particularly popular in America.

Although any piece of furniture directly associated with any of the three is today worth a fortune, they were more admired than celebrated in their own lifetimes, and at times not even all that admired. Chippendale's fortunes slipped first. He was an outstanding furniture maker but hopeless at running a business, a deficiency that became acutely evident upon the death of his business partner, James Rannie, in 1766. Rannie was the brains of the operation and without him Chippendale lurched from crisis to crisis for the rest of his life. All this was painfully ironic, for as he struggled to pay his men and keep himself out of a debtor's cell, Chippendale was producing items of the highest quality for some of England's richest households, and working closely with the leading architects and designers – Robert Adam, James Wyatt, Sir William Chambers and others. Yet his personal trajectory was relentlessly downwards.

It was not an easy age in which to do business. Customers were routinely slow in paying. Chippendale had to threaten David Garrick, the actor and impresario, with legal action for chronic unpaid bills, and stopped work at Nostell Priory, a stately home in Yorkshire, when the debt there reached £6,838 – a whopping liability. 'I have not a single guinea to pay my men with tomorrow', he wrote in despair at one point. It is clear that Chippendale spent much of his life in a froth of anxiety, scarcely for a moment enjoying any sense of security at all. At his death in 1779, his personal worth had sunk to just £28 2s 9d – not enough to buy a modest piece of ormolu from his own showrooms. The firm struggled on under the directorship of his son, but finally succumbed to bankruptcy in 1804.

When Chippendale died, the world barely noticed. No obituary appeared in any paper. Fourteen years after his death, Sheraton wrote of Chippendale's designs that 'they are now wholly antiquated and laid aside'. By the late 1800s, his reputation had fallen so low that the first edition of the *Dictionary of National Biography* gave him just one paragraph – much less than it gave Sheraton or Hepplewhite – and much of that was critical and a good deal of it was wrong. The author was so little absorbed by the facts of Chippendale's life that he had him coming from Worcestershire, not Yorkshire.

Sheraton (1751–1806) and Hepplewhite (1727?–1786) could hardly boast of magnificent success themselves. Hepplewhite's shop was in a down-at-heel district, Cripplegate, and his identity sufficiently obscure that his contemporaries referred to him variously as Kepplewhite and Hebblethwaite. Almost nothing is known of his personal life. He had actually been dead for two years by the time his own book of patterns was published. Sheraton's fate was even more curious. He seems never to have opened a shop, and no piece of furniture that can be attributed to him has ever been found. He may never have made any, but acted merely as a draughtsman and designer. Though his book sold well, it appears not to have enriched him, for he had to supplement his income by teaching drawing and perspective. At some point he gave up furniture design, trained as a minister for a non-conformist sect known as the Narrow Baptists, and became essentially a street-corner preacher. He died in complete squalor, 'among dirt and bugs', in London in 1806, leaving a wife and two children.

As furniture makers, Chippendale and his contemporaries were masters without any doubt, but they enjoyed one special advantage that can never be replicated: the use of the finest furniture wood that has ever existed, a species of mahogany called *Swietenia mahogani*. Found only on parts of Cuba and Hispaniola (the island today shared by Haiti and the Dominican Republic) in the Caribbean, *Swietenia mahogani* has never been matched for richness, elegance and utility. Such was the demand for it that it was entirely used up – irremediably extinct – within fifty years of its discovery. Some two hundred other species of mahogany exist in the world, and most are very good woods, but they have nothing like the richness and smooth workability of the departed *S. mahogani*. The world may one day produce better chairmakers than Chippendale and his peers, but it will never produce finer chairs.

Curiously, no one at all appreciated this for the longest time. Many Chippendale chairs and other pieces, now considered priceless, spent a century or more being casually knocked about in the servants' quarters before they were rediscovered and returned to the main house in the Edwardian era. Some six hundred pieces of Chippendale furniture have now been confirmed altogether. Others, handed down or disposed of in estate sales, could easily sit unregarded in some country cottage or suburban semi, more valuable than the houses that contain them.

III

If we were to go back in time to a house in Chippendale's day, one difference that would immediately strike us would be that chairs and other furniture were generally pushed up against the walls, giving every room the aspect of a waiting room. Chairs or tables in the middle of the room would have looked as out of place to Georgians as a wardrobe left in the middle of a room would look to us today. (One reason for pushing them to the side was to make it easier to walk through rooms without tripping over furniture in the dark.) Because they were kept against the wall, the backs of early upholstered chairs and settees were often left unfinished, just as we leave bare the backs of chests and wardrobes today.

When one had visitors, the custom was to bring an appropriate number of chairs forward and arrange them in a circle or semicircle, rather like storytime in a primary school. This had the inevitable effect of making nearly all conversations strained and artificial. Horace Walpole, after sitting for four and a half hours in an agonizing circle of fatuous conversation, declared: 'We wore out the Wind and the Weather, the Opera and the Play . . . and every topic that would do in a formal circle.' Yet when daring hostesses tried to introduce spontaneity by arranging chairs into more intimate clusters of threes and fours, many felt the result was tantamount to pandemonium and more than a few could never get used to the idea of conversations taking place behind their backs.

The one problem with the chairs of the age was that they weren't terribly comfortable. The obvious solution was to pad them, but that proved more difficult than one might have thought because few craftsmen had all the skills necessary to make a good padded chair. Manufacturers struggled to get square edges where fabric met wood – piping and cording were originally brought in as a way of disguising these inadequacies – and were frequently out of their depth at producing padding that would maintain a permanent domed shape on the seat. Only saddlers could reliably provide the requisite durability, which is why so much early upholstered furniture was covered in leather. Fabric upholsterers also had the problem that many pre-industrial fabrics could be produced only in widths of about twenty inches, creating a need for seams in awkward places. Only after the invention of the flying shuttle by John Kay in 1733 did it become possible to produce fabrics in widths of three feet or so.

Improvements in textile and printing technologies transformed decorative possibilities beyond furniture as well. This was the age that saw the widespread introduction of carpets, wallpapers and bright fabrics. Paint, too, became available in a range of rich colours for the first time. The upshot is that by late in the eighteenth century, households were full of features that would have been the wildest indulgences a century before. The modern house – a house such as we would recognize today – had begun to emerge. At last, some fourteen hundred years after the

Romans withdrew, taking their hot baths, padded sofas and central heating with them, the British were rediscovering the novel condition of being congenially situated. They hadn't entirely mastered comfort yet, but they had certainly discovered an alluring concept. Life, and the expectations that went with it, would never be the same again.

There was, however, one consequence in all this. The advent of comfort in the home, in particular the widespread use of soft furnishings, made furniture much more vulnerable to stains, burns and other careless abuses. In an effort to save the most valuable furniture from the worst of the risks, a new type of room was created, and it is there, conveniently, that we go next.

CHAPTER EIGHT

The Dining Room

I

BY THE TIME Mr Marsham came to build his house, it would have been unthinkable for a man of his position not to have a formal dining room in which to entertain, but just how formal and how spacious and whether situated at the front of the house or the back are all matters that would have required some reflection since dining rooms were still novel enough that their dimensions and situation could not be assumed. In the end, as we have seen, Mr Marsham decided to eliminate the proposed servants' hall and give himself a thirty-foot-long dining room – big enough to accommodate eighteen or twenty guests, a very large number for a country parson. Even if he entertained frequently, as would seem to be indicated, it must have been a lonely room on the nights he dined alone. At least the view across to the churchyard was a pleasant one.

We know almost nothing about how Mr Marsham used this room, not simply because we know so little about Mr Marsham but also because we know surprisingly little about certain aspects of dining rooms themselves. In the middle of the table was likely to have stood an object of costly elegance known as an epergne (pronounced 'ay-pairn'), consisting of dishes connected by ornamental branches, each dish containing a selection of fruits or nuts. For a century or so no table of discernment was without its epergne, but why it was called an epergne no one remotely knows. The word doesn't exist in French. It just seems to have popped into being from nowhere.

Around the epergne on Mr Marsham's table are likely to have been cruet stands – elegant little racks, usually of silver, holding condiments – and these too have a mystery. Traditional cruet stands came with two glass bottles with stoppers, for oil and vinegar, and three matching casters – that is, bottles with perforated tops for sprinkling (or casting) flavourings on to food. Two of the casters contained salt and pepper, but what went into the third caster is unknown. It is generally presumed to have been dried mustard, but that is really because no one can think of anything more likely. 'No satisfactory alternative has ever been suggested' is how the food historian Gerard Brett has put it. In fact, there is no evidence to suggest that mustard was ever desired or utilized in such ready fashion by diners at any time in history. Probably for this reason, by Mr Marsham's day the third caster was rapidly disappearing from tables – as indeed were cruet stands themselves. Condiments now increasingly varied from meal to meal as certain ones became associated with particular foods – mint sauce with lamb, mustard with ham, horseradish with beef and so on. Scores of other flavourings were applied in the kitchen. But just two were considered so indispensable that they never left the table at all. I refer of course to salt and pepper.

Why it is that these two, out of all the hundreds of spices and flavourings available, have such a durable venerability is one of the questions with which we began the book. The answer is a complicated one, but a dramatic one. I can tell you at once that nothing you touch today will have more bloodshed, suffering and woe attached to it than the innocuous twin pillars of your salt and pepper set.

Start with salt. Salt is a cherished part of our diet for a very fundamental reason. We need it. We would die without it. It is one of about forty tiny specks of incidental matter – odds and ends from the chemical world – that we must get into our bodies to give ourselves the necessary zip and balance to sustain daily life. Collectively they are known as vitamins and minerals, and there is a great deal – a really quite surprising amount – that we don't know about them, including how many of them we need, what exactly some of them do, and in what amounts they are optimally consumed.

That they were needed at all was a piece of knowledge that was an amazingly long time coming. Until well into the nineteenth century, the notion of a well-balanced diet had occurred to no one. All food was believed to contain a single vague but sustaining substance – 'the universal aliment'. A pound of beef had the same value for the body as a pound of apples or parsnips or anything else, and all that was required of a human was to make sure that an ample amount was taken in. The idea that embedded within particular foods were vital elements that were central to one's well-being had not yet been thought of. That's not altogether surprising because the symptoms of dietary deficiency – lethargy, aching joints, increased suscepti- bility to infection, blurred vision – seldom suggest dietary imbalance. Even today if your hair started to fall out or your ankles swelled alarmingly, it is unlikely your first thoughts would turn to what you had eaten lately. Still less would you think about what you *hadn't* eaten. So it was with bewildered Europeans, who for a very long time died in often staggering numbers without knowing why.

Of scurvy alone it has been suggested that as many as two million sailors died between 1500 and 1850. Typically it killed about half the crew on any long voyage. Various desperate expedients were tried. Vasco da Gama on a cruise to India and back encouraged his men to rinse their mouths with urine, which did nothing for their scurvy and can't have done much for their spirits either. Sometimes the toll was truly shocking. On a three-year voyage in the 1740s, a British naval expedition under the command of Commodore George Anson lost 1,400 men out of 2,000 who sailed. Four were killed by enemy action; virtually all the rest died of scurvy.

Over time people noticed that sailors with scurvy tended to recover when they got to a port and received fresh foods, but nobody could agree what it was about those foods that helped them. Some thought it wasn't the foods at all, but just a change of air. In any case, it wasn't possible to keep foods fresh for weeks on long voyages, so simply identifying efficacious vegetables and the like was slightly pointless. What was needed was some kind of distilled essence – an antiscorbutic, as the medical men termed it – that would be effective against scurvy but portable too. In the 1760s, a Scottish doctor named

William Stark, evidently encouraged by Benjamin Franklin, conducted a series of patently foolhardy experiments in which he tried to identify the active agent by, somewhat bizarrely, depriving himself of it. For weeks he lived on only the most basic of foods – bread and water chiefly – to see what would happen. What happened was that in just over six months he killed himself, from scurvy, without coming to any helpful conclusions at all. In roughly the same period, James Lind, a naval surgeon, conducted a more scientifically rigorous (and personally less risky) experiment by finding twelve sailors who had scurvy already, dividing them into pairs, and giving each pair a different putative elixir – vinegar to one, garlic and mustard to another, oranges and lemons to a third, and so on. Five of the groups showed no improvement, but the pair given oranges and lemons made a swift and total recovery. Amazingly, Lind decided to ignore the significance of the result and doggedly stuck with his personal belief that scurvy was caused by incompletely digested food building up toxins within the body.

It fell to the great Captain James Cook to get matters on to the right course. On his circumnavigation of the globe in 1768–71, Captain Cook packed a range of antiscorbutics to experiment on, including thirty gallons of carrot marmalade and a hundred pounds of sauerkraut for every crew member. Not one person died from scurvy on his voyage – a miracle that made him as much a national hero as his discovery of Australia or any of his other many achievements on that epic undertaking. The Royal Society, Britain's premier scientific institution, was so impressed that it awarded him the Copley Medal, its highest distinction. The British navy itself was not so quick, alas.

In the face of all the evidence, it prevaricated for another generation before finally providing citrus juice to sailors as a matter of routine.*

The realization that an inadequate diet was the cause not only of scurvy but of a range of common diseases was remarkably slow in coming. Not until 1897 did a Dutch physician named Christiaan Eijkman, working in Java, notice that people who ate wholegrain rice didn't get beriberi, a debilitating nerve disease, while people who ate polished rice very often did. Clearly some thing or things were present in some foods and missing in others, and served as a determinant of well-being. It was the beginning of an understanding of 'deficiency disease', as it was known, and it won him the Nobel Prize in medicine even though he had no idea what these active agents were.

The real breakthrough came in 1912, when Casimir Funk, a Polish biochemist working at the Lister Institute in London, isolated thiamine, or Vitamin B1, as it is now more generally known. Realizing it was part of a family of molecules, he combined the terms 'vital' and 'amines' to make the new word 'vitamines'. Although Funk was right about the vital part, it turned out that only some of the vitamines were amines (that is to say, nitrogen-bearing), and so the name was changed to 'vitamins' to make it 'less emphatically inaccurate', in Anthony Smith's nice phrase.

Funk also asserted that there was a direct correlation between a deficiency of specific amines and the onset of certain diseases – scurvy, pellagra and rickets in particular.

* The Naval Board used lime juice rather than lemon juice because it was cheaper, which is why British sailors became known as limeys. Lime juice wasn't nearly as effective as lemon juice.

This was a huge insight and had the potential to save millions of shattered lives, but unfortunately it wasn't heeded. The leading medical textbook of the day continued to insist that scurvy was caused by any number of factors – 'insanitary surroundings, overwork, mental depression and exposure to cold and damp' were the principal ones its authors thought worth listing – and only marginally by dietary deficiency. Worse still, in 1917 America's leading nutritionist, E. V. McCollum of the University of Wisconsin – the man who actually coined the terms Vitamins A and B – declared that scurvy was not in fact a dietary deficiency disease at all, but was caused by constipation.

Finally, in 1939 a Harvard Medical School surgeon named John Crandon decided to settle matters once and for all by the age-old method of withholding Vitamin C from his diet for as long as it took to make himself really ill. It took a surprisingly long time. For the first eighteen weeks, his only symptom was extreme fatigue. (Remarkably, he continued to operate on patients throughout this period.) But in the nineteenth week he took an abrupt turn for the worse – so much so that he would almost certainly have died had he not been under close medical supervision. He was injected with 1,000 milligrams of Vitamin C and was restored to life almost at once. Interestingly, he had never acquired the one set of symptoms that everyone associates with scurvy: the falling out of teeth and bleeding of gums.

Meanwhile, it turned out that Funk's vitamines were not nearly as coherent a group as originally thought. Vitamin B proved to be not one vitamin but several, which is why we have B1, B2 and so on. To add to the confusion, Vitamin K has nothing to do with an alphabetical sequence. It was called K because its Danish discoverer, Henrik Dam, dubbed it *Koagulations vitamin* for its role in blood clotting. Later, folic acid was added to the group. Sometimes it is called Vitamin B9, but more often it is just called folic acid. Two other vitamins – pantothenic acid and biotin – don't have numbers or, come to that, much profile, but that is because they only very rarely cause us problems.

The vitamins are, in short, a disorderly bunch. It is almost impossible to define them in a way that comfortably embraces them all. A standard textbook definition is that a vitamin is 'an organic molecule not made in the human body which is required in small amounts to sustain normal metabolism', but in fact Vitamin K *is* made in the body, by bacteria in the gut. Vitamin D, one of the most vital substances of all, is actually a hormone, and most of it comes to us not through diet but through the magical action of sunlight on skin.

Vitamins are curious things. It is odd, to begin with, that we cannot produce them ourselves when we are so very dependent on them for our well-being. If a potato can produce Vitamin C, why can't we? Within the animal kingdom only humans and guinea pigs are unable to synthesize Vitamin C in their own bodies. Why us and guinea pigs? No point asking. Nobody knows. The other remarkable thing about vitamins is the striking disproportion between dosage and effect. Put simply, we need vitamins a lot, but we don't need a lot of them. Three ounces of Vitamin A, lightly but evenly distributed, will keep you purring for a lifetime. Your B1 requirement is even less – just one ounce spread over seventy or eighty years. But just try doing without those energizing specks and see how long it is before you start to fall to pieces.

The same considerations exactly apply with the vitamins' fellow particles the minerals. The fundamental difference between vitamins and minerals is that vitamins come from the world of living things – from plants and bacteria and so on – and minerals do not. In a dietary context, 'minerals' is simply another name for the chemical elements – calcium, iron, iodine, potassium and the like – that sustain us. Ninety-two elements occur naturally on earth, though some in only very tiny amounts. Francium, for instance, is so rare that it is thought that the whole planet may contain just twenty francium atoms at any given time. Of the rest, most pass through our bodies at some time or other, sometimes quite regularly, but whether they are important or not still is often not known. You have a lot of bromine distributed through your tissues. It behaves as if it is there for a purpose, but nobody yet has worked out what that purpose might be. Remove zinc from your diet and you will get a condition known as hypogeusia in which your taste buds stop working, making food boring or even revolting, but until as recently as 1977 zinc was thought to have no role in diet at all.

Several elements, like mercury, thallium and lead, seem to do nothing good for us and are positively detrimental if consumed excessively.* Others are also unnecessary but far more benign, of which the most notable is gold. That is why gold can be used as a filling

* Mercury especially so. It has been estimated that as little as $1/25$ of a teaspoon of mercury could poison a sixty-acre lake. It is fairly amazing that we don't get poisoned more often. According to one computation, no fewer than 20,000 chemicals in common use are also poisonous to humans if 'touched, ingested or inhaled'. Most are twentieth-century creations.

for teeth: it doesn't do you any harm. Of the rest, some twenty-two elements are known or thought to be of central importance to life, according to *Essentials of Medical Geology*. We are certain about sixteen of them; the other six we merely think are vital. Nutrition is a remarkably inexact science. Consider magnesium, which is necessary for the successful management of proteins within the cells. Magnesium abounds in beans, cereals and leafy vegetables, but modern food processing reduces the magnesium content by up to 90 per cent – effectively annihilates it. So most of us are not taking in anything like the recommended daily amount – not that anyone really knows what that amount should be. Nor can anybody specify the consequences of magnesium deficiency. We could be taking years off our lives, or points off our IQ, or the edge off our memory, or almost any other bad thing you care to suggest. We just don't know. Arsenic is similarly uncertain. Obviously if you get too much in your system you will very quickly wish you hadn't. But we all get a *little* arsenic in our diets, and some authorities are absolutely certain it is vital to our well-being in these tiny amounts. Others are not so sure.

Which brings us back, in a very roundabout way, to salt. Of all the minerals the most vital in dietary terms is sodium, which we mostly consume in the form of sodium chloride – table salt.* Here the problem is not that we are

---

* Sodium chloride is strange stuff because it is made up of two extremely aggressive elements: sodium and chlorine. Sodium and chlorine are the Hell's Angels of the mineral kingdom. Drop a lump of pure sodium into a bucket of water and it will explode with enough force to kill. Chlorine is even more deadly. It was the active ingredient in the poison gases of the First World War and, as swimmers know, even in very dilute form it makes the eyes sting. Yet put these two volatile elements together and what you get is innocuous sodium chloride – common table salt.

getting too little, but possibly way too much. We don't need all that much – 200 milligrams a day, about what you would get with six or eight vigorous shakes of a salt cellar – but we take in about sixty times that amount on average. In a normal diet it is almost impossible not to because there is so much salt in the processed foods we eat with such ravenous devotion. Often it is heaped into foods that don't seem salty at all – breakfast cereals, prepared soups and ice creams, for instance. Who would guess that an ounce of cornflakes contains more salt than an ounce of salted peanuts? Or that the contents of one can of soup – almost any can at all – will considerably exceed the total daily recommended salt allowance for an adult?

Archaeological evidence shows that once people settled down in agricultural communities they began to suffer salt deficiencies – something that they had not experienced before – and so had to make a special effort to find salt and get it into their diet. One of the mysteries of history is how they knew they needed to do so because the absence of salt in the diet awakes no craving. It makes you feel bad and eventually it kills you – without the chloride in salt, cells simply shut down, like an engine without fuel – but at no point would a human being think: 'Gosh, I could sure do with some salt.' So how they knew to go searching for it is an interesting question, particularly as in some places getting it required some ingenuity. Ancient Britons, for instance, heated sticks on a beach, then doused them in the sea and scraped the salt off. Aztecs, by contrast, acquired salt by evaporating their own urine. These are not intuitive acts, to put it mildly. Yet getting salt into the diet is one of the most profound urges in nature and it is a universal one. Every society in the world in which salt is freely available consumes, on average, forty times the amount needed to sustain life. We just can't get enough of the stuff.

Salt is now so ubiquitous and cheap that we forget how intensely desirable it was once, but for much of history it drove men to the edges of the world. Salt was needed to preserve meats and other foods, and so was often required in vast quantities: Henry VIII had 25,000 oxen slaughtered and salted for one military campaign in 1513. So salt was a hugely strategic resource. In the Middle Ages caravans of as many as forty thousand camels – enough to form a column seventy miles long – conveyed salt across the Sahara from Timbuktu to the lively markets of the Mediterranean.

People have fought wars over it and been sold into slavery for it. So salt has caused some suffering in its time. But that is nothing compared with the hardship and bloodshed and murderous avarice associated with a range of tiny foodstuffs that we don't need at all and could do perfectly well without. I refer to salt's complements in the condiment world: the spices.* Nobody would die without spices, but plenty have died for them.

A very big part of the history of the modern world is the history of spices, and the story starts with an unprepossessing vine that once grew only on the coast of southwest India. The vine is called *Piper nigrum*. If presented with it in its natural state you would almost certainly struggle to guess its importance, but it is the

---

* The difference between herbs and spices is that herbs come from the leafy part of plants and spices from the wood, seed, fruit or other non-leafy part.

source of all three 'true' peppers – black, white and green. The little round hard peppercorns that we pour into our household pepper mills are actually the vine's tiny fruit, dried to pack a gritty kick. The difference between the varieties is simply a function of when they are picked and how they are processed.

Pepper has been appreciated since time immemorial in its native territory, but it was the Romans who made it an international commodity. Romans loved pepper. They even peppered their desserts. Their attachment to it kept the price high and gave it a lasting value. Spice traders from the distant east couldn't believe their luck. 'They arrive with gold and depart with pepper,' one Tamil trader remarked in wonder. When the Goths threatened to sack Rome in 408, the Romans bought them off with a tribute that included three thousand pounds of pepper. For his wedding meal in 1468, Duke Karl of Bourgogne ordered 380 pounds of black pepper – far more than even the largest wedding party could eat – and displayed it conspicuously so that people could see how fabulously wealthy he was.

Incidentally, the long-held idea that spices were used to mask rotting food doesn't stand up to much scrutiny. The only people who could afford most spices were the ones least likely to have bad meat, and anyway spices were too valuable to be used as a mask. So when people had spices they used them carefully and sparingly, and not as a sort of flavoursome cover-up.

Pepper accounted for some 70 per cent of the spice trade by bulk, but other commodities from further afield – nutmeg and mace, cinnamon, ginger, cloves and turmeric, as well as several largely forgotten exotics such as calamus, asafoetida, ajowan, galangal and zedoary – began to find their way to Europe, and these became even more valuable. For centuries spices were not just the world's most valued foodstuffs, they were the most treasured commodities of any type. The Spice Islands, hidden away in the Far East, remained so desirable and prestigious and exotic that when James I gained possession of two small islets, it was such a coup that for a time he was pleased to style himself 'King of England, Scotland, Ireland, France, Puloway and Puloroon'.

Nutmeg and mace were the most valuable because of their extreme rarity.* Both came from a tree, *Myristica fragrans*, which was found on the lower slopes of just nine small, volcanic islands rising sheer from the Banda Sea, amid a mass of other islands – none with quite the right soils and microclimates to support the nutmeg tree – between Borneo and New Guinea in what is now Indonesia. Cloves, the dried flower buds of a type of myrtle tree, grew on six similarly selective islands some two hundred miles to the north in the same chain, known to geography as the Moluccas but to history as the Spice Islands. Just to put this in perspective, the Indonesian archipelago consists of sixteen thousand islands scattered over 735,000 square miles of sea, so it is little wonder that the locations of fifteen of them remained a mystery to Europeans for so long.

All of these spices reached Europe through a

---

* Nutmeg is the seed of the tree; mace is part of the flesh that surrounds the seed. Mace was actually the rarer of the two. About a thousand tons of nutmeg were harvested annually, but only about a hundred tons of mace.

complicated network of traders, each of whom naturally took a cut. By the time they reached European markets, nutmeg and mace fetched as much as sixty thousand times what they sold for in the Far East. Inevitably, it was only a matter of time before those at the end of the supply chain concluded it would be a lot more lucrative to cut out the intermediate stages and get all the profits at the front end.

So began the great age of exploration. Christopher Columbus is the best remembered of the early explorers but not the first. In 1487, five years ahead of him, Fernão Dulmo and João Estreito set off from Portugal into the uncharted Atlantic, vowing to turn back after forty days if they hadn't found anything by then. That was the last anyone ever saw of them. It turned out that finding the right winds to bring one back to Europe wasn't at all easy. Columbus's real achievement was managing to cross the ocean successfully in both directions. Though an accomplished enough mariner, he was not terribly good at a great deal else, especially geography, the skill that would seem most vital in an explorer. It would be hard to name any figure in history who has achieved more lasting fame with less competence. He spent large parts of eight years bouncing around Caribbean islands and coastal South America convinced that he was in the heart of the Orient and that Japan and China were at the edge of every sunset. He never worked out that Cuba is an island and never once set foot on, or even suspected the existence of, the land mass to the north that everyone thinks he discovered: the United States. He filled his holds with valueless iron pyrite thinking it was gold and with what he confidently believed to be cinnamon and pepper. The first was actually a worthless tree bark and the second were not true peppers but chilli peppers – excellent when you have grasped the general idea of them, but a little eye-wateringly astonishing on first hearty chomp.

Everyone but Columbus could see that this was not the solution to the spice problem, and in 1497 Vasco da Gama, sailing for Portugal, decided to go the other way to the Orient, around the bottom of Africa. This was a much trickier proposition than it sounds. Contrary prevailing winds and currents wouldn't allow a southern-sailing vessel to simply follow the coastline, as logic would indicate. Instead it was necessary for Gama to sail far out into the Atlantic Ocean – almost to Brazil, in fact, though he didn't know it – to catch westerly breezes that would shoot his fleet around the southern cape. This made it a truly epic voyage. Europeans had never sailed this far before. Gama's ships were out of sight of land for as much as three months at a time. This was the voyage that effectively discovered scurvy. No earlier sea voyages had been long enough for the symptoms of scurvy to take hold.

It also brought two other unhappy traditions to the maritime world. One was the introduction of syphilis to Asia – just five years after Columbus's men conveyed it to Europe from the Americas – helping to make it a truly international disease. The other was the casual infliction of extreme violence on innocent people. Vasco da Gama was a breathtakingly vicious man. On one occasion he captured a Muslim ship carrying hundreds of men, women and children, locked the passengers and crew in the hold, carried off everything of value, and then – gratuitously, appallingly – set the ship ablaze. Almost everywhere he went Gama abused or slaughtered the people he encountered, and so set a tone of distrust and brutish violence that would characterize and diminish the whole of the age of discovery.

Gama never got to the Spice Islands. Like most others, he thought the East Indies were just a little east of India – hence their name, of course – but in fact they proved to be *way* beyond India, so far beyond that Europeans arriving there began to wonder if they had sailed most of the way around the world and were almost back to the Americas. If so, then a trip to the Indies for spices would be more simply effected by sailing west, past the new lands lately discovered by Columbus, rather than going all the way around Africa and across the Indian Ocean.

In 1519, Ferdinand Magellan set off in five leaky ships, in a brave but seriously underfunded operation, to find a western route. What he discovered was that between the Americas and Asia was a greater emptiness than anyone had ever imagined Earth had room for: the Pacific Ocean. No one has ever suffered more in the quest to get rich than Ferdinand Magellan and his crew as they sailed in growing disbelief across the Pacific in 1521. Their provisions all but exhausted, they devised perhaps the least appetizing dish ever served: rat droppings mixed with wood shavings. 'We ate biscuit which was no longer biscuit but powder of biscuits swarming with worms,' recorded one crew member. 'It stank strongly of the urine of rats. We drank yellow water that had been putrid for many days. We also ate some ox hides that covered the top of the mainyard . . . and often we ate sawdust from boards.' They went three months and twenty days without fresh food or water before finding relief and a shoreline in Guam – and all in a quest to fill the ships' holds with dried flower buds, bits of tree bark and other aromatic scrapings to sprinkle on food and make into pomanders.

In the end, only eighteen out of two hundred and sixty men survived the voyage. Magellan himself was killed in a skirmish with natives in the Philippines. The surviving eighteen did very well out of the voyage, however. In the Spice Islands they loaded up with 53,000 pounds of cloves, which they sold in Europe for a profit of 2,500 per cent, and almost incidentally in the process became the first human beings to circle the globe. The real significance of Magellan's voyage was not that it was the first to circumnavigate the planet, but that it was the first to realize just how big that planet was.

Although Columbus had little idea of what he was doing, it was his voyages that ultimately proved the most important, and we can date the moment that that became so with precision. On 5 November 1492, on Cuba, two of his crewmen returned to the ship carrying something no one from their world had ever seen before: 'a sort of grain [that the natives] call maiz which was well tasted, bak'd, dry'd and made into flour'. In the same week, they saw some Taino Indians sticking cylinders of smouldering weed in their mouths, drawing smoke into their chests and pronouncing the exercise satisfying. Columbus took some of this odd product home with him too.

And so began the process known to anthropologists as the Columbian Exchange – the transfer of foods and other materials from the New World to the old and vice versa. By the time the first Europeans arrived in the New World, farmers there were harvesting more than a hundred kinds of edible plants – potatoes, tomatoes, sunflowers, marrows, aubergines, avocados, a whole slew of beans and squashes, sweet potatoes, peanuts, cashews, pineapples, papaya, guava, yams, manioc (or cassava), pumpkins, vanilla, four types of chilli pepper and chocolate, among rather a lot else – not a bad haul.

It has been estimated that 60 per cent of all the crops grown in the world today originated in the Americas. These foods weren't just incorporated into foreign cuisines. They effectively *became* the foreign cuisines. Imagine Italian food without tomatoes, Greek food without aubergines, Thai and Indonesian foods without peanut sauce, curries without chillies, hamburgers without French fries or ketchup, African food without cassava. There was scarcely a dinner table in the world in any land to east or west that wasn't drastically improved by the foods of the Americas.

No one foresaw this at the time, however. For the Europeans the irony is that the foods they found they mostly didn't want, while the ones they wanted they didn't find. Spices were what they were after and the New World was dismayingly deficient in those, apart from chillies, which were too fiery and startling to be appreciated at first. Many promising New World foods failed to attract any interest at all. The indigenous people of Peru had 150 varieties of potato, and valued them all. An Incan of five hundred years ago would have been able to identify varieties of potato in much the way that a modern wine snob identifies grapes. The Quechuan language of Peru still has a thousand words for different types or conditions of potatoes. *Hantha*, for instance, describes a potato that is distinctly on the old side but still has edible flesh. The conquistadores, however, brought home only a few varieties, and there are those who say they were by no means the most delicious. Further north, the Aztecs had a great fondness for amaranth, a cereal that produces a nutritious and tasty grain. It was as popular a foodstuff in Mexico as maize, but the Spanish were offended by the way the Aztecs used it, mixed with blood, in rites involving human sacrifice, and refused to touch it.

The Americas, it may be said, gained much from Europe in return. Before the Europeans stormed into their lives, people in Central America had only five domesticated creatures – the turkey, duck, dog, bee and cochineal insect – and no dairy products. Without European meat and cheese, Mexican food as we know it could not exist. Wheat in Kansas, coffee in Brazil, beef in Argentina and a great deal more would not be possible.

Less happily, the Columbian Exchange also involved disease. With no immunity to many European diseases, the natives sickened easily and 'died in heapes'. One epidemic, probably viral hepatitis, killed an estimated 90 per cent of the natives in coastal Massachusetts. A once-mighty tribal group in the region of modern Texas and Arkansas, the Caddo, saw its population fall from an estimated 200,000 to just 1,400 – a drop of over 99 per cent. An equivalent outbreak in modern New York would reduce the population to 56,000 – 'not enough to fill Yankee Stadium' in the chilling phrase of Charles C. Mann. Altogether disease and slaughter reduced the native population of Mesoamerica by an estimated 90 per cent in the first century of European contact. In return they gave Columbus's men syphilis.*

* Amerindians got syphilis too, but suffered less from it, in much the way that Europeans suffered less from measles and mumps.

Over time the Columbian Exchange also of course involved the wholesale movement of peoples, the setting up of colonies, the transfer – sometimes enforced – of language, religion and culture. Almost no single act in history has more profoundly changed the world than Columbus's blundering search for eastern spices.

There is another irony in all this. By the time the age of exploration was fully under way, the heyday of spices was coming to an end anyway. In 1545, just twenty years or so after Magellan's epic voyage, an English warship, the *Mary Rose*, sank in mysterious circumstances off the English coast near Portsmouth. More than four hundred men died. When the ship was recovered in the late twentieth century, marine archaeologists were surprised to find that almost every sailor owned a tiny bag of black pepper, which he kept attached to his waist. It would have been one of his most prized possessions. The fact that even a common sailor of 1545 could now afford a supply of pepper, however modest, meant that pepper's days of hyper-rarity and extreme desirability were at an end. It was on its way to taking its place alongside salt as a standard and comparatively humble condiment.

People continued to fight over the more exotic spices for another century or so, and sometimes even over the more common ones. In 1599, eighty British merchants, exasperated by the rising cost of pepper, formed the British East India Company with a view to getting a piece of the market for themselves. This was the initiative that brought King James the treasured isles of Puloway and Puloroon, but in fact the British never had much success in the East Indies, and in 1667, in the Treaty of Breda, they ceded all claims to the region to the Dutchin return for a small piece of land of no great significance in North America. The piece of land was called Manhattan.

By now, however, there were new commodities that people wanted even more, and the quest for these was, in the most unexpected ways, about to change the world still further.

II

Two years before his unhappy adventure with 'many worms creeping', Samuel Pepys recorded in his diary a rather more prosaic milestone in his life. On 25 September 1660, he tried a new hot beverage for the first time, recording in his diary: 'And afterwards I did send for a cup of tee (a China drink), of which I never had drank before.' Whether he liked it or not Pepys didn't say, which is a shame as it is the first mention we have in English of anyone's drinking a cup of tea.

A century and a half later, in 1812, a Scottish historian named David Macpherson, in a dry piece of work called *History of the European Commerce with India*, quoted the tea-drinking passage from Pepys's diary. That was a very surprising thing to do because in 1812 Pepys's diaries were supposedly still unknown. Although they resided in the library of Magdalene College, Cambridge, and so were available for inspection, no one had ever looked into them – so it was thought – because they were written in a private code that had yet to be deciphered. How Macpherson managed to find and translate the relevant passage in six volumes of dense and secret scribblings, and what gave him the inspiration to look there in the first place, are mysteries that are some distance beyond being answerable.

By chance, a Cambridge scholar, the Reverend George Neville, master of Magdalene, saw Macpherson's passing reference to Pepys's diaries and grew intrigued to know what else might be in them. Pepys after all had lived through momentous times – through the restoration of the monarchy, the last great plague epidemic, the Great Fire of London of 1666 – so their content was bound to be of interest. He commissioned a clever but penurious student named John Smith to see if he could crack the code and transcribe the diaries. The work took Smith three years. The result of course was the most celebrated diaries in the English language. Had Pepys not had that cup of tea, Macpherson not mentioned it in a dull history, Neville been less curious and young Smith less intelligent and dogged, the name Samuel Pepys would mean nothing to anyone but naval historians, and a very considerable part of what we know about how people lived in the second half of the seventeenth century would in fact be unknown. So it was a good thing that he had that cup of tea.

Normally, like most other people of his class and period, Pepys drank coffee, though coffee itself was still pretty novel in 1660. Britons had been vaguely familiar with coffee for decades, but principally as a queer, dark beverage encountered abroad. A traveller named George Sandys in 1610 grimly described coffee as being 'blacke as soot, and tasting not much unlike it'. The word was spelled in any number of imaginative ways – as 'coava', 'cahve', 'cauphe', 'coffa' and 'cafe', among others – before finally coming ashore as 'coffee' in about 1650.

Credit for coffee's popularity in England belongs to a man named Pasqua Rosee, who was Sicilian by birth and Greek by background, and who worked as a servant for Daniel Edwards, a British trader in Smyrna, now Izmir, in Turkey. Moving to England with Edwards, Rosee served coffee to Edwards's guests, and this proved so popular that he was emboldened to open a café – the first in London – in a shed in the churchyard of St Michael Cornhill in the City of London in 1652. Rosee promoted coffee for its health benefits, claiming that it cured or prevented headaches, 'defluxion of rheums', wind, gout, scurvy, miscarriages, sore eyes and much else.

Rosee did very well out of his business, but his reign as premier coffee-maker didn't last long. Some time after 1656 he was compelled to leave the country 'for some misdemeanour', which the record unfortunately doesn't specify. All that is known is that he departed suddenly and was heard of no more. Others swiftly moved in to take his place. By the time of the Great Fire, more than eighty coffee houses were in business in London and they had become a central part of the life of the city.

The coffee served in the coffee houses wasn't necessarily very good coffee. Because of the way coffee was taxed in Britain (by the gallon) the practice was to brew it in large batches, store it cold in barrels and reheat it a little at a time for serving. So coffee's appeal in Britain was less to do with its being a quality beverage than a social lubricant. People went to coffee houses to meet people of shared interests, to gossip, read the latest journals and news-papers – a brand-new word and concept in the 1660s – and exchange information of value to their lives and busi-ness. When people wanted to know what was going on in the world, they went to a coffee house to find out. People took to using coffee houses as their offices – as, most famously, at Lloyd's Coffee House on Lombard Street, which gradually evolved into Lloyd's insurance market. William Hogarth's father hit on the idea of opening a coffee house in which only Latin would be spoken. It failed spectacularly – *toto bene*, as Mr Hogarth himself might have said – and he spent years in debtors' prison in unhappy consequence.

Although it was pepper and spices that brought the East India Company into being, its destiny was tea. In 1696, the government introduced the first in a series of cuts in the tea tax, and the effect on consumption was immediate. Between 1699 and 1721 tea imports increased almost a hundredfold, from 13,000 pounds to 1.2 million pounds, then quadrupled again in the thirty years to 1750. Tea was slurped by labourers and daintily sipped by ladies. It was taken at breakfast, dinner and supper. It was the first beverage in history to belong to no class, and the first to have its own ritual slot in the day: teatime. It was easier to make at home than coffee, and it also went especially well with another great gustatory treat that was suddenly becoming affordable for the average wage earner: sugar. Britons came to adore sweet, milky tea as no other nation had (or even perhaps could). For something over a century and a half, tea was at the heart of the East India Company, and the East India Company was at the heart of the British Empire.

Not everyone got the hang of tea immediately. The poet Robert Southey related the story of a lady in the country who received a pound of tea as a gift from a city friend when it was still a novelty. Uncertain how to engage with it, she boiled it up in a pot, spread the leaves on toast with butter and salt, and served it to her friends, who nibbled it gamely and declared it interesting but not quite to their taste. Elsewhere, however, it raced ahead, in tandem with sugar.

The British had always loved sugar, so much so that when they first got easy access to it, about the time of Henry VIII, they put it on almost everything – on eggs, meat, and into their wine. They scooped it on to potatoes, sprinkled it over greens, ate it straight off the spoon if they could afford to. Even though sugar was very expensive, people consumed it till their teeth turned black, and if their teeth didn't turn black naturally they blackened them artificially to show how wealthy and marvellously self-indulgent they were. But now, thanks to plantations in the West Indies, sugar was becoming increasingly affordable, and people were discovering that it went particularly well with tea.

Sweet tea became a national indulgence. By 1770 per capita consumption of sugar was running at 20 pounds a head and most of that, it seems, was spooned into tea. (That sounds like quite a lot until you realize that Britons today eat 80 pounds of sugar per person annually, while Americans pack away a decidedly robust 126 pounds of sugar per head.) As with coffee, tea was held to confer health benefits; among much else, it was said that it 'assuageth the pains of the Bowels'. A Dutch doctor, Cornelius Bontekoe, recommended drinking fifty cups of tea a day – and in extreme cases as many as two hundred – in order to keep oneself sufficiently primed.

Sugar also played a big role in a less commendable development: the slave trade. Nearly all the sugar Britons consumed was grown on West Indian estates worked by slaves. We have a narrow tendency to associate slavery exclusively with the plantation economy of the southern US, but in fact plenty of other people got rich from slavery, not least the traders who shipped 3.1 million Africans across the ocean before the trade in humans was abolished in 1807.

Tea was adored and esteemed not just in Great Britain but in her overseas dominions, too. Tea was taxed in America as part of the hated Townshend duties. In 1770 these duties were repealed on everything but tea in what proved to be a fatal misjudgement. They were kept on tea partly to remind colonists of their subjugation to the crown and partly to help the East India Company out of a deep and sudden hole. The company had become hopelessly overextended. It had accumulated 17 million pounds of tea – a huge amount of a perishable product – and, perversely, had tried to create an air of well-being by paying out more in dividends than it could really afford. Bankruptcy loomed unless it could reduce its stockpiles. Hoping to ease it through the crisis, the British government gave the company an effective monopoly on tea sales in America. Every American knows what happened next.

On 16 December 1773, a group of eighty or so colonists dressed as Mohawk Indians boarded British ships in Boston Harbor, broke open 342 tea chests and dumped the contents overboard. That sounds like a fairly moderate act of vandalism. In fact, it was a year's supply of tea for Boston, with a value of £18,000, so it was a grave and capital offence, and everyone involved knew so. Nobody at the time, incidentally, called it the Boston Tea Party; that name wasn't first used until 1834. Nor could the behaviour of the crowds be characterized as one of good-natured high spirits, as we Americans rather like to think. The mood was murderously ugly. The unluckiest person in all this was a British customs agent named John Malcolm. Malcolm had recently been hauled from a house in Maine and tarred and feathered, a blisteringly painful punishment since it involved the application of hot tar to bare skin. Usually it was applied with stiff brushes, which were painful enough in themselves, though in at least one instance the victim was simply held by his ankles and dunked head first into a barrel of tar. To the coating of tar was added handfuls of feathers before the victim was paraded through the streets, and often beaten or even hanged. So there was nothing at all jovial about tarring and feathering, and we can only imagine Malcolm's dismay as he was hauled wriggling from his house a second time and given another 'Yankee jacket', as it was also known. Once dried, it took days of delicate picking and scrubbing to get the tar and feathers off. Malcolm sent a square of charred and blackened epidermis back to England with a note asking if he could please come home. His wish was granted. Meanwhile, however, America and Britain were implacably on the road to war. Fifteen months later the first shots were fired. As a versifier of the day noted:

> What discontents, what dire events,
> From trifling things proceed?
> A little Tea, thrown in the Sea,
> Has thousands caused to bleed.

At the same time that Britain was losing its American

colonies, it was facing serious problems connected to tea from the other direction as well. By 1800 tea was embedded in the British psyche as the national beverage, and imports were running at 23 million pounds a year. Virtually all that tea came from China. This caused a large and chronic trade imbalance. The British resolved this problem in part by selling opium produced in India to the Chinese. Opium was a very considerable business in the nineteenth century, and not just in China. People in Britain and America – women in particular – took a lot of opium, too, mostly in the form of medicinal paregoric and laudanum. Imports of opium to the United States went from 24,000 pounds in 1840 to no less than 400,000 pounds in 1872, and it was women who mostly sucked it down, though quite a lot was given to children, too, as a treatment for croup. Franklin Delano Roosevelt's grandfather Warren Delano made much of the family's fortune by trading opium, a fact that the Roosevelt family has never exactly crowed about.

To the unending exasperation of the Chinese authorities, Britain became particularly skilled at persuading Chinese citizens to become opium addicts – university courses in the history of marketing really ought to begin with British opium sales – so much so that by 1838 Britain was selling almost five million pounds of opium to China every year. Unfortunately, this still wasn't enough to offset the huge costs of importing tea from China. An obvious solution was to grow tea in some warm part of the expanding British empire. The problem was that the Chinese had always been secretive about the complicated processes of turning tea leaves into a refreshing beverage, and no one outside China knew how to get an industry going.

Enter a remarkable Scotsman named Robert Fortune.

For three years in the 1840s, Fortune travelled around China, disguised as a native, collecting information on how tea was grown and processed. It was risky work: had he been caught he would certainly have been imprisoned and could well have been executed. Although Fortune spoke none of the languages of China, he got around that problem by pretending always to come from a distant province where another dialect prevailed. In the course of his travels, he not only learned the secrets of tea production, but also introduced to the West many valuable plants, among them the fan palm, the kumquat and several varieties of azaleas and chrysanthemums.

Under his guidance, tea cultivation was introduced to India in that curiously inevitable year 1851 with the planting of some 20,000 seedlings and cuttings. In half a century, from a base of nothing in 1850, tea production in India rose to 140 million pounds a year.

As for the East India Company, however, its period of glory came to an abrupt and unhappy conclusion. The precipitating event, unexpectedly enough, was the introduction of a new kind of rifle, the Enfield P53, at just about the time that tea cultivation was starting. The rifle was an old-fashioned type that was loaded by tipping powder down the barrel. The powder came in grease-coated paper cartridges which had to be bitten open. A rumour spread among the native sepoys, as the soldiers were known, that the grease used was made from the fat of pigs and cows – a matter of profoundest horror for Muslim and Hindu soldiers alike since the consumption of such fats, even unwittingly, would condemn them to eternal damnation. The East India Company's officers handled the matter with stunning insensitivity. They court-martialled several Indian soldiers who refused to handle the new cartridges, and threatened to punish any others who didn't fall into line. Many sepoys became convinced that it was all part of a plot to replace their own faiths with Christianity. By unfortunate coincidence, Christian missionaries had recently become active in India, fanning suspicions further. The upshot was the Sepoy Rebellion of 1857, in which the native soldiers turned on their British masters, whom they very much outnumbered, and killed them in large numbers. At Cawnpore, the rebels gathered together two hundred women and children in a hall and hacked them to pieces. Other innocent victims, it was reported, were thrown into wells and left to drown.

When news of these cruelties reached British ears, retribution was swift and unforgiving. Rebellious Indians were tracked down and executed in ways calculated to instil terror and regret. One or two were even fired from cannons, or so it is often recorded. Untold numbers were shot or summarily hanged. The whole episode left Britain profoundly shaken. More than five hundred books appeared on the uprising in its immediate aftermath. India, it was commonly agreed, was too big a country and too big a problem to leave in the hands of a business. Control of India passed to the British crown and the East India Company was wound up.

III

All of these foods, all of these discoveries, all of this end-less fighting made its way back to England and ended up on dinner tables, and in a new kind of room: the dining room. The dining room didn't acquire its modern mean-ing until the late seventeenth century and didn't become general in houses until even later. In fact, it only just made it into Samuel Johnson's dictionary of 1755. When Thomas Jefferson put a dining room in Monticello, it was quite a dashing thing to do. Previously meals had been served at little tables in any convenient room.

What caused dining rooms to come into being wasn't a sudden universal urge to dine in a space exclusively dedicated to the purpose, but rather, by and large, a simple desire on the part of the mistress of the house to save her lovely new upholstered furniture from greasy desecration. Upholstered furniture, as we have lately seen, was expensive, and the last thing a proud owner wanted was to have anyone wiping fingers on it.

The arrival of the dining room marked a change not only in where the food was served, but how it was eaten and when. For one thing, forks were now suddenly becom-ing common. Forks had been around for a long time, but took for ever to gain acceptance. 'Fork' originally signified an agricultural implement and nothing more; it didn't take on a food sense until the mid-fifteenth century, and then it described a large implement used to pin down a bird or joint for carving. The person credited with intro-ducing the eating fork to England was Thomas Coryate, an author and traveller from the time of Shakespeare who was famous for walking huge distances – to India and back on one occasion. In 1611 he produced his magnum opus, called *Coryate's Crudities*, in which he gave much praise to the dinner fork, which he had first encountered in Italy. The same book was also notable for introducing English readers to the Swiss folk hero William Tell and to a new device called the umbrella.

Eating forks were thought comically dainty and unmanly – and dangerous too, come to that. Since they had only two sharp tines, the scope for spearing one's lip or tongue was great, particularly if one's aim was impaired by wine and jollity. Manufacturers experimented with additional numbers of tines – sometimes as many as six – before settling, late in the nineteenth century, on four as the number that people seemed most comfortable with. Why four should induce the optimum sense of security isn't easy to say, but it does seem to be a fundamental fact of flatware psychology.

The nineteenth century also marked a time of change for the way food was served. Before the 1850s, nearly all the dishes of the meal were placed on the table at the outset. Guests would arrive to find the food waiting. They would help themselves to whatever was nearby and ask for other dishes to be passed or call a servant over to fetch one for them. This style of dining was traditionally known as *service à la française*, but now a new practice came in known as *service à la russe* in which food was delivered to the table in courses. A lot of people hated the new practice because it meant everyone had to eat everything in the same order and at the same pace. If one person was slow, it held up the next course for everyone else, and meant that food lost heat. Dinners now sometimes dragged on for

The overdressed dining table: table glass including decanters, claret jugs and a carafe, from Mrs Beeton's The Book of Household Management.

hours, putting a severe strain on many people's sobriety and nearly everyone's bladders.

The nineteenth century also became the age of the overdressed dining table. A diner at a formal gathering might sit down to as many as nine wine glasses just for the main courses – more were brought for dessert – and a blinding array of silverware with which to conduct an assault on the many dishes put before him. The types of specialized eating implements for cutting, serving, probing, winkling and otherwise getting viands from serving dish to plate and from plate to mouth became almost numberless. As well as a generous array of knives, forks and spoons of a more or less conventional nature, the diner needed also to know how to recognize and manipulate specialized cheese scoops, olive spoons, terrapin forks, oyster prongs, chocolate muddlers, gelatin knives, tomato slices, and tongs of every size and degree of springiness. At one point, a single manufacturer offered no fewer than 146 different types of flatware for the table. Curiously, one of the few survivors from this culinary onslaught is one that is most difficult to understand: the fish knife. No one has ever identified a single advantage conferred by its odd scalloped shape or worked out the original thinking behind it. There isn't a single kind of fish that it cuts better or bones more delicately than a conventional knife does.

Dining was, as one book of the period phrased it, 'the great trial', with rules 'so numerous and so minute in respect of detail that they require the most careful study; and the worst of it is that none of them can be violated without exposing the offender to instant detection'. Protocol ruled every action. If you wished to take a sip of wine, you needed to find someone to drink with you. As one foreign visitor explained it in a letter home: 'A messenger is often sent from one end of the table to the other to announce to Mr B—— that Mr A—— wishes to take wine with him; whereupon each, sometimes with considerable trouble, catches the other's eye . . . When you raise your glass, you look fixedly at the one with whom you are drinking, bow your head, and then drink with great gravity.'

Some people needed more help with the rules of table behaviour than others. John Jacob Astor, one of the richest men in America but not evidently the most cultivated, astounded his hosts at one dinner party by leaning over and wiping his hands on the dress of the lady sitting next to him. One popular American guidebook, *The Laws of Etiquette; or, Short Rules and Reflections for Conduct in Society*, informed readers that they 'may wipe their lips on the table cloth, but not blow their noses with it'. Another solemnly reminded readers that it was not polite in refined circles to smell a piece of meat while it was on one's fork. It also explained: 'The ordinary custom among well-bred persons is as follows: soup is taken with a spoon.'

Mealtimes moved around, too, until there was scarcely an hour of the day that wasn't an important time to eat for somebody. Dining hours were dictated to some extent by the onerous and often preposterous obligations of making and returning social calls. The convention was to drop in on others between twelve and three each day. If someone called and left a card but you were out, etiquette dictated that you must return the call the next day. Not to do so was the gravest affront. What this meant in practice was that most people spent their afternoons dashing around trying to catch up with people who were dashing around in a similarly unproductive manner trying to catch up with them.

Partly for this reason the dinner hour moved later and later – from midday to mid-afternoon to early evening – though the new conventions were by no means taken up uniformly. One visitor to London in 1773 noted that in a single week he was invited to dinners that started successively at 1 p.m., 3 p.m., 5 p.m. and 'half after six, dinner on table at seven'. Eighty years later when John Ruskin informed his parents that it had become his habit to dine at six in the evening, they received the news as if it marked the most dissolute recklessness. Eating so late, his mother told him, was dangerously unhealthy.

Another factor that materially influenced dining times was theatre hours. In Shakespeare's day performances began about two o'clock, which kept them conveniently out of the way of mealtimes, but that was dictated largely by the need for daylight in open-air arenas like the Globe. Once plays moved indoors, starting times tended to get later and later and theatre-goers found it necessary to adjust their dining times accordingly – though this was done with a certain reluctance and even resentment. Eventually, unable or unwilling to modify their personal habits any further, the beau monde stopped trying to get to the theatre for the first act and took to sending a servant to hold their seats for them till they had finished dining. Generally they would show up – noisy, drunk and disinclined to focus – for the later acts. For a generation or so it was usual for a theatrical company to perform the first half of a play to an auditorium full of dozing servants who had no attachment to the proceedings and to perform the second half to a crowd of ill-mannered inebriates who had no idea what was going on.

Dinner finally became an evening meal in the 1850s, influenced by Queen Victoria. As the distance between breakfast and dinner widened, it became necessary to create a smaller meal around the middle of the day, for which the word 'luncheon' was appropriated. 'Luncheon' originally signified a lump or portion (as in 'a luncheon of cheese'). In that sense it was first recorded in English in 1580. In 1755 Samuel Johnson was still defining it as a quantity of food – 'as much food as one's hand can hold' – and only slowly over the next century did it come to signify, in refined circles at least, the middle meal of the day.

One consequential change is that where people used to get most of their calories at breakfast time and midday, with only a small evening top-up at suppertime, now those intakes are almost exactly reversed. Most of us consume the bulk – a sadly appropriate word here – of our calories in the evening and take them to bed with us, a practice that doesn't do us any good at all. The Ruskins, it turns out, were right.

CHAPTER NINE

The Cellar

I

IF YOU HAD SUGGESTED to anyone in 1783, at the end of the American War of Independence, that New York would one day be the greatest city in the world, you would possibly have been marked out as a fool. New York's prospects in 1783 were not promising. It had been more loyalist than any other city, so the war had had an unhappy effect on its standing within the new republic. In 1790, its population was just 10,000. Philadelphia, Boston and even Charleston were all busier ports.

The state of New York had just one important advantage – an opening to the west through the Appalachian Mountains, the chain that runs in rough parallel to the Atlantic Ocean. It is hard to believe that those soft and rolling mountains, often little more than big hills, could ever have constituted a formidable barrier to movement, but in fact they afforded almost no usable passes along the whole of their 2,500-mile length and were such an obstruction to trade and communications that many people believed that the pioneers living beyond the mountains would eventually, of practical necessity, form a separate nation. For farmers it was cheaper to ship their produce downriver to New Orleans, via the Ohio and Mississippi rivers, then by sea around Florida and up the Atlantic seaboard to Charleston or one of the other eastern ports – a distance of three thousand miles or more – than it was to haul it three hundred miles overland across the mountains.

But in 1810, De Witt Clinton, then mayor of New York City and soon to become governor of the state, produced an idea that many thought was possibly mad but certainly delusional. He proposed building a canal across the state to Lake Erie, connecting New York City with the Great Lakes and rich farmlands beyond. People called it Clinton's Folly, and not surprisingly. The canal would have to be dug with picks and shovels, to a width of forty feet, through 363 miles of rough wilderness. It would need eighty-three locks, each ninety feet long, to manage all the changes of elevation. Along some stretches the slope would have to average no more than one inch per mile. No canal of even close to this degree of challenge had ever been attempted anywhere in the settled world, much less in a wilderness.

And here was the thing. America didn't have a single native-born engineer who had ever worked on a canal. Thomas Jefferson, who normally venerated ambition, thought the whole idea insane. 'It is a splendid project, and may be executed a century hence,' he allowed after reviewing the plans, but added at once: 'It is little short of madness to think of it at this day.' President James Madison refused to give federal aid, at least partly motivated by a desire to keep the centre of commercial gravity further south and away from that old loyalist stronghold.

So New York's options were to proceed alone or do without. Despite the costs, risks and almost total absence of necessary skills, it decided to fund the project itself. Four men – Charles Broadhead, James Geddes, Nathan Roberts and Benjamin Wright – were appointed to get the work done. Three of them were judges; the fourth was a schoolteacher. None had ever even *seen* a canal, much less tried to build one. All that they had in common was some experience of surveying. Yet somehow through reading, consultation and inspired experimentation, they managed to design and supervise the greatest engineering project the New World had ever seen. They became the first people in history to learn how to build a canal by building a canal.

Early on it became apparent that one problem threatened the viability of the whole enterprise – a lack of hydraulic cement. Half a million bushels of hydraulic cement (a bushel is 32 US quarts or about 35 litres, so 500,000 bushels is a lot) were needed to make the canal watertight. If water seeped away on any section, it would be a disaster for the whole canal, so clearly it was a problem that had to be fixed. Unfortunately no one knew how to overcome it.

A young canal employee named Canvass White volunteered to travel to England at his own expense to see what he could learn. For nearly a year White walked the length and breadth of Britain – two thousand miles in all – studying canals and learning all he could about how they were built and kept together, with a particular eye on waterproofing. By chance, it turned out that Parker's Roman cement, which, as we have seen, played a central role in the downfall of William Beckford's Fonthill Abbey because of its lack of strength as a building material, worked unexpectedly well as a hydraulic cement, where it needed only to be used as a water-resistant mortar. Its inventor, the Reverend Mr Parker of Gravesend, didn't grow rich from this, unfortunately, as he sold his patent within a year of taking it out, and then, rather ironically, emigrated to America where he soon died. His cement, however, did very well till it was superseded by superior varieties in the 1820s, and gave Canvass White hope to suppose that he might come up with something similar using American materials.

Returning home, and now armed with some knowledge of the scientific principles of adhesion, White experimented with various native ingredients, and quickly formulated a compound that worked even better than Parker's cement. It was a great moment in American technological history – indeed, it could be said to be the beginning of American technological history – and it deserved to make White rich and celebrated. In fact, it did neither. White's patents entitled him to a royalty of four cents on each bushel sold – a small enough sum as it was – but the manufacturers declined to share their profits. He pressed his claims through the courts, but was unable to enforce any judgments that went his way. The result was a long slide into penury.

The manufacturers, meantime, grew rich making what was now the best hydraulic cement in the world. Thanks in large part to White's invention, the canal opened early, in 1825, after just eight years of construction. It was a triumph from the start. So many boats used it – 13,000 in the first year – that at night their running lights looked like swarms of fireflies on the water, according to one captivated witness. With the canal, the cost of shipping a ton of flour from Buffalo to New York City fell from $120 a ton to $6 a ton, and the carrying time was reduced from three weeks to just over one. The effect on New York's fortunes was breathtaking. Its share of national exports leapt from less than 10 per cent in 1800 to over 60 per cent by the middle of the century; in the same period, even more dazzlingly, its population went from 10,000 to well over half a million.

Probably no manufactured product in history – certainly none of greater obscurity – has done more to change a city's fortunes than Canvass White's hydraulic cement. The Erie Canal not only secured the economic primacy of New York within the United States, but, very possibly, of the United States within the world. Without the Erie Canal, Canada would have been ideally positioned to become the powerhouse of North America, with the St Lawrence River serving as the conduit to the Great Lakes and the rich lands beyond.

So the great unsung Canvass White didn't just make New York rich, more profoundly he helped to make America. In 1834, exhausted by his legal battles and suffering from some serious but unspecified malady – probably consumption – he travelled to St Augustine, Florida, in the hope of restoring his health, but died there soon after arriving. He was already forgotten by history and so poor that his wife could barely afford to bury him. And that is probably the last time you will ever hear his name.

*   *   *

I mention all this here because we have descended to the cellar, an unfinished and basic space in the Old Rectory, as in most English houses of the period. Originally it served primarily as a coal store. Today it holds the boiler, idle suitcases, out-of-season sporting equipment and many sealed cardboard boxes that are almost never opened but are always carefully transferred from house to house with every move in the belief that one day someone might want some baby clothes that have been kept in a box for twenty-five years. It isn't a very congenial space, but it does have the compensating virtue of providing some sense of the superstructure of the house – the things that hold it up and keep it together, which is the subject of this chapter – and the reason I have prefaced it all with the story of the Erie Canal is to make the point that building materials are more important, and even, dare I say, interesting than you might think. They certainly help to make history in ways that don't often get mentioned in books.

Indeed, the history of early America is really a history of coping with shortages of building materials. For a country famed for being rich in natural resources, America along the eastern seaboard proved to be appallingly deficient in many basic commodities necessary to an independent civilization. One was limestone, as the first colonists discovered to their dismay. In England, you could build a reasonably secure house with wattle and daub – essentially mud and sticks – if it was sufficiently bound with lime. But in America there was no lime (or at least none found before 1690), so the colonists used dried mud and this was woefully lacking in sturdiness. During the first century of colonization, it was a rare house that lasted more than ten years. This was the period of the Little Ice Age, when a century or so of bitterly cold winters and howling storms battered the temperate world. A hurricane in 1634 blew away – literally just lifted up and carried off – half the houses of Massachusetts. Barely had people rebuilt when a second storm of similar intensity blew in, 'overturning sundry howses, uncovering [i.e. unroofing] diverse others', in the words of one diarist who lived through it. Even decent building stone was not available in many areas. When George Washington wanted to pave his loggia at Mount Vernon with simple flagstones, he had to send to England for them.

The one thing America had in quantity was wood. When Europeans arrived in the New World it was to a continent containing an estimated 950 million acres of woodland – enough to seem effectively infinite – but in fact the woods that greeted the newcomers were not quite as boundless as they first appeared, particularly as one moved inland. Beyond the mountains of the eastern seaboard, large expanses had been cleared already by Indians, and much of the forest undergrowth burned to make hunting easier. In Ohio, early settlers were astonished to find that the woods were more like English parks than primeval forests, and roomy enough to allow the driving of carriages through the trees. Indians created these parks for the benefit of bison, which they effectively harvested.

The colonists positively devoured wood. They used it to build houses, barns, wagons, boats, fences, furniture and every possible sort of daily utensil, from buckets to spoons. They burned it in copious amounts for warmth and for cooking. According to the historian of early American life Carl Bridenbaugh, the average colonial house required fifteen to twenty cords of firewood a year, enough to deplete local supplies quickly in most places. Bridenbaugh mentions one village on Long Island where every stick of wood to the horizon in every direction was exhausted in just fourteen years, and there must have been many others like it.

Huge additional acreages were cleared for fields and pastures, and even roadways resulted in literally widespread clearances. Highways in colonial America tended to be inordinately wide – 165 feet across was not unusual – to provide safety from ambush and room to drive and graze herds of animals en route to market. By 1810 barely a quarter of Connecticut's original woods remained. Further west, Michigan's seemingly inexhaustible stock of white pine – 170 billion board feet of it when the first colonists arrived – shrank by 95 per cent in just a century. Much American wood was exported to Europe, particularly in the form of shingles and weatherboards.* As Jane Jacobs noted in *The Economy of Cities*, a lot of American wood fuelled the Great Fire of London.

One common assumption is that the early settlers built log cabins. They didn't. They didn't know how. Log cabins were introduced by Scandinavian immigrants in the late eighteenth century, at which point they did rapidly catch on. Although log cabins were comparatively straightforward productions – that was of course their appeal – there was some complexity to them, too. Where the logs

---

* Weatherboards became known as clapboards in America; no one knows why.

locked in place at the corners, the builders could use any of several types of notch – V notch, saddle notch, diamond notch, square notch, full dovetail, half dovetail and so on – and these, it turns out, had curiously particular geographical affinities, which no one has ever been able to entirely explain. Saddle notching, for instance, was the preferred method in the Deep South and in homes in central Wisconsin and southern Michigan, but was found almost nowhere else. Residents of New York State, meanwhile, overwhelmingly went for a method of notching called false corner-timbering, but abandoned that style almost completely when they moved on. A history of American migration can be plotted – in fact has been plotted – by working out which notches appeared where, and whole careers have been spent trying to account for the different distribution patterns.

When you consider how quickly the American colonists scythed their way through the towering forests that greeted them upon arrival, it is hardly surprising that a shortage of timber was a chronic and worrisome problem in the much more confined and crowded landscape of England. Legend and fairy tales may have left us with an ineradicable popular image of medieval England as a land of dark and brooding forests, but in fact there weren't many trees for the likes of Robin Hood and his merry men to hide behind. As long ago as the time of the Domesday Book, in 1086, just 15 per cent of the English countryside was wooded.

Throughout history Britons have used and needed a lot of wood. A typical farmhouse of the fifteenth century contained the wood of 330 oak trees. Ships used even more. Nelson's flagship, *Victory*, consumed probably three thousand mature oaks – the equivalent of a good-sized woodland. Oak was also used in large quantities in industrial processes. Oak bark, mixed with dog faeces, was used in the tanning of leather. Ink was made from oak galls, a kind of flesh wound in trees created by a parasitic wasp. But the real consumer of wood was the charcoal industry. By the time of Henry VIII, nearly 200 square miles a year of forest were required to produce sufficient charcoal for the iron industry, and by the late eighteenth century the figure had grown to 540 square miles a year, or about one-seventh of the total woodland in the country.

Most woodlands were managed through coppicing – cutting them back, then letting them grow out again – so it wasn't as if great swathes were being clear-felled every year. In fact, the charcoal industry, far from being a culprit, was responsible for a great deal of woodland maintenance – though what it preserved, it must be said, tended to be characterless, small-rise woods rather than mighty sun-pierced stands of forest primeval. Even with careful management, the demand for wood was so relentlessly upwards that by the 1500s Britain was using timber faster than it could replenish it, and by 1600 wood for building was in desperately short supply. The half-timbered houses that we associate with this period in England are not a reflection of abundance of timber but of paucity. They were the owners' way of showing that they could afford a scarce resource.

Only necessity finally made people turn to stone. England had the most wonderful building stone in the world, but took for ever to discover it. For nearly a thousand years, from the collapse of the Roman Empire to the age of Chaucer, wood was the almost invariable building material of England. Only the most important buildings – cathedrals, palaces, castles, churches – were accorded stone. When the Normans came to England there wasn't a single stone house in the country. This was slightly remarkable because just underneath nearly everyone's feet was sublime building stone thanks to the existence of a great belt of hard-wearing oolitic limestones (that is, ones containing lots of spherical ooliths, or grains), running in a broad arc across the body of the country, from Dorset on the south coast to the Cleveland Hills of Yorkshire in the north. This is known as the Jurassic belt, and all the most famous building stones of England, from Purbeck marble and the white stone of Portland to the honeyed blocks of Bath and the Cotswolds, are found within its sweep. These immensely ancient stones, squeezed out of primeval seas, are what give so much of the British landscape its soft and timeless feel. In fact, timelessness with respect to English buildings is a distinct illusion.

The reason stone wasn't used more was that it was expensive – expensive to extract because of the labour involved, and expensive to move because of its enormous weight. Hauling a cartload of stone ten or twelve miles could easily double its cost, so medieval stone didn't travel far, which is why there are such appealing and specific regional differences of stone use and architectural style throughout Britain. A good-sized stone building – a Cistercian monastery, say – might require 40,000 cartloads of stone to build. A stone building was literally awesome, not just because it was massive but because it was massively stony. The stone itself was a statement of power, wealth and splendour.

Domestically, stone was hardly used at all until the eighteenth century, but then it caught on fast, even for simple buildings like cottages. Unfortunately, large areas outside the limestone belt had no local stone, and this included the most important and building-hungry place of all: London. The environs of London did, however, hold huge reserves of iron-rich clay, so the city rediscovered an ancient building material: brick. Bricks have been around for at least six thousand years, though in Britain they date only from Roman times, and Roman bricks were not actually very good. For all their other building skills, the Romans lacked the ability to fire bricks in a way that would allow big ones to be baked all the way through, so they made thinner bricks which were more like tiles. After the Romans departed, bricks fell out of use in England for the better part of a thousand years.

Bricks began to appear in some English buildings by about 1300, but for the next two hundred years native skills were so lacking that it remained usual to bring in Dutch brickmakers and bricklayers when building a brick house. As a home-produced building material, brick came into its own in the time of the Tudors. Many of the great brick buildings like Hampton Court Palace date from this period. Bricks had one great advantage: they could frequently be made on site. The moats and ponds that we associate with Tudor manor houses often denote where clay was dug out to be made into brick. But bricks had drawbacks too. To create a decent brick the brickmaker had to get every stage exactly right. He had first to mix carefully two or more types of clay to ensure the right consistency to prevent warping and shrinkage when fired. The prepared clay was then formed into brick shapes in moulds, which had to be air-dried for two weeks. Finally, the bricks were stacked and fired in an oven. If any of these stages was flawed – if the moisture content was too high or the heat of the kiln not exactly right – the result was imperfect bricks. And imperfect bricks were common. So bricks in medieval and renaissance Britain had a high prestige value. They were novel and stylish and generally only appeared in the smartest and most important structures.

Perhaps the greatest demonstration of the difficulty of making bricks – or possibly just the greatest demonstration of single-minded futility – was in the 1810s when Sydney Smith, the well-known wit and cleric, decided to make his own bricks for the rectory he was building for himself at Foston le Clay in Yorkshire. He was said to have unsuccessfully fired 150,000 bricks before finally conceding that he probably wasn't going to get the hang of it.

The golden age of English brick was the century from 1660 to 1760. 'Nowhere in the world can more beautiful brickwork be seen than in the best English examples of this age,' Brunskill and Clifton-Taylor wrote in their definitive *English Brickwork*. A big part of the beauty of bricks of this period was their subtle lack of uniformity. Because it was impossible to make really uniform ones, bricks were of a lovely range of hues – from pinkish red to deepest plum. Minerals in the clay give bricks their colour, and the predominance of iron in most soil types accounts for the disproportionate weighting towards red. The classic London yellow stock bricks, as they are known, take their colour from the presence of chalk in the soil.

Bricks had to be laid in a staggered pattern so that the vertical joins didn't form continuous straight lines (which would weaken the structure), and a range of styles arose, all fundamentally dictated by considerations of strength but also by a pleasant impulse to provide variety and beauty. English bond is a style in which one row is made up entirely of stretchers (the long side of bricks) and the next is made only of headers (the end side). In Flemish bond, headers alternate with stretchers from brick to brick. Flemish bond is much more popular than English not because it is stronger but because it is more economical, since every façade has more long faces than short ones, and thus requires fewer bricks. But there were many other patterns – Chinese bond, Dearne's bond, English garden-wall bond, cross bond, rat-trap bond, monk bond, flying bond and so on, each signifying a different configuration of headers and stretchers – and these elemental patterns could be additionally enhanced by making some of the bricks stick out slightly, like little steps (a practice known as corbelling), or by inserting different-coloured bricks to form a diamond pattern, known as a diaper. (The relationship between a pattern of bricks and a baby's undergarment is that the baby garment was originally made from linen threads woven in a diamond pattern.)

Brick remained an eminently respectable material for the smartest homes right up into the Regency period, but then there suddenly arose a cold distaste for it, especially for red brick. 'There is something harsh in the transition' from stone to brick, mused Isaac Ware in his highly influential *Complete Body of Architecture* (1756). Red brick, he went on, was 'fiery and disagreeable to the eye . . . and most improper in the country' – the very place it was mostly being put to use.

Suddenly stone became the only acceptable material for the surface of a building. In the Georgian period stone was so fashionable that owners would go to almost any lengths to disguise the nature of their house if it wasn't stone at all. Apsley House, at Hyde Park Corner in London, was built of brick but then encased in Bath stone when brick suddenly became unfashionable.

America played an indirect and unexpected role in brick's falling fortunes. The loss of tax revenue from the American colonies after the American War of Independence, as well as the cost of paying for that war, meant that the British government urgently needed funds, and in 1784 it introduced a stiff brick tax. Manufacturers made bricks larger to reduce the impact of the tax, but these were so awkward to work with that the effect was to depress sales further. To counter this decline in revenue, the government raised the brick tax twice more, in 1794 and 1803. Brick went into a headlong retreat. Bricks were out of fashion and people couldn't afford them anyway.

The problem was that a lot of the buildings already in existence were inescapably of brick. In Britain a simple expedient was to give the houses a kind of permanent facial by applying a creamy layer of stucco – a kind of exterior plaster compounded from lime, water and cement, from the Old German *stukki*, or covering – over the original brick surface. As the stucco dried, lines could be neatly incised to make it look like blocks of stone. The Regency architect John Nash became especially associated with stucco, as a famous line of doggerel records:

> But isn't our Nash . . . a very great master?
> He found us all brick and he leaves us all plaster!

Nash is yet another of the people in this story who rather came from out of nowhere, and his climb to greatness could not easily have been predicted. He grew up in poverty in south London and was not a particularly imposing figure to behold. He had 'a face like a monkey's', in the startlingly cruel description of a contemporary, and none of the breeding that could help smooth the way to success. But somehow he managed to land a plum traineeship in the office of Sir Robert Taylor, one of the leading architects of the day.

After completing his apprenticeship, he embarked on a career that showed more enterprise than triumphs, at least in its early days. In 1778, as a career-starting speculation he designed and built two groups of houses in Bloomsbury, which were among the very first (if not *the* very first) in London to be covered in stucco. Unfortunately, the world was not yet ready for stucco-clad houses and they didn't sell. (One of them remained empty for twelve years.) Such a setback would have been challenging enough in propitious circumstances, but in fact Nash's private life was simultaneously unravelling in a rather spectacular manner. His young wife turned out to be not quite the catch he had hoped for. She ran up stupendous, unpayable bills at dressmakers and milliners all over London, and twice he found himself arrested for debt. Worse, he discovered that while he was extricating himself from these legal difficulties, she had been engaged in energetic frolics with others, including one of his oldest friends, and that the two children of his marriage were not in all likelihood his (or indeed any one man's).

Bankrupted and presumably just a touch glum, Nash shed his wife and children – what became of them is unknown – and moved to Wales, where he built a new, less ambitious career and seemed poised to play out his life as a moderately successful architect of provincial town halls and other municipal structures.

And so his life passed for some years. But in 1797, at the clearly advanced age of forty-six, he returned to London, married a much younger woman, became a close friend of the Prince of Wales – the future King George IV – and embarked on one of the most important and influential architectural careers anyone has ever had. What accounted for these sudden changes has always been a mystery. The rumour, widely circulated, was that his new wife was the Prince Regent's mistress and that Nash was merely a convenient cover. It is a not unreasonable presumption for she was a real beauty and time had not made Nash any handsomer. He was, in his own words, a 'thick, squat, dwarf figure, with round head, snub nose and little eyes'. But as an architect he was a wizard, and almost at once he began to produce a string of exceptionally bold and confident buildings. At Brighton he transformed a staid existing property known as the Marine Pavilion into the colourful domed fireworks of a building known as the Brighton Pavilion. But the real changes were in London.

No one, other than perhaps the Luftwaffe, has done more to change the look of London than John Nash did over the next thirty years. He created Regent's Park and

Regent Street and a good many of the streets and terraces around, which gave London a rather grand and imperial look that it had not had before. He built Oxford Circus and Piccadilly Circus. He created Buckingham Palace out of the lesser Buckingham House. He planned, though he did not live long enough to build, Trafalgar Square. And he covered almost every bit of everything he built with stucco.

II

Brick might have been permanently marginalized as a domestic building material but for one important, unexpected consideration: pollution. By the early Victorian era coal was being burned in England in positively prodigious quantities. A typical middle-class family could burn a ton a month and nineteenth-century Britain suddenly had lots of middle-class families. By 1842, Britain was using two-thirds of all the coal produced in the western world. In London the result was a near-impenetrable gloom through much of the year. In one of the Sherlock Holmes stories Holmes has to strike a match – in daytime – to read something written on a London wall. So hard was it to find one's way that people not infrequently walked into walls or tumbled into unseen voids. In one famous incident, seven people in a row fell into the Thames, one after the other. In 1854, when Joseph Paxton suggested building an eleven-mile-long 'Grand Girdle Railway' to link all the principal railway termini in London, he proposed to build it under glass, so that passengers would be insulated from London's unwholesome air. It was more desirable evidently to be inside with the thick smoke of trains than outside with the thick smoke of everything else.*

Coal was hard on practically everything – on clothes, paintings, plants, furniture, books, buildings and respiratory systems. During weeks of really bad fog, the number of recorded deaths in London could easily increase by a thousand. Even pets and animals at the Smithfield meat market died in disproportionately increased numbers.

Coal smoke was particularly hard on stone buildings. Structures that looked radiant when new often deteriorated with alarming swiftness. Portland stone took

---

* One man more than any other fixed our visual image of what Victorian London was like: the French illustrator Gustave Doré (1833–83), whose illustration of London back streets appears on page 298. Doré's illustrative dominance was a little unexpected because he spoke barely a word of English and actually didn't spend much time in Britain. Doré's private life was slightly bizarre in that he conducted a number of torrid affairs with actresses – Sarah Bernhardt was his most celebrated conquest – but lived with his mother and for the whole of his life slept in a room adjoining hers. Doré viewed himself as a great artist, but the rest of the world did not, and he had to settle for being an extremely successful illustrator for books and magazines. He was very popular in England – for many years there was a Doré Gallery in Mayfair that dealt exclusively in his works – and is best remembered now for his dark drawings of London life, particularly for the scenes of squalor along the back streets. It is interesting to reflect that a very large part of our visual impression of nineteenth-century London before photography is based on the drawings of an artist who worked from memory in a studio in Paris, and got much of it wrong. Blanchard Jerrold, the man who supplied the text for the drawings, was driven to despair by many of his inaccuracies. (If that name Jerrold seems vaguely familiar, he is the son of the *Punch* journalist who first called the Great Exhibition hall the 'Crystal Palace'.)

on a disturbing piebald appearance, assuming a brilliant whiteness on every face that was exposed to winds and rain, but becoming a filthy black under every sill, lintel and sheltered corner. At Buckingham Palace Nash employed Bath stone because he thought it would wear better; he was wrong. Almost immediately it began to crumble. A new architect, Edward Blore, was brought in to fix the building. He enclosed Nash's courtyard with a new frontage built out of Caen stone. It too began to fall apart almost at once. Most alarming of all were the new Houses of Parliament, where the stone began to blacken and develop shocking pits and gouges, as if raked with gunfire, even while the building was going up. Desperate remedies were attempted to halt the deterioration. Various combinations of gums, resins, linseed oil and beeswax were painted on to the surface, but these either did nothing or produced new and even more alarming stains.

Just two materials seemed to be impervious to the insult of corrosive acids. One was a remarkable artificial stone known as Coade stone and named after Eleanor Coade, who owned the factory that made it. Coade stone was immensely popular and was used by every leading architect from about 1760 to 1830. It was practically indestructible and could be shaped into any kind of ornamental object – friezes, arabesques, capitals, modillions or any other decorative thing that would normally be carved. The best known Coade object is the large lion on Westminster Bridge near the Houses of Parliament, but Coade stone can be found all over – at Buckingham Palace, Windsor Castle, the Tower of London, on the tomb of Captain Bligh in the churchyard of St Mary-at-Lambeth, London.

The back streets of Victorian London as illustrated by Gustave Doré.

Coade stone looks and feels exactly like worked stone, and weathers as hard as the hardest stone, but it isn't stone at all. It is, surprisingly, a ceramic. Ceramics are baked clay. Depending on the type of clay and how intensely they are fired they yield three different materials: earthenware, stoneware or porcelain. Coade stone is a type of stoneware, but an especially hard and durable type. Most Coade stone is so resistant to weather and pollution that it looks almost brand new even after nearly two and a half centuries of exposure to the elements.

Considering its ubiquity and remarkable character-istics, surprisingly little is known about Coade stone and its eponymous maker. Where and when it was invented, how Eleanor Coade became involved with it, why the firm came to a sudden end some time in the late 1830s are all matters that have failed to excite much scholarly interest. Mrs Coade receives only half a dozen paragraphs in the *Dictionary of National Biography* and the only full-scale history of her and her firm was a work self-published by the historian Alison Kelly in 1999.

What can be said for certain is that Eleanor Coade was the daughter of a failed businessman from Exeter, who came to London in about 1760 and ran a successful business selling linens. Towards the end of the decade she met one Daniel Pincot, who was already engaged in the manufacture of artificial stone. They opened a factory on the south side of the Thames about where Waterloo Station stands today and began producing an unusually high-grade material. Mrs Coade is often credited as its inventor, but it seems more likely that Pincot had the method and she the money. In any case, Pincot left the firm after just two years and is heard from no more.

Eleanor Coade ran the business very successfully for fifty-two years until her death at the age of eighty-eight in 1821 – an especially remarkable achievement for a woman in the eighteenth century. She never married. Whether she was sweet and beloved or a raging harridan we have no idea. All that can be said is that the Coade company's sales dwindled without her. Eventually the firm went under, but so quietly that no one is sure now when exactly it ceased production.

There is an enduring myth that the secret of Coade stone died with Eleanor Coade. In fact, the process has been reproduced experimentally on at least two occasions. Nothing is stopping people from making it commercially now. The only reason it isn't made is that nobody bothers.

Coade stone could only ever be used for incidental decorative purposes. Fortunately, there was one venerable building material that also stood up to pollution very well: brick. Pollution was the making of modern brick, though several other timely factors helped. The development of canals made it economical to ship bricks over considerable distances. The invention of the Hoffmann kiln (named for Friedrich Hoffmann, its German inventor) allowed bricks to be produced continuously, and thus more cheaply, along a sort of production line. The removal of the brick tax in 1850 reduced costs further still. The biggest spur of all was simply Britain's phenomenal growth in the nine-teenth century – the growth of cities, of industry, of people needing housing. In the lifetime of Queen Victoria, London's population went from one million to nearly seven million, and newly industrialized cities like Manchester, Leeds and Bradford had growth rates greater still. Overall, the number of houses in Britain quadrupled in the century, and the new housing stock overwhelmingly was of brick, as were most of the mills, chimneys, railway stations, sewers, schools, churches, offices and other new infrastructure that leapt into being in that frantically busy age. Brick was too versatile and economical to resist. It became the default building material of the Industrial Revolution.

According to one estimate, more bricks were laid in Britain in the Victorian period than in all of previous history together. The growth of London meant the spread of suburbs of more or less identical brick houses – mile after mile of 'dreary repetitious mediocrity', in Disraeli's bleak description. The Hoffmann kiln had much to answer for here since it introduced absolute uniformity of size, colour and appearance to bricks. Buildings made of the new-style bricks had much less subtlety and character than buildings of earlier eras, but they were much cheaper, and there has hardly ever been a time in the conduct of human affairs when cheapness didn't triumph.

There was just one problem with brick that became increasingly apparent as the century wore on and building space grew constrained. Bricks are immensely heavy, and you can't make really tall buildings with them – not that people didn't try. The tallest brick building ever built was the sixteen-storey Monadnock Building, a general purpose office building erected in Chicago in 1893 and designed shortly before his death by the architect John Root of the famous firm of Burnham and Root. The Monadnock Building still stands, and is an extraordinary edifice to behold. Such is its weight that the walls at street level are six feet thick, making the ground floor – normally the most welcoming part of a building – into a dark and forbidding vault.

The Monadnock Building would be exceptional anywhere, but it is particularly so in Chicago where the earth
is essentially a large sponge. Chicago is built on mudflats:
anything heavy deposited on Chicago soil wants to sink –
and, in the early days, pretty generally *did* sink. Most architects allowed for a foot or so of settling in Chicago's soils.
Pavements were built with a severe slant, running upwards
from the kerb to the building. The hope was that as the
building settled the pavement would come down with
it into a position of perfect horizontality. In practice, it
seldom did.

To ameliorate the sinking problem, nineteenth-
century architects developed a technique of constructing a
'raft' on which the building could stand, rather as a surfer
stands on a surfboard. The raft under the Monadnock
Building extends eleven feet beyond the building in every
direction, but even with the raft the building sank almost
two feet after construction – something you really don't
want a sixteen-storey building to do. It is a testimony to
the skills of John Root that the building still stands. Many
others weren't so fortunate. A government office block
called the Federal Building, constructed at a staggering cost
of $5 million in 1880, took on such a swift and dangerous
pitch that it didn't last two decades. Many other smaller
buildings had similarly abbreviated lives.

What architects needed was some kind of lighter and
more flexible building material, and for a long time it
seemed that that would be the one that Joseph Paxton first
brought to large-scale fame with the Crystal Palace: iron.

As a building material iron was of two types: cast iron
and wrought iron. Cast iron (so called because it is cast in
moulds) was great at compression – supporting its own

weight – but not so good under tension and tended to snap like a pencil when stressed horizontally. So it made excellent pillars, but not beams. Wrought iron, in contrast, was strong enough for horizontal duty, but more expensive because it was more complicated and time-consuming to manufacture since it had to be repeatedly folded and stirred while it was still molten. As well as making it comparatively strong, the folding and stirring made it ductile – that is, capable of being pulled, rather like taffy, and bent into shapes, which is why decorative objects like gates are made of wrought iron. Together they were used in large-scale construction and engineering projects all over the world.

Curiously, the one place iron never caught on except incidentally was in housing. Elsewhere, however, iron went from strength to strength – until, that is, it was realized that strength was not actually its most dependable quality. The disturbing fact was that iron sometimes failed spectacularly. Cast iron in particular tended to splinter or fracture if it wasn't cast perfectly, and imperfections could be impossible to detect. That became tragically manifest in the winter of 1860 at a textile mill in Lawrence, Massachusetts. There, one cold morning, nine hundred women, mostly Irish immigrants, were at work at their clattering machines when one of the cast-iron columns supporting the roof gave way. After a moment's hesitation, the other columns in the row failed one by one, like buttons popping on a shirt. The terrified workers rushed for the exits, but before many could get out of the doors the building collapsed with a roar that none who heard it would ever forget. As many as two hundred workers died, though remarkably no one bothered, then or afterwards, to make a formal count. Hundreds more were injured. Many of those trapped inside were hideously incinerated as fires spread from broken lamps.

In the following decade iron's standing suffered a further blow when a bridge over the Ashtabula River in Ohio collapsed as a passenger train crossed over it. Seventy-six people were killed. That accident was recalled with uncanny precision three years later, almost to the day, on the Tay Bridge in Scotland. As a train crossed it in bad weather, a portion of the bridge gave way, hurling the carriages into the waters far below and killing almost an identical number of people as had died at Ashtabula. Those were the most notorious of the tragedies, but in fact iron mishaps on a smaller scale were almost routine. Railway boilers made of cast iron sometimes exploded, and rails commonly worked loose or buckled under the strain of heavy loads or shifting weather, causing derailments. It was in fact iron's shortcomings that in large part allowed the Erie Canal to remain successful as long as it did. Well into the railway age it continued to thrive, which is surprising on the face of it because it was frozen over and unusable for months each winter. Trains could run all year round and, as engines steadily improved, could theoretically carry more freight. In practice, however, iron rails weren't strong enough to support really heavy loads.

Something much stronger was needed, and that material was steel – which is just another kind of iron but with a different input of carbon. Steel was a superior material in every way, but couldn't be made in bulk because of the high volume of heat required. It was fine for things like swords and razors, but not for large-scale industrial products like beams and rails. In 1856, the problem was unexpectedly – and indeed improbably – solved by an English businessman who knew nothing at all of metallurgy, but loved to tinker and experiment. His name was Henry Bessemer and he was already eminently successful from having invented a product known as bronze powder. This was used to apply a fake gilt finish to a wide range of materials. Victorians loved gilt finishes, so Bessemer's powder made him rich and gave him the leisure to indulge his inventive instincts. During the Crimean war he decided he wanted to build heavy guns, but he could see that he needed a better material than cast or wrought iron, and so began experimenting with new methods of production. Having no real idea what he was doing, he blew air into molten pig iron to see what would happen. What should have happened, according to conventional predictions, was an almighty explosion, which is why no qualified person had tried such a foolhardy experiment before. In fact it didn't explode but produced a flame of very high intensity, which burned out impurities and resulted in hard steel. Suddenly it was possible to make steel in bulk. Steel was the material the Industrial Revolution had been waiting for. Everything from railway lines to ocean-going ships to bridges could be built faster, stronger and cheaper. Skyscrapers became possible and so cityscapes were transformed. Railway engines became robust enough to pull mighty loads at speed across continents. Bessemer grew immensely rich and famous, and many towns in America (as many as thirteen, according to one source) named themselves Bessemer or Bessemer City in his honour.

Less than a decade after the Great Exhibition, iron as a structural material was finished – which makes it slightly odd that the most iconic structure of the entire century, about to rise over Paris, was made of that doomed material. I refer of course to the soaring wonder of the age known as the Eiffel Tower. Never in history has a structure been more technologically advanced, materially obsolescent and gloriously pointless all at the same time. And for that remarkable story, it is necessary to go back upstairs and into a new room.

CHAPTER TEN

The Passage

I

HIS FULL NAME WAS Alexandre Gustave Boenickhausen-Eiffel, and he was headed for a life of respectable obscurity in his uncle's vinegar factory in Dijon when the factory failed and he took up engineering.

He was, to put it mildly, very good at it. He built bridges and viaducts across impossible defiles, railway concourses of stunning expansiveness and other grand and challenging structures that continue to impress and inspire, including, in 1884, one of the trickiest of all, the internal supporting skeleton for the Statue of Liberty. Everybody thinks of the Statue of Liberty as the work of the sculptor Frédéric Bartholdi, and it is of course his design. But without ingenious interior engineering to hold it up, the Statue of Liberty is merely a hollow structure of beaten copper barely one-tenth of an inch thick. That's about the thickness of a chocolate Easter bunny – but an Easter bunny 151 feet high, which must stand up to wind, snow, driving rain and salt spray, the expansion and

Eiffel's Tower under construction, Paris, 1888.

contraction of metal in sun and cold, and a thousand other rude, daily physical assaults.

None of these challenges had ever been faced by an engineer before, and Eiffel solved them in the neatest possible way: by creating a skeleton of trusses and springs on which the copper skin is worn like a suit of clothes. Although he wasn't thinking of what this technique could do for more conventional buildings, it marked the invention of curtainwall construction, the most important building technique of the twentieth century – the form of construction that made skyscrapers possible. (The builders of Chicago's early skyscrapers also independently invented curtainwall construction, but Eiffel got there first.) The ability of the metal skin to twist under pressure neatly anticipated the design of aircraft wings long before anyone was seriously thinking about aircraft at all. So the Statue of Liberty is quite a piece of work, but because all that ingenuity is underneath Liberty's gowns almost no one appreciates it.

Eiffel was not a vain man, but in his next big project he made sure no one would fail to appreciate his role in its construction by creating something that was nothing *but* skeleton. The event that brought it into being was the Paris Exposition of 1889. As is usual with these things, the organizers wanted an iconic centrepiece and invited proposals. A hundred or so were submitted, including a design for a 900-foot-high guillotine, to commemorate France's unrivalled contribution to decapitation. For many that was scarcely more preposterous than Eiffel's winning entry. Large numbers of Parisians could not see the point of placing an enormous functionless derrick in the middle of the city.

The Eiffel Tower wasn't just the largest thing that anyone had ever proposed to build, it was the largest completely useless thing. It wasn't a palace or burial chamber or place of worship. It didn't even commemorate a fallen hero. Eiffel gamely insisted that his tower would have many practical applications – that it would make a terrific military lookout and that one could do useful aeronautical and meteorological experiments from its upper reaches – but eventually even he admitted that mostly he wished to build it simply for the slightly strange pleasure of making something really quite enormous.

Many people loathed it, especially artists and intellectuals. A group of notables that included Alexandre Dumas, Emile Zola, Paul Verlaine and Guy de Maupassant submitted a long, rather overexcited letter protesting at 'the deflowering of Paris' and arguing that 'when foreigners come to see our exhibition they will cry out in astonishment, "What! This is the atrocity which the French have created to give us an idea of their boasted taste!"' The Eiffel Tower, they continued, was 'the grotesque, mercenary invention of a machine builder'. Eiffel accepted the insults with cheerful equanimity and merely pointed out that one of the outraged signatories of the petition, the architect Charles Garnier, was in fact a member of the commission that had approved the tower in the first place.

In its finished state, the Eiffel Tower seems so singular and whole, so couldn't-be-otherwise, that we have to remind ourselves that it is an immensely complex assemblage, a fretwork of 18,000 intricately fitted parts, which only come together because of an immense amount of the very cleverest thought. Consider just the first 180 feet of the structure, up to the first platform – already the height of a fifteen-storey building. Up to that height the legs lean steeply inwards at an angle of fifty-four degrees. They would clearly fall over if they weren't braced by the platform. The platform just as clearly couldn't be up there without the four legs underneath to support it. The parts work flawlessly when brought together, but *until* they are brought together they cannot work at all. Eiffel's first challenge, therefore, was to devise some way to brace four immensely tall and heavy legs, each straining to topple inwards; then, at the right moment, be able to ease them into position so that all four came together at exactly the right points to support a large and very heavy platform. An incorrect alignment of as little as one-tenth of one degree would have put any leg out by a foot and a half – far more than could be corrected without taking everything down and starting all over again. Eiffel effected the delicate operation by anchoring each leg in a giant container of sand, like a foot in a large boot. Then, when work on them was complete, the legs could be eased into position by letting sand out of the boxes in a carefully controlled manner. The system worked perfectly.

However, that was only the start of things. Above the first platform came another eight hundred feet of iron framework made from fifteen thousand mostly large, unwieldy pieces, all of which had to be swung into place at increasingly challenging heights. Tolerances in some places were as little as one-tenth of a millimetre. Some observers were convinced that the tower couldn't support its own weight. A professor of mathematics filled reams of paper with fevered calculations and declared that when the tower was two-thirds up the legs would splay and the whole would collapse in a thunderous fury, crushing the neighbourhood below. In fact, the Eiffel Tower is pretty light at just 9,500 tons – it is mostly air, after all – and needed foundations just seven feet deep to support its weight.

More time was spent designing the Eiffel Tower than building it. Erection took under two years and came in well under budget. Just 130 workers were needed on site, and none died in the building process – a magnificent achievement for a project this large in that age. Until the erection of the Chrysler Building in New York in 1930, it would be the tallest structure in the world. Although by 1889 steel was displacing iron everywhere, Eiffel rejected it because he had always worked in iron and didn't feel comfortable with steel. So there is a certain irony in the thought that the greatest edifice ever built of iron was also the last.

The Eiffel Tower was the most striking and imaginative large structure in the world in the nineteenth century, and perhaps the greatest structural achievement too, but it wasn't the most expensive building of its century or even of its year. At the very moment that the Eiffel Tower was rising in Paris, two thousand miles away in the foothills of the Appalachian Mountains in North Carolina an even more expensive structure was going up – a private residence on rather a grand scale. It would take more than twice as long to complete as the Eiffel Tower, employ four times as many workers, cost three times as much to build, and was intended to be lived in for just a few months a year by one man and his mother. Called Biltmore, it was (and remains) the largest private house ever built in North America. Nothing can say more about the shifting economics of the late nineteenth century than that the residents of the New World were now building houses greater than the greatest monuments of the Old.

America in 1889 was in the sumptuous midst of the period of hyper-self-indulgence known as the Gilded Age. There would never be another time to equal it. Between 1850 and 1900 every measure of wealth, productivity and well-being skyrocketed in America. The country's population in the period tripled, but its wealth increased by a factor of thirteen. Steel production went from 13,000 tons a year to 11.3 million. Exports of metal products of all kinds – guns, rails, pipes, boilers, machinery of every description – went from $6 million to $120 million. The number of millionaires, fewer than twenty in 1850, rose to forty thousand by the century's end.

Europeans viewed America's industrial ambitions with amusement, then consternation and finally alarm. In Britain, a National Efficiency Movement arose with the idea of recapturing the bulldog spirit that had formerly made Britain pre-eminent. Books with titles like *The American Invaders* and *The 'American Commercial Invasion' of Europe* sold briskly. But actually what Europeans were seeing was only the beginning.

By the early twentieth century America was producing more steel than Germany and Britain combined – a circumstance that would have seemed inconceivable half a century before. What particularly galled the Europeans was that nearly all the technological advances in steel production were made in Europe, but it was America that made the steel. In 1901, J. P. Morgan absorbed and amalgamated a host of smaller companies into the mighty US Steel Corporation, the largest business enterprise the world had ever seen. With a value of $1.4 billion it was worth more than all the land in the United States west of the Mississippi and twice the size of the US federal government if measured by annual revenue.

America's industrial success produced a rollcall of financial magnificence: Rockefellers, Morgans, Astors, Mellons, Morgans, Fricks, Carnegies, Goulds, du Ponts, Belmonts, Harrimans, Huntingtons, Vanderbilts and many more basked in dynastic wealth of essentially inexhaustible proportions. John D. Rockefeller made $1 billion a year, measured in today's money, and paid no income tax. No one did, for income tax did not yet exist in America. Congress tried to introduce an income tax of 2 per cent on earnings over $4,000 in 1894, but the Supreme Court ruled it unconstitutional. Income tax wouldn't become a regular part of American life until 1914, and in the meantime any money that was made was kept. People would never be this rich again.

Spending all this wealth became for many a more or less full-time occupation. A kind of desperate, vulgar edge became attached to almost everything they did. At one New York dinner party, guests found the table heaped with sand and at each place a little gold spade; upon a signal, they were invited to dig in and search for diamonds and other costly glitter buried within. At another party – possibly the most preposterous ever staged – several dozen horses wearing padded hooves were led into the ballroom of Sherry's, a vast and esteemed eating establishment, and tethered around the tables so that the guests, dressed as cowboys and cowgirls, could enjoy the novel and

sublimely pointless pleasure of dining in a New York ballroom on horseback. Many parties cost tens of thousands
of dollars. On 26 March 1883, Mrs William K. Vanderbilt
broke all precedent by throwing a party that cost
$250,000, though as the *New York Times* judiciously con-
ceded it did mark the end of Lent. Easily dazzled in those
days, the *Times* ran 10,000 words of unrestrained gush
reporting every detail of the event. This was the party
which Mrs Cornelius Vanderbilt attended as an electric
light (possibly the only occasion in her life on which she
could be described as radiant).

Many of the nouveaux riches travelled to Europe and
began buying up fine art, furniture and whatever else
could be crated up and shipped home. Henry Clay Folger,
president of Standard Oil (and distantly related to the
Folger's coffee family), began collecting First Folios of
William Shakespeare, usually from hard-up aristocrats,
and eventually acquired about a third of all surviving
copies, which today form the basis of the great Folger
Shakespeare Library in Washington, DC. Many others, like
Henry Clay Frick and Andrew Mellon, built up great art
collections, while some simply bought indiscriminately,
none more so than the newspaper magnate William
Randolph Hearst, who acquired treasures so freely that he
needed two warehouses in Brooklyn to store them all.
Hearst and his wife were not, evidently, the most
sophisticated of buyers: when he told her that the Welsh
castle he had just bought was Norman, she reportedly
replied: 'Norman who?'

The new rich began to collect not just European art
and artefacts, but actual Europeans. During the last
quarter of the nineteenth century, it became a fashion to

identify cash-starved aristocrats and marry one's daughters off to them. No fewer than five hundred rich young American women accepted such an arrangement. In almost every instance the event was not so much a marriage as a transaction. May Goelet, who stood to inherit $12.5 million, was wooed by a Captain George Holford, who was rich and had three great houses. 'Unfortunately,' she noted wistfully in a letter home, 'the dear man has no title.' So she married the Duke of Roxburghe instead and thereby got a rotten life but a terrific title. For some families, marrying rich Americans wasn't so much a habit as a syndrome. Lord Curzon married two Americans (serially, of course). The eighth Duke of Marlborough married Lily Hammersley, an American widow who was not hugely attractive (one newspaper described her as 'a badly dressed woman with a moustache') but was fabulously wealthy, while the ninth duke wed Consuelo Vanderbilt, who was good-looking *and* came with $4.2 million of railway stock. Meanwhile, his uncle, Lord Randolph Churchill, married the American Jennie Jerome, who didn't bring the family as much money but did produce Winston Churchill. By the early twentieth century, 10 per cent of all British aristocratic marriages were to Americans – an extraordinary proportion.

At home, the newly wealthy of America built houses on a grand scale. Grandest of all were the Vanderbilts. They built ten mansions on Fifth Avenue in New York alone. One had 137 rooms, making it one of the largest city houses ever built. But they had even more palatial homes outside the city, particularly at Newport, Rhode Island. In possibly the only example ever of the super-rich being ironic, they called their Newport homes 'cottages'. In fact, these were houses so big that even the servants needed servants. They contained acres of marble, the most glittery chandeliers, tapestries the size of tennis courts, fittings heavily wrought from silver and gold. It has been estimated that if built today the Breakers would cost half a billion dollars – rather a lot for a summer home. The ostentation of these properties generated such widespread disapproval that a Senate committee for a time seriously considered introducing a law limiting how much any person could spend on a house.

The architect responsible for much of this was a man named Richard Morris Hunt. Hunt grew up in Vermont, the son of a Congressman, but at nineteen went to Paris and became the first American to study architecture at the Ecole des Beaux Arts – in effect, was the first American to be formally trained as an architect. He was charming and good-looking – 'the handsomest American in Paris' in the view of one observer – but until 1881, when he was well into his fifties, his career was prosperous and respectable but a touch mundane. Typical of his projects was design-ing the base of the Statue of Liberty – a lucrative commission, but hardly one on which to hang a repu-tation. Then he discovered rich people. In particular he discovered the Vanderbilts.

The Vanderbilts were the richest family in America, with an empire founded on railways and shipping by Cornelius Vanderbilt, 'a coarse, tobacco-chewing, profane oaf of a man' in the estimation of one of his con-temporaries. Cornelius Vanderbilt – 'the Commodore' as he liked to be known, though he had no actual entitle-ment to the name – didn't offer much in the way of sophistication or intellectual enchantment, but he had a positively uncanny gift for making money.* At one time he personally controlled some 10 per cent of all the money in circulation in the United States. The Vanderbilts between them owned some twenty thousand miles of railway line and most of what rolled along it, and that provided them with more money than they really knew what to do with. And Richard Morris Hunt became, in the nicest possible way, the man who helped them spend it. He built houses for them of sumptuous grandeur on Fifth Avenue in New York, in Bar Harbor in Maine, on Long Island and in Newport. Even the family mausoleum on Staten Island was, at $300,000, as costly as many an outsized mansion. Whatever architectural whims fluttered through their brains Hunt was there to satisfy. Oliver Belmont, husband of Alva Vanderbilt, was crazy about horses. He had Hunt design for him a fifty-two-room mansion, Belcourt Castle, in which the whole of the ground floor was stables, so that Belmont could drive his coach straight through the massive front doors and into the house. The horses had stalls that were panelled in teak with sterling silver fittings. The living area was above.

In one of the many Vanderbilt mansions, a breakfast nook was adorned with a Rembrandt painting. At the Breakers a children's playhouse was larger and better appointed than most people's actual houses; it came complete with bell pulls connected to the main house so that

---

* The Commodore was also intimately acquainted with the frailties of iron mentioned in the previous chapter. In 1838, a train on the Camden and Amboy Railroad on which he was riding derailed when an axle broke and Vanderbilt's carriage was sent crashing down a thirty-foot embankment. Two passengers were killed. Vanderbilt was seriously injured but survived. Also on the train but uninjured was the former president John Quincy Adams.

servants could be summoned if the children suddenly required refreshments, needed a shoelace tied or suffered some other crisis of comfort. The Vanderbilts grew so powerful and spoiled that they could get away, literally, with murder. Reggie Vanderbilt, son of Cornelius and Alice Vanderbilt, was a notoriously reckless driver (as well as insolent, idle, stupid and without redeeming feature) who ran through or over pedestrians on five separate occasions in New York. Two of those he flung aside were killed; a third was crippled for life. He was never charged with any offence.

The one member of the family who seemed immune from the urge to be extravagant or revolting was George Washington Vanderbilt, a member of the clan so painfully shy and quiet that people sometimes assumed him to be simple-minded. In fact, he was exceedingly intelligent and spoke eight languages. He lived at home well into adulthood, and passed his time translating modern literature into ancient Greek and vice versa. He had a collection of over twenty thousand books, giving him probably the largest private library in America. At the age of twenty-three, George's father died, leaving a fortune of some $200 million. George inherited $10 million of that, which doesn't sound a huge amount, but it's equivalent to $300 million in modern money.

In 1888 he decided finally to build a place of his own. He bought 130,000 acres of wooded retreat in North Carolina and engaged Richard Morris Hunt to build him something suitably comfy. Vanderbilt decided he wanted a Loire chateau – but grander, of course, and with better plumbing – and so he built more with Biltmore (though he seems never to have noticed the pun). Closely

modelled on the famous Chateau de Blois, it is a
rambling, gloriously excessive mountain of Indiana limestone, comprising 250 rooms, a frontage 780 feet long and
a footprint of five acres. It was, and remains, the largest
house ever built in America. For its construction,
Vanderbilt employed a thousand workers at an average
wage of 90 cents a day.

He filled Biltmore with the finest of everything
Europeans would sell him, which in the late 1880s was
practically everything – tapestries, furnishings, classic
works of art. The scale recalls, and in some crucial respects
exceeds, the manic excesses of William Beckford at
Fonthill Abbey. The dining-room table could seat seventy-
six. The ceiling was seventy-five feet above the floor. It
must have been like living on the concourse of a major
railway station.

For the grounds he brought in the ageing Frederick
Law Olmsted, designer of Central Park in New York, who
persuaded Vanderbilt to turn much of the estate into
experimental forest. The Secretary of Agriculture, J. Sterling
Morton, marvelled that Vanderbilt employed more men
and had a larger budget for his single forest than Morton
had for an entire federal department. The estate had two
hundred miles of roads. It included a town – a small city
really – complete with schools, a hospital, churches, railway station, banks and shops to serve the estate's two
thousand employees and their families. Workers lived a
prosperous but semi-feudal existence, bound by many
rules. They were not allowed to keep dogs, for instance. To
support the estate, Vanderbilt's forests were logged for
timber, and his many farms produced fruit, vegetables,
dairy products, eggs, poultry and livestock. He

also engaged in some manufacturing and processing.
George intended to live there with his mother for
several months a year, but she died soon after Biltmore
was completed, so he resided alone, in massive solitude,
until 1898 when he married Edith Stuyvesant Dresser,
with whom he produced a single child, Cornelia. By this
point it was becoming clear that the estate was an
economic disaster. Annual losses were running at
$250,000 and George had to keep it afloat out of a dwin-
dling stock of capital. In 1914 he died suddenly. His wife
and daughter sold as much of the estate as they could as
quickly as they could, and declined ever to have anything
to do with it again.

II

We might pause here for a moment to consider where we
are and why. We are in the passage, as domestic corridors
were called on most architectural plans in the nineteenth
century. It is the least congenial and most gloomy space in
the Old Rectory since it has no windows and must take
whatever natural light it can through the open doors of
neighbouring rooms. Slightly more than halfway along is
a door that could be shut – and in earlier days no doubt
was – to divide the service side of the house from the
private domain beyond. Just beyond that, near the back
staircase, is a niche in the wall that can't have been there
when the house was built, for it is clearly designed to hold
something that didn't exist in 1851, but that would change

the world and more quickly than anyone imagined. It is that niche in particular that has brought us here.

If you have wondered in recent pages what the abundant wealth of Americans in the Gilded Age has to do with a downstairs corridor in an English house, the answer is: more than you might think. From this point onwards, the direction and momentum of modern life was determined increasingly by American events, American inventions, American interests and demands. For Europeans that was a source of some dismay, but a little exciting, too, for Americans did things in ways no one had before.

They were, for one thing, so smitten with the idea of progress that they invented things without having any idea whether they would be of any use or not. The absolute quintessence of the phenomenon was Thomas Edison. Nobody was better (or worse, depending on how you choose to view it) at inventing things that had no obvious need or purpose. Overall, Edison was of course immensely successful and a huge generator of wealth. By 1920, it has been estimated, the industries his inventions and refinements spawned were worth, in aggregate, $21.6 billion. But he was terrible at working out which of his interests had the best commercial prospects. He simply persuaded himself, as no human being ever had before, that whatever he invented would make money. In fact, more often than not it didn't, and nowhere was that more true than with his long and costly dream to fill the world with concrete homes.

Concrete was one of the most exciting products of the nineteenth century. As a material it had been around for a very long time – the great dome of the Pantheon in Rome is made of concrete; Salisbury Cathedral stands on concrete foundations – but the modern breakthrough for it came in 1824 when Joseph Aspdin, a humble bricklayer in Leeds, invented Portland cement, so called to suggest that it was as attractive and durable as Portland stone. Portland cement was vastly superior to any existing product. It even performed better in water than the Reverend James Parker's Roman cement. How Aspdin invented his product has always been something of a mystery because making it required certain precisely measured steps – namely, pulverizing limestone to a particular degree of fineness, mixing it with clay of a certain moistness, and baking the whole at temperatures much higher than would be found in a normal lime kiln. What gave Aspdin the hunch to alter the constituents as he did and then to conclude that they would make a product that would set harder and smoother if heated to an extreme degree is a puzzle that cannot be answered, but somehow he did it and it made him rich.

For years, Edison was captivated by concrete's possibilities, and around the turn of the century he decided to act upon the impulse in a big way. He formed the Edison Portland Cement Company and built a huge plant near Stewartsville, New Jersey. By 1907 Edison was the fifth biggest cement producer in the world. His researchers patented more than four dozen improved ways of making quality cement in bulk. Edison cement built Yankee Stadium and the world's first stretch of concrete highway, but his abiding dream was to fill the world with concrete houses.

The plan was to make a mould of a complete house into which concrete could be poured in a continuous flow, forming not just walls and floors but every interior structure – baths, toilets, sinks, cabinets, doorjambs, even picture frames. Apart from a few odds and ends like doors and light switches, everything would be made of concrete. The walls could even be tinted, Edison suggested, to make painting forever unnecessary. A four-man team could build a new house every two days, he calculated. Edison expected his concrete houses to sell for $1,200, about a third of the cost of a conventional home of the same size.

It was a wild and ultimately unrealizable dream. The technical problems were overwhelming. The moulds, which were of course the size of the house itself, were ridiculously cumbersome and complex, but the real problem was filling them smoothly. Concrete is a mixture of cement, water and aggregates – that is, gravel and small stones – and it is in the nature of aggregates to want to sink. The challenge for Edison's engineers was to formulate a mixture liquid enough to flow into every corner of every mould but thick enough to hold its aggregates in suspension in defiance of gravity, while hardening to a smooth, uniform consistency of sufficient quality to persuade people that they were purchasing a home and not a bunker. It proved an impossible ambition. Even if all else went well, the engineers calculated, the house would weigh 450,000 pounds, causing all manner of ongoing structural strains.

All the technical challenges, plus problems of over-supply generally within the industry (which Edison's huge plant did much to aggravate), guaranteed that Edison would always struggle to make money on the enterprise. Cement-making was a difficult business anyway because it was so seasonal. But Edison pressed on and designed a range of concrete furnishings – bureaus, cupboards, chairs, even a concrete piano – to go with his concrete houses. He promised that soon he would offer a double bed that would never wear out for just $5. The entire range was to be unveiled at a cement industry show in New York in 1912. In the event, when the show opened, the Edison stand was bare. No one from the Edison company ever offered an explanation. It was the last anyone heard of concrete furniture. As far as is known, Edison never discussed the matter.

A few concrete houses were built and some actually still stand in New Jersey and Ohio, but the general concept clearly never caught on, and concrete houses became one of Edison's more costly failures. That is really saying something for Edison was good at making things the world didn't yet have, but terrible at seeing how it would choose to make use of them. He completely failed, for instance, to see the potential of the phonograph as a medium for entertainment, but thought of it only as a device for taking dictation and archiving voices – he actually called it 'the speaking machine'. For years he refused to accept that the future of motion pictures lay in projecting images on screens because he hated the thought that they could become visible to someone who had slipped into the viewing chamber without buying a ticket. For a long time he held out for the idea of keeping them securely inside hand-cranked peepshow boxes. In 1908 he confidently declared that aircraft had no future.

After his costly failures with cement, Edison moved on to other ideas that mostly proved to be impractical or demonstrably hare-brained. He developed an interest in warfare and predicted that soon he would be able to induce mass comas in enemy troops through 'electrically charged atomizers'. He also concocted a plan to build giant electromagnets that would catch enemy bullets in flight and send them back the way they had come. He invested heavily in an automated general store in which customers would put a coin in a slot and a moment later a bag of coal, potatoes, onions, nails, hairpins or some other desired commodity would come sliding down a chute to them. The system never worked. It never came close to working.

Which brings us at last to the niche in the wall and the world-changing object it contained: the telephone. When Alexander Graham Bell invented the telephone in 1876, no one anywhere saw its full potential, Bell included. Many didn't see any potential for it at all. Executives from Western Union famously dismissed the phone as 'an electrical toy'. So Bell proceeded independently and did rather well out of it, to say the least. The Bell patent (No. 174,465) became the single most valuable patent ever granted. All Bell did really was put together existing technologies. The components necessary to make telephones had existed for thirty years and the principles were understood. The problem wasn't so much with getting a voice to travel along a wire – children had been doing that with two tin cans and a length of string for years – as with amplifying it so that it could be heard at a distance.

In 1861 a German schoolteacher named Philipp Reis built a prototype device, and even called it a 'Telephon', for which reasons Germans naturally tend to credit him with the invention. The one thing Reis's phone didn't do, however, was actually work, at least as far as could be told at the time. It could send only simple signals – primarily clicks and a small range of musical tones – and not effectively enough to let it challenge the pre-eminence of the telegraph. Ironically, it was later discovered that when the contact points on Reis's device became fouled with dust or dirt they were able to transmit speech with startling fidelity. Unfortunately Reis, with Teutonic punctiliousness, had always kept his equipment impeccably shiny and clean, and so went to his grave never knowing how close he had come to producing a working instrument. At least three other men, including the American Elisha Gray, were well on the road to building working phones when Bell had his breakthrough moment in Boston in 1876. Gray actually filed something called a patent caveat – a sort of holding claim that allowed one to protect an invention that wasn't quite yet perfected – on the very day that Bell filed his own, more formal patent, but, unfortunately for Gray, Bell beat him by a few hours.

Bell was born in 1847, the same year as Thomas Edison, and grew up in Edinburgh, but emigrated to Canada with his parents in 1870 partly in response to a family tragedy after his two brothers died just three years apart from tuberculosis.* While his parents settled on a farm in Ontario, Bell took up the post of professor of vocal physiology at the recently founded Boston University – a rather surprising appointment as he had no training in vocal physiology and no university degree of his own. All he had, really, was a sympathetic interest in communications and a long-standing family attachment to the field.

* Edison's family was also in Canada till shortly before he was born. It is interesting to consider how different North American history might have been if Edison and Bell had both stayed north of the border and done their inventing there.

His mother was deaf and his father was a world expert on speech and elocution at a time when elocution was regarded with something close to awe. The senior Bell's book *The Standard Elocutionist* had recently sold 250,000 copies in the US alone. In any case, Bell's position at BU was not quite as grand as it sounds. He was employed to give just five hours of lectures a week at a salary of $25. Luckily, this suited Bell because it gave him time to get on with his experimental work.

Bell sought ways to amplify sounds electrically as an aid to the hard of hearing. Soon it occurred to him that this work could equally be used to send voices across distances to make 'speaking telegraphs', as he termed them. To assist in this new line of development he hired a young man named Thomas A. Watson. Together the two threw themselves at the problem in early 1875. Just over a year later, on 10 March 1876, a week to the day after Bell's twenty-ninth birthday, the most famous moment in telecommunications history occurred in a small lab at 5 Exeter Place in Boston, when Bell spilled some acid on his lap and sputtered, 'Mr Watson, come here, I want to see you,' and an astonished Watson in a separate room heard the message clearly. At least that was the story Watson related fifty years later in a series of anniversary advertisements commemorating the telephone's invention. Bell, who had died four years before the anniversary, had never actually mentioned spilled acid to anyone, and it would be odd, when you think about it, for a person startled by a searing pain in his lap to voice such a calm request, at normal volume, to someone who was not in fact present. Moreover, because of the prototype phone's primitiveness, Watson could only hear a message when his ear was pressed to a vibrating reed, and it seems a touch unlikely that he would have had an ear cocked to a listening device on the off chance that Bell, seized by acidic pain, would call out to him. Whatever the precise circumstances, Bell's notes confirmed that he did ask Watson to come to him and that Watson, in a separate room, heard the request clearly. History's first telephone call had been made.

Watson deserves more attention than history has given him. Born in Salem, Massachusetts, in 1854, seven years after Bell was born in Scotland, he left school at fourteen and worked in various undistinguished jobs before hooking up with Bell. The two men were bound by the deepest feelings of respect and even affection, yet they never progressed to first-name terms, despite half a century's friendship. It is impossible to say exactly how vital Watson's role was in the invention of the phone, but he was certainly far more than a mere assistant. During the seven years he worked for Bell, he secured sixty patents in his own name, including one for the distinctive ringing bell that was for decades an invariable part of every phone call made. Remarkably, before this the only way to know if someone was trying to get through to you was to pick up the phone from time to time and see if anyone was there.

For most people the telephone was such an incomprehensible novelty that Bell had to explain exactly what it did. 'The telephone,' he wrote, 'may be briefly described as an electrical contrivance for reproducing in different places the tones and articulations of a speaker's voice so that Conversations can be carried on by word of mouth between persons in different rooms, in different streets or in different Towns . . . The great advantage it possesses over every other form of electrical apparatus is that it requires no skill to operate the instrument.'

Displayed at the Centennial Exhibition in Philadelphia that summer, it attracted little attention. Most visitors were far more impressed by an electric pen invented by Thomas Edison. The pen worked by rapidly punching holes in a sheet of paper to form an outline of letters in a stencil fashion, permitting ink to be injected on to the pages below, which allowed multiple copies of a document to be made quickly. Edison, ever misguided, was confident that the invention would be 'bigger than telegraphy'. Of course it wasn't, but someone else was taken with the idea of the rapidly punching pen and re-developed it to inject ink under skin. The modern tattoo gun was born.

As for the telephone, Bell persevered and gradually built up a following. The first telephone installation began functioning in Boston in 1877. It allowed three-way communications between two banks (one of them the interestingly named Shoe and Leather Bank) and a private company. By July of that year Bell had two hundred phones in operation in the city and by August the number had leapt to 1,300, though mostly these were two-way connections within offices – more like intercoms than telephones. The real breakthrough was the invention of the switchboard the following year. This allowed any phone user to talk to any other phone user in his district – and soon there were lots of those. By the early 1880s America had sixty thousand telephones in operation. In the next twenty years that figure would increase to over six million.

Phones were originally seen as providing services –

weather reports, stock market news, fire alarms, musical entertainment, even lullabies to soothe restless babies. Nobody saw them as being used primarily for gossip, social intercourse or keeping in touch with friends and family. The idea that you would chat by phone to someone you saw regularly anyway would have struck most people as absurd.

Because it was based on so many existing technologies, and because it proved so swiftly lucrative, a stream of people and companies challenged Bell's patents or simply ignored them. Luckily for Bell, his father-in-law, Gardiner Hubbard, was a brilliant and tireless lawyer. He launched or defended six hundred legal actions and won every one. The biggest was against the great and monolithic Western Union, which teamed up with Edison and Elisha Gray to try to get control of the phone business by whatever means it could. Western Union was by now a central component of the Vanderbilt empire, and the Vanderbilts just hated not to come first. They had every advantage – financial resources, an existing network of wires, technicians and engineers of the highest calibre – whereas Bell had only two things: a patent and Gardiner Hubbard. Hubbard sued for patent infringement and won the case in less than a year.

By the early twentieth century Bell's telephone company, renamed American Telephone & Telegraph, was the largest corporation in America, with stock worth $1,000 a share. (When the company was finally broken up in the 1980s to satisfy antitrust regulators, it was worth more than General Electric, General Motors, Ford, IBM, Xerox and Coca-Cola combined, and employed a million people.) Bell moved to Washington, DC, became a US citizen and devoted himself to worthwhile pursuits. Among other things, he invented the iron lung and experimented with telepathy. When President James A. Garfield was shot by a disgruntled lunatic in 1881, Bell was called in to see if he could help locate the bullet. He invented a metal detector, which worked beautifully in the laboratory but gave confused results at Garfield's bedside. It wasn't until much later it was realized that it had been reading the presidential bedsprings. In between these pursuits he helped found the journal *Science* and the National Geographic Society, for whose magazine he wrote under the memorable nom de plume of H. A. Largelamb (an anagram of 'A. Graham Bell').

Bell treated his friend and colleague Watson generously. Though he had no legal obligation to do so, he awarded Watson 10 per cent of the company, allowing Watson to retire rich at the age of just twenty-seven. Able to do anything he wanted, he devoted the rest of his life to doing just that. He travelled the world, read widely and took a degree in geology at MIT. He then started a shipyard, which quickly grew to employ four thousand men, producing a scale of stress and obligation that he hadn't wished for at all. So he sold the business, converted to Islam and became a follower of Edward Bellamy, a radical philosopher and quasi-Communist who for a short period in the 1880s enjoyed phenomenal esteem and popularity. Tiring of Bellamy, Watson moved to England in early middle age and took up acting, for which he showed an unexpected talent. He proved particularly adept at Shakespearean roles and performed many times at Stratford-upon-Avon before returning to America and a life of quiet retirement. He died, contented and rich, at his winter home on Pass-Grille Key, Florida, just shy of his eighty-first birthday in 1934.

Two other names deserve passing mentions with respect to the telephone. The first is Henry Dreyfuss. A young theatrical designer whose previous experience had been exclusively with designing stage sets and the interiors of cinemas, he was commissioned by the new AT&T in the early 1920s to design a new type of phone to replace the upright 'candlestick'. Dreyfuss came up with a startlingly squat, slightly boxy, sleekly modern design in which the handset rested laterally in a cradle slightly above and behind a large dial. This of course became the standard model throughout most of the world for most of the twentieth century. It was one of those things – rather like the Eiffel Tower – that did its job so well and seemed so inevitable that it takes some effort to remember that someone had to conceive it, but in fact nearly everything about it – the amount of resistance built into the dial, the low centre of gravity that made it next to impossible to knock over, the brilliant notion of having the hearing and speaking functions contained in a single handset – was the result of conscious and inspired thinking by a man who would normally never have been allowed anywhere near industrial design. Why AT&T engineers chose the youthful Dreyfuss for the project is forgotten, but they could not have made a better choice.

Dreyfuss didn't design the dial itself. That had already been designed in-house, in 1917, by a Bell employee, William G. Blauvelt. It was Blauvelt who decided to put three letters with most, but not all, of the numbers. He assigned no letters to the first hole because in those early days the telephone dial needed to be rotated slightly beyond the first hole to generate a signal initiating a call. So the sequence ran 2 (ABC), 3 (DEF), 4 (GHI) and so on. Blauvelt left out Q from the outset, because it would have always to be followed by a U, limiting its utility, and eventually dropped Z as well because it didn't feature enough in English to be useful. Every exchange was given a name, usually derived from the street or district in which it stood – Bensonhurst, Hollywood, Pennsylvania Avenue, for instance, though some exchanges used the names of trees or other objects – and the caller would ask the operator to be connected to 'Pennsylvania 6-5000' (as in the Glenn Miller tune) or 'Bensonhurst 5342'. When direct dialling was introduced in 1921, the names were reduced to two-letter prefixes and the convention became to capitalize those letters, as in HOllywood and BEnsonhurst.

The system had a certain charm, but became increasingly impractical. A lot of names – RHinelander or SYcamore, say – were susceptible to confusion among those whose spelling was not of the first order. Letters also made it difficult to introduce direct dialling from abroad since foreign phones didn't always come with letters, or had letters and numbers placed in different arrays. So the old system was slowly phased out in America, beginning in 1962. Today the letters serve only as a mnemonic device, enabling users to remember to dial 1-800-BUY-PIZZA or whatever.

As for the rectory, it is impossible to say when the telephone first came to the house, but its installation was almost certainly an event of great excitement for some early-twentieth-century rector and his family. The niche today is empty, however. The days when houses had a single phone at the foot of the stairs are long gone, and these days no one wants to talk in such an exposed and comfortless place.

III

For many people, the new age of enormous wealth in America meant being able to indulge slightly peculiar whims. George Eastman of Kodak film and camera fame never married and lived in an enormous house in Rochester, New York, with his mother, but kept many servants, including a house organist, who woke him – and presumably quite a lot of the rest of Rochester – with a dawn recital on a giant Aeolian organ. Eastman's other endearing quirk was that he had a private kitchen in the upstairs of the house where he liked to go and put on an apron and bake pies. Rather more extreme was John M. Longyear, of Marquette, Michigan, who, upon discovering that the Duluth, Mesabi & Iron Range Railroad had won the right to lay tracks to carry iron ore right past his house, had the entire property dismantled and packed up – 'house, shrubs, trees, fountains, ornamental waters, hedges and drives, gatekeeper's lodge, porte-cochere, greenhouses, and stables', in the words of one admiring biographer – and had the whole transferred to Brookline, Massachusetts, where he replicated his previous tranquil existence down to the last flower bulb, but without trains running past his windows. By comparison, the practice of one Frank Huntington Beebe of keeping two mansions side by side – one to live in, one to decorate over and over – seems admirably restrained.

For pure commitment to spending, it would be hard to beat Mrs E. T. Stotesbury – Queen Eva, as she was known. As an economic entity she was a wonder. She once spent half a million dollars taking a party of friends on a hunting trip simply to kill enough alligators to make a set of suitcases and hatboxes. On another occasion, she had the whole of the ground floor of El Mirasol, her Florida home, redecorated overnight, but neglected to inform her long-suffering husband so that when he awoke the next morning and came downstairs he was for some time not at all certain where he was.

The husband in question, Edward Townsend Stotesbury, made his fortune as an executive in the banking empire of J. P. Morgan. Though a distinguished banker, he didn't have a lot of presence: he was, in the words of one chronicler, 'a dignified hole in the atmosphere, the invisible hand that wrote the checks'. Mr Stotesbury was worth $75 million when he met Mrs Stotesbury in 1912 – she had recently exhausted the good will and bank balance of her first husband, Mr Oliver Eaton Cromwell – and with dizzying efficiency she helped him to spend $50 million of his fortune on new houses. She began with Whitemarsh Hall in Philadelphia, a house so big that no two accounts ever describe it in quite the same way. Depending on whose figures you credit, it had 154, 172 or 272 rooms. All agree that it had fourteen lifts, considerably more than most hotels. It cost Mr Stotesbury nearly $1 million a year just to maintain. He employed forty gardeners and ninety other staff there. The Stotesburys also had a summer cottage at Bar Harbor in Maine with a mere eighty rooms and twenty-eight baths, and their even more palatial Florida home, El Mirasol.

The architect of this last-named extravaganza was Addison Mizner, who is now almost entirely forgotten but was for a brief and glittering period perhaps the most sought-after, and certainly the most extraordinary, architect in America.

Mizner was born into an old and distinguished family in northern California. His brother was the playwright and impresario Wilson Mizner, who, among much else, co-wrote the song 'Frankie and Johnnie'. Before becoming an architect Addison led a remarkably exotic life: he painted magic lantern slides in Samoa, sold coffin handles in Shanghai, peddled Asian antiquities to rich Americans, panned for gold in the Klondike. Returning to the United States, he became a landscape architect on Long Island and finally took up conventional architecture in New York City, though he had to abandon that career abruptly when the authorities realized he had no training in the field – 'not even a correspondence course', in the words of one amazed observer – and no licence. So in 1918 he took his architectural practice to Palm Beach, Florida, which wasn't so fussy about qualifications, and began to build houses for very, very, very rich people.

In Palm Beach he befriended a young man named Paris Singer, one of twenty-four children of the sewing machine magnate Isaac M. Singer. Paris was an artist, aesthete, poet, businessman and gadfly who wielded mighty power in the neurotic world of Palm Beach society. Mizner designed for him the Everglades Club, which instantly became the most exclusive outpost south of the Mason-Dixon line. Only three hundred members were permitted, and Singer was ruthlessly selective in whom he allowed in. One woman was banished because he found her laugh annoying. When another member pleaded for clemency on behalf of her distressed friend, Singer told her to back off or be banished herself. She backed off.

Mizner sealed his success by securing a commission from Eva Stotesbury to build El Mirasol, a winter home of predictably vast extent. (The garage alone held forty cars.) It became a more or less permanent project because each time anyone else in Palm Beach threatened to build something bigger Mrs Stotesbury had Mizner slap on an extension, so that El Mirasol remained ever supreme.

It is fair to say that there has almost certainly never been another architect like Addison Mizner. He didn't believe in blueprints and was notoriously approximate in his instructions to his workmen, using expressions like 'about so high' and 'right about here'. He was famously forgetful too. Sometimes he installed doors that opened on to blank walls or, in one interesting case, revealed the interior of a chimney. The owner of a smart new boathouse on Lake Worth took possession of his prize only to discover that it had four blank walls and no way in at all. For a client named George S. Rasmussen, Mizner forgot to include a staircase and so put an external one up on an outside wall as an afterthought. This compelled Mr and Mrs Rasmussen to put on rainwear or other appropriate attire when they wished to go from floor to floor in their own home. When asked about this oversight, Mizner reportedly said it didn't matter because he didn't like Rasmussen anyway.

According to the *New Yorker*, his clients were expected to accept whatever he felt like building for them. They would present him with a large cheque, disappear for a

year or so and come back to take possession of a completed house, not knowing whether it was a Mexican-style
hacienda, a Venetian Gothic palace, a Moorish castle or
some festive combination of the three. Mizner was particularly infatuated with the worn look of Italian palazzos,
and 'aged' his own creations by boring artificial worm-
holes in the woodwork with a hand drill and defacing the
walls with artful stains meant to suggest some vague but
attractive Renaissance fungal growth. After his workmen
had created a well-crafted mantelpiece or doorway he
would often pick up a sledgehammer and knock off a
corner to give it an air of careworn venerability. Once he
used quicklime and shellac to age some leather chairs at
the Everglades Club. Unfortunately the body heat from the
guests warmed the shellac to a renewed gooeyness and
several found themselves stuck fast. 'I spent the whole
night pulling dames out of those goddam chairs,' recalled
a club waiter years later. Several women left the backs of
their dresses behind. Despite his idiosyncrasies, Mizner
was widely admired. He sometimes had as many as a
hundred projects on the go at once and was known to
design more than one house in a day. 'Some authors,'
wrote one chronicler in 1952, 'have classed his Everglades
Club, in Palm Beach, and his Cloister, in Boca Raton,
among the most beautiful buildings in America.' Frank
Lloyd Wright was a fan. As time passed, Addison Mizner
grew increasingly stout and eccentric. He was often seen
shopping in Palm Beach in his dressing gown and pyjamas. He died of a heart attack in 1933.

The Wall Street crash of 1929 brought an end to most
of the more notable excesses of the day. E. T. Stotesbury
was hit particularly hard. In a futile effort to calm his bank

balances, he begged his wife to limit her expenditure on entertainment to no more than $50,000 a month, but the redoubtable Mrs Stotesbury found that a cruel and impossible restriction. Mr Stotesbury was well on his way to insolvency when, providentially, he too dropped dead of a heart attack on 16 May 1938. Eva Stotesbury lived on until 1946, but had to sell jewellery, paintings and houses to keep herself modestly afloat. After her death a property developer bought El Mirasol and demolished it to put more houses on the same piece of land. Some twenty other Mizner houses in Palm Beach – the greater part of what he built, in short – have since been torn down as well.

The Vanderbilt mansions with which we began this survey didn't fare much better. The first of the Vanderbilt mansions on Fifth Avenue was built in 1883 and they were already being demolished by 1914. By 1947 all had gone. Not one of the family's country houses was lived in for a second generation.

Remarkably, almost nothing was saved from inside the buildings either. When the eponymous head of the Jacob Volk Wrecking Company was asked why he didn't salvage the priceless Carrara marble fireplaces, the Moorish tiles, the Jacobean panelling and other treasures contained within the William K. Vanderbilt residence on Fifth Avenue, he gave the questioner a withering look. 'I don't deal in second-hand stuff,' he said.

CHAPTER ELEVEN

The Study

I

IN 1897 A YOUNG ironmonger in Leeds named James Henry Atkinson took a small piece of wood, some stiff wire and not much else, and created one of the great contraptions of history: the mousetrap. It is one of several useful items – the paper clip, zip and safety pin are among the many others – that were invented in the late nineteenth century and were so nearly perfect from the outset that they have scarcely been improved upon in all the decades since. Atkinson sold his patent for £1,000, a very considerable sum for the time, and went on to invent other things, but nothing that secured him more money or immortality.

His mousetrap, manufactured under the proprietary name Little Nipper, has sold in the tens of millions, and continues to dispatch mice with brisk and brutal efficiency all over the world. We own several Little Nippers ourselves, and hear the dreadful snap of a terminal event far more often than we would wish to. Two or three times a week in

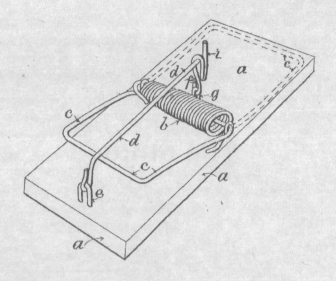

James Henry Atkinson's patent drawing for the 'Little Nipper'
mousetrap, 1899.

winter we catch them, nearly always in the same place, in this bleak, small room at the end of the house.

Although 'study' makes it sound like a significant space, it is really just a glorified storeroom, too dark and cold even in mild months to encourage much lingering. This is another room that doesn't appear on Edward Tull's original plans. Presumably Mr Marsham had it added because he needed an office in which to write his sermons and receive parishioners – particularly, I daresay, the more unrefined and muddy-booted of them; the squire's wife would almost certainly have been invited into the more comfortable parlour next door. These days the study is the final refuge of old furniture and pictures that one member of the marriage partnership admires and the other would happily see on a bonfire. Almost the only reason we go in there now is to check the mousetraps.

Mice are not easy creatures to figure. There is for a start their remarkable gullibility. When you consider how easily they are taught to find their way around mazes and other complex environments in labs, it is surprising that nowhere have they grasped that a dab of peanut butter on a wooden platform is a temptation worth resisting. No less mysterious in our house is their predilection – I might almost say their determination – for dying in this room, the study. It is not only the coldest room in the house but the furthest from the kitchen and all the biscuit crumbs and fugitive grains of rice and other morsels that end up on the floor and are there for the taking. Mice give the kitchen a wide berth (probably, it has been suggested to us, because our dog sleeps there) and mousetraps placed there, however sumptuously baited, capture nothing but dust. It is to the study that our mice seem fatefully drawn, which is why I thought this might be the appropriate place to consider some of the many living things that dwell with us.

Wherever there are humans there are mice. No other creatures live in more environments than the two of us do. House mice – *Mus musculus*, as they are known on formal occasions – are wondrously adaptable with regard to environment. Mice have even been found living in a refrigerated meat locker kept permanently chilled at −10C. They will eat almost anything. They are next to impossible to keep out of a house: a normal-sized adult can squeeze through an opening just ten millimetres (or three-eighths of an inch) wide, a gap so very tight that you would almost certainly bet good money that no grown mouse could possibly squeeze through it. They could. They can. They very often do.

Once in, mice breed prodigiously. In optimum conditions (and in most houses conditions seldom are other than optimal) a female mouse will produce her first litter six to eight weeks after birth and then monthly thereafter. A typical litter consists of six to eight offspring, so numbers can very quickly mount up. Two mice, breeding prolifically, could theoretically produce a million descendants in a year. That doesn't happen in our homes, thank goodness, but very occasionally mouse numbers do get completely out of control. Australia seems to be particularly propitious in this respect. In one famous outbreak in 1917, the town of Lascelles, in western Victoria, was literally overrun with mice after an unusually warm winter. For a short but memorably lively period, mice existed in Lascelles in such densities that every horizontal surface became a frantic mass of darting bodies. Every inanimate object writhed under a furry coating. There was nowhere to sit. Beds were unusable. 'The people are sleeping on tables to avoid the mice,' one newspaper reported. 'The women are kept in a constant state of terror, and the men are kept busy preventing the mice from crawling down their coat collars.' Over 1,500 tons of mice – perhaps a hundred million individuals – were killed before the outbreak was defeated.

Even in comparatively small numbers mice can do a lot of damage, particularly in food storage areas. Mice and other rodents consume about a tenth of America's annual grain crop – an astonishing proportion. Each mouse voids about fifty pellets a day, and that results in a lot of contamination, too. Because of the impossibility of achieving perfection in storage, hygiene regulations in most places allow up to two faecal pellets per pint of grain – a thought to bear in mind the next time you look at a loaf of whole-grain bread.

Mice are notable vectors of disease. Hantavirus, a family of respiratory and renal disorders that are always disagreeable and often lethal, is particularly associated with mice and their droppings. (The name *hanta* comes from a river in Korea where the disease was first noted by Westerners during the Korean War.) Fortunately hantavirus is fairly rare since few of us breathe in the frail vapours of mouse droppings, but if you get down on your hands and knees in the vicinity of infected waste – to crawl around in an attic, say, or set a trap in a cupboard – you run the risk in many countries of infection. Globally, over 200,000 people a year are infected and it kills between 30 and 80 per cent of victims, depending on how quickly and well they are treated. In the United States, between thirty and forty people a year contract hantavirus, and about a third die. In Great Britain, happily, the disease remains unrecorded. Mice have also been implicated in occurrences of salmonellosis, leptospirosis, tularemia, plague, hepatitis, Q fever and murine typhus, among many other diseases. In short, there are very good reasons for not wanting mice in your house.

Almost everything that could be said of mice applies equally, but with multiples, to their cousins the rats. Rats are more common in and around our houses than we care to think. Even the best homes sometimes have them. They come in two principal varieties in the temperate world: the emphatically named *Rattus rattus*, which is alternatively (and tellingly) known as the roof rat, and *Rattus norvegicus*, or the Norway rat.* The roof rat likes to be up high – in trees and attics principally – so the scurryings you hear across your bedroom ceiling late at night may not be, I'm sorry to say, mice. Fortunately, roof rats are rather more retiring than Norway rats, which live in burrows and are the ones you see scuttling through sewers in movies or prowling around rubbish bins in back alleys.

We associate rats with conditions of poverty, but rats are no fools and they sensibly prefer a well-heeled home to a poor one. What's more, modern homes make a delectable environment for rats. 'The high protein content that characterizes the more affluent neighbourhoods is particularly enticing,' James M. Clinton, a US health official, wrote some years ago in a public health report that remains one of the most compelling, if unnerving, surveys ever taken of the behaviour of domestic rats. It isn't merely that modern houses are full of food, but that many of them dispose of it in ways that make it practically irresistible. As Clinton put it: 'Today's garbage disposals in homes pour out a bountiful, uniform, and well-balanced food supply for rats.' According to Clinton, one of the oldest of all urban legends, that rats come into homes by way of toilets, is in fact true. In one outbreak, rats in Atlanta invaded several homes in wealthy neighbourhoods, and bit more than a few people. 'On several occasions,' Clinton reported, 'rats were found alive in covered toilet bowls.' If ever there was a reason to put the lid down, this could be it.

---

* The Norway rat was often in the past called the brown rat and the roof rat has been called the black rat, but the names are misleading – the colour of a rat's fur isn't a reliable indicator of anything – so rodentologists now nearly always avoid the terms.

Once in a domestic environment, most rats show little fear 'and will even deliberately approach and make contact with motionless persons'. They are particularly emboldened in the presence of infants and the elderly. 'I have verified the case of a helpless woman attacked by rats while she slept,' Clinton reported. He went on: 'The victim, an elderly hemiplegic, haemorrhaged extensively from multiple rat-bite wounds and died despite emergency hospital treatment. Her 17-year-old granddaughter asleep in the same room at the time of the attack was unharmed.'

Rat bites are almost certainly under-reported because only the most serious cases attract attention, but even using the most conservative figures at least 14,000 people in the United States are attacked by rats each year. Rats have very sharp teeth and can become aggressive if cornered, biting 'savagely and blindly, in the manner of mad dogs', in the words of one rat authority. A motivated rat can leap as high as three feet – high enough to be considerably unnerving if it is coming your way and is out of sorts.

The usual defence against rat outbreaks is poison. Poisons are often designed around the curious fact that rats cannot regurgitate, so they will retain poisons that other animals – pet dogs and cats, for instance – would quickly throw up. Anti-coagulants are commonly used too, but there is evidence to suggest that rats are developing resistance to them.

Rats are smart, too, and often work cooperatively. At the former Gansevoort poultry market in Greenwich Village, New York, pest control authorities could not understand how rats were stealing eggs without breaking them, so one night an exterminator sat in hiding to watch.

What he saw was that one rat would embrace an egg with all four legs, then roll over on his back. A second rat would then drag the first rat by its tail to their burrow, where they could share their prize in peace. In similar manner workers at a packing plant discovered how sides of meat, hanging from hooks, were knocked to the floor and devoured night after night. An exterminator named Irving Billig watched and found that a swarm of rats formed a pyramid underneath a side of meat, and one rat scrambled to the top of the heap and leapt on to the meat from there. He then climbed to the top of the side of meat and gnawed his way through it around the hook until the meat dropped to the floor, at which point hundreds of waiting rats fell ravenously upon it.

When eating, rats will unhesitatingly gorge if plenty is available, but they can also get by on very little if necessary. An adult rat can survive on less than an ounce of food a day and as little as half an ounce of water. For pleasure they seem to enjoy gnawing on wires. Nobody knows why because wires clearly are not nutritious and offer nothing in return except the very real prospect of a fatal shock. Still rats can't stop themselves. It is believed that as many as a quarter of all fires that can't otherwise be explained may be attributed to rats chewing on wires.

When they are not eating, rats are likely to be having sex. Rats have a lot of sex – up to twenty times a day. If a male rat can't find a female, he will happily – or at least willingly – find relief in a male. Female rats are robustly fecund. The average adult female Norway rat produces 35.7 offspring a year, in litters of six to nine at a time. In the right conditions, however, a female rat can produce a new litter of up to twenty babies every three weeks.

Theoretically a pair of breeding rats could start a dynasty of 15,000 new rats in a year. In practice, that doesn't happen because rats die a lot. Like many animals, they are more or less programmed by evolution to expire fairly easily. The annual mortality rate is 95 per cent. A determined extermination campaign will normally reduce rat populations by 75 per cent or so, but once the campaign stops the rat population will recover in six months or less. In short, an individual rat hasn't got great prospects in life, but his family is effectively ineradicable.

Mostly, however, rats are just immensely lazy. They spend up to twenty hours a day asleep, normally emerging to look for food just after sunset. They seldom venture more than 150 feet if they can possibly help it. This may be part of a survival policy, for mortality rates rocket whenever they are compelled to migrate.

When rats are mentioned in a historical context, the one topic that invariably follows is plague. This may be not quite fair. For one thing, rats don't actually infect us with plague. Rather, they harbour the fleas (that harbour the bacteria) that spread the disease. Plague kills rats just as energetically as it kills us. Indeed, it kills many other things, too. One of the signs of a plague outbreak is lots of dead dogs, cats, cows and other animals scattered about. Fleas much prefer the blood of furry creatures to the blood of humans, and generally turn to us only when nothing better is available. For that reason, modern epidemiologists in places where plague is still common – notably parts of Africa and Asia – generally avoid culling rats and other rodents too enthusiastically during outbreaks. In a very real sense there is no more welcome time for rats to be around than when plague is rampant. Anyway, more than seventy other creatures besides rats – including rabbits, voles, marmots, squirrels and mice – have been implicated in the spread of plague. Moreover, possibly the very worst plague outbreak in history doesn't seem to have involved rats at all, at least not in England. Long before the notorious Black Death of the fourteenth century, an even more ferocious plague devastated Europe in the seventh century. In some places almost everyone died. Bede, in his history of England written in the following century, says that when the pestilence reached his monastery at Jarrow, it killed everyone except the abbot and one boy – a mortality rate considerably over 90 per cent. Whatever was the source of its spread, it wasn't rats, it seems. No rat bones from the seventh century have been found anywhere in Britain – and people have looked hard. One excavation in Southampton collected fifty thousand animal bones from in and around a cluster of dwellings; none came from a rat.

It has been suggested that some outbreaks attributed to plague may not have been plague at all, but ergotism, a fungal disease of grain. Plague didn't come at all to many cold, dry northern places – Iceland escaped entirely, as did much of Norway, Sweden and Finland – even though those places had rats. At the same time, plague was associated with miserably wet years almost everywhere it appeared – the very circumstances that would tend to produce ergotism. The one problem with the theory is that the symptoms of ergotism are not much like those of plague. It may be that the term 'pestilence' was used loosely or vaguely and simply misinterpreted by later historians.

Even just a generation or two ago, rat numbers in urban areas may have been considerably higher than now. The *New Yorker* reported in 1944 that a team of exterminators working in a well-known (but carefully unidentified) hotel in Manhattan caught 236 rats in the basement and sub-basement in three nights. At about the same time, rats all but took over the aforementioned Gansevoort poultry market. They invaded in such numbers that secretaries sometimes found rats leaping out of their desks when the drawers were opened. Exterminators were called in and caught four thousand rats in a matter of days, but they couldn't make the market rat-proof. In the end it was shut down.

It is commonly written that there is one rat for every human being in a typical city, but studies have shown that to be an exaggeration. The actual figure is more like one rat for every three dozen people. Unfortunately, that still adds up to a lot of rats – roughly a quarter of a million for greater London, for instance.

II

The real life in your house is on a much smaller scale. Down at the realm of the very tiny, your house teems with life: it is a veritable rainforest for crawling, clambering things. Armies of tiny creatures patrol the boundless jungles of your carpet fibres, paraglide amid floating motes of dust, crawl across the bedsheets at night to graze upon the vast, delicious, gently heaving mountain of slumbering flesh that is you. These creatures exist in numbers you cannot comfortably imagine. Your bed alone, if it is averagely clean, averagely old, averagely dimensioned and turned averagely often (which is to say almost never), is likely to be home to some two million tiny bed mites, too small to be seen with the naked eye but unquestionably there. It has been calculated that if your pillow is six years old (which is the average age for a pillow), one-tenth of its weight will be made up of sloughed skin, living and dead mites, and mite dung – or frass, as it is known to entomologists.

Clambering among the bed mites, on a much more gigantic scale, might also these days be lice, for it appears that these once-nearly-vanquished creatures are making a comeback. Like rats, lice come in two principal varieties: *Pediculus capitas*, or head lice, and *Pediculus corporis*, or body lice. These latter are relative newcomers on the bodily irritants scene. They evolved some time in the last 50,000 years from head lice. Of the two, head lice are much smaller (they are about the size of a sesame seed, and actually look much the same) and so harder to detect. An adult female head louse will lay three to six eggs per day. Each louse can live for about thirty days. The empty shells of dead lice are called nits. Lice have developed an increasing resistance to pesticides, but the greatest reason for their increase, it seems, is low-temperature wash cycles in washing machines. As Dr John Maunder of the British Medical Entomology Centre has put it: 'If you wash lousy clothing at low temperatures, all you get is cleaner lice.'

Historically, the most common bedroom dread was bedbugs – *Cimex lectularius*, as the little bloodsuckers are scientifically known. Bedbugs made sure that no one ever slept alone. In former times, people were driven half mad by bugs and the desire to be rid of them. When Jane

Carlyle discovered that bedbugs had invaded her house-keeper's bed, she had the bed taken to pieces and carried to the garden where each piece was washed with chloride of lime, then immersed in water for two days to drown any bugs that survived the disinfectant. The bedding mean-while was taken to a sealed room and dusted repeatedly with disinfectant powder until no more bugs emerged. Only then was it put back together and the housekeeper allowed to resume a normal night's sleep, in a bed that was now almost certainly at least mildly toxic to her as well as to any insect life that dared to creep back in.

Even when beds weren't actively infested, it was routine to take them apart at least once a year and paint them with disinfectant or varnish as a precaution. Manufacturers often advertised how quickly and easily their beds could be dismantled for an annual maintenance. Brass beds became popular in the nine-teenth century not because brass was suddenly thought a stylish metal for bedsteads but because it gave no harbour to bedbugs.

Like lice, bedbugs are making an unwelcome come-back. For most of the twentieth century they were virtually extinct in most of Europe and America thanks to the rise of modern insecticides, but in recent years they have been vigorously rebounding. No one is sure why. It may have something to do with more international travel – people bringing them home in their suitcases and so on – or that they are developing greater resistance to the things we spray at them. Whatever it is, they are suddenly being noticed again. 'Some of the best hotels in New York have them,' the *New York Times* quoted one expert as saying in a report in 2005. The *Times* article went on to note that because most people have no experience of bedbugs and don't know what to look out for, they are likely to discover they are infested only when they wake up and find themselves lying in a swarm of them.

If you had the right equipment and a peculiar measure of motivation, you could find numberless millions of other dinky creatures living with you – vast tribes of isopods, pleopods, endopodites, myriapods, chilopods, pauropods and other all-but-invisible specks. Some of these little creatures are practically ineradicable. An insect named *Niptus hololeucus* has been found living in cayenne pepper and in the cork stoppers of cyanide bottles. Some, like flour mites and cheese mites, dine with you pretty regularly.

Move down to the next level of living things, to the world of microbes, and the numbers swell beyond counting. Your skin alone is home to about a trillion bacteria. Inside you are many thousands of trillions more, many of them engaged in necessary and helpful tasks like breaking down food in the gut. Altogether you hold about a hundred quadrillion bacterial cells in your body. If you took them out and put them in a pile they would weigh about four pounds. Microbes are so ubiquitous that we easily forget that a large part of every modern house is taken up with heavy metal objects – refrigerators, dishwashers, washing machines – that exist exclusively to kill or suppress them. Getting germs out of our lives is a kind of endless daily quest for most of us.

The most celebrated germ expert in the world is almost certainly Dr Charles P. Gerba of the University of Arizona who is so devoted to the field that he gave one of his children the middle name Escherichia, after the bacterium *Escherichia coli*. Dr Gerba established some years ago that household germs are not always most numerous where you would expect them to be. In one famous survey he measured bacterial content in different rooms in various houses and found that typically the cleanest surface of all in the average house was the toilet seat. That is because it is wiped down with disinfectant more often than any other surface. By contrast the average desktop has five times more bacteria living on it than the average toilet seat.

The dirtiest area of all was the kitchen sink, closely followed by the kitchen counter, and the filthiest object was the kitchen wash cloth. Most kitchen cloths are drenched in bacteria, and using them to wipe counters (or plates or breadboards or greasy chins or any other surface) merely transfers microbes from one place to another, affording them new chances to breed and proliferate. The second most efficient way of spreading germs, Gerba found, is to flush a toilet with the lid up. That spews billions of microbes into the air. Many stay in the air, float-ing like tiny soap bubbles, waiting to be inhaled, for up to two hours; others settle on things like your toothbrush. That is, of course, yet another good reason for putting the lid down.

Almost certainly the most memorable finding of all of recent years with respect to microbes was when an enter-prising middle-school student in Florida compared the quality of water in the toilets at her local fast food restaurants with the quality of the ice in the soft drinks, and found that in 70 per cent of outlets she surveyed the toilet water was cleaner than the ice.

What is perhaps most remarkable about all these

multitudinous life forms is how little we sometimes know about them – and how recently what we do know has been learned. Bed mites weren't discovered at all until 1965, even though millions of them exist in every bed. As late as 1947, a medical correspondent for the *New Yorker* could write: 'Mites are only infrequently found in this country and until recently were practically unknown in New York City.' Then in the late 1940s residents of an apartment complex called Kew Gardens in Queens, New York, began sickening in large numbers with flu-like symptoms. The malady was known as 'the Kew Gardens mystery fever' until an astute exterminator noticed that mice were also getting sick and discovered on close inspection that tiny mites living in their fur – the very mites that were supposed not to exist in America in large numbers – were transmitting rickettsial pox to apartment dwellers.

Similar degrees of ignorance have long applied to many larger creatures, not least one of the most important and least understood of all animals that are sometimes found in modern houses: bats. Hardly anybody likes bats, which is truly unfortunate because bats do much more good than harm. They eat enormous quantities of insects, to the benefit of crops and people alike. Brown bats, the most common species in America, consume up to six hundred mosquitoes per hour. Tiny pipistrelle bats – which weigh no more than a small coin – hoover up three thousand insects apiece in the course of a night's swoopings. Without bats there would be a lot more midges in Scotland, chiggers in North America and fevers in the tropics. Forest trees would be chewed to pieces. Crops would need more pesticides. The natural world would become a very stressed place. Bats are also vital to the life cycles of many wild plants through pollination and seed dispersal. A seba bat – a tiny bat in South America – will eat as many as sixty thousand tiny seeds per night. The seed distribution of a single colony of seba bats – about four hundred bats – can produce nine million seedlings of new fruit trees a year. Without the bats, those fruit trees wouldn't happen. Bats are also critical to the survival in the wild of avocados, balsa, bananas, breadfruit, cashews, cloves, dates, figs, guavas, mangoes, peaches and saguaro cactus, among others.

There are far more bats in the world than most people realize. In fact, about a quarter of all mammal species – some eleven hundred in all – are bats. They range in size from tiny bumblebee bats, which really are no bigger than bumblebees and therefore are the smallest of all mammals, up to the magnificent flying foxes of Australia and south Asia, which can have wingspans of six feet.

At times in the past attempts have been made to capitalize on bats' special qualities. In the Second World War, the American military invested a great deal of time and money in an extraordinary plan to arm bats with tiny incendiary bombs and to release them in vast numbers – as many as one million at a time – from planes over Japan. The idea was that the bats would roost in eaves and roof spaces, and that soon afterwards tiny detonators on timers would go off and they would burst into flames, causing hundreds of thousands of fires.

Creating sufficiently tiny bombs and timers required a great deal of experiment and ingenuity, but finally in the spring of 1943 work had progressed sufficiently that a trial was set to take place at Muroc Lake, California. It would be putting it mildly to say that matters didn't go quite to plan.

Remarkably for an experiment, the bats were fully armed with live bomblets when released. This proved not to be a good idea. The bats failed to light on any of the designated targets, but did destroy all the hangars and most of the storage buildings at the Muroc Lake airport, as well as an army general's car. The general's report on the day's events must have made interesting reading. In any case, the programme was cancelled soon afterwards.

A rather less hare-brained but ultimately no more successful plan to make use of bats was conceived by a Dr Charles A. R. Campbell of Tulane University Medical School. Campbell's idea was to build giant 'bat towers', where bats would roost and breed, and then go out to eat mosquitoes. This, Campbell believed, would substantially reduce malaria and also provide guano in commercially worthwhile quantities. Several of the towers were built and some actually still stand, if precariously, but they never worked. Bats, it turns out, don't like to be told where to live.

In America, bats were persecuted by health officials for years because of inflated – and at times irrational – concerns that they carried rabies. The story began in October 1951 when an anonymous woman in west Texas, the wife of a cotton planter, came across a bat in the road outside her house. She thought it was dead, but when she bent to look at it, it leapt up and bit her on the arm. This was highly unusual. American bats are all insectivores and had never been known to bite a human. She and her husband disinfected and dressed the wound – it was just a small one – and didn't think anything more of it. Three weeks later the woman was admitted to a hospital in Dallas in a delirious condition. She was 'wildly agitated' and unable to speak or swallow. Her eyes were filled with terror. She was beyond help. Rabies can be successfully treated, but only if the treatment is immediate. Once symptoms start, it's too late. After four days of unutterable distress, the woman slipped into a coma and died.

Now scattered cases of people being bitten by rabid bats began to crop up in other locations – two in Pennsylvania, one each in Florida, Massachusetts and California, two more in Texas. All this was over the space of four years, so it was hardly rampant, but it did cause concern. Finally, on New Year's Day 1956, a public health official in Texas, Dr George C. Menzies, entered a hospital in Austin with rabies symptoms. Menzies had been studying caves in central Texas for evidence of rabies-bearing bats, but hadn't been bitten or otherwise exposed to rabies as far as anyone knew. Yet somehow he became infected, and after just two days in care he died in the usual hideous manner, in discomfort and terror, his eyes like saucers.

The case was widely reported and resulted in a kind of vengeful hysteria. Officials at the highest levels concluded that extermination was an urgent and necessary step. Bats became the most friendless creatures in America. Years of steady persecution followed, and bat populations in many places suffered shocking depredations. In one case, the largest bat colony in the world, at Eagle Creek, Arizona, experienced a population fall from thirty million to three thousand in a matter of years.

Merlin D. Tuttle, America's leading bat authority and founder of Bat Conservation International, a charity for bats, related a story, reported in the New Yorker in 1988, of a case in which public health officials in Texas told a farmer that if he didn't kill the bats in a cave on his land,

he and his family and their livestock would be at grave risk
of contracting rabies. On their instructions, the farmer
filled the cave with kerosene and lit it. The conflagration
killed about a quarter of a million bats. When Tuttle interviewed the farmer later, he asked him how long his family
had owned the property. About a century, the farmer
replied. And in all that time, Tuttle went on, had they ever
been troubled by rabies? No, the farmer responded.

'And when I explained to him the value of the bats and
what he'd done, he actually broke down and cried,' Tuttle
said. In fact, as Tuttle pointed out, 'more people die of
food poisoning at church picnics annually than have died
in all history from contact with bats'.

Today bats are among the most endangered of all
animals. About a quarter of bat species are on extinction
watch lists – that is an amazingly and indeed appallingly
high proportion for such a vital creature – and over forty
species teeter on the very edge of extinction. Because bats
are so reclusive and often so difficult to study, much about
their population numbers remains uncertain. In Britain,
for example, it is uncertain whether there are seventeen
surviving species of bat or sixteen. Authorities haven't got
enough evidence to decide whether the greater mouse-
eared bat is extinct or just lying very low.

What *is* certain is that matters everywhere may be
about to get much worse. In early 2006 a highly lethal new
fungal disease, called white-nose syndrome (because it
turns the hair around the victims' noses white), was discovered among hibernating bats in a cave in New York.
The disease kills up to 95 per cent of the bats that it infects.
It has now spread to half a dozen other states and will
almost certainly spread further. As of late 2009, scientists

still had no idea what it is about the fungus that kills its host, how it spreads, where it originated or how to stop it. All that is certain is that the fungus is specially adapted to survive in cold conditions – not good news for the bats of much of North America, Europe and Asia.

Lots of creatures are so unassuming, and often so little studied, that we barely notice when they go extinct. Britain lost twenty species of moth in the twentieth century, and yet there was hardly an outcry. About 75 per cent of species of British moth have undergone a population decline. Agricultural intensification and more powerful pesticides are among the probable causes for population declines, but no one actually knows. Butterfly species are similarly suffering, with at least eight populations at all-time lows in Britain, again for reasons that can only be supposed. The knock-on effects may be considerable. Birds are often perilously dependent on healthy moth and butterfly populations. A single family of blue tits can require 15,000 caterpillars in a season. So declines in insect populations will mean declines in bird populations, too.

III

The direction of movement for populations is not always downwards, it must be said. Sometimes populations boom, occasionally in ways that shape history. Never has that been more true than in 1873, when farmers in the western United States and across the plains of Canada experienced a devastating visitation unlike anything anyone had ever seen before. From out of nowhere came swarms of Rocky Mountain locusts – great chirring masses of motion and appetite that blotted out the sun and devoured everything in their path. Wherever the swarms landed, the effects were appalling. They stripped clean fields and orchards, and devoured almost everything they lighted on. They ate leather and canvas, laundry off lines, the wool off the backs of living sheep, even the handles of wooden tools. One amazed witness reported them landing in such numbers that they put out a good-sized fire. It was, according to most witnesses, like experiencing the end of the world. The noise was deafening. One swarm was estimated as being 1,800 miles long and perhaps 110 miles wide. It took five days to pass. It is thought to have contained at least 10 billion individual insects, but other estimates have put the figure as high as 12.5 *trillion*, with a massed weight of 27.5 million tons. It was almost certainly the largest gathering of living things ever seen on Earth. Nothing would deflect them. When two swarms met, they would push through each other and emerge in unbroken ranks on the other side. No amount of battering them with shovels or spraying with insecticide made any measurable impact.

This was exactly at a time when people were moving in vast numbers into the western United States and Canada, and creating a new wheatbelt across the great plains. Nebraska's population, for instance, went from 28,000 to over a million in one generation. Altogether four million new farms were created west of the Mississippi in the period after the US Civil War, and many of these new farmers were heavily indebted with mortgages on their houses and land and with loans on flotillas of new equipment – reapers, threshers, harvesters and so on – needed to farm on an industrial scale. Hundreds of thousands of others had invested huge sums in railways, grain silos and businesses of every type to support the booming populations of the west. Now vast numbers of people were being literally wiped out.

At the end of the summer, the locusts vanished, and a measure of hopeful relief crept in. But the optimism was misplaced. The locusts returned in the following three summers, each time in larger numbers than before. The unnerving thought that life in the west might become untenable began to take hold. No less alarming was the thought that the locusts could spread eastwards and begin to devour the even richer farmlands of the Midwest and east. There has never been a darker or more helpless moment in the whole of American history.

And then it all just came to an end. In 1877, the swarms were much reduced and the locusts within them seemed curiously lethargic. The next year they didn't come at all. The Rocky Mountain locust (its formal name was *Melanoplus spretus*) didn't just retreat, but vanished altogether. It was a miracle. The last living specimen was found in Canada in 1902. None has been seen since.

It took more than a century for scientists to work out what had happened, but it appears that the locusts retired every winter to hibernate and breed in the loamy soils abutting the winding rivers of the high plains east of the Rockies. These, it turned out, were the very places where new waves of incoming farmers were transforming the land through ploughing and irrigation – actions that killed the locusts and their pupae as they slept. They couldn't have devised a more effective remedy if they had spent millions of dollars and studied the matter for years. No extinction can ever be called a good thing, but this was probably as close to positive as such an event can get.

Had the locusts continued to thrive, the world would have been a very different place. Global agriculture and commerce, the peopling of the west and ultimately the fate of our old rectory, as well as almost everything else beyond, connected to and in between, would have been profoundly reshaped in ways we can scarcely imagine. American farmers in the last quarter of the nineteenth century were already gripped with a form of angry populism that was deeply resentful of banks and big business, and these feelings were widely echoed in the cities, particularly among newly arrived immigrants. Had agriculture collapsed sufficiently to produce widespread hardship and hunger, there might well have been an overwhelming rush to socialism. There were certainly many who ardently desired such an outcome.

Instead, of course, matters settled down, the west resumed its long expansion, America became the breadbasket of the world and the British countryside went into a long tailspin from which it has never entirely recovered. That is a story that we shall get to in due course, but meanwhile let's step into the garden and consider why so much of that landscape was, and indeed remains, so very attractive to be in.

CHAPTER TWELVE

The Garden

I

IN 1730, QUEEN CAROLINE of Anspach, the industrious and ever-improving wife of King George II, did a rather daring thing. She ordered the diversion of the little River Westbourne in London to make a large pond in the middle of Hyde Park. The pond, called the Serpentine, is still there and still much admired by visitors, though almost none realize quite how historic a body of water it is.

This was the first manmade pond in the world designed not to look manmade. It is hard to imagine now quite what a radical step this was. Previously all artificial bodies of water were rigorously geometrical – either boxily rectangular, in the manner of a reflecting pool, or circular, like the Round Pond in neighbouring Kensington Gardens, built just two years earlier. Now here was an artificial body of water that was curvilinear and graceful, that meandered beguilingly and looked as if it had been formed, in a moment of careless serendipity, by nature.

People were enchanted by the deception and flocked to admire it. The royal family were so pleased that for a time they kept two outsized yachts on the Serpentine even though there was barely space for them to turn without colliding.

For Queen Caroline, it was a rare popular triumph, for her gardening ambitions were often ill-judged. In the same period, she appropriated two hundred acres of Hyde Park for the grounds of Kensington Palace, banishing private citizens from its leafy paths except on Saturdays, and then only for part of the year and only if they looked respectable. This became, not surprisingly, a source of widespread resentment. The queen also toyed with the idea of making the whole of St James's Park private, and asked her prime minister, Robert Walpole, how much that would cost. 'Only a crown, madam,' he replied with a thin smile.

So the Serpentine was an immediate success, and the credit for it – certainly for its engineering, probably also for its conception – belongs to a shadowy figure named Charles Bridgeman. Where exactly this man of dashing genius came from has always been a mystery. He appeared, seemingly from out of nowhere, in 1709 with a set of signed drawings of an expert calibre for some proposed landscaping works at Blenheim Palace. Everything about him before this is conjectural: where he was born, the timing and circumstances of his upbringing, where he acquired his considerable skills. Historians can't even agree whether to spell his name Bridgeman or Bridgman. Yet for the thirty years after he came on this scene he was everywhere that gardening of a high order was needed. He worked with all the leading architects – John Vanbrugh,

Charles Bridgeman (fourth from left, holding garden plan) in William Hogarth's The Rake's Levée.

William Kent, James Gibbs, Henry Flitcroft – on projects all over England. He was largely responsible for designing and laying out Stowe, the most celebrated garden of the day. He was appointed royal gardener and managed the gardens at Hampton Court, Windsor, Kew and all the royal parks throughout the king's domain. He created Richmond Gardens. He designed the Round Pond and the Serpentine. He surveyed and designed for estates all over the south of England. Wherever there was important gardening to be done, Bridgeman was there. No individual portrait of him exists, but he does appear, rather unexpectedly, in the second picture of Hogarth's sequence *The Rake's Progress*, where he is one of several people, including a tailor, dancing instructor and jockey, importuning the young rake to invest his money with them.* Even there, however, Bridgeman looks uncomfortable and stiff, as if he has somehow wandered into the wrong painting.

Gardening was already a huge business in England when Bridgeman came along. London's Brompton Park Nursery, which stood on land now occupied by the mighty museums of South Kensington, covered one hundred acres, and produced enormous volumes of shrubbery, exotic plants and other green things for stately homes up and down the country. But these were gardens of a very different type from those we know today. For one thing, they were luridly colourful: paths were filled with coloured gravel, statues were brightly painted, bedding plants were chosen for the intensity of their hues. Nothing was natural

---

* The pictures chart the decline of a wealthy young man, so there is a certain aptness in the fact that they were owned, before his (and his house's) downfall, by William Beckford of Fonthill Abbey.

or understated. Hedges were shaped into galloping topiary. Paths and borders were kept rigorously straight and lined with fastidiously clipped box or yew. Formality ruled. The grounds of stately homes weren't so much parks as exercises in geometry.

Now quite suddenly all of that order and artificiality was being swept away, and the fashion became to make things look natural. Where this impulse came from isn't at all easy to say. The early eighteenth century was a time when nearly all young men of privileged bearing travelled through Europe on grand tours. Practically without exception they returned home full of enthusiasm for the formal orders of the classical world and a burning desire to reproduce them in an English setting. Architecturally, they longed for nothing more than to be proudly and unimaginatively derivative. Where the grounds were concerned, however, they rejected rigidity and began to build an entirely new kind of world outdoors. For those who believe the British have gardening genius embedded in their chromosomes, this was the age that seemed to prove it.

One of the heroes of this movement was our old friend Sir John Vanbrugh. Because he was self-taught, he was able to bring a fresh perspective to matters. He considered the setting of his houses as no architect had before, for instance. At Castle Howard, almost the first thing he did was rotate the house ninety degrees on its axis, so that it faced north–south rather than east–west, as it had under earlier plans drawn up by William Talman. This made it impossible to provide the traditional long approach to the house, with glimpsed views across fields as a kind of visual foreplay, but had the compensating virtue that the house sat far more comfortably in the landscape and the occupants enjoyed an infinitely more satisfying outlook on the world beyond. This was a radical reversal of traditional orientation. Before this, houses weren't built to enjoy a view. They *were* the view.

To maximize important prospects, Vanbrugh introduced another inspired feature – the folly, a building designed with no other purpose in mind than to complete a view and provide a happy spot for the wandering eye to settle. His Temple of the Four Winds at Castle Howard was the first of its type. To this he added the most ingenious and transformative innovation of all: the ha-ha. A ha-ha is a sunken fence, a kind of palisade designed to separate the private part of an estate from its working parts without the visual intrusion of fence or hedge. It was an idea adapted from French military fortifications (where Vanbrugh would have first encountered them during his years of imprisonment). Because they were unseen until the last instant, people tended to discover them with a startled cry of 'Ha-ha!' – and hence, so it is said, the name. The ha-ha wasn't simply a practical device for keeping cows off the lawn, but an entirely new way of perceiving the world. Grounds, garden, parkland, estate – all became part of a continuous whole. Suddenly the attractive part of a property didn't have to end at the lawn's edge. It could run on to the horizon.

One less happy practice Vanbrugh introduced with Carlisle at Castle Howard was that of razing estate villages and moving the occupants elsewhere if they were deemed to be insufficiently picturesque or too intrusive. At Castle Howard, Vanbrugh cleared away not only an existing village but also a church and the ruined castle from which the new house took its name. Soon villages up and down the country were being levelled to make way for more extensive houses and unimpeded views. It was almost as if a rich person couldn't begin work on a grand house until he had thoroughly disrupted at least a few dozen menial lives. Oliver Goldsmith lamented the practice in a long, sentimental poem, 'The Deserted Village', inspired by a visit to Nuneham Park in Oxfordshire when the first Earl Harcourt was in the process of erasing an ancient village to create a more picturesque space for his new house. Here at least fate exacted an interesting revenge. After completing the work, the earl went for a stroll around his newly reconfigured grounds, but failed to recall where the old village well had been, fell into it and drowned.*

Vanbrugh didn't necessarily invent any of these things. Horace Walpole for one credited Bridgeman with inventing the ha-ha, and it may be for all we know that he gave the idea to Vanbrugh. But then it may equally be, for all we know, that Vanbrugh gave it to him. All that can be said is that by the early 1710s people suddenly had lots of ideas for how to improve the landscape, principally by giving it an air of greater naturalism. One event that seems to have contributed was a storm of 1711 known as the Great Blow, which knocked down trees all over the country and caused a lot of people to notice, evidently for the first time, how agreeable a backdrop they had made. In any case, people suddenly became unusually devoted to nature.

* In the following century Nuneham Park gained a second distinction. On a visit there in the summer of 1862, with a party that included Alice Liddell, daughter of the dean of his Oxford college, Christ Church, Charles Lutwidge Dodgson began the stories that became *Alice's Adventures in Wonderland*.

Joseph Addison, the essayist, became the voice of the movement with a series of articles in the *Spectator* called 'The Pleasures of the Imagination', in which he suggested that nature provided all the beauty one could want already. It just needed a bit of management, or as he put it in a famous line: 'A Man might make a pretty Landskip of his own Possessions.' (The newish word 'landscape', you will gather, hadn't quite settled in yet.) 'I do not know whether I am singular in my Opinion,' he went on, 'but, for my own part, I would rather look upon a Tree in all its Luxuriancy and Diffusion of Boughs and Branches, then when it is thus cut and trimmed into a Mathematical Figure,' and all at once the world seemed to agree with him.

Stately homeowners everywhere gladly followed these precepts, introducing curving paths and wandering lakes, but for a time the improvements were mostly architectural. All across the country rich landowners packed their grounds with grottoes, temples, prospect towers, artificial ruins, obelisks, castellated follies, menageries, orangeries, pantheons, amphitheatres, exedra (curved walls with niches for busts of heroic figures), the odd nymphaeum and whatever other architectural caprices came to mind. These were not ornamental trifles but hefty monuments. The Mausoleum at Castle Howard, designed by Nicholas Hawksmoor (and where Vanbrugh's patron the third earl is now passing eternity), was as large and as costly as any of Christopher Wren's London churches. Robert Adam drew up a plan to erect a complete walled Roman town, picturesquely ruined and entirely artificial, across a dozen acres of meadowy hillside in Herefordshire simply to give a minor noble named Lord Harley something diverting to gaze upon from his breakfast table. That was never built, but other diversions of startling magnificence were. The famous pagoda at Kew Gardens, rising to a height of 163 feet, was for a long time the tallest freestanding structure in England. Until the nineteenth century it was sumptuously gilded and covered with painted dragons – eighty in all – and tinkling brass bells, but these were sold off by King George IV to reduce his debts, so what we see today is really a stripped-down shell. At one time the grounds of Kew had nineteen other fantasy structures scattered about, including a Turkish mosque, an Alhambra Palace, a miniature Gothic cathedral and temples to Aeolus, Arethusa, Bellona, Pan, peace, solitude and the sun – all so that some members of the royal family would have a selection of diversions with which to punctuate their walks.

For a time it was highly fashionable to build a hermitage and install in it a live-in hermit. At Painshill in Surrey, one man signed a contract to live seven years in picturesque seclusion, observing a monastic silence, for £100 a year, but was fired after just three weeks when he was spotted drinking in the local pub. An estate owner in Lancashire promised £50 a year for life to anyone who would pass seven years in an underground dwelling on his estate without cutting his hair or toenails or talking to another person. Someone took up the offer and actually lasted four years before deciding he could take no more; whether he was given at least a partial pension for his efforts is sadly unknown. Queen Caroline – she of the Serpentine in Hyde Park – had the architect William Kent build for her a hermitage at Richmond into which she installed a poet named Stephen Duck, but that was not a success either, for Duck decided he didn't like the silence or being looked at by strangers, so he quit. Somewhat improbably, he went on to become the rector of a church at Byfleet in Surrey. Unfortunately he appears not to have been happy there – he appears not to have been happy anywhere – and drowned himself in the Thames.

The ultimate expression of folly building was surely at Chiswick, then a village west of London, where the third Earl of Burlington (and yet another Kit-Cat member) built Chiswick House, which was not a house at all and never intended to be lived in, but a place to look at art and listen to music, a kind of glorified summer house, built on a literally palatial scale. This was the property from which, you may just recall, the eighth Duke of Devonshire stepped out and had his happy first encounter with Joseph Paxton.

Meanwhile, Charles Bridgeman and his successors were extensively reworking whole landscapes. At his masterpiece grounds, Stowe in Buckinghamshire, everything was done on a monumental scale. One of the ha-has stretched for four miles. Hills were reshaped, valleys flooded, temples of marbled magnificence strewn about almost carelessly. Stowe was unlike anything that had ever been built before. For one thing, it was one of the world's first true tourist attractions. It was the first garden in Britain to attract sightseers and the first to have its own guidebook. It became so popular that in 1717 Lord Cobham, its owner, had to buy a neighbouring inn to accommodate visitors.

In 1738, Bridgeman died and soon after was succeeded by a person so youthful that he hadn't even been born when Bridgeman began work on Stowe. The young man's name was Lancelot Brown, and he was exactly the man the landscape movement needed.

Brown's life story closely recalls that of Joseph Paxton. Both were the sons of yeoman farmers, both were exceptionally bright and hard-working, both went into gardening as boys and both distinguished themselves swiftly in the employ of rich men. In Brown's case, the story began in Northumberland, where his father was a tenant farmer on an estate called Kirkharle. Brown was apprenticed as a gardener there at fourteen and served the full seven years, but then left Northumberland and moved south, possibly looking for a better climate for his asthma. What he did for the next period of his life is unknown but he must have distinguished himself, for soon after the death of Charles Bridgeman Lord Cobham selected him to be the new head gardener at Stowe. He was just twenty-four years old.

Brown found himself in charge of a staff of forty, serving as paymaster as well as head gardener. Gradually he took on the management of the whole estate, building projects as well as gardening ones. By such means, and no doubt additional study, he acquired the skills to become an entirely competent, if workmanlike, architect. In 1749, Lord Cobham died and Brown decided to become independent. He moved to Hammersmith, then a village west of London, and embarked on a freelance career. At the age of thirty-five he was about to become the man history knows as Capability Brown.

His vision was sweeping. He didn't make gardens, he made landscapes. It was his habit, upon seeing an estate, to announce that it had capabilities, and so he acquired his famous nickname. There has long been a tendency to portray Brown as a mere tinkerer, an incidental improver, who did little more than arrange trees into attractive clumps. In fact, no one shifted more earth or operated on a larger scale than he did. To make the Grecian Valley at Stowe his workmen took away, in barrows, 23,500 cubic yards of soil and rock and scattered it elsewhere. At Heveningham in Suffolk he raised a large lawn by twelve feet. He happily moved fully grown trees and sometimes fully grown villages too. To aid the former, he devised a wheeled machine that could move trees up to thirty-six feet high without harming them – a piece of horticultural engineering that was seen as almost miraculous. He planted tens of thousands of trees – 91,000 in a single year at Longleat. He built lakes that covered a hundred acres of productive farmland (a fact that almost certainly gave some of his clients pause). At Blenheim Palace, a magnificent bridge crossed a piddling stream; Brown flanked it with lakes and made it glorious.

He saw in his mind's eye exactly how landscapes could look a hundred years hence. Long before anyone else thought of doing so, he used native trees almost exclusively. It is such touches that make his landscapes look as if they evolved naturally when in fact they were designed almost down to the last cowpat. He was far more of an engineer and landscape architect than he was a gardener. He had a particular gift for 'confusing the eye' – by, for instance, making two lakes on different levels look like a much larger single lake. Brown created landscapes that were in a sense 'more English' than the countryside they replaced, and did it on a scale so sweeping and radical that it takes some effort now to imagine just how novel it was. He called it 'place-making'. The landscape of much of lowland England today may look timeless, but it was in large part an eighteenth-century creation, and it was

Brown more than anyone who made it. If that is tinkering, it is on a grand scale.

Brown provided a full service – design, provision of plants, planting, maintenance afterwards. He worked hard and fast and so could manage a lot of commitments. It was said that an hour's brisk tour of an estate was all it took for him to form a comprehensive scheme for improvements. A big part of the appeal of Brown's approach was that it was cheap in the long run. Manicured grounds with their parterres and topiary and miles of clipped hedges needed a lot of maintenance. Brown's landscapes looked after themselves by and large. He was also emphatically practical. Where others built temples, pagodas and shrines, Brown put up buildings that *looked* like extravagant follies but actually were dairies or kennels or housing for estate workers. Having grown up on a farm he actually understood farming, and often introduced changes that improved efficiency. If not a great architect, he was certainly a competent one and for one thing understood drainage better than perhaps any other architect of his time thanks to his work in landscaping. He was a master of soil engineering long before such a discipline existed. Unseen beneath his dozing landscapes can be complex drainage systems that turned bogs into meadows, and have kept them that way for 250 years. He might just as well have been called Drainage Brown.

Brown was once offered £1,000 to do an estate in Ireland, but declined, saying that he hadn't done all of England yet. In his three decades of self-employment he undertook some 170 commissions, and so transformed a good portion of the English countryside. He also grew rich doing so. Within a decade of going independent, he was earning £15,000 a year, enough to put him in the top ranks of the newly emergent middle class.

His achievements were by no means unreservedly admired by all. The poet Richard Owen Cambridge once declared to Brown: 'I very earnestly wish I may die before you, Mr Brown.'

'Why?' asked Brown, surprised.

'Because I should like to see heaven before you had improved it,' Cambridge answered drily.

The artist John Constable hated Brown's work. 'It is not beauty because it is not nature,' he declared. But Brown's most devoted antagonist was the snobbish Sir William Chambers. He dismissed Brown's landscapes as unimaginative, insisting they 'differ very little from common fields'. But then Chambers's idea of improving a landscape was to cover it with garish buildings. It was he who designed the pagoda, mock Alhambra and other diversions at Kew. Chambers thought Brown little more than a peasant because his speech and manners lacked refinement, but Brown's clients loved him. One, Lord Exeter, hung a portrait of Brown in his house where he could see it every day. Brown also seems to have been just a very nice man. In one of his few surviving letters, he tells his wife how, separated from her by business, he passed the day in imaginary conversation with her, 'which has every charm except your dear company, which will ever be the sincere and the principal delight, my dear Biddy, of your affectionate husband'. That's not bad for someone who was barely schooled. They were certainly not the words of a peasant. He died in 1783 aged sixty-six and was much missed by many.

II

Just as Capability Brown was rejecting flowers and ornamental shrubs, others were finding new ones in magnificent abundance. The period that lay fifty years to either side of Brown's death was one of unprecedented discovery in the botanical world. The hunt for plants became a huge driver of both science and commerce.

The person who can reasonably be said to have started it all was Joseph Banks, the brilliant botanist who accompanied Captain James Cook on his voyage to the South Seas and beyond from 1768 to 1771. Banks packed Cook's little ship with specimen plants – thirty thousand in all – including fourteen hundred never previously recorded, at a stroke increasing the world's stock of known plants by about a quarter. He would almost certainly have found more on Cook's second voyage, but Banks alas was spoiled as well as brilliant. He insisted on taking seventeen servants this time, including two horn players to entertain him in the evenings. Cook politely demurred, and Banks declined to go. Instead he privately financed an expedition to Iceland. En route the party stopped at the Bay o' Skaill in Orkney and Banks did some excavating there, but overlooked the grassy knoll that covered Skara Brae, and so just missed the chance to add one of the great archaeological discoveries of the age to his many other accomplishments.

Meanwhile, dedicated plant hunters were fanning out across the world, not least in North America, which proved to be especially productive of plants that were not only lovely and interesting but would bloom in British soil. The first Europeans to penetrate America's interior from the east weren't looking for lands to settle or passages to the west. They were looking for plants they could sell on, and they found wondrous new species by the score – the azalea, aster, camellia, catalpa, euphorbia, hydrangea, rhododendron, rudbeckia, Virginia creeper, wild cherry and many types of ferns, shrubs, trees and vines. Fortunes could be made from finding new plants and getting them safely back to the nurseries of Europe for propagation. Soon the woods of North America were so full of plant hunters that it is impossible to tell now who exactly discovered what. John Fraser, after whom is named the Fraser fir, discovered either 44 new species or 215, depending on which botanical history you credit.

The dangers of plant hunting were considerable. Joseph Paxton dispatched two men to North America to see what they could find; both drowned when their heavily laden boat overturned on a foaming river in British Columbia. The son of André Michaux, a French hunter, was hideously mangled by a bear. In Hawaii, David Douglas, discoverer of the Douglas fir, fell into an animal trap at a particularly unpropitious moment: it was already occupied by a wild bull, which proceeded to trample him to death. Others got lost and starved, or died of malaria, yellow fever or other diseases, or were killed by suspicious natives. Those who succeeded, however, often acquired considerable wealth – perhaps none more notably than Robert Fortune, last encountered in Chapter 8 travelling riskily around China disguised as a native to discover how tea was produced. His introduction of tea-growing to India possibly saved the British Empire, but it was the bringing of chrysanthemums and azaleas to British nurseries that allowed him to die wealthy.

Others were driven by a simple quest for adventure – sometimes dangerously misguided, it would seem. Perhaps the most notable – and on the face of it most unlikely – in this category were the young friends Alfred Russel Wallace and Henry Walter Bates, both the sons of English businessmen of modest means. Though neither had ever even been abroad, they decided in 1848 to voyage to Amazonia to search for botanical specimens. Soon afterwards, they were joined by Wallace's brother Herbert and by another keen amateur, Richard Spruce, a schoolmaster on the Castle Howard estate in Yorkshire who had never tackled anything more challenging than an English meadow. None seemed remotely prepared for life in the tropics, and poor Herbert demonstrated as much by catching yellow fever and expiring almost as soon as he was ashore. The others, however, persevered, though for reasons unknown they elected to split up and head off in different directions.

Wallace plunged into the jungles along the Rio Negro and spent the next four years doggedly collecting specimens. The challenges he faced were numberless. Insects made his life a torment. He broke his glasses, on which he was highly dependent, during a lively encounter with a hornets' nest, and lost a boot in some other moment of mayhem and for some time had to clomp around the jungles half shod. He bewildered his Indian guides by preserving his specimens in jars of *caxaca*, an alcohol fermented from sugar cane, instead of drinking it as any sensible man would. Thinking him mad, they appropriated the remaining *caxaca* and melted into the forest. Undeterred – undeterrable – Wallace pressed on.

After four years, he stumbled from the steamy jungles

exhausted, his clothes in tatters, trembling and half
delirious from a recurrent fever, but with a rare collection
of specimens. In the Brazilian port city of Pará he secured
passage home on a barque called the *Helen*. Midway across
the Atlantic, however, the *Helen* caught fire and Wallace
had to scramble into a lifeboat, leaving his precious cargo
behind. He watched as the ship, consumed by flames, slid
beneath the waves, taking his treasures with it. Undaunted
(well, perhaps just a little daunted), Wallace allowed himself a spell of convalescence, then sailed to the other ends
of the earth, to the Malay Archipelago, where he roamed
ceaselessly for eight years and collected a staggering
127,000 specimens, including a thousand insects and two
hundred species of birds never before recorded, all of
which he managed to get safely back to England.

Bates, meanwhile, stayed on in South America for
seven years after Wallace's departure, exploring mostly by
boat on the Amazon and its tributaries, and eventually
brought home almost 15,000 specimens of animals and
insects, which seems a modest number compared with
Wallace's 127,000, but some 8,000 of his – more than
half, a phenomenal proportion – were new to science.

But the most remarkable of all in many ways was
Richard Spruce. He stayed on in South America for a full
eighteen years, exploring areas never before visited by a
European, and assembling vast stores of information,
including glossaries of twenty-one native Indian
languages. Among much else, he discovered a commercially important rubber plant, the species of coca from
which is derived modern cocaine, and the variety of
cinchona that produced quinine – for a century the only
effective remedy against malaria and other tropical fevers

– as well as the flavoured tonic water that is vital for a good gin and tonic.

When at last he returned home to Yorkshire, he discovered that all the money he had earned from his endeavours over twenty years had been misinvested by the people to whom he had entrusted it, and he was now penniless. His health was so ruined that he spent most of the next twenty-seven years in bed, listlessly cataloguing his findings. He never did find the strength to write his memoirs.

Thanks to the efforts of these daring men and scores of others like them, the number of plants available to English gardeners soared amazingly – from about one thousand in 1750 to well over twenty thousand a hundred years later. Newly found exotic plants became hugely prized. A small monkey puzzle tree, a decorative conifer discovered in Chile in 1782, could by the 1840s easily fetch £5 in Britain, roughly the annual cost of keeping a maid. Bedding plants, too, became a huge industry. All of this gave a mighty boost to amateur gardening.

So, too, much more unexpectedly, did the rise of the railways. Railways allowed people to move out to distant suburbs and commute in to work. Suburbs gave home-owners greater space. More spacious properties allowed – indeed, all but required – the new breed of suburbanites to take an interest in gardening.

But one other change was even more profoundly consequential than all others: the rise of female gardening at home. The catalyst was a woman named Jane Webb who had no background in gardening, and whose improbable fame was as the author of a potboiler in three volumes called *The Mummy! A Tale of the Twenty-second Century*, which she published anonymously in 1827, when she was just twenty years old. Her description of a steam lawn-mower so excited (seriously) the gardening writer John Claudius Loudon that he sought her out for friendship, thinking she was a man. Loudon was even more excited when he discovered she was a woman and rather swiftly proposed marriage, even though he was at that point exactly twice her age.

Jane accepted, and so began a touching and productive partnership. John Claudius Loudon was already a man of great stature in the world of horticulture. Born on a farm in Scotland in 1783, the year Capability Brown died, he had passed his youth in a fever of self-improvement, teaching himself six languages, including Greek and Hebrew, and absorbing from books as much as was to be known about botany, horticulture, natural history and all else related to the verdant arts. In 1804 at the age of twenty-one he began to produce a seemingly endless stream of stout books with earnest, daunting titles – *A Short Treatise on Several Improvements Recently Made in Hothouses*; *Observations on the Formation and Management of Useful and Ornamental Plantations*; *The Different Modes of Cultivating the Pine-Apple* – all of which sold considerably better than they sound as if they ought to have. He also edited, largely wrote and in effect single-handedly produced a string of popular gardening magazines – as many as five at once – and all this, it may be noted, despite being almost staggeringly unlucky with his health. He had a particular knack, it seems, for getting ill and then developing appalling complications. His right arm, for instance, had to be amputated as a result of a bad bout of rheumatic fever.

Soon afterwards, his knee ankylosed, leaving him with a permanent limp. As a consequence of his chronic pains, he became for a time addicted to laudanum. This was not a man for whom life was ever easy.

Mrs Loudon was even more successful than her husband thanks to a single work, *Practical Instructions in Gardening for Ladies*, published in 1841, which proved to be magnificently timely. It was the first book of any type ever to encourage women of elevated classes to get their hands dirty and even to take on a faint glow of perspiration. This was novel almost to the point of eroticism. *Gardening for Ladies* bravely insisted that women could manage gardening independent of male supervision if they simply observed a few sensible precautions – working steadily but not too vigorously, using only light tools, never standing on damp ground because of the unhealthful emanations that would rise up through their skirts. The book appeared to assume that the reader had scarcely ever been outdoors, much less laid hands on a gardening tool. Here, for instance, is Mrs Loudon explaining what a spade does:

> The operation of digging, as performed by a gardener, consists of thrusting the iron part of the spade, which acts as a wedge, perpendicularly into the ground by the application of the foot, and then using the long handle as a lever, to raise up the loosened earth and turn it over.

The whole book is like that, describing in almost painful detail the most mundane and obvious actions, like which end of the spade to put into the ground. It is practically unreadable now and it probably wasn't greatly read then. The value of *Gardening for Ladies* wasn't what it contained so much as what it represented: permission to go outside and *do* something. It came at exactly the right moment to catch the nation's fancy. In 1841, middle-class women everywhere were bored out of their skulls by the rigidities of life, and grateful for any suggestion of diversion. *Gardening for Ladies* remained lucratively in print for the rest of the century. And it really did encourage them to get their hands dirty. The whole of the second chapter was devoted to manure.

Apart from its appeal as a recreation, there was a second, rather more unexpected impetus behind the rise of the garden movement in the nineteenth century, and one in which John Claudius Loudon also played a central role. The age was vividly marked by epidemics of cholera and other contagions, which killed vast numbers. This didn't make people want to garden exactly, but it did lead to a general longing for fresh air and open spaces, particularly as it became inescapably evident that urban graveyards were on the whole squalid, overcrowded and unhealthy.

In the middle of the nineteenth century, London had just 218 acres of burial grounds. People were packed into them in densities almost beyond imagining. When the poet William Blake died in 1827, he was buried, at Bunhill Fields, on top of three others; later, four more were placed on top of him. By such means London's burial places absorbed staggering heaps of dead flesh. St Marylebone Parish Church packed an estimated one hundred thousand bodies into a burial ground of just over an acre. Where the National Gallery now stands on

Trafalgar Square was the modest burial ground of St Martin-in-the-Fields church. It held seventy thousand bodies in an area about the size of a modern bowling green, and uncounted thousands more were interred in the crypts inside. In 1859, when St Martin's announced its intention to clear out the crypts, the naturalist Frank Buckland decided to find the coffin of the great surgeon and anatomist John Hunter so that his remains could be reinterred at Westminster Abbey, and Buckland left a riveting account of what he found inside.

'Mr Burstall having unlocked the ponderous oak door of the vault No. 3,' Buckland wrote, 'we threw the light of our bull's eye lantern into the vault, and then I beheld a sight I shall never forget.' In the shadowy gloom before him were thousands upon thousands of jumbled and broken coffins, crammed everywhere, as if deposited by a tsunami. It took Buckland sixteen days of dedicated searching to find his quarry. Unfortunately no one took similar pains with any of the other coffins and they were roughly carted off to unmarked graves in other cemeteries. In consequence the whereabouts of the mortal remains of quite a number of worthies – the furniture maker Thomas Chippendale, the royal mistress Nell Gwyn, the scientist Robert Boyle, the miniaturist Nicholas Hilliard, the highwayman Jack Sheppard and the original Winston Churchill, father of the first Duke of Marlborough, to name just some – are today quite unknown.

Many churches made most of their money from burials, and were loath to give up such lucrative business. At the Enon Baptist Chapel on Clement's Lane in Holborn (now the site of the London School of Economics), the church authorities managed to cram a colossal twelve thousand bodies in the cellar in just nineteen years. Not surprisingly, such a volume of rotting flesh created odours that could not well be contained. It was a rare service in which several worshippers didn't faint. Eventually, most stopped coming altogether, but still the chapel kept accepting bodies for interment. The parson needed the income.

Burial grounds grew so full that it was almost impossible to turn a spade of soil without bringing up some decaying limb or other organic relic. Bodies were buried in such shallow and cursory graves that often they were exposed by scavenging animals or rose spontaneously to the surface, the way rocks do in fields, and had to be re-deposited. Mourners in cities almost never attended at graveside to witness a burial itself. The experience was simply too upsetting, and widely held to be dangerous in addition. Anecdotal reports abounded of graveyard visitors struck down by putrid emanations. A Dr Walker testified to a parliamentary inquiry that graveyard workers, before disturbing a coffin, would drill a hole in the side, insert a tube and burn off the escaping gases – a process that could take twenty minutes, he reported. He knew of one man who failed to observe the usual precautions and was felled instantly – 'as if struck with a cannon-ball' – by the gases from a fresh grave. 'To inhale this gas, undiluted with atmospheric air, is instant death,' confirmed the committee in its written report, adding grimly, 'and even when much diluted it is productive of disease which commonly ends in death.' Till late in the century, the medical journal the *Lancet* ran occasional reports of people overcome by bad air while visiting graveyards.

The sensible solution to all this horrid foulness, it

seemed to many, was to move cemeteries out of the cities altogether, and to make them more like parks. Joseph Paxton was an enthusiast for the idea, but the person principally behind the movement was the tireless and ubiquitous John Claudius Loudon. In 1843 he wrote and published *On the Laying Out, Planting, and Managing of Cemeteries; and on the Improvement of Churchyards* – an unexpectedly timely book, as it happened, since he would need a cemetery himself before the year was out. One of the problems with London cemeteries, Loudon pointed out, was that they were mostly built on heavy clay soils, which didn't drain well and thus promoted festering and stagnation. Suburban cemeteries, he suggested, could be sited on sandy or gravel soils where the bodies planted within them would become, in effect, wholesome compost. Liberal plantings of trees and shrubs would not only create a bucolic air, but would soak up any miasmas that leaked out of the graves and replace foul airs with fresh ones. Loudon designed three of these new model cemeteries and made them practically indistinguishable from parks. Unfortunately he was not able to rest eternally in one of his own creations as he died, worn out by overwork, before they could be built, but he was buried at Kensal Green Cemetery, in west London, which was founded on similar principles.

Cemeteries became, improbably, de facto parks. On Sunday afternoons, people went to them not just to pay their respects to the dear departed but to stroll, take the air and have picnics. Highgate Cemetery in north London, with its long views and imposing monuments, became a tourist attraction in its own right. People living nearby purchased gate keys so that they could let themselves in and out whenever it suited them. The largest of all was Brookwood Cemetery in Surrey, opened by the London Necropolis and National Mausoleum Company in 1854, which grew to hold almost a quarter of a million bodies on its two thousand bucolic acres. It became such a large operation that the company ran a private railway between London and Brookwood, twenty-three miles to the west, with three classes of service and two stations at Brookwood: one for Anglicans and one for Nonconformists. Railway workers knew it affectionately as the 'Stiffs Express'. The service lasted until 1941 when it was dealt what proved to be a mortal blow by German bombers.

Gradually it dawned on the authorities that what was wanted really wasn't cemeteries that were like parks, but parks that were like parks. In the year that Loudon died, an entirely new phenomenon – the municipal park – opened at Birkenhead, across the River Mersey from Liverpool. Built on 125 acres of wasteland, it was an instant success and a much acclaimed marvel, and it almost goes without saying that it was designed by the ever industrious, ever inventive, ever reliable Joseph Paxton.

Parks already existed at this time, but they were not like parks as we know them today. For one thing, they tended to be exclusive. Only people of fashion and rank (plus a smattering of impudently bold courtesans from time to time) were allowed into the big London parks until well into the nineteenth century. There was a 'tacit understanding', as it is always termed, that parks were not for people of the lower or even middle classes, however those rankings were defined. Some parks didn't even bother to make it tacit. Regent's Park charged an admission fee until 1835 expressly to discourage common people from cluttering the paths and lowering the tone. Many of the new industrial cities had almost no parks anyway, so most working people had nowhere to go for fresh air and recreation other than for a walk along the dusty roads that led out of town into the country, and anyone foolhardy enough to step off these rutted tracks and on to private land – to admire a view, empty a straining bladder, take a drink from a stream – could well find his foot painfully clamped in a steel trap. This was an age in which people were routinely transported to Australia for poaching, and any form of trespass, however innocent or slight, was bound to be regarded as nefarious.

So the idea of a park built by a city for the free use of all its citizenry, whatever their station in life, was almost indescribably exciting. Paxton eschewed the formal avenues and ordered vistas that parks normally embraced and created instead something more natural and inviting. Birkenhead Park brought to mind the grounds of a private estate, but for the use of all people. In the spring of 1851 (that year!), a young American journalist and author named Frederick Law Olmsted, while on a walking holiday in the north of England with two friends, stopped to buy provisions for lunch at a Birkenhead bakery and the baker spoke of the park with such enthusiasm and pride that they decided to go and have a look. Olmsted was enchanted. The quality of landscape design 'had here reached a perfection that I had never before dreamed of', he recalled in *Walks and Talks of an American Farmer in England*, his popular account of the trip. At that time, many people in New York were actively pressing for a decent public park for the city, and this, thought Olmsted, was the very park they needed. He could have no idea that six years later he would design that park himself.

Frederick Law Olmsted was born in 1822 in Hartford, Connecticut, the son of a prosperous dry goods merchant, and passed his early adulthood flitting from job to job. He worked for a textile firm, went to sea as a merchant seaman, ran a small farm and finally turned to writing. After his return to America from England, he joined the fledgling *New York Times* and went off to tour the southern states, producing a series of celebrated newspaper articles which were later published as a successful book, *The Cotton Kingdom*. He became something of a gadfly, social-izing with the likes of Washington Irving, Henry Wadsworth Longfellow and William Makepeace Thackeray when they were in town, and joined the publishing firm of Dix & Edwards, where he became a partner. For a time everything seemed to be going his way, but then the firm suffered a series of financial setbacks and in 1857 – a year of economic depression and widespread bank failures – he found himself abruptly broke and unemployed.

At just this moment, the city of New York was about to begin converting 840 acres of hayfields and scrubland into the long-awaited Central Park. It was an enormous site, stretching nearly 2.5 miles from top to bottom and half a mile across. Olmsted, in some desperation, applied for the job of superintendent of the workforce and got it. He was thirty-five years old, and this was not a step up for him. Becoming the superintendent of a municipal park was, for someone who had enjoyed as much success as he had, a humbling comedown, particularly as Central Park was a far from assured success. For one thing, in those days it wasn't actually central at all. 'Uptown' Manhattan was still nearly two miles to the south. The area of the proposed park was an uninhabited wasteland – a forlorn expanse of abandoned quarries and 'pestiferous swamps', in the words of one observer. The idea of it becoming a popular beauty spot seemed almost ludicrously ambitious.

No design had been agreed for the park – which was, not incidentally, always called *the* Central Park, with a definite article, in its early days. A prize of $2,000 awaited the winning entry and Olmsted needed the money. He teamed up with a young British architect, only recently arrived in America, named Calvert Vaux and submitted a plan.* Vaux (pronounced 'vawks') was a slight figure, just four feet ten inches tall. He had grown up in London, the son of a doctor, but emigrated to America in 1850 soon after qualifying. Olmsted had passion and vision, but lacked draughting skills, which Vaux could supply. It was the start of an immensely successful partnership. To satisfy the design brief, all the proposals were required to incorporate certain features – parade ground, playing fields, skating pond, at least one flower garden and a lookout tower, among rather a lot else – and they also had to incorporate four crossing streets at intervals so that the park wouldn't act as a barrier to east–west traffic along its entire length. What set Olmsted and Vaux's design apart more than anything else was their decision to place the cross streets in trenches, below the line of sight, physically

---

* Vaux would also have a successful independent career. Among much else, he co-designed, with another Englishman, Jacob Wrey Mould, the American Museum of Natural History overlooking Central Park.

segregating them from park visitors, who passed safely above on bridges. 'This also had the advantage of allowing the park to be closed at night without interrupting traffic,' writes Witold Rybczynski in his biography of Olmsted. Theirs was the only proposal with this feature.

It is easy to suppose that park-making consists essentially of just planting trees, laying paths, setting out benches and digging the odd pond. In fact, Central Park was an *enormous* engineering project. Over twenty thousand barrels of dynamite were needed to reconfigure the terrain to Olmsted and Vaux's specifications, and over half a million cubic yards of fresh topsoil had to be brought in to make the earth rich enough for planting. At the peak of construction in 1859, Central Park had a workforce of 3,600 men. The park opened bit by bit, so it never had a grand opening. Many people found it disordered and confusing. And it is true, Central Park has little in the way of dominant focal points. As Adam Gopnik has put it: 'The Mall is oriented toward nothing much and goes nowhere in particular. The lakes and ponds are all nestled in their own places, and are not part of a continuous waterway. The main areas are not neatly marked off but dribble away into one another. There is a deliberate absence of orientation, of clear planning, of a familiar, reassuring lucidity. Central Park is without a central place.'

But people grew to love it anyway, and soon Olmsted was receiving commissions from all over America. This is slightly surprising because Olmsted was not much good at building the kind of parks that people actually wanted – and the more parks he built, the more evident this became. Olmsted was convinced that all the ills of urban life were owing to bad air and a lack of exercise, producing 'a premature failure of the vigour of the brain'. Quiet walks and tranquil reflection were what was needed to restore health, energy and even moral tone to a jaded citizenry. So Olmsted was absolutely against anything that was noisy, vigorous or fun. He especially didn't want diversions like zoos and boating lakes – the very sorts of amusements park users craved. At Franklin Park in Boston he had base-ball playing banned, along with all other 'active recreations', as he disdainfully called them, for anyone except children under sixteen. Fourth of July celebrations were flatly forbidden.

People responded by ignoring the rules, and park authorities obliged them by turning a blind eye, so that everywhere Olmsted's parks ended up as much more pleasurable places than he wanted them to be, though still considerably more restrictive than the parks of Europe with their lively beer gardens and bright-lit rides.

Although he didn't start landscaping until he was well on the way to middle age, Olmsted's career was breath-takingly productive. He built over a hundred municipal parks all over North America – in Detroit, Albany, Buffalo, Chicago, Newark, Hartford and Montreal. Though Central Park is his most famous creation, many think Prospect Park in Brooklyn his masterpiece. He also executed more than two hundred private commissions for estates and institutions of every kind, including some fifty university campuses. Biltmore was Olmsted's last project – and in fact one of his last rational acts. Very soon afterwards he slid into a helpless and progressive dementia. He spent the last five years of his life at the McLean Asylum in Belmont, Massachusetts, where, it almost goes without saying, he had designed the grounds.

III

Though there are obvious dangers in speculating too freely about the style of life adopted by the good Reverend Mr Marsham in his rectory, something he will very probably have dreamed about, if not actually owned, was a greenhouse, for greenhouses were the great new toy of the age. Inspired by Joseph Paxton's Crystal Palace in London, and neatly coinciding with the timely abolition of duties on glass, greenhouses soon were popping up all over and being filled with all the exciting new specimens of plant that were pouring into Britain from around the globe. This widespread transfer of living things between continents was not without consequences, however. In the summer of 1863 a keen gardener in Hammersmith, west London, found a prize vine in his greenhouse sickening. He was unable to identify the malady, but saw that the leaves were covered with galls from which sprang insects of a kind he had not seen before. He collected a few and sent them to John Obadiah Westwood, professor of zoology at Oxford and an international authority on insects.

The identity of the vine owner is now lost, alas, which is unfortunate as he was a significant human being: the first in Europe to suffer from an infestation of phylloxera, a tiny, all-but-invisible aphid that would shortly devastate the European wine industry. About Professor Westwood we know a great deal, however. He had been born in modest circumstances – his father was a diemaker in Sheffield – and was entirely self-taught. He became the leading authority in Britain not only on insects – and really no one could come near him for entomological expertise – but also on Anglo-Saxon writings. In 1849, he was appointed the first professor of zoology at Oxford.

Almost exactly three years after phylloxera's discovery in Hammersmith, wine growers in the Bouches-du-Rhône region near Arles in southern France found that their vines were withering and dying. Soon vineyard death was spreading across France. Vineyard owners were impotent. Because the insects infested the roots, the first sign of mortal illness was the first sign of anything. Farmers couldn't dig up the vines to see if phylloxera was present without killing the vines, so they just had to wait and hope. Mostly they were disappointed.

Forty per cent of France's vines were killed in fifteen years. Eighty per cent were 'reconstituted' through the grafting on of American roots. In among the general devastation were small, mysterious areas of apparent immunity. All the champagne region was wiped out but for two tiny vineyards outside Reims, which for some reason successfully resisted infection and still produce champagne grapes from their original roots – the only French champagnes that do.

Phylloxera aphids from the New World had almost certainly reached Europe before, but would have arrived as little corpses because they were unable to survive the long sea voyage. The introduction of fast steamships at sea and even faster trains on land meant that the little aphids could arrive refreshed and ready to conquer new territory.

Phylloxera originated in America and had killed off all attempts to introduce European vines on to American soils – a matter that had caused consternation and despair from French New Orleans to Thomas Jefferson's Monticello and on through Ohio and the rolling uplands of New York.

American vines were immune to phylloxera, but didn't make very good wine. Then someone realized that if you grafted European vines on to American roots, you got vines that could successfully resist phylloxera. The question was whether they produced wine as good as they had before.

In France, many vineyard owners couldn't bear the thought of corrupting their vines with American stock. Burgundy, fearful that its beloved and exceedingly valuable grand crus would be irreparably compromised, refused for fourteen years to allow American roots to besmirch its ancient vines, even though those vines were puckering and dying on every hillside. Many growers almost certainly engaged in a bit of illicit grafting anyway, which may have saved their noble wines from extinction.

But it is thanks to American roots that French wines still exist. It is impossible to say whether wines are worse now than they were before. Most authorities think not, but such a desperate remedy is bound to nurture lingering doubts among those who are inclined to have them. What is certainly true is that surviving pre-phylloxera wines have attracted a cachet that has led people to part with a good deal of their money and much of their common sense in a quest to possess something so deliciously irreplaceable. In 1985, Malcolm Forbes, the American publisher, paid $156,450 for a bottle of Château Lafite 1787. This made it much too valuable to drink, so he put it on display in a special glass case. Unfortunately, the spotlights that artfully lit the precious bottle caused the ancient cork to shrink and it fell with a $156,450 splash into the bottle. Even worse was the fate of an eighteenth-century Château Margaux reputed to have once been owned by Thomas

Jefferson and valued, very precisely, at $519,750. While showing off his acquisition at a New York restaurant in 1989, William Sokolin, a wine merchant, accidentally knocked the bottle against the side of a serving cart and it broke, in an instant converting the world's most expensive bottle of wine into the world's most expensive carpet stain. The restaurant manager dipped a finger in the wine and declared that it was no longer drinkable anyway.

IV

While the Industrial Revolution was producing wondrous machines that transformed how people (and sometimes pests) lived, horticultural science lagged appallingly. Well into the nineteenth century no one had any real idea even of something as basic as what made plants grow. Everyone knew that soil needed fertilizing, but there was little agreement on *why* it did or what constituted an effective fertilizer. A survey of farmers in the 1830s showed that the fertilizers in use at that time included sawdust, feathers, sea sand, hay, dead fish, oyster shells, woollen rags, ashes, horn shavings, coal tar, chalk, gypsum and cotton seeds, among other products. Some of these worked better than you might expect – farmers were no fools, after all – but no one could rank them in order of effectiveness or say in what proportions they worked best. In consequence the overall trajectory of farm yields was relentlessly downwards. Corn harvests in upstate New York went from 30 bushels an acre in 1775 to barely a quarter of that half a century later. (A bushel is 35.2 litres or 32 US quarts.) A few eminent scientists, notably Nicholas-Théodore de Saussure in Switzerland, Justus Liebig in Germany and Humphry Davy in England, established a relationship between nitrogen and minerals on the one hand and soil fertility on the other, but how you got the former into the latter was still a matter of debate, so farmers almost everywhere continued to cast desperate and often ineffective dressings on to their fields.

Then in the 1830s there suddenly came the miracle product the world had been waiting for: guano. Guano – bird droppings – had been used in Peru since the time of the Incas, and its efficacy had been remarked upon by explorers and travellers ever since, but it wasn't until now that anyone thought to scoop it into bags and sell it to desperate farmers in the northern hemisphere. Once guano was discovered by outsiders, however, they couldn't get enough of it. A dressing of guano re-energized fields and increased crop yields by up to 300 per cent. The world was seized with what came to be known as 'guano mania'. Guano worked because it was packed with nitrogen, phosphorus and potassium nitrate – which coincidentally were also vital ingredients in gunpowder. The uric acid in guano was also much valued by dyemakers. So guano became prized from lots of different directions. Suddenly there was almost nothing in the world people wanted more.

Guano was often enormously abundant where seabirds nested. Many rocky islands were literally smothered in it: deposits 150 feet deep were not unknown. Some Pacific islands were essentially nothing *but* guano. Trading in guano made a lot of people very rich. Schroder's, the British merchant bank, was founded largely on the guano trade. For thirty years Peru earned practically all its foreign exchange from bagging up and selling bird droppings to a grateful world. Chile and Bolivia went to war over guano claims. The US Congress brought in the Guano Islands Act, which allowed private interests to claim as US territory any guano-bearing islands they found that weren't already claimed. The US acquired more than fifty islands.

While guano was making life better for farmers, it had one very serious effect on city life. It killed the market in human waste. Previously, the people who emptied city cesspits – nightsoil men, as they were called – had sold their waste to farmers just outside the cities. That had helped to keep costs down. But after 1847 the market for human waste collapsed, so disposal became a problem that was generally solved by tipping the collected waste into the nearest convenient river, with consequences that, as we shall see, would take decades to sort out.

The inevitable problem with guano was that it had taken centuries to accumulate, but no time at all to be used up. One island off the coast of Africa containing an estimated 200,000 tons of guano was scraped bare in just over a year. Prices soared to almost $80 a ton. By 1850, the average farmer had the dispiriting choice of spending roughly half his income on guano or watching his yields wither. Clearly what was needed was a synthetic fertilizer – something that would feed crops reliably and economically. It was just at this point that a curious figure named John Bennet Lawes steps into the story.

Lawes was the son of a wealthy landowner in Hertfordshire, and from boyhood had a passion for chemical experimentation. He turned a spare room in the family home into a laboratory and spent most of his time locked away there. In about 1840, aged in his mid-twenties, he became curious about a puzzling quirk of bone meal fertilizers – namely that bone meal spread on certain soils like chalks and peats raised turnip yields wondrously, but the same meal on a clay soil had no effect at all. No one knew why. Lawes began to conduct experiments on the family farm, using various combinations of soils, plants and manures to try to get to the bottom of the problem. It was essentially the start of scientific farming. In 1843, the year that Loudon died, he turned part of the farm into the Rothamstead Experimental Station – the world's first agricultural research station.

Lawes was gloriously obsessed with fertilizers and manures. Nobody has ever taken a deeper – a more literally hands-on – interest in them than Lawes did. There wasn't an aspect of their powers that didn't excite his fascination. He fed his animals different diets, then studied their dung to see how they affected yields. He doused plants in every combination of chemicals he could think of, and in so doing discovered that mineral phosphates treated with acid made bone meal effective in all soils, though he didn't know why. (The answer came much later from elsewhere and was explained by the fact that the active fertilizing agent in animal bones, calcium phosphate, was inert in alkaline soils, and needed acid to be activated.) Nonetheless Lawes had created the first chemical fertilizer, which he called super-phosphate of lime. The world had the fertilizer it desperately needed. Such was his devotion to his business that on his honeymoon he took his bride on an extended tour of the industrial reaches of the Thames and its tributaries looking for a site for a new factory. He died in 1900 very rich.

*   *   *

All of these developments – the rise of amateur gardening, the growth of suburbs, the development of potent fertilizers – led to one final momentous development that transformed the way the world looks but is hardly ever noted: the rise of the household lawn.

Before the nineteenth century lawns in any meaningful sense were the preserve almost exclusively of owners of stately homes and institutions with large grounds because of the cost of maintaining them. For those who wished to have a greensward of grass, there were only two options. The first was to keep a flock of sheep. That was the option chosen for Central Park in New York, which until the end of the nineteenth century was home to a roaming flock of two hundred sheep superintended by a shepherd who lived in the building that was until recently the Tavern-on-the-Green. The other option was to employ a dedicated team of people who would spend the whole of every growing season scything, gathering and carting away grass. Both options were expensive and neither gave a very good finish. Even the most carefully scythed lawn was, by modern standards, rough and clumpy, and a sheep-grazed lawn was even worse. Which of these options Mr Marsham went for is impossible to say, but as he employed a gardener, James Baker, it is likely that the lawn was scythed. In any case, it almost certainly looked pretty terrible.

There is a very slight possibility that Mr Marsham made use of an exciting and slightly unnerving new contraption: the lawnmower. The lawnmower was the invention of one Edwin Beard Budding, a foreman in a cloth factory in Stroud, Gloucestershire, who in 1830, while staring at a machine used to trim cloth, hit on the idea of turning the cutting mechanism on its side, putting it into a smaller contraption with wheels and a handle and using it to cut grass. Considering that no one had ever thought to mow grass before, this was quite a novel concept. Even more remarkable was that Budding's machine, as eventually patented, anticipated the look and operation of the modern cylinder mower to a startling degree.

It differed in just two critical respects. First, it was immensely heavy and difficult to manoeuvre. James Ferrabee & Co., the manufacturer of Budding's machine, promised in a prospectus that owners of their new machine – not, interestingly, gardeners or estate workers but the owners themselves – would find that it provided 'an amusing, useful and healthy exercise', and included illustrations showing happy purchasers walking with the machine as if pushing a baby carriage across a smooth surface. In fact, the Budding machine was exhausting. The operator had not only to engage a heavy clutch, and grip it fiercely, but then had to lean into the machine with all his might to make it move. Manhandling it into a new position at the end of each row was barely possible without assistance.

The other distinctive problem with Budding's machine was that it didn't cut very well. Because it was so heavy and poorly balanced, the blades often either spun helplessly above the grass or bit savagely into the turf. Only intermittently did they leave in their wake smoothly cropped grass. The machine was also expensive. In consequence of all this, it failed to sell in any great numbers, and Budding and Ferrabee soon parted ways.

Other manufacturers, however, took Budding's concept and slowly but doggedly improved it. The main problem was weight. Cast iron is immensely heavy. To overcome this, many of the early mechanical lawnmowers were designed to be pulled by horses. One enterprising manufacturer, the Leyland Steam Power Company, took up the idea first suggested by Jane Loudon in 1827 and built a steam-powered mower, but this proved so unwieldy and massive – it weighed over one and a half tons – that it was only ever barely under control and in constant danger of ploughing through fences and hedges.* Finally, the introduction of simple drive chains (borrowed from the other new wonder of the age, the bicycle) and Henry Bessemer's new lightweight steels made the small push-along mower a practical proposition, and that was just what the small suburban garden needed. By the last quarter of the nineteenth century, the lawnmower was comfortably established as a part of gardening life. On even the most modest properties, a good, well-cut lawn became the ideal. For one thing, it was a way of announcing to the world that the householder was prosperous enough that he didn't need to use the space to grow vegetables for his dinner table.

Apart from coming up with the initial idea, Budding himself had nothing more to do with lawnmowers, but he did go on to create another invention that proved of lasting benefit to humanity: the adjustable spanner. But it was his lawnmower that for ever changed the world beneath our feet.

Today for many people gardening is about lawns and

---

* Eventually Leyland abandoned steam and mowers, and developed an interest in the new internal combustion engine. It finished life as British Leyland, the car manufacturer.

almost nothing else. In the United States lawns cover more surface area – 50,000 square miles – than any single farm crop. Grass on domestic lawns wants to do what wild grasses do in nature – namely, grow to a height of about two feet, flower, turn brown and die. To keep it short and green and continuously growing means manipulating it fairly brutally and pouring a lot of stuff on to it. In the western United States about 60 per cent of all the water that comes out of taps for all purposes is sprinkled on lawns. Worse still are the amounts of herbicides and pesticides – 70 million pounds of it a year – that are soaked into lawns. It is a deeply ironic fact that for most of us keeping a handsome lawn is about the least green thing we do.

And on that somewhat dispiriting note, let's return to the house and the last room we'll visit before we head upstairs.

CHAPTER THIRTEEN

The Plum Room

I

WE CALL IT THE PLUM ROOM for no other reason than that the walls were painted that colour when we moved in, and by accident the name stuck. There is no telling what the Reverend Mr Marsham called this room. It appeared on the original plans as 'the Drawing Room', but then that key room was moved next door during the reshuffle that deprived the servants of the proposed 'Footman's Pantry' and gave Mr Marsham a spacious dining room instead. Whatever it was called, this room was clearly intended as a kind of parlour, probably for the receiving of favoured guests. Mr Marsham might have called it the library, for one section of wall is filled with a built-in bookcase reaching from floor to ceiling and large enough to hold about 600 books, a respectable number for a man of his profession in that day. By 1851, books for reading were widely affordable but books for show remained expensive, so if Mr Marsham's shelves held a collection of tooled calfskin it is entirely possible that that was display enough to give the room its name.

Mr Marsham seems to have lavished a good deal of care on this room. The cornice mouldings, wooden fireplace surround and bookshelves are all in a semi-exuberant classical style that bespeaks expense and thoughtful selection. Nineteenth-century pattern books offered homeowners an almost infinite array of shapely, esoterically named motifs – ovolos, ogees, quirks, crockets, scotias, cavettos, dentils, evolute spirals, even a 'Lesbian cymatium', and at least two hundred more – with which to individualize projecting surfaces of wood or plaster, and Mr Marsham chose liberally, opting for bubble-like beading around the doorcase, fluted columns at the windows, ribbony swags fluttering across the fireplace breast and a stately show of repeating demi-hemispheres in a style known as egg-and-dart around the ceiling trim.

Such decorative gusto was actually out of fashion by this time and marks Mr Marsham out as something of a rustic, but we may be grateful to him now, for the classical styles he selected take us in a straight line to the most influential architect in history – himself a rustic, as it happens – and onward to two of the most interesting houses ever built, both in America, both the work of rustics there. So this is really a chapter about architectural style in a domestic setting and some rustics who changed the world. It touches in passing on books, too – not inappropriately, I hope, for a chapter coming from a room that may or may not once have been a library.

For the story of how the plum room's stylistic features, and a great deal else in the built world beyond, got to look the way they do, we need to leave Norfolk and England, and take ourselves to the sunny plains of northern Italy and the pleasant and ancient city of Vicenza, halfway between Verona and Venice in the region known as the Veneto. At first glance, Vicenza seems much like any other northern Italian city of its size, but almost all visitors are soon overtaken by an odd sense of familiarity. Again and again, you turn corners to find yourself standing before buildings that you feel, in an almost uncanny way, you have seen before.

In a sense you have. For these buildings were the templates from which other important buildings all over the western world were derived: the Louvre, the White House, Buckingham Palace, the New York Public Library, the National Gallery of Art in Washington and uncountable numbers of banks, police stations, courthouses, churches, museums, hospitals, schools, stately homes and unassuming houses. The Palazzo Barbarano and Villa Piovene clearly share architectural DNA with the New York Stock Exchange, the Bank of England and the Berlin Reichstag, among many others. The Villa Capra, on a hillside on the edge of town, brings to mind a hundred domed structures, from Vanbrugh's Temple of the Four Winds at Castle Howard to the Jefferson Memorial in Washington, DC. The Villa Chiericati, with its striking portico of triangular pediment and four severe columns, isn't just rather *like* the White House, it *is* the White House, but weirdly transferred to what is still a working farm a little beyond the city's eastern edge.

The person responsible for all this architectural prescience was a stonemason named Andrea di Pietro della Gondola who in 1524, aged not quite sixteen, arrived in Vicenza from his native Padua. There he befriended an influential aristocrat, Giangiorgio Trissino.

Had it not been for this lucky acquaintanceship, the young man would very probably have passed his life as a dusty hewer of stone, his genius unplumbed, and the world today would be a very different-looking place. Happily for posterity, Trissino perceived some talent worth nurturing within the boy. He brought him into his home, had him schooled in mathematics and geometry, took him to Rome to see the great buildings of antiquity and put before him every other possible advantage that would allow him to become the greatest, most confident, most improbably influential architect of his age. In the course of things, he also bestowed upon him the name by which we all know him now: Palladio, after Pallas Athene, the goddess of wisdom in ancient Greece. (Their relationship, I feel oddly bound to note, seems to have been entirely platonic. Trissino was a well-known ladies' man and his young mason was happily married and en route to becoming the father of five children. Trissino just liked Palladio a good deal. It seems that most people in Palladio's life did.)

And so under the older man's tutelage Palladio became an architect – an unusual step for someone of his background, for architects at that time normally began their careers as artists, not artisans. Palladio didn't paint or sculpt or draw; he just designed buildings. But his practical training as a mason gave him one invaluable advantage: it permitted him an intimate understanding of structures, and allowed him, in the phrase of Witold Rybczyński, to understand the *how* of a building as much as the *what*.

Palladio was a classic case of right talents, right place, right time. Vasco da Gama's epic voyage to India a quarter of a century earlier had broken Venice's monopoly over the European end of the spice trade, undermining its commercial dominance, and now the wealth of the region was migrating inland. Suddenly there was a new breed of gentleman farmers who had both wealth and architectural ambitions, and Palladio knew exactly how to take the one to satisfy the other. He began to dot Vicenza and the district around with the most perfect and agreeable houses ever built. His particular genius lay in the ability to design buildings that were faithful to the classical ideals yet were more beguiling and inviting, more endowed with comfort and élan, than the more severe ancient forms from which they derived. It was a reinvigoration of classical ideals and the world would come to love it.

Palladio didn't design many structures – a few palazzos, four churches, a convent, a basilica, two bridges and thirty villas, of which only seventeen still stand today. Of the missing thirteen villas, four were never finished, seven were destroyed, one was never built, and one is missing and unaccounted for. Called the Villa Ragona, if it was ever built it has never been found.

Palladio's methods were based on rigorous adherence to rules, and were modelled on the precepts of Vitruvius, a Roman architect of the first century BC. Vitruvius wasn't a particularly distinguished architect. He was really more of a military engineer. What made him valuable to history was the accidental fact that his writings survived – the only architectural work from classical antiquity to do so. A lone copy of Vitruvius's text on architecture was found on a shelf at a monastery in Switzerland in 1415. Vitruvius laid down exceedingly specific rules regarding proportions, orders, shapes, materials and anything else that could be quantified. Formulas ruled everything in his world. The amount of spacing between columns in a row, say, could never be left to instinct or feeling, but was dictated by strict formulas designed to confer an automatic and reliable harmony. This could be dizzyingly particular. For instance:

> The height of all oblong rooms should be calculated by adding together their measured length and width, taking one half of this total, and using the result for the height. But in the case of exedrae or square oeci, let the height be brought up to one and a half times the width . . . The height of the tablinum at the lintel should be one eighth more than its width. Its ceiling should exceed this height by one third of the width. The fauces in the case of smaller atriums should be two thirds, and in the case of larger one half, the width of the tablinum . . . Let the busts of ancestors with their ornaments be set up at a height corresponding to the width of the alae. The proportionate width and height of doors may be settled, if they are Doric, in the Doric manner, and if Ionic, in the Ionic manner, according to the rules of symmetry which have been given about portals in the Fourth Book.

Palladio, following Vitruvius, believed that all rooms should be one of seven elementary shapes – circular, square or five types of rectangle – and that particular rooms needed always to be built in particular proportions. Dining rooms, for example, had to be twice as long as they were wide. These shapes alone made for pleasing spaces, though why they did exactly he didn't say. (Neither, come to that, did Vitruvius.) In fact, however, Palladio followed his own precepts only about half the time. Some of the

rules Palladio decreed are doubtful, in any case. The idea
of a hierarchy among column types – Corinthian always
above Ionic and Ionic always above Doric – appears to be
the invention of Sebastiano Serlio, a contemporary of
Palladio's. The rule isn't mentioned by Vitruvius at all.
Palladio also made one very fundamental error. He put a
portico with columns on every villa he built, unaware that
these were found only on Roman temples and never on
homes. This is probably his most copied device and yet it
is, from the perspective of fidelity, completely wrong. But
it may also be the happiest error in architectural history.

Had he merely built a scattering of fine homes around
Vicenza, Palladio's name would never have become an
adjective. What made him famous was a book published
in 1570, towards the end of his life. Called *I Quattro Libri
dell'architettura (The Four Books of Architecture)*, it is partly a
book of floor plans and elevations, partly a declaration of
principles and partly a collection of practical advice. It is
full of rules and particulars – 'Of the height of the rooms',
'of the dimensions of the doors and windows' – but also
useful tips. (For example: don't place windows too near
corners, for they weaken the overall structure.) It was the
perfect book for gentlemen amateurs.

Palladio's first and greatest champion in the English-
speaking world was Inigo Jones, the theatrical designer
and self-taught architect, who discovered Palladio's work
on a visit to Italy twenty years after Palladio's death and
was smitten to the point of obsessiveness. He bought every
Palladio drawing he could lay his hands on – some two
hundred in all – learned to speak Italian, and even
modelled his signature on Palladio's. On his return to
England, he began putting up Palladian buildings at every

opportunity. The first was the Queen's House in Greenwich, built in 1616. To modern eyes, it is a rather dull square block that brings to mind the central police station in a small Midwestern city, but it was stunningly crisp and modern in Stuart England. Every building in the country suddenly seemed to belong to another, fussier age.

Palladianism became particularly associated with – and largely indistinguishable from – the Georgian period. This era of architectural orderliness began in 1714 with the accession of George I and lasted through the reigns of three more Georges and the son of a George, William IV, whose death in 1837 brought in Queen Victoria and a new dynastic era. In practice, of course, things were not that precise. Architectural style doesn't change just because a monarch dies. Nor does it stay still during the course of a long dynasty.

Because the Georgian period went on so long, various architectural refinements and elaborations arose and either fell away or prospered independently, so that it is sometimes impossible to distinguish meaningfully between Neoclassical, Regency, Italianate Revival, Greek Revival and other terms intended to denote a particular style, aesthetic or block of time. In America, Georgian became an unappealing label after independence (it wasn't actually much liked before), so there Colonial was coined for buildings pre-dating independence, and Federal for those built after.

What all these styles had in common was an attachment to classical ideals, which is to say to strict rules, and that wasn't always a terribly good thing. Rules meant that architects sometimes scarcely had to think at all. Mereworth, a stately home in Kent designed by Colen

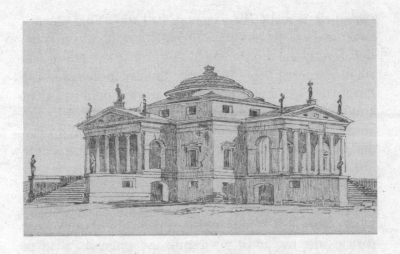

Palladio's Villa Capra ('La Rotonda') (top), and Thomas Jefferson's Monticello (bottom).

Campbell, is really just a copy of Palladio's Villa Capra – only the dome is somewhat altered – and many others are not a great deal more original. 'Fidelity to the canon was what mattered,' as Alain de Botton noted in *The Architecture of Happiness*. Though some splendid Palladian buildings were built – Chiswick House, Lord Burlington's outsized folly in west London, springs shiningly to mind – the overall effect over time was repetitious and just a little numbing. As the architectural historian Nikolaus Pevsner observed, 'it is not easy to keep apart in one's mind the various villas and country houses built during the period'.

So there is a certain satisfaction in the thought that perhaps the two most interesting and original Palladian houses of the age were built not in Europe by trained architects, but in a distant land by amateurs. But what amateurs they were.

II

In the autumn of 1769, on a hilltop in the piedmont of Virginia, on what was then the very edge of the civilized world, a young man began building his dream home. It would consume more than half a century of his life and nearly all his resources, and he would never see it finished. His name was Thomas Jefferson. The house was Monticello.

There had never been a house like it. This was, almost literally, the last house in the world. Before it lay an unexplored continent. Behind it was all the known world.

Perhaps nothing says more about Jefferson and his house than that it faces away from that old world and into the unknown emptiness of the new.

What was really distinctive about Monticello was that it was built on a hilltop. People didn't do that in the eighteenth century, and for good practical reasons. Jefferson created many disadvantages for himself by building where he did. For one thing, he had to run a road to the top, then clear and level acres of rocky summit – both huge jobs. He also had constantly to deal with the problem of water supplies. Water is always a problem on hilltops since it is in its nature to run downhill, so wells had to be dug unusually deep. Even then they ran dry on average about one year in five and water had to be carted up. Lightning was a chronic worry, too, as his house was the highest point for miles.

Monticello is Palladio's Villa Capra, but reinterpreted, built of different materials, standing in another continent – gloriously original, but faithful to the original too. The Age of Enlightenment was the perfect time for Palladian ideals. It was an intensely scientific period in which it was believed that everything, including beauty and its appreciation, could be reduced to scientific principles. That Palladio's book of plans was also a suitable primer for amateur architects made him practically, as well as spiritually, indispensable to a man like Jefferson. About 450 handbooks of architecture were produced in the half-century or so before Jefferson began work on Monticello, so he had plenty to choose from, but it was Palladio to whom he was devoted. 'Palladio is the Bible,' he wrote simply.

Jefferson, at the time he began Monticello, had never

been anywhere larger than Williamsburg, the colonial capital, where he had attended the College of William and Mary, and Williamsburg, with some two thousand people, was hardly a metropolis. Although he later travelled to Italy, he never saw the Villa Capra and would almost certainly have been astounded by it because the Villa Capra is enormous compared with Monticello. Though they look very similar in illustrations, Palladio's version is built on a scale that makes Monticello seem almost cottage-like. Partly this is because Monticello's service areas – the dependencies, as they were known – are built into the slope of the hill and are invisible from the house and garden. A lot of Monticello is essentially underground.

The Monticello visitors see today is a house Jefferson never saw but only dreamed of. It was never finished in his lifetime, or even in really good shape. For fifty-four years Jefferson inhabited a building site. 'Putting up and pulling down is one of my favourite amusements,' he remarked cheerfully, and it was just as well for he never stopped tinkering and messing. Because work was so protracted, some parts of Monticello were actively deteriorating while others were still a-building.

Many aspects of Jefferson's designs were tricky. The roof was a builder's nightmare because it involved un-necessarily complicated joining of hips to slopes. 'It was one place where he was definitely more amateur than pro-fessional,' Bob Self, architectural conservator of Monticello, told me while showing me around. 'The design was perfectly sound, but just a lot more compli-cated than it needed to be.'

As an architect, Jefferson was fastidious to the point of weirdness. Some of his plans specified measurements to seven decimal points. Self showed me one measuring a strangely precise 1.8991666 inches. 'Nobody, even now, could measure anything to that degree of accuracy,' he said. 'You are talking millionths of an inch. I suspect it was just a kind of intellectual exercise. There isn't anything else it could be really.'

The oddest feature of the house was the two staircases. Jefferson thought staircases a waste of space, so he made them only two feet wide and very steep – 'a little ladder of a staircase', as one visitor put it. The stairs were so narrow and twisting that almost everything that needed to go up them, including all but the smallest pieces of visitors' luggage, had to be winched up and hauled in through a window. The stairs were buried so deep in the house that no natural light reached them, so they were forbiddingly dark as well as steep. Negotiating them, particularly in descent, is an unnerving experience even now. Because of the danger, visitors are not allowed to go up to the first or second floors, so much of Monticello is, of unhappy necessity, off limits. (The space is mostly used for offices.) This means that visitors cannot see the most agreeable room in the house – the sky room, as Jefferson called it, occupying the space within the dome. With its yellow walls and green floor, its cool breezes and sumptuous views, this would make a perfect study or studio or retreat of any kind. But it has always been difficult to get to and in Jefferson's day it was unusable for about a third of the year because there was no effective way to heat it. In consequence, it became an attic room used for storage.

In other ways, the house was a marvel. The dome, Monticello's defining feature, had to be built in an odd way to fit on to existing load-bearing walls at the back. 'So although it looks completely regular,' Self said, 'it isn't. The whole thing was a huge exercise in calculus. The ribs that support it are all of different lengths but they had to span the same radius, so its design was all about sines and cosines. Not many people could have got that dome up there.' Other flourishes were generations ahead of their time. For one thing, Jefferson put thirteen skylights into the house, so it is unusually bright and airy.

Outside on the terrace Self pointed out to me a very beautiful spherical sundial in the garden that Jefferson had made himself. 'It's not just that it is a terrific piece of crafts-manship,' he said, 'but it's also that it couldn't be built without a thorough understanding of astronomy. It is quite amazing what he had the time and capacity to fit into his brain.'

Monticello became famous for its novelties – a dumb-waiter built into a fireplace, indoor privies, a device called a polygraph which used two pens to make a copy of any letter written on it. One feature, a pair of doors in which both opened when only one – either one – was pushed, charmed and mystified experts for a century and a half. It wasn't until the inner mechanisms were exposed during remodelling in the 1950s that renovators discovered that the doors were invisibly linked by a rod and pulleys under the floor – a fairly straightforward arrangement, as it turned out, but astounding because it represented a lot of cost and enterprise for very little effort saved.

Jefferson was amazingly energetic. His boast was that in fifty years the sun had never caught him in bed, and he scarcely wasted a moment of his eighty-three years. He was an obsessive record keeper. He had seven notebooks

on the go at any one time and into each of these he
recorded the most microscopic details of daily life. He
fully noted each day's weather, the migratory patterns of
birds, the dates on which flowers blossomed. He not only
kept copies of 18,000 letters he wrote, and saved the 5,000
he was sent, but also diligently logged them all in an
'Epistolary Record' which itself ran to more than 650
pages. He kept a record of every cent earned and spent. He
recorded how many peas it took to fill a pint pot. He kept
full, individual inventories for his slaves, giving an unusually complete record of how they were treated and
what they owned.

Yet, strangely, he didn't keep a diary or an inventory of
Monticello itself. 'We know more about Jefferson's house
in Paris than this one, oddly enough,' Susan Stein, the
senior curator, told me when I visited Monticello. 'We
don't know what kind of floor coverings he had in most
rooms and can't always be sure about a lot of the furnishings. We know the house had two indoor privies, but we
don't know who got to use them or what they used for
toilet paper. These things don't get recorded.' So we are in
the strange position with Jefferson that we know everything about the 250 types of edible plant he grew (he
organized them by whether they were eaten for their roots,
fruits or leaves), but surprisingly little about many aspects
of his life indoors.

The house was always terribly self-indulgent. When
Jefferson brought his young bride, Martha, to Monticello
in 1772, it was already three years into its building and
clear at a glance that this was *his* house. His private study,
for instance, was almost twice the size of both the dining
room and marital bedroom. The things that featured in

the house were designed to meet his needs and whims. He could, for instance, check the wind direction and speed from any of five locations in the house – not something that Mrs Jefferson was crying out for.

After Martha's early death, just ten years into their marriage, the house became even more decidedly his. Guests were not permitted into any of the private parts of the house – which is to say most of it – except under escort. Those who wished to browse in the library had to wait for Mr Jefferson to take them in personally.

Of all the puzzling lapses in Jefferson's record-keeping, the most surprising perhaps is that he didn't keep a record of his books, and had no idea how many he actually had. Jefferson loved books and was very lucky to live in a generation when books were becoming commonplace. Until comparatively recently books had been really quite rare. When Jefferson's father died in 1757, he left a library of forty-two books, and that was regarded as pretty impressive. A library of four hundred books – the number that John Harvard left at his death – was considered so colossal that they named Harvard College after him. Over the course of his life, Harvard had acquired books at the rate of about twelve a year. Jefferson, over the course of *his* life, bought books at the rate of about twelve a *month*, accumulating a thousand every decade on average.

Without his books, Thomas Jefferson could not have been Thomas Jefferson. For someone like him living on a frontier, remote from actual experience, books were vital guides to how life might be lived, and none gave him greater inspiration, satisfaction and useful instruction than I *Quattro Libri*.

III

Because of financial constraints and his endless tinkering, Monticello never looked its best or even close to it. In 1802 when a Mrs Anna Maria Thornton came to visit she was shocked to find she still had to enter across wobbly planks. By this time Jefferson had been working on the house for over thirty years. 'Tho' I had been prepared to see an unfinished house, still I could not help being struck with . . . the general gloom,' she marvelled in her diary. Jefferson himself never much minded the inconvenience. 'We are now living in a brick kiln,' he wrote happily at one point to a friend. Jefferson was not a great caretaker either. In Virginia's muggy climate exterior wood needs repainting at least once every five years. As far as can be determined, Jefferson never repainted at all. Termites began chewing up structural timbers almost as soon as they went up, and dry rot swiftly set in too.

Jefferson was constantly in financial difficulties, but they were difficulties of his own making. He was a breathtaking spender. When he returned from five years in France in 1790, he brought back a shipload of furniture and household goods – five stoves, fifty-seven chairs, assorted mirrors, sofas and candlesticks, a coffee urn that he had designed himself, clocks, linens, crockery of every description, 145 rolls of wallpaper, a supply of Argand lamps, four waffle irons and much more – enough to fill eighty-six large crates. In addition he brought home a horse-drawn carriage. All of this he had delivered to his residence in Philadelphia, then the nation's capital, and went straight out to buy more.

Although personally ascetic – Jefferson dressed less showily than his own household servants – he spent colossal sums on food and drink. During his first term as president he spent $7,500 – equivalent to about $120,000 in today's money – on wine alone. During one eight-year period, he purchased no fewer than twenty thousand bottles of wine. Even aged eighty-two and hopelessly saddled with debts, he was 'still ordering Muscat de Rivesaltes in 150-bottle lots', as one biographer notes with undisguised wonder.

Many of Monticello's quirks spring from the limitations of Jefferson's workmen. He had to stick to a simple Doric style for the exterior columns because he could find no one with the skills to handle anything more complex. But the greatest problem of all, in terms of both expense and frustration, was a lack of home-grown materials. It is worth taking a minute to consider what the American colonists were up against in trying to build a civilization in a land without infrastructure.

Britain's philosophy of empire was that America should provide it with raw materials at a fair price and take finished products in return. The system was enshrined in a series of laws known as the Navigation Acts, which stipulated that any product bound for the New World had either to originate in Britain or pass through it on the way there, even if it had been created in, say, the West Indies, and ended up making a pointless double crossing of the Atlantic. The arrangement was insanely inefficient, but gratifyingly lucrative to British merchants and manufacturers, who essentially had a fast-growing continent at their commercial mercy. By the eve of the revolution America effectively *was* Britain's export market. It took 80 per cent of British linen exports, 76 per cent of exported nails, 60 per cent of wrought iron and nearly half of all the glass sold abroad. In bulk terms, America annually imported 30,000 pounds of silk, 11,000 pounds of salt and over 130,000 beaver hats, among much else. Many of these things – not least the beaver hats – were made from materials that originated in America in the first place and could easily have been manufactured in American factories – a point that did not escape the Americans.

America's small internal market and problems of distribution over such a large area meant that Americans couldn't compete even when they dared to try. Several fairly substantial glass-making operations were set up in the 1700s, and some even prospered briefly, but by the time of the revolution no glass was being made in the colonies. In most households a broken window stayed broken. Glass was so rare everywhere that immigrants were advised to bring their own window glass with them. Iron, likewise, was in chronic short supply. Paper was often so scarce as to be effectively non-existent. Only the most basic pottery was made in America – jugs, crocks and the like; anything of quality, like porcelain and bone china, had to come from (or, even more expensively, through) Britain. For Jefferson and other Virginia planters the problem was compounded by the absence of towns. It was easier to communicate with London than with other colonies.

The consequence of this was that practically everything had to be ordered through a distant agent. Every wish had to be made known in exhaustive detail, but ultimately one had to trust to a stranger's judgement and honest devotion. The scope for disappointment was vast. A typical order from George Washington (this one in 1757) gives some sense of the innumerable things Americans were unable to produce for themselves. Washington requested six pounds of snuff, two dozen sponge tooth-brushes, twenty sacks of salt, fifty pounds of raisins and almonds, a dozen mahogany chairs, two tables ('4½ feet square when spread, and to join occasionally'), a large Cheshire cheese, some marble for a chimney, a quantity of papier mâché and wallpaper, one cask of cider, fifty pounds of candles, twenty loaves of sugar and 250 panes of glass, among much else.

'N.B. Let it be carefully pack'd,' he added just a touch plaintively, but futilely, for nearly every shipment came with goods broken, spoiled or missing. When you have waited the better part of a year for, say, twenty panes of glass only to find half of them broken and the others of the wrong size, even the most stoic temperaments tended to unravel.

From the merchants' and agents' point of view, the orders were sometimes mystifyingly ambiguous. One from Washington instructed his London agent to acquire for him 'two Lyons after the Antique Lyon's in Italy'. The agent correctly surmised that Washington meant statuary, but could only guess the types and sizes. Since Washington had never been within an ocean's breadth of Italy, it is likely that he wasn't entirely sure himself. Washington's letters to his London agency, Robert Cary & Co., constantly asked for items that were 'fashionable' and 'in the latest taste' or 'uniformly handsome and genteel', but his follow-up letters indicate that he only seldom felt that he had got it.

Even the most carefully drawn instructions were dangerously susceptible to misinterpretation. Edwin Tunis relates the story of a man who enclosed with his order a drawing of the family crest that he wanted on his dinner service. To make sure his directions were fully understood, he appended a bold arrow to emphasize some detail. When the plates arrived the man discovered to his horror that the arrow had been faithfully copied on to every piece.

It was easy – and for many agents irresistibly tempting – to offload on to Americans clothes and furnishings that were unsold because they were no longer fashionable in England. 'You cannot really form an idea of the trash that is to be found in the best shops,' an English visitor named Margaret Hall wrote home to a friend. A cheerful catch-phrase of English factories became: 'It's good enough for America.' Being overcharged was a constant suspicion. Washington wrote furiously to Cary after one consignment that many of the products supplied were 'mean in quality but not in price, for in this they excel indeed far above any I have ever had'.

The carelessness of agents and merchants drove Americans half mad with exasperation. Colonel John Tayloe, while building the famous Octagon House in Washington, ordered a fireplace from the Coade factory in London, waited a year or so for its delivery, and was reduced to helpless sputters when he opened the crate and found that they had forgotten to pack the mantelshelf. Rather than wait for the shelf to arrive, he had a new one made from wood by a trustworthy American carpenter. The fireplace – still with a wooden top – remains one of the few Coade pieces in America.

Because of the difficulties of supply, plantation owners often had little choice but to make their own. Jefferson fired his own bricks – altogether some 650,000 of them –

but this was a difficult business as only about half from any load were usable because the heating was so uneven in his home-built kilns. He also began manufacturing his own nails. As tensions with Britain increased, matters grew more difficult still. In 1774, the Continental Congress passed a non-importation agreement. Jefferson discovered to his dismay that fourteen pairs of very expensive sash windows he had ordered from England, and really quite earnestly needed, could not now reach him.

This suppression of free trade greatly angered the Scottish economist Adam Smith (whose *Wealth of Nations*, not coincidentally, came out the same year that America declared its independence) but not nearly as much as it did the Americans, who naturally resented the idea of being kept eternally as a captive market. It would be overstating matters to suggest that the exasperations of commerce were the cause of the American revolution, but they were certainly a powerful component.

IV

While Thomas Jefferson was endlessly tinkering with Monticello, 120 miles to the north-east his colleague and fellow Virginian George Washington was facing similar obstacles and setbacks, and responding with the same kind of adaptive genius, with the rebuilding of Mount Vernon, his plantation home on the banks of the Potomac River near the modern District of Columbia. (The proximity is not coincidental. Washington was given the job of choosing the site of a new national capital, and chose one that was an easy ride from his plantation.)

When Washington moved to Mount Vernon in 1754 after the death of his half-brother Lawrence, it was a modest farmhouse of eight rooms. He spent the next thirty years rebuilding and expanding it into a stately mansion of twenty rooms – all elegantly proportioned and beautifully finished (and with many nods to Palladio). Washington enjoyed one brief youthful trip to Barbados but otherwise never left his 'Infant Woody Country', as he once called it. Yet a visitor to Mount Vernon was struck by its sophistication, as if Washington had toured the great houses and gardens of Europe and carefully selected the finest aspects of each.

He fussed over every detail. For eight years during the Revolutionary War, through all the hardships and distractions of battle, he wrote home weekly to enquire how things were going and to issue new or modified instructions for some element of design. Washington's foreman wondered, understandably, whether this was a good time to be investing money and energy in a house that the enemy might at any moment capture and destroy. Washington spent most of the war bogged down in fighting in the north, leaving his own part of the country chronically exposed to attack. Luckily the British never reached Mount Vernon. Had they got there, they almost certainly would have spirited off Mrs Washington and put the house and estate to the torch.

Despite the risks, Washington pressed on. Indeed, it was at the very lowest point of the war, in 1777, that Mount Vernon acquired its two most daring architectural features: its cupola and the open-air front porch, known as the piazza, with its distinctive rectangular pillars running the length of the east front of the house. The piazza was Washington's own design and it was his masterstroke. 'To this day,' writes Stewart Brand, 'it is one of the nicest places in America to just sit.' The cupola was Washington's idea too. It not only adds a jaunty cap to the roofline but served as a very effective air conditioner, catching passing breezes and directing them into the body of the house.

'The piazza is a really ingenious way of keeping the house shaded and cool and keeping the frontage attractive,' Dennis Pogue, associate director for preservation at Mount Vernon, told me when I was there. 'He was a much, much better architect than he is nearly always given credit for.'

Because he was continually adding to an existing structure, Washington had to make constant compromises. For structural reasons, he had to choose between redoing much of the interior or abandoning symmetry on the back end of the house – which is to say the side of the house that arriving visitors first saw. He chose to abandon symmetry. 'That was quite a brave and unusual thing to do in that age, but Washington was always pragmatic,' says Pogue. 'He preferred a sensible interior layout to an imposed symmetry without. He hoped people wouldn't notice.' In Pogue's experience about half of visitors don't. It has to be said the absence of symmetry is not particularly jarring, though for anyone who values balance it is hard not to notice that the cupola and pediment are a good foot and a half out of alignment.

Lacking building stone of any kind, Washington faced his house with planks of wood, carefully chamfered at the edges to look like blocks of cut stone and painted to disguise knots and grain. While the paint was still drying, sand was gently blown on to them to give a gritty, stone-like texture. The deception was so successful that even now guides point out the real nature of the building to visitors by rapping on it with their knuckles.

Washington didn't get to spend a lot of time enjoying Mount Vernon, and even when he was at home he didn't get much peace. One of the conventions of the age was to feed and put up any respectable-looking person who presented himself at the door. Washington was plagued with guests – he had 677 of them in one year – and many of those stayed for more than one night.

Washington died in 1799, just two years after retiring, and Mount Vernon began a long decline. By the middle of the following century, it was virtually derelict. Washington's heirs offered it to the nation at a reasonable price, but Congress didn't believe that its role included managing the homes of ex-presidents and declined to provide funds. In 1853, a woman named Louisa Dalton Bird Cunningham, while cruising up the Potomac on a passenger steamer, was so appalled by its condition that she started a foundation, the Mount Vernon Ladies' Association, which bought the place and began its long and heroic restoration. It still looks after it with intelligence and affection. Even more miraculous in its way is the survival of the peerless view across the Potomac. In the 1950s, a plan was unveiled to build a massive oil refinery on the opposite shore. A Congresswoman from Ohio, Frances Payne Bolton, successfully intervened and managed to save eighty square miles of Maryland foreshore for posterity, so that today the view remains as agreeable and satisfying as it was in Washington's day.

*   *   *

Monticello suffered similarly after Jefferson's death, though in fact it was already in a pretty decrepit state. A shocked visitor in 1815 recorded that nearly all the chairs were worn through and had pieces of stuffing sticking out of them. When Jefferson died at the age of eighty-three on 4 July 1826 – fifty years to the day after the signing of the Declaration of Independence – he had debts of more than $100,000, a colossal sum, and Monticello was looking threadbare.

Unable to afford the considerable upkeep on the house, Jefferson's daughter put it on the market for $70,000, but there were no takers. In the end it was sold for just $7,000 to a man named James Barclay who tried to make it into a silk farm. The enterprise failed miserably. Barclay ran off to the Holy Land to do missionary work, and the house became derelict. Weeds grew through the floorboards. Doors fell off. Cows wandered through empty rooms. Houdon's famous bust of Voltaire was found lying in a field. In 1836, just ten years after Jefferson died, Monticello was bought for $2,500 – a paltry sum for such a house even then – by an improbable figure named Uriah Phillips Levy. Nearly everything about Levy made him an unusual owner of a Virginian estate, but then nearly everything about him was unusual anyway. To begin with, he was a Jewish naval officer – the only one in the US Navy. He was also difficult and obstreperous – qualities that his superiors didn't like to see in any naval officer but ones that neatly fed any anti-Semitic prejudices they were inclined to hold already. Five times in his career Levy was court-martialled, and five times exonerated. Of equal consideration to his new neighbours was that he was from New York. A Jewish Yankee didn't have many friends in Virginia. At the outbreak of the Civil War, Monticello was seized by the Confederate government and Levy fled to Washington, the nearest safe refuge. He appealed to President Lincoln for help, and Lincoln, with a neat appreciation of aptness, appointed him to a seat on the federal court-martial board.

The Levy family owned Monticello for ninety years – far longer than Jefferson himself did. Without them, the house would never have survived. In 1923, they sold Monticello for $500,000 to the newly formed Thomas Jefferson Memorial Foundation, which embarked on a long programme of renovation. Not until 1954 was the work complete. Nearly two hundred years after Jefferson started on it, Monticello was finally the house he had intended it to be.

Had Thomas Jefferson and George Washington merely been plantation owners who built interesting houses, that would have been accomplishment enough, but in fact of course between them they also instituted a political revolution, conducted a long war, created and tirelessly served a new nation, and spent years away from home. Despite these distractions, and without proper training or materials, they managed to build two of the most satisfying houses ever built. That really is quite an achievement.

Monticello's celebrated contraptions – its silent dumbwaiters and dual-action doors and the like – are sometimes dismissed as gimmicks, but in fact they anticipated by 150 years or so the American love for labour-saving devices, and helped to make Monticello not just the most stylish house ever built in America but also

the first modern one. But it is Mount Vernon that has
been the more influential of the two. It became the ideal
from which countless other houses, as well as drive-
through banks, motels, restaurants and other roadside
attractions, derive. Probably no other single building in
America has been more widely copied – almost always,
alas, with a certain robust kitschiness, but that is hardly
Washington's fault and decidedly unfair to his reputation.
Not incidentally, he also introduced the first ha-ha into
America and can reasonably claim to be the father of the
American lawn; among all else he did, he devoted years of
meticulous effort to trying to create the perfect bowling
green, and in so doing became the leading authority in the
New World on grass seed and grass.

It is remarkable to think that much less than a century
separated Jefferson and Washington living in a wilderness
without infrastructure from a Gilded Age America that
dominated the world. At probably no time in history has
daily life changed more radically and comprehensively
than in the seventy-four years between the death of
Thomas Jefferson in 1826 and the beginning of the
following century – very nearly the same years, as it coincidentally happens, that marked the boundaries of our
own Mr Marsham's quietly uneventful life in England.

There is a small postscript to all this. In the summer of
1814 the British burned down America's Capitol Building
(an act of vandalism so infuriating to Jefferson that he
wanted to send American agents to London to set fire to
landmarks there) and with it went the Congressional
Library. Jefferson immediately, and generously, offered his
own library to the nation 'on whatever terms the Congress

might think proper'. Jefferson thought he had about ten thousand books, but when a delegation from the federal government came to survey the collection, they found that the number was in fact 6,487. Worse, when they had a look at the books, they weren't at all sure they wanted them. Many, they felt, were of no use to Congress as they covered topics like architecture, wine-making, cooking, philosophy and art. About a quarter were in foreign languages, 'which cannot be read', the delegation noted grimly, while a good many more were of an 'immoral and irreligious nature'. In the end, the Congressmen allotted Jefferson $23,900 for the library – considerably less than half its value – and rather grudgingly took it away. Jefferson, as might have been expected, immediately embarked on building a new library, and had accumulated about a thousand new books by the time of his death the following decade.

Congress may not have been especially grateful for this windfall, but the purchase gave the infant United States the most sophisticated governmental library in the world and completely redefined such a library's role. Government libraries previously had been mere reference rooms, designed for strictly utilitarian purposes, but this was to be a comprehensive, universal collection – an entirely different concept.

Today the Library of Congress is the largest library in the world, with more than 115 million books and related items. Unfortunately, Jefferson's part of it didn't last long. Thirty-six years after the Jefferson library was purchased, early on a Christmas Eve morning, one of the chimneys in the Capitol library caught fire. Because it was early and a holiday no one was around to notice the fire or check its spread. By the time the blaze was discovered and brought under control, most of the collection was destroyed, including Jefferson's precious copy of *I Quattro Libri*.

The year of the fire, it almost goes without saying, was 1851.

CHAPTER FOURTEEN

The Stairs

I

WE NOW COME to the most dangerous part of the house – in fact, one of the most hazardous environments anywhere: the stairs. No one knows exactly how dangerous the stairs are because records are curiously deficient. Most countries keep records of deaths and injuries sustained in falls, but not of what caused the falls in the first place. So in the United States, for instance, it is known that about 12,000 people a year hit the ground and never get up again, but whether that is because they have fallen from a tree, a roof or off the back porch is unknown. In Britain, fairly scrupulous stair-fall figures were kept until 2002, but then the Department for Trade and Industry decided that keeping track of these things was an extravagance it could no longer afford, which seems a fairly misguided economy considering how much fall injuries cost society. The last set of figures indicated that a rather whopping 306,166 Britons were injured seriously enough in stair falls to require medical attention

'Perspective of a staircase' by Thomas Malton.

that year, so it is clearly more than a trifling matter.

John A. Templer of MIT, author of the definitive (and, it must be said, almost only) scholarly text on the subject, *The Staircase: Studies of Hazards, Falls, and Safer Design*, suggests that all fall-injury figures are probably severely underestimated anyway. Even on the most conservative calculations, however, stairs rank as the second most common cause of accidental death, well behind car accidents but far ahead of drownings, burns and other similarly grim misfortunes. When you consider how much falls cost society in lost working hours and the strains placed on health systems it is curious that they are not studied more attentively. Huge amounts of money and bureaucratic time are invested in fire prevention, fire research, fire codes and fire insurance, but almost none is spent on the understanding or prevention of falls.

Everybody trips on stairs at some time or other. It has been calculated that you are likely to miss a step once in every 2,222 occasions you use stairs, suffer a minor accident once in every 63,000 uses, a painful accident once in every 734,000, and need hospital attention once every 3,616,667 uses.

Eighty-four per cent of people who die in stair falls at home are sixty-five or older. This is not so much because the elderly are more careless on stairs, but because they don't get up so well afterwards. Children, happily, only very rarely die in falls on stairs, though households with young children in them have by far the highest rates of injuries, partly because of high levels of stair usage and partly because of the startling things children leave on steps. Unmarried people are more likely to fall than married people, and previously married people fall more

than both of those. People in good shape fall more
often than people in bad shape, largely because they do a
lot more bounding and don't descend as carefully and
with as many rest stops as the tubby or infirm.

The best indicator of personal risk is whether you have
fallen much before. Accident proneness is a slightly
controversial area among stair-injury epidemiologists, but
it does seem to be a reality. About four persons in ten
injured in a stair fall have been injured in a stair fall
before.

People fall in different ways in different countries.
Someone in Japan, for instance, is far more likely to be
hurt in a stair fall in an office, department store or railway
station than is anyone in the United States. This is not
because the Japanese are more reckless stair users, but
simply because Americans don't much use stairs in public
environments. They rely on the ease and safety of lifts and
escalators. American stair injuries overwhelmingly happen
in the home – almost the only place where many
Americans submit themselves to regular stair use. For the
same reason, females are far more likely to fall down stairs
than men: they use stairs more, especially at home where
falls most commonly occur.

When we fall on stairs, we tend to blame ourselves and
generally attribute the fall to carelessness or inattentiveness.
In fact, design substantially influences the likelihood of
whether you will fall, and how hurt you will feel when you
have stopped bouncing. Poor lighting, absence of handrails,
confusing patterns on the treads, risers that are unusually
high or low, treads that are unusually wide or narrow and
landings that interrupt the rhythm of ascent or descent are
the principal design faults that lead to accidents.

According to Templer, stair safety is not one problem but two: 'avoiding the circumstances that cause accidents and designing stairs that will minimize injuries if an accident occurs'. He notes how at one New York City railway station (he doesn't say which) the stair edges had been given a non-slip covering with a pattern that made it difficult to discern the stair edge. In six weeks, more than fourteen hundred people – a truly astonishing number – fell down these stairs, at which point the problem was fixed.

Stairs incorporate three pieces of geometry: rise, going and pitch. The rise is the height between steps, the going is the step itself (technically, the distance between the leading edges, or nosings, of two successive steps measured horizontally) and the pitch is the overall steepness of the stairway. Humans have a fairly narrow tolerance for differing pitches. Anything more than 45 degrees is uncomfortably taxing to walk up, and anything less than 27 degrees is tediously slow. It is surprisingly hard to walk on steps that don't have much pitch, so our zone of comfort is a small one. An inescapable problem with stairs is that they have to convey people safely in both directions, whereas the mechanics of locomotion require different postures in each direction. (You lean into the stairs when climbing but hold your centre of gravity back in descent, as if applying a brake.) So stairs that are safe and comfortable in the ascent may not be so good for going down and vice versa. How far the nosing projects outward from the tread, for one thing, can materially affect the likelihood of a mishap. In a perfect world, stairs would change shape slightly depending on whether a user was going up or down them. In practice, every staircase is a compromise.

Let's look at a fall in slow motion. Descending a staircase is in a sense a controlled fall. You are propelling your body outwards and downwards in a manner that would clearly be dangerous if you weren't fully on top of things. The problem for the brain is distinguishing the moment when a descent stops being controlled and starts being a kind of unhappy mayhem. The human brain responds very quickly to danger and disarray, but it still takes a fraction of a moment – 190 milliseconds to be precise – for the reflexes to kick in and for the mind to assimilate that something is going wrong (that you have just stepped on a skate, say) and to clear the decks for a tricky landing. During this exceedingly brief interval the body will descend, on average, seven more inches – too far, generally, for a graceful landing. If this event happens on the bottom step you come down with an unpleasant jolt – more of an affront to your dignity than anything else. But if it happens higher up, your feet simply won't be able to make a stylish recovery, and you had better hope that you can catch the handrail – or indeed that there *is* a handrail. One study in 1958 found that in three-quarters of all stair falls no handrail was available at the point of the fall's origin.

The two times to take particular care on staircases are at the beginning and end of a journey. It is then that we seem to be most inclined to be distracted. As many as one-third of all stair accidents occur on the first or last step, and two-thirds occur on the first or last *three* steps. The most dangerous circumstance of all is having a single step in an unexpected place. Nearly as dangerous are stairs with four or fewer risers. They seem to inspire overconfidence.

Not surprisingly, going downstairs is much more

dangerous than going up. Over 90 per cent of injuries occur during descent. The chances of having a 'severe' fall are 57 per cent on straight flights of stairs, but only 37 per cent on stairs with a dogleg. Landings too need to be of a certain size – the width of a step plus the width of a stride is considered about right – if they are not to break the rhythm of the stair user. A broken rhythm is a prelude to a fall.

For a long time it was recognized that people going up and down steps appreciate being able to do so with a certain rhythm, and that this instinct could most readily be satisfied by having broad treads on short climbs and narrower treads on steeper climbs. Classical writers on architecture had surprisingly little to say on the design of stairs, however. Vitruvius merely suggested that stairs should be well lit. His concern was not to reduce the risk of falls but to keep people moving in opposite directions from colliding (another reminder of just how dark it could be in the pre-electrical world). It wasn't until the late seventeenth century that a Frenchman named François Blondel devised a formula that mathematically fixed the relationship between riser and tread. Specifically he suggested that for every unit of increased height the depth of tread should be decreased by two units. The formula was widely adopted and even now, more than three hundred years later, remains enshrined in many building codes even though it doesn't actually work very well – or indeed at all – on stairs that are either unusually high or unusually low.

In modern times, the person who took the design of stairs most seriously was, surprisingly, Frederick Law Olmsted. Although almost nothing in his work required it of him, Olmsted measured risers and treads fastidiously – sometimes obsessively – for nine years in an attempt to arrive at a formula that ensured staircase comfort and safety in both directions. His findings were converted into a pair of equations by a mathematician named Ernest Irving Freeze. They are:

$$R = 9 - \sqrt{1/7\ (G - 8)\ (G - 2)}$$

and

$$G = 5 + \sqrt{7\ (9 - R)^2 + 9}$$

The first, I am told, is for when the going is fixed, and the second for when it is not.

In our own time, Templer suggests that risers should be between 6.3 inches and 7.2 inches and that goings should never be less than nine inches, but ought to be more like eleven, but if you look around you will see that there is huge variability. In general, according to the *Encyclopaedia Britannica*, US steps tend to be slightly higher, per unit of tread, than British ones, and European ones higher still, but it doesn't quantify the statement.

In terms of the history of stairs, not a great deal can be said. No one knows where stairs originated or when, even roughly. The earliest, however, may not have been designed to convey people upwards to an upper storey, as you might expect, but rather *downwards*, into mines. In 2004, the most ancient wooden staircase yet found, dating from about three thousand years ago, was discovered a hundred metres underground in a Bronze Age salt mine at Hallstatt in Austria. It was possibly the first environment in which an ability to ascend and descend by foot alone (as opposed to a ladder, where hands are needed, too) was a positive and necessary advantage since it would leave both arms free to carry heavy loads.

In passing, one linguistic curiosity is worth noting. As nouns, 'upstairs' and 'downstairs' are surprisingly recent additions to the language. 'Upstairs' isn't recorded in English until 1842 (in a novel called *Handy Andy* by one Samuel Lover), and 'downstairs' is first seen the following year in a letter written by Jane Carlyle. In both cases, the context makes clear that the words were already in existence – Jane Carlyle was no coiner of terms – but no earlier written records have yet been found. The upshot is that for at least three centuries people lived on multiple floors, yet had no convenient way of expressing it.

II

While we are on the topic of how our houses can hurt us, we might pause on the landing for a moment and consider one other architectural element that has throughout history proved lethal to a startlingly large number of people: the walls, or more specifically the things that go on the walls, namely paint and wallpaper. For a very long time both were, in various ways, robustly harmful.

Consider wallpaper, a commodity that was just becoming popular in ordinary homes at the time Mr Marsham built his rectory. For a long time wallpaper – or 'stained paper', as it was still sometimes called – had been very expensive. It was heavily taxed for over a century, but it was also extremely labour-intensive to make. It was made not from wood pulp but from old rags. Sorting through rags was a dirty job that exposed the sorters to a range of infectious diseases. Until the invention of a machine that could create continuous lengths of paper in 1802, the maximum size of each sheet was only two feet or so, which meant that paper had to be joined with great skill and care. The Countess of Suffolk paid £42 to wall paper a single room at a time (the 1750s) when a good London house cost just £12 a year to rent. Flocked wallpaper, made from dyed stubbles of wool stuck to the surface of wallpaper, became wildly fashionable after about 1750 but presented additional dangers to those involved in its manufacture as the glues were often toxic.

When the wallpaper tax was finally lifted, in 1830, wallpaper really took off (or perhaps I should say really went on). The number of rolls sold in Britain leapt from one million in 1830 to thirty million in 1870, and this was when it really started to make a lot of people sick. From the outset wallpaper was often coloured with pigments that used large doses of arsenic, lead and antimony, but after 1775 it was frequently soaked in an especially insidious compound called copper arsenite, which was invented by the great but wonderfully hapless Swedish chemist Karl Scheele.* The colour was so popular that it became known as Scheele's green. Later, with the addition

---

* Scheele independently discovered eight elements – chlorine, fluorine, manganese, barium, molybdenum, tungsten, nitrogen and oxygen – but received credit for none of them in his lifetime. He had an unfortunate habit of tasting every substance he worked with, as a way of familiarizing himself with its properties, and eventually the practice caught up with him. In 1786, he was found slumped at his workbench, dead from an accidental overdose from some toxic compound or other.

of copper acetate, it was refined into an even richer pigment known as emerald green. This was used to colour all kinds of things – playing cards, candles, clothing and curtain fabrics, and even some foods. But it was especially popular in wallpaper. This was dangerous not only to the people who made or hung the wallpaper, but also to those who lived with it afterwards.

By the late nineteenth century, 80 per cent of English wallpapers contained arsenic, often in very significant quantities. A particular enthusiast was the designer William Morris, who not only loved rich arsenic greens but was on the board of directors of (and heavily invested in) a company in Devon that made arsenic-based pigments. Especially when damp was present – and in English homes it seldom was not – the wallpaper gave off a peculiar musty smell that reminded many people of garlic. People noticed that bedrooms with green wallpapers usually had no bedbugs. It has also been suggested that poisonous wallpaper could well account for why a change of air was so often beneficial for the chronically ill. In many cases they were doubtless simply escaping a slow poisoning. One such victim was Frederick Law Olmsted, a man we seem to be encountering more often than might be expected. He suffered apparent arsenic poisoning from bedroom wallpaper in 1893, at just the time people were finally figuring out what was making them unwell in bed, and needed an entire summer of convalescence – in another room.

Paints were surprisingly dangerous, too. The making of paints involved the mixing of many toxic products – in particular lead, arsenic and cinnabar (the parent ore of mercury). Painters commonly suffered from a vague but embracing malady called painters' colic, which was essentially lead poisoning with a flourish.* Painters purchased white lead as a block, then ground it to a powder, usually by rolling an iron ball over it repeatedly. This got a lot of dust on to their fingers and into the air, and the dust so created was highly toxic. Among the many symptoms painters tended to come down with were palsies, racking cough, lassitude, melancholy, loss of appetite, hallucinations and blindness. One of the quirks of lead poisoning is that it causes an enlargement of the retina that makes some victims see halos around objects – an effect Vincent Van Gogh famously exploited in his paintings. It is probable that he was suffering lead poisoning himself. Artists often did. One of those made seriously ill by white lead was James McNeill Whistler, who used a lot of it in creating the lifesized painting 'The White Girl'.

Today lead paint is banned almost everywhere except for certain very specific applications, but it is much missed by conservators because it gave a depth of colour and a mellow air that modern paints really can't match. Lead paint looks especially good on wood.

Painting also involved many problems of demarcation. Who was allowed to do what in England was

* Although lead's dangers have been well known for a long time, it continued to be used in many products well into the twentieth century. Food came in cans sealed with lead solder. Water was often stored in lead-lined tanks. Lead was sprayed on to fruit as a pesticide. Lead was even used in the manufacture of toothpaste tubes. It was banned from domestic paints in the United States in 1978 and in Britain in 1992. Although lead has been removed from most consumer products, it continues to build up in the atmosphere because of industrial applications. The average person of today has about 625 times more lead in his system than someone of fifty years ago.

very complicated thanks to the system of craft guilds, which meant that some practitioners could apply paint, some could apply distempers and some could do neither. Painters did most of the painting, as you would naturally expect, but plasterers were allowed to apply distemper (a kind of thin paint) to plastered walls – but only a few shades. Plumbers and glaziers, by contrast, could apply oil paints but not distemper. The reason for this is slightly uncertain, but it is probably attached to the fact that window frames were often made of lead – a material in which both plumbers and glaziers specialized.

Distemper was made from a mixture of chalk and glue. It had a softer, thinner finish that was ideal for plastered surfaces. By the mid-eighteenth century distempers normally covered walls and ceilings and heavier oil paints covered the woodwork. Oil paints were a more complex proposition. They consisted of a base (usually lead carbonate, or 'white lead'), a pigment for colour, a binder such as linseed oil to make it stick, and thickening agents like wax or soap, which is slightly surprising because eighteenth-century oil paints were already pretty glutinous and difficult to apply – 'like spreading tar with a broom', in the words of the writer David Owen. It wasn't until someone discovered that adding turpentine, a natural thinner distilled from the sap of pine trees, made the paint easier to apply that painting became smoother in every sense. Turpentine also gave paint a matt finish, and this became a fashionable look by the late eighteenth century.

Linseed oil was the magical ingredient in paint because it hardened into a tough film – essentially made paint paint. Linseed oil is squeezed from the seeds of flax, the plant from which linen comes (which is why flaxseeds are also called linseeds). Its one dramatic downside was that it is extremely combustible – a pot of linseed oil could in the right conditions burst into flame spontaneously – and so almost certainly was the source of many devastating house fires. It had to be used with special caution in the presence of open flames.

The most elementary finish of all was limewash, or whitewash, which was generally applied to more basic areas, like service rooms and servants' quarters. Whitewash was just a simple mix of quicklime and water (sometimes mixed with tallow to enhance adhesion); it didn't last long, but it did have the practical benefit of acting as a disinfectant. Despite the name whitewash, it was often tinted (if rather feebly) with colouring agents.

Painting was especially skilful because painters ground their own pigments and mixed their own paints – in other words created their own colours – and generally did so in great secrecy in order to maintain a commercial advantage over their rivals. (Add resins to linseed oil instead of pigment and you get varnish. Painters made this in great secrecy too.) Paint had to be mixed in small portions and used at once, so the ability to make matching batches from day to day was a real skill. They also had to apply several coats since even the best paints had little opacity. Generally, at least five coats were needed to cover a wall. So painting was a big and disruptive and fairly technical undertaking.

Pigments varied in price very significantly. Duller colours, like off-white and stone, could be had for four or five pence a pound. Blues and yellows were two to three times as expensive, and so tended to be used only by the middle classes and above. Smalt, a shade of blue made with ground glass which gave a glittery effect, and azurite, made from a semi-precious stone, were dearer still. The most expensive of all was verdigris, which was made by hanging copper strips over a vat of horse dung and vinegar and then scraping off the oxidized copper that resulted. It is the same process that turns copper domes and statues green – just quicker and more commercial – and it made 'the delicatest Grass-green in the world', as one eighteenth-century admirer enthused. A room painted in verdigris always produced an appreciative 'ah' in visitors.

When paints became popular, people wanted them to be as vivid as they could possibly be made. The restrained colours that we associate with the Georgian period in Britain, or Colonial period in America, are a consequence of fading, not decorative restraint. In 1979, when Mount Vernon began a programme of repainting the interiors in faithful colours, 'people came and just yelled at us', Dennis Pogue, the curator, told me with a grin when I visited. 'They told us we were making Mount Vernon garish. They were right – we were. But that's just because that's the way it was. It was hard for a lot of people to accept that what we were doing was faithful restoration.

'Even now paint charts for Colonial-style paints virtually always show the colours from the period as muted. In fact, colours were actually nearly always quite deep and sometimes even startling. The richer a colour you could get, the more you tended to be admired. For one thing, rich colours generally denoted expense, since you needed a lot of pigment to make them. Also, you need to remember that often these colours were seen by candlelight, so they needed to be more forceful to have any kind of impact in muted light.'

The effect is now repeated at Monticello, where several of the rooms are of the most vivid yellows and greens. Suddenly George Washington and Thomas Jefferson come across as having the decorative instincts of hippies. In fact, however, compared with what followed they were exceedingly restrained.

When the first ready-mixed paints came on to the market in the second half of the nineteenth century, people slapped them on with something like wild abandon. It became fashionable not just to have powerfully bright colours in the home, but to have as many as seven or eight colours in a single room.

If we looked closely, however, we would be surprised to note that two very basic colours didn't exist at all in Mr Marsham's day: a good white and a good black. The brightest white available was a rather dull off-white, and although whites improved through the nineteenth century, it wasn't until the 1940s, with the addition of titanium dioxide to paints, that really strong, lasting whites became available. The absence of a good white paint would have been doubly noticeable in early New England, for the Puritans not only had no white paint but didn't believe in painting anyway. (They thought it was showy.) So all those gleaming white churches we associate with New England towns are in fact a comparatively recent phenomenon.

Also missing from the painter's palette was a strong black. Permanent black paint, distilled from tar and pitch, wasn't popularly available until the late nineteenth century. So all the glossy black front doors, railings, gates, lampposts, gutters, downpipes and other fittings that are such an elemental feature of London's streets today are actually quite recent. If we were to be thrust back in time to Dickens's London, one of the most startling differences to greet us would be the absence of black painted surfaces. In the time of Dickens, almost all ironwork was green, light blue or dull grey.

Now we may proceed up the stairs to a room that may never actually have killed anyone but has probably been the seat of more suffering and despair than all the other rooms of the house put together.

CHAPTER FIFTEEN

The Bedroom

I

THE BEDROOM IS a strange place. There is no space within the house where we spend more time doing less, and doing it mostly quietly and unconsciously, than here, and yet it is in the bedroom that many of life's most profound and persistent unhappinesses are played out. If you are dying or unwell, exhausted, sexually dysfunctional, tearful, racked with anxiety, too depressed to face the world or otherwise lacking in equanimity and joy, the bedroom is the place where you are most likely to be found. It has been thus for centuries, but at just about the time that the Reverend Mr Marsham was building his house an entirely new dimension was added to life behind the bedroom door: dread. Never before had people found more ways to be worried in a small, confined space than Victorians in their bedrooms.

The beds themselves became a particular source of disquiet. Even the cleanest people became a steamy mass of toxins once the lights went out, it seemed. 'The water given

out in respiration,' explained Shirley Forster Murphy in
Our Homes, and How to Make Them Healthy (1883), 'is
loaded with animal impurities; it condenses on the inner
walls of buildings, and trickles down in foetid streams,
and . . . sinks into the walls,' causing damage of a grave but
unspecified nature. Why it didn't cause this damage when
it was in one's body in the first place was never explained
or evidently considered. It was enough to know that
breathing at night was a degenerate practice.

Twin beds were advocated for married couples, not
only to avoid the shameful thrill of accidental contact but
also to reduce the mingling of personal impurities. As one
medical authority grimly explained: 'The air which
surrounds the body under the bed clothing is exceedingly
impure, being impregnated with the poisonous substances
which have escaped through the pores of the skin.' Up to
40 per cent of deaths in America, one doctor estimated,
arose from chronic exposure to unwholesome air while
sleeping.

Beds were hard work, too. Turning and plumping
mattresses was a regular chore – and a heavy one, too. A
typical feather bed contained forty pounds of feathers.
Pillows and bolsters added about as much again and all of
these had to be emptied out from time to time to let the
feathers air, for otherwise they began to stink. Many
people kept flocks of geese, which they plucked for fresh
bedding perhaps three times a year (a job that must have
been as tiresome for the servants as it was for the geese). A
plumped feather bed may have looked divine, but
occupants quickly found themselves sinking into a hard,
airless fissure between billowy hills. Support was on a
lattice of ropes, which could be tightened with a key when

they began to sag (hence the expression 'sleep tight') but in no degree of tension did they offer much comfort. Spring mattresses were invented in 1865, but didn't work reliably at first because the coils would sometimes turn, confronting the occupant with the very real danger of being punctured by his own bed.

A popular American book of the nineteenth century, *Goodholme's Cyclopedia*, divided mattress types into ten levels of comfort. In descending order they were:

Down
Feathers
Wool
Wool-flock
Hair
Cotton
Wood-shavings
Sea-moss
Sawdust
Straw

When wood-shavings and sawdust make it into a top ten list of bedding materials you know you are looking at a rugged age. Mattresses were havens not only for bedbugs, fleas and moths (which loved old feathers when they could get at them) but for mice and rats as well. The sound of furtive rustlings beneath the coverlet was an unhappy accompaniment to many a night's sleep.

Children who were required to sleep in trundle beds low to the floor were likely to be especially familiar with the whiskery closeness of rats. Wherever people were, were rats. An American named Eliza Ann Summers reported in

1867 how she and her sister took armloads of shoes to bed each night to throw at the rats that ran across the floor. Susanna Augusta Fenimore Cooper, daughter of James Fenimore Cooper, said that she never forgot, or indeed ever quite got over, the experience of rats scuttling across her childhood bed.

Thomas Tryon, author of a book on health and well-being in 1683, complained of the 'Unclean, fulsom Excrement' of feathers as being attractive to bugs. He suggested fresh straw, and lots of it, instead. He also believed (with some justification) that feathers tended to be polluted with faecal matter from the stressed and unhappy birds from which they were plucked.

Historically, the most basic common filling was straw, whose pricks through the ticking were a celebrated torment, but people often used whatever they could. In Abraham Lincoln's boyhood home, dried cornhusks were used, an option that must have been as crunchily noisy as it was uncomfortable. If one couldn't afford feathers, wool or horsehair were cheaper alternatives, but they tended to smell. Wool often became infested with moths, too. The only certain remedy was to take the wool out and boil it, a tedious process. In poorer homes, cow dung was sometimes hung from the bedpost in the belief that it deterred moths. In hot climates, summertime insects coming through the windows were a nuisance and hazard. Netting was sometimes draped around beds, but always with a certain uneasiness as all netting was extremely flammable. A visitor to upstate New York in the 1790s reported how his hosts, in a well-meaning stab at fumigation, filled his room with smoke just before bedtime, leaving him to grope his way through a choking fog to his bed. Wire screens to keep out insects were invented early – Jefferson had them at Monticello – but not widely used because of the expense.

For much of history a bed was, for most homeowners, the most valuable thing they owned. In William Shakespeare's day, for instance, a decent canopied bed cost £5, half the annual salary of a typical schoolmaster. Because they were such treasured items, the best bed was often kept downstairs, sometimes in the living room, where it could be better shown off to visitors or seen through an open window by passers-by. Generally, such beds were notionally reserved for really important visitors, but in practice were hardly used, a fact that adds some perspective to the famous clause in Shakespeare's will in which he left his second-best bed to his wife, Anne. This has often been construed as an insult, when in fact the second-best bed was almost certainly the marital one and therefore the one with the most tender associations. Why Shakespeare singled out that particular bed for mention is a separate mystery since Anne would in the normal course of things have inherited all the household beds, but it was by no means the certain snub that some interpretations have made it.

Privacy was a much different concept in former times. In inns, sharing beds remained common into the nineteenth century, and diaries frequently contain entries lamenting how the author was disappointed to find a late-arriving stranger clambering into bed with him. Benjamin Franklin and John Adams were required to share a bed at an inn in New Brunswick, New Jersey, in 1776, and passed a grumpy and largely sleepless night squabbling over whether to have the window open or not.

Even at home, it was entirely usual for a servant to sleep at the foot of his master's bed whatever his master might be up to within the bed. The records make clear that King Henry V's steward and chamberlain both were present when he bedded Catherine of Valois. Samuel Pepys's diaries show that a servant slept on the floor of his and his wife's bedroom, and that he regarded her as a kind of living burglar alarm. In such circumstances, bed curtains provided a little privacy and cut down on draughts, too, but increasingly came to be seen as unhealthy refuges of dust and insects. Bed curtains could be a fire hazard, too – no small consideration when everything in the bedroom, from the rush matting on the floor to the thatch overhead, was energetically combustible. Nearly every household book cautioned against reading by candlelight in bed, but many people did anyway.

In one of his works, John Aubrey, the seventeenth-century historian, relates an anecdote concerning the marriage of Thomas More's daughter Margaret to a man named William Roper. In the story Roper calls one morning and tells More that he wishes to marry one of the latter's daughters – either one will do – upon which More takes Roper to his bedroom where the daughters are asleep in a truckle bed wheeled out from beneath the parental bed.* Leaning over, More deftly takes 'the sheet by the

* 'Truckle bed' and 'trundle bed' are two words for the same thing. 'Truckle' comes from the Greek *trochlea*, signifying something that slides, and 'trundle' is related to the Old English words *trindle* and *trendle*, all meaning something that moves along by rolling. 'Truckle bed' dates from 1459; 'trundle bed' followed about a hundred years later.

corner and suddenly whippes it off', Aubrey relates with words that all but glisten lustily, revealing the girls to be fundamentally naked. Groggily protesting at the disturbance, they roll on to their stomachs, and after a moment's admiring reflection Sir William announces that he has seen both sides now and with his stick lightly taps the bottom of sixteen-year-old Margaret. 'Here was all the trouble of the wooeing,' writes Aubrey with clear admiration.

However true or not the episode – and it is worth noting that Aubrey was writing more than a century after the fact – what is clear is that no one in his day thought it odd that More's grown daughters would sleep beside the parental bed.

The real problem with beds, certainly by the Victorian period, was that they were inseparable from that most troublesome of activities, sex. Within marriage, sex was of course sometimes necessary. Mary Wood-Allen in the popular and influential *What a Young Woman Ought to Know* assured her young readers that it was permissible to take part in physical intimacies within marriage, so long as it was done 'without a particle of sexual desire'. The mother's moods and musings at the time of conception and throughout pregnancy were thought to affect the foetus profoundly and irremediably. Partners were advised not to have intercourse unless they were 'in full sympathy' with each other at the time for fear of producing a failed child.

To avoid arousal more generally, women were instructed to get plenty of fresh air, avoid stimulating pastimes like reading and card games, and above all never to use their brains more than was strictly necessary.

Educating them was not simply a waste of time and resources but dangerously bad for their delicate constitutions. In 1865, John Ruskin opined in an essay that women should be educated just enough to make themselves practically useful to their spouses, but no further. Even the American Catherine Beecher, who was by the standards of the age a radical feminist, argued passionately that women should be accorded full and equal educational rights, so long as it was recognized that they would need extra time to do their hair.

For men, the principal and preoccupying challenge was not to spill a drop of seminal fluid outside the sacred bounds of marriage – and not much there either if one could decently manage it. As one authority explained, seminal fluid, when nobly retained within the body, enriched the blood and invigorated the brain. The consequence of discharging this natural elixir illicitly was to leave one literally enfeebled in mind and body. So even within marriage one should be spermatozoically frugal, as more frequent sex produced 'languid' sperm, which resulted in listless offspring. Monthly intercourse was recommended as a safe maximum.

Self-abuse was of course out of the question at all times. The well-known consequences of masturbation covered virtually every undesirable condition known to medical science, not excluding insanity and premature death. Self-polluters – 'poor creeping tremulous, pale, spindle-shanked, wretched creatures who crawl upon the earth', as one chronicler described them – were to be pitied. 'Every act of self-pollution is an earthquake – a blast – a deadly paralytic stroke,' declared another. Case studies vividly drove home the risks. A medical man named Samuel Tissot described how one of his patients drooled continuously, dripped watery blood from his nose and 'defecated in his bed without noticing it'. It was those last three words that were particularly crushing.

Worst of all, an addiction to self-abuse would automatically be passed on to offspring, so that every incident of wicked pleasure not only softened one's own brain but sapped the vitality of generations yet unborn. The most thorough analysis of sexual hazards, not to mention most comprehensive title, was provided by Sir William Acton in *The Functions and Disorders of the Reproductive Organs, in Childhood, Youth, Adult Age, and Advanced Life, Considered in Their Physiological, Social and Moral Relations*, first published in 1857. He it was who decided that masturbation would lead to blindness. He was also responsible for the oft-quoted assertion: 'I should say that the majority of women are not very much troubled with sexual feeling of any kind.'

Such beliefs held sway for an amazingly long time. 'Many of my patients told me that their first masturbatory act took place while witnessing some musical show,' Dr William Robinson reported grimly, and perhaps just a bit improbably, in a 1916 work on sexual disorders.

Fortunately, science was standing by to help. One remedy, described by Mary Roach in *Bonk: The Curious Coupling of Sex and Science*, was the Penile Pricking Ring, developed in the 1850s, which was slipped over the penis at bedtime (or indeed any time) and was lined with metal prongs that bit into any penis that impiously swelled beyond a very small range of permissible deviation. Other devices used electrical currents to jerk the subject into a startled but penitent wakefulness.

Penile pricking ring.

Not everyone agreed with these conservative views, it must be noted. As early as 1836, a French medical authority named François Lallemand published a three-volume study equating frequent sex with robust health. This so impressed a Scottish medical expert named George Drysdale that he formulated a philosophy of free love and uninhibited sex called *Physical, Sexual and Natural Religion*. Published in 1855, it sold 90,000 copies and was translated into eleven languages, 'including Hungarian', as the *Dictionary of National Biography* notes with its usual charming emphasis on pointless detail. Clearly, there was *some* kind of longing for greater sexual freedom in society. Unfortunately, society at large was still a century or so away from granting it.

In such a perpetually charged and confused atmosphere, it is perhaps little wonder that for many people successful sex was an unrealizable aspiration – and in no case more resoundingly than that of John Ruskin himself. In 1848, when the great art critic married nineteen-year-old

Euphemia 'Effie' Chalmers Gray, things got off to a bad start and never recovered. The marriage was never consummated. As she later related, Ruskin confessed to her that 'he had imagined women were quite different to what he saw I was and that the reason he did not make me his Wife was because he was disgusted with my person the first evening . . .'

Eventually able to take no more (or actually wanting to take a lot more, but with someone else) Effie filed a nullity suit against Ruskin, the details of which became a happy titillation for devotees of the popular press in many lands, and then ran off with the artist John Everett Millais, with whom she had a happy life and eight children. The timing of her virtual elopement with Millais was unfortunate as Millais was at that time engaged in painting a portrait of Ruskin. Ruskin, a man of honour, continued to sit for Millais, but the two men never again spoke. Ruskin sympathizers, of whom there were many, responded to the scandal by pretending there wasn't one. By 1900 the whole episode had been so effectively expunged from the record that W. G. Collingwood could, without a blush of embarrassment, write *The Life of John Ruskin* without hinting that Ruskin had ever been married, much less sent crashing from a room at the sight of female pubic hair.

Ruskin never overcame his prudish ways or gave any indication of desiring to. After the death of J. M. W. Turner – in 1851 – he was given the job of going through the works left to the nation by the great artist, and found several watercolours of a cheerfully erotic nature. Horrified, Ruskin decided that they could only have been drawn 'under a certain condition of insanity', and for the good of the nation destroyed almost all of them, robbing posterity of several priceless works.

Effie Ruskin's escape from her unhappy marriage was both lucky and unusual, for nineteenth-century divorce acts, like everything else to do with marriage, were overwhelmingly biased in favour of men. To obtain a divorce in Victorian England a man had merely to show that his wife had slept with another man. A woman, however, had to prove that her spouse had compounded his infidelity by committing incest, bestiality or some other dark and inexcusable transgression drawn from a very small list. Until 1857, a divorcee forfeited all her property and generally she lost the children too. Indeed, in law a wife had no rights at all – no right to property, no right of expression, no freedoms of any kind beyond those her husband chose to grant her. According to the great legal theorist William Blackstone, upon marriage a woman relinquished her 'very being or legal existence'. A wife had no legal personhood at all.

Some countries were slightly more liberal than others. In France, exceptionally, a woman could divorce a man on grounds of adultery alone, though only as long as the infidelity had occurred in the marital home. In England, however, standards were brutally unfair. In one well-known case, a woman named Martha Robinson was for years beaten and physically misused by a cruel and unstable husband. Eventually he infected her with gonorrhoea and then poisoned her almost to the point of death by slipping anti-venereal powders into her food without her knowledge. Her health and spirit broken, she sued for divorce. The judge listened carefully to the arguments, then dismissed the case and sent Mrs Robinson home with instructions to try to be more patient.

Even when things went well, it was difficult being a woman, for womanhood was automatically deemed to be a pathological condition. There was a belief, more or less universal, that women after puberty were either ill or on the verge of being ill almost permanently. The development of breasts, womb and other reproductive apparatus 'drained energy from the finite supply each individual possessed', in the words of one authority. Menstruation was described in medical texts as if it were a monthly act of wilful negligence. 'Whenever there is actual pain at any stage of the monthly period, it is because something is wrong either in the dress, or the diet, or the personal and social habits of the individual,' wrote one (male, of course) observer.

The painful irony is that women frequently *were* unwell because considerations of decorum denied them proper medical care. In 1856, when a young housewife in Boston, from a respectable background, tearfully confessed to her doctor that she sometimes found herself involuntarily thinking of men other than her husband, the doctor ordered a series of stringent emergency measures, which included cold baths and enemas, the removal of all stimulus, including spicy foods and the reading of light fiction, and the thorough scouring of her vagina with borax. Light fiction was commonly held to account for promoting morbid thoughts and a tendency to nervous hysteria. As one author gravely summarized: 'Romance-reading by young girls will, by this excitement of the bodily organs, tend to create their premature development, and the child becomes physically a woman months or even years before she should.'

As late as 1892, Judith Flanders reports, a man who took his wife to have her eyes tested was told that the problem was a prolapsed womb and that until she had a hysterectomy her vision would remain impaired.

Sweeping generalizations were about as close as any medical man would permit himself to get to women's reproductive affairs. This could have serious medical consequences since no doctor could make a proper gynaecological examination. In extremis, he might probe gently beneath a blanket in an underlit room, but this was highly exceptional. For the most part, women who had any medical complaint between neck and knees were required to point blushingly to the affected area on a dummy.

One American physician in 1852 cited it as a source of pride that 'women prefer to suffer the extremity of danger and pain rather than waive those scruples of delicacy which prevent their maladies from being fully explored'. Some doctors opposed forceps delivery on the grounds that it allowed women with small pelvises to bear children, thus passing on their inferiorities to their daughters.

The inevitable consequence of all this was that ignorance of female anatomy and physiology among medical men was almost medieval. The annals of medicine hold no better example of professional gullibility than the celebrated case of Mary Toft, an illiterate rabbit breeder from Godalming, in Surrey, who for a number of weeks in the autumn of 1726 managed to convince medical authorities, including two physicians to the royal household, that she was giving birth to a series of rabbits. The matter became a national sensation. Several of the medical men attended at the births, and professed total amazement. It was only when yet another of the king's physicians, a German named Cyriacus Ahlers, investigated more closely and pronounced the whole matter a hoax that Toft at last admitted the deception. She was briefly imprisoned for fraud but then sent home to Godalming, and that was the last that anyone ever heard of her.

An understanding of female anatomy and physiology was still a long way off, however. As late as 1878 the *British Medical Journal* was able to run a spirited and protracted correspondence on whether a menstruating woman's touch could spoil a ham. Judith Flanders notes that one British doctor was struck off the medical register for noting in print that a change in coloration around the vagina soon after conception was a useful indicator of pregnancy. The conclusion was entirely valid; the problem was that it could only be discerned by looking. The doctor was never allowed to practise again. In America, meanwhile, James Platt White, a respected gynaecologist, was expelled from the American Medical Association for allowing his students to observe a woman – with her permission – give birth.

Against this, the actions of a surgeon named Isaac Baker Brown become all the more extraordinary. In an age in which doctors normally didn't go within an arm's length of a woman's reproductive zone, and would have little idea of what they had found if they went there, Baker Brown became a pioneering gynaecological surgeon. Unfortunately, he was motivated almost entirely by seriously disturbed notions. In particular he was convinced that nearly every female malady was the result of 'peripheral excitement of the pudic nerve centring on the clitoris'. Put more bluntly, he thought women were masturbating and that this was the cause of insanity, epilepsy, catalepsy, hysteria, insomnia and countless other nervous disorders. The solution was to remove the clitoris surgically, and thus take away any possibility of wayward excitation. He also developed the conviction that the ovaries were mostly bad and were better off removed. Since no one had ever tried to remove ovaries before, it was an exceptionally delicate and risky operation. Baker Brown's first three patients died on the operating table. Undaunted, he performed his fourth experimental operation on, of all people, his sister. She lived.

When it was discovered that he had for years been removing women's clitorises without their permission or prior knowledge, the reaction of the medical community was swift and furious. In 1867, Baker Brown was expelled from the Obstetrical Society of London, which effectively ended his ability to practise. On the plus side, doctors did at last accept that it was time to become scientifically attentive to the private parts of female patients. So ironically, by being such a poor doctor and dreadful human being, Baker Brown did more than any other person to bring the study and practice of female medicine up to modern standards.

II

There was, it must be said, one very sound reason for being fearful of sex in the pre-modern era: syphilis. There has never been a more appalling disease, at least for the unlucky portion who get what is known as third-stage syphilis. This is a milestone you just don't want to experience. Syphilis gave sex a real dread. To many, it seemed a clear message from God that sex outside the bounds of marriage was an invitation to divine retribution.

Syphilis, as we have seen, had been around for a long time. As early as 1495, just three years after the voyage of Christopher Columbus that introduced it to Europe, some soldiers in Italy developed pustules 'like grains of millet' all over their faces and bodies, which is thought to be the first medical reference to syphilis in Europe. It spread rapidly – so rapidly that people couldn't agree where it came from. The first recorded mention of it in English is as 'the French pox' in 1503. Elsewhere it was known as the Spanish disease, the Celtic humours, the Neapolitan pox or, perhaps most tellingly, 'the Christian disease'. 'Syphilis' was coined in a poem by the Italian Hieronymus Fracastorius in 1530 (in his poem Syphilis is the name of a shepherd who gets the disease), but does not appear in English until 1718.

Syphilis was for a long time a particularly unnerving disease because of the way it came and went in three stages, each successively worse than the last. The first stage usually showed itself as a genital chancre, ugly but painless. This was followed some time later by a second stage that involved anything from aches and pains to hair loss. Like first-stage syphilis, this would also resolve itself after a month or so whether it was treated or not. For two-thirds of syphilis sufferers, that was it. The disease was over. For the unfortunate one-third, however, the real dread was yet to come. The infection would lie dormant for as long as twenty years before erupting in third-stage syphilis. This is the stage nobody wants to go through. It eats away the body, destroying bones and tissue without pause or mercy. Noses frequently collapsed and vanished. (London for a time had a 'No-Nose'd Club'.) The mouth may lose its roof. The death of nerve cells can turn the victim into a stumbling wreck. Symptoms vary, but every one of them is horrible. Despite the dangers, people put up with the risks to an amazing degree. James Boswell contracted venereal diseases nineteen times in thirty years.

Treatments for syphilis were severe. In the early days a lead solution was injected into the bladder via the urethra. Then mercury became the drug of choice and remained so right up to the twentieth century and the invention of the first antibiotics. Mercury produced all kinds of toxic symptoms – bones grew spongy, teeth fell out – but there was no alternative. 'A night with Venus and a lifetime with Mercury' was the axiom of the day. Yet the mercury didn't actually cure the disease but merely moderated the worst of the symptoms while inflicting others.

Perhaps nothing separates us more completely from the past than how staggeringly ineffectual – and often petrifyingly disagreeable – medical treatments once were. Doctors were lost in the face of all but a narrow range of maladies. Often their treatment merely made matters worse. The luckiest people in many ways were those who suffered in private, and recovered without medical intervention.

The worst outcome of all, for obvious reasons, was to have to undergo surgery. In the centuries before anaesthetic, many ways of ameliorating pain were tried out. One method was to bleed the patient to the point of faintness. Another was to inject an infusion of tobacco into the rectum (which, at the very least, must have given the patient something else to think about). The most common treatment was to administer opiates, principally in the form of laudanum, but even the most liberal doses couldn't mask real pain.

During amputations, limbs were normally removed in less than a minute, so the most traumatizing agony was over quickly, but vessels still had to be tied off and the wound stitched, so there remained much scope for lingering pain. Working quickly was the trick of it. When Samuel Pepys underwent a lithotomy – the removal of a kidney stone – in 1658 the surgeon took just fifty seconds to get in and find and extract a stone about the size of a tennis ball. (That is, a seventeenth-century tennis ball, which was rather smaller than a modern one, but still a sphere of considerable dimension.) Pepys was extremely lucky, as Liza Picard points out, because his operation was the surgeon's first of the day so his instruments were reasonably clean. Despite the quickness of the operation, Pepys needed more than a month to recover.

More complicated procedures were almost unbelievably taxing. They are painful enough to read about now, but what they must have been like to live through simply cannot be conceived. In 1806, the novelist Fanny Burney, while living in Paris, suffered a pain in her right breast, which gradually grew so severe that she could not lift her arm. The problem was diagnosed as breast cancer and a mastectomy was ordered. The job was given to a celebrated surgeon named Baron Larrey, whose fame was based not so much on his skill at saving lives as on his lightning speed. He would later become famous for conducting two hundred amputations in twenty-four hours after the battle of Borodino in 1812.

Burney's account of the experience is almost un-
bearably excruciating because of the very calmness with
which she relays its horrors. Almost as bad as the event
itself was the torment of awaiting it. As the days passed the
anxiety of apprehension became almost crushing, and was
made worse when she learned on the morning of the
appointed day that the surgeons would be delayed by
several hours. In her diary she wrote: 'I walked backwards
and forwards till I quieted all emotions, and became, by
degrees, nearly stupid – torpid, without sentiment or
consciousness – and thus I remained till the clock struck
three.'

At that point she heard four carriages arrive in quick
succession. Moments later, seven grave men in black came
into the room. Burney was given a drink to calm her nerves
– she didn't record what, but wine mixed with laudanum
was the usual offering. A bed was moved into the middle
of the room; old bedding was placed on it so as not to
spoil a good mattress or linens.

'I now began to tremble violently,' Burney wrote, 'more
with distaste and horror of the preparations even than of
the pain . . . I mounted, therefore, unbidden, the bedstead,
and M. Dubois placed me upon the mattress, and spread a
cambric handkerchief upon my face. It was transparent,
however, and I saw through it that the bedstead was
instantly surrounded by the seven men and my nurse. I
refused to be held; but when, bright through the cambric,
I saw the glitter of polished steel – I closed my eyes . . .'
Learning that they intended to remove the whole breast,
she surrendered herself to 'a terror that surpasses all
description'. As the knife cut into her, she emitted 'a
scream that lasted intermittingly during the whole time of

the incision – and I almost marvel that it rings not in my ears still, so excruciating was the agony. When the wound was made, and the instrument was withdrawn, the pain seemed undiminished . . . but when again I felt the instrument – describing a curve – cutting against the grain, if I may say so, while the flesh resisted in a manner so forcible as to oppose and tire the hand of the operator, who was forced to change from the right to the left – then, indeed, I thought I must have expired. I attempted no more to open my eyes.'

But still the operation went on. As the surgeons dug away diseased tissue, she could feel and hear the scrape of the blade on her breastbone. The entire procedure lasted seventeen and a half minutes, and it took her months to recover. But the operation saved her life. She lived another twenty-nine years and the cancer never came back.

Not surprisingly, people were sometimes driven by pain and a natural caution regarding doctors to attempt extreme remedies at home. Gouverneur Morris, one of the signatories of the Declaration of Independence, killed himself by forcing a whalebone up his penis to try to clear a urinary blockage.

The advent of surgical anaesthetics in the 1840s didn't eliminate the agony of medical treatments very often so much as postpone it. Surgeons still didn't wash their hands or clean their instruments, so many of their patients survived the operations only to die of a more prolonged and exquisite agony through infection. This was generally attributed to 'blood poisoning'. When President James A. Garfield was shot in 1881, it wasn't the bullet that killed him but doctors sticking their unwashed fingers in the wound. Because anaesthetics encouraged the growth of surgical procedures, there was in fact probably a considerable net increase in the amount of pain and suffering *after* the advent of anaesthetics.

Even without the unnerving interventions of surgeons, there were plenty of ways to die in the pre-modern world. For the City of London, the death rolls – or Bills of Mortality as they were known in England – for 1758 list 17,576 deaths from more than eighty causes. Most deaths, as might be expected, were from smallpox, fever, consumption or old age, but among the more miscellaneous causes listed (with original spellings) were:

choaked with fat	1
itch	2
froze to death	2
St Anthony's fire	4
lethargy	4
sore throat	5
worms	6
killed themselves	30
French pox	46
lunatick	72
drowned	109
mortification	154
teeth	644

How exactly 'teeth' killed so many seems bound to remain for ever a mystery. Whatever the actual causes of death, it is clear that expiring was a commonplace act and that people were prepared for it to come from almost any direction. Death rolls from Boston in the same period show people dying from such unexpected causes as 'drinking cold water', 'stagnation of the fluids', 'nervous fevers' and 'fright'. It is interesting too that many of the more expected forms of death feature only marginally. Of the nearly 17,600 people whose deaths were recorded in London in 1758, just fourteen were executed, five murdered and four starved.

With so many lives foreshortened, marriages in the pre-industrial world tended to be brief. In the fifteenth and sixteenth centuries, the average marriage lasted just ten years before one or the other of the partners expired. It is often assumed that because people died young they also married young in order to make the most of the short life that lay in front of them. In fact, that seems not to be so. For one thing, people still saw the normal span of life – one's theoretical entitlement – as the biblical three score years and ten. It was just that not so many people made it to that point. Nearly always cited in support of the contention that people married early are the tender ages of the principal characters in Shakespeare's *Romeo and Juliet* – Juliet just thirteen, Romeo a little older. Putting aside the consideration that the characters were fictitious and hardly proof of anything, what is always overlooked in this is that in the poem by Arthur Brooke on which Shakespeare based the story, the characters were actually sixteen. Why Shakespeare reduced their ages is, like most of what Shakespeare did, unknowable. In any case, Shakespeare's youthful ages are not supported by documentary evidence in the real world.

In the 1960s, the British historian Peter Laslett did a careful study of British marriage records and found that at no time in the recorded past did people regularly marry at very early ages. Between 1619 and 1660, for instance,

85 per cent of women were nineteen or older when married; just one in a thousand was thirteen or under. The median age at marriage for brides was twenty-three years and seven months and for men it was nearly twenty-eight years – not very different from the ages of today. William Shakespeare himself was unusual in being married at eighteen, while his wife, Anne, was unusually old at twenty-six. Most really youthful marriages were formalities known as *espousals de futuro*, which were more declarations of future intentions than licences to hop into bed.

What is true is that there were a lot more widowed people out there and that they remarried more often and more quickly after bereavement. For women, it was frequently an economic necessity. For men, it was the desire to be looked after. In short, it was often as much a practical consideration as an emotional one. One village surveyed by Laslett had, in 1688, seventy-two married men, of whom thirteen had been married twice, three had been married three times, three married four times and one married five times, all as the result of widowhood. Altogether about a quarter of all marriages were re-marriages following bereavement, and those proportions remained unchanged right up to the first years of the twentieth century.

With so many people dying, mourning became a central part of most people's lives. The masters of mourning were of course the Victorians. Never have a people become more morbidly attached to death or found more complicated ways to mark it. The master practitioner was Victoria herself. After her beloved Prince Albert died in December 1861, the clocks in his bedroom were stopped at the minute of his death, 10.50 p.m., but at the queen's behest his room continued to be serviced as if he were merely temporarily absent rather than permanently interred in a mausoleum across the grounds. A valet laid out clothes for him each day, and soap, towels and hot water were brought to the room at the appropriate times, then taken away again.

At all levels of society mourning rules were strict and exhaustingly comprehensive. Every possible permutation of relationship was considered and ruled upon. If, for example, the dearly departed was an uncle by marriage, he was to be mourned for two months if his wife survived him, but for just one month if he were unmarried or widowed himself. So it went through the entire canon of relationships. One needn't even have met the people being mourned. If one's husband had been married before and widowed – a fairly common condition – and a close relative of his first wife's died, the second wife was expected to engage in 'complementary mourning' – a kind of proxy mourning on behalf of the deceased earlier partner.

Exactly how long and in what manner mourning clothes were worn was determined with equally meticulous precision by the degree of one's bereavement. Widows, already swaddled in pounds of suffocating broadcloth, had additionally to drape themselves in black crêpe, a type of crimped silk. Crêpe was scratchy, rustly and maddeningly difficult to maintain. Raindrops on crêpe left whitish blotches wherever they touched it, and the crêpe in turn ran on to fabric or skin underneath. A crêpe stain ruined any fabric it touched and was nearly impossible to wash off skin. The amounts of crêpe worn were strictly dictated by the passage of time. One could tell at a glance how long a woman had been widowed by how much crêpe she had at each sleeve. After two years, a widow moved into a phase known as 'half-mourning' when she could begin to wear grey or pale lavender, so long as they weren't introduced too abruptly.

Servants were required to mourn when their employers died, and a period of national mourning was decreed when a monarch died. Much consternation ensued when Queen Victoria expired in 1901, because it had been over sixty years since the last regal departure and no one could agree what level of mourning was appropriate to such a long-lasting monarch in such a new age.

If Victorians didn't have enough to worry about already, they developed some peculiar anxieties about death. Fear of premature burial became widespread – a fear that Edgar Allan Poe exploited to vivid effect in his story of the same name in 1844. Catalepsy, a condition of paralysis in which the victim merely *seemed* dead while actually being fully conscious, became the dread disease of the day. Newspapers and popular magazines abounded with stories of people who suffered from its immobilizing effects. One well-known case was that of Eleanor Markham of upstate New York who was about to be buried in July 1894 when anxious noises were heard coming from her coffin. The lid was lifted and Miss Markham cried out: 'My God, you are burying me alive!'

She told her saviours: 'I was conscious all the time you were making preparations to bury me. The horror of my situation is altogether beyond description. I could hear everything that was going on, even a whisper outside the door.' But no matter how much she willed herself to cry out, she said, she was powerless to utter a noise. According to one report, of 1,200 bodies exhumed in New York City for one reason or another between 1860 and 1880, six showed signs of thrashing or other post-interment distress. In London, when the naturalist Frank Buckland went looking for the coffin of the anatomist John Hunter at St Martin-in-the-Fields church, he reported coming upon three coffins that showed clear evidence of internal agitation (or so he was convinced). Anecdotes of premature burials were numerous. A correspondent to the popular journal *Notes and Queries* offered this contribution in 1858:

> A rich manufacturer named Oppelt died about fifteen years since at Reichenberg, in Austria, and a vault was built in the cemetery for the reception of the body by his widow and children. The widow died about a month ago and was taken to the same tomb; but, when it was opened for that purpose, the coffin of her husband was found open and empty, and the skeleton discovered in a corner of the vault in a sitting posture.

For at least a generation such stories became routine in even serious periodicals. So many people became morbidly obsessed with the fear of being interred before their time that a word was coined for it: *taphephobia*. The novelist Wilkie Collins placed on his bedside table each night a letter bearing standing instructions of the tests he wished carried out to ensure that he really had died in his sleep if he was found in a seemingly corpse-like state. Others directed that their heads be cut off or their hearts removed before burial, to put the matter comfortably (if that is the right word) beyond doubt. One author proposed the construction of 'Waiting Mortuaries', where the departed could be held for a few days to ensure they really were quite dead and not just unusually still. Another more entrepreneurial type designed a device that allowed someone awaking within a coffin to pull a cord, which opened a breathing tube for air and simultaneously set off a bell and started a flag waving at ground level. An Association for Prevention of Premature Burial was established in Britain in 1899 and an American society was formed the following year. Both societies suggested a number of exacting tests to be satisfied by attending physicians before they could safely declare a person dead – holding a hot iron against the deceased's skin to see if it blistered was one – and several of these tests were actually incorporated into medical schools' curricula for a time.

Grave robbing was another great concern – and not without reason, for the demand for fresh bodies in the nineteenth century was considerable. London alone was home to twenty-three schools of medicine or anatomy, each requiring a steady supply of cadavers. Until the passing of the Anatomy Act in 1832 only executed criminals could be used for experiment and dissection, and executions in England were much rarer than is commonly supposed. In 1831, a typical year, 1,600 people were condemned to death in England, but only fifty-two executed. So the demand for bodies was way beyond what could be legally supplied. Grave robbery in consequence became an irresistibly tempting business, particularly as stealing a body was, thanks to a curious legal quirk, a misdemeanour rather than a felony. At a time when a well-paid working man might earn a pound in a week, a fresh corpse could fetch eight or ten pounds and sometimes as much as twenty, and, at least initially, without much risk as long as the culprits were careful to remove only the bodies and not shrouds, coffins or keepsakes, for which they *could* be charged with a felony.

It wasn't just a morbid interest in dissection that drove the market. In the days before anaesthetics surgeons really needed to be closely acquainted with bodies. You can't poke thoughtfully among arteries and organs when the patient is screaming in agony and spurting blood. Speed was of the essence and the essential part of speed was familiarity, which could only come with much devoted practice on the dead. And of course the lack of refrigeration meant that flesh began to spoil quickly, so the need for fresh supplies was constant.

To thwart robbers, the poor in particular often held on to the bodies of departed loved ones until they had begun to putrefy and so had lost their value. Edwin Chadwick's *Report on the Sanitary Condition of the Labouring Classes of Great Britain* was full of gruesome and shocking details about the practice. In some districts, he noted, it was common for families to keep a body in the front room for a week or more while waiting for putrefaction to get a good hold. It was not unusual, he said, to find maggots dropping on to the carpet and infants playing among them. The stench, not surprisingly, was powerful.

Graveyards also improved their security, employing armed nightwatchmen. That severely elevated the risk of being apprehended and beaten, so some 'resurrection men', as they were popularly known, turned to murder as safer. The most notorious and devoted were William Burke and William Hare, Irish immigrants in Edinburgh, who killed at least fifteen people in a period of less than a year, beginning in November 1827. Their method was crudely effective. They befriended sad wastrels, got them drunk and suffocated them, the stout Burke sitting on the victim's chest and Hare covering the mouth. The bodies were taken at once to Professor Robert Knox, who paid from £7 to £14 for each fresh, pink corpse. Knox must have known that something exceedingly dubious was going on – two Irish alcoholics turning up with a succession of extremely fresh bodies, each having expired in seemingly tranquil fashion – but maintained that it was not his business to ask questions. He was widely condemned for his part in the affair, but never charged or penalized. Hare escaped hanging by turning king's evidence and offering to testify against his friend and partner. This proved unnecessary as Burke made a full confession, and was swiftly hanged. His body was delivered to another anatomy school for dissection, and pieces of his skin were pickled and for years handed out as keepsakes to favoured visitors.

Hare spent only a couple of months in prison before being released, though his fate was not a happy one. He took a job at a lime kiln, where his co-workers recognized him and thrust his face into a heap of quicklime, permanently blinding him. He is thought to have spent his last years as a wandering beggar. Some reports had him returning to Ireland, others place him in America, but how long he lived and where he was buried are unknown.

All this gave a great spur to an alternative way of disposing of bodies that was surprisingly controversial in the nineteenth century: cremation. The cremation movement had nothing to do with religion or spirituality. It was all about creating a practical way to get rid of a lot of bodies in a clean, efficient and non-polluting manner. Sir Henry Thompson, founder of the Cremation Society of England, demonstrated the efficacy of his ovens by cremating a horse at Woking in 1874. The demonstration worked perfectly but caused an outcry among those emotionally opposed to the idea of burning a horse or any animal. In Dorset a certain Captain Hanham built his own crematorium and used it very efficiently to dispose of his wife and mother in defiance of the laws. Others, fearful of arrest, sent their loved ones to countries where cremation was legal. Charles Wentworth Dilke, the writer and politician who was one of the co-founders of the *Gardener's Chronicle* with Joseph Paxton, shipped his late wife to Dresden to be cremated in 1874 after she died in childbirth. Another early exponent was Augustus Pitt Rivers, one of the nineteenth century's leading archaeologists, who not only desired cremation for himself but insisted upon it for his wife, despite her continued objections. 'Damn it, woman, you shall *burn*,' he declared to her whenever she raised the matter. Pitt Rivers died in 1900 and was cremated, even though it wasn't yet legal. His wife outlived him, however, and was given the peaceful burial she had always longed for.

In Britain, on the whole, opposition remained entrenched for a long time. Many people thought the wilful destruction of a corpse immoral. Others cited practical considerations. A point made often by opponents was that it would destroy evidence in cases of murder. The movement also wasn't helped by the fact that one of its principal proponents was essentially mad. His name was William Price. He was a doctor in rural Wales noted for his eccentricities, which were exhaustive. He was a druid, a vegetarian and a militant Chartist; he refused to wear socks or to touch coins. In his eighties he fathered a son by his housekeeper and named it Jesus Christ. When the baby died in early 1884 Price decided to cremate it on a pyre on his land. When villagers saw the flames and went to investigate they found Price, dressed as a druid, dancing around the bonfire and reciting strange chants. Outraged and flustered, they stepped in to stop him and in the confusion Price snatched the half-burned baby from the fire and retired with it to his house, where he kept it in a box under his bed until arrested a few days later. Price was brought to trial, but released when the judge decided that nothing he had done was conclusively criminal, since the baby was not actually cremated. He did, however, set back the cause of cremation very severely.

While cremation became routine elsewhere, it wasn't formally legalized in Britain until 1902, just in time for our Mr Marsham to exercise that option if he chose to. He didn't.

CHAPTER SIXTEEN

The Bathroom

I

IT WOULD NOT BE EASY to find a statement on hygiene more wrong, or at least more incomplete, than this one by the celebrated architectural critic Lewis Mumford in his classic work *The City in History*, published in 1961:

> For thousands of years city dwellers put up with defective, often quite vile, sanitary arrangements, wallowing in rubbish and filth they certainly had the power to remove, for the occasional task of removal could hardly have been more loathsome than walking and breathing in the constant presence of such ordure. If one had any sufficient explanation of this indifference to dirt and odor that are repulsive to many animals, even pigs, who take pains to keep themselves and their lairs clean, one might also have a clue to the slow and fitful nature of technological improvement itself, in the five millennia that followed the birth of the city.

In fact, as we have already seen with Skara Brae in Orkney, people have been dealing with dirt, rubbish and wastes, often surprisingly effectively, for a very long time – and Skara Brae is by no means unique. A home of 4,500 years ago from the Indus Valley, at a place called Mahenjo-Daro, had a nifty system of rubbish chutes to get waste out of the living area and into a midden. Ancient Babylon had drains and a sewage system. The Minoans had running water, bathtubs and other civilizing comforts well over 3,500 years ago. In short, cleanliness and generally looking after one's body have been important to a lot of cultures for so long that it is hard to know where to begin.

The ancient Greeks were devoted bathers. They loved to get naked – 'gymnasium' means 'the naked place' – and work up a healthful sweat, and it was their habit to conclude their daily workouts with a communal bath. But these were primarily hygienic plunges. For them bathing was a brisk business, something to be got over quickly. Really serious bathing – languorous bathing – starts with Rome. Nobody has ever bathed with as much devotion and precision as the Romans did.

The Romans loved water altogether – one house at Pompeii had thirty taps – and their network of aqueducts provided their principal cities with a superabundance of fresh water. The delivery rate to Rome worked out at an intensely lavish three hundred gallons per head per day, seven or eight times more than the average Roman needs today.

To Romans the baths were more than just a place to get clean. They were a daily refuge, a pastime, a way of life. Roman baths had libraries, shops, exercise rooms, barbers, beauticians, tennis courts, snack bars and brothels. People from all classes of society used them. 'It was common, when meeting a man, to ask where he bathed,' writes Katherine Ashenburg in her sparkling history of cleanliness, *The Dirt on Clean*. Some Roman baths were built on a truly palatial scale. The great baths of Caracalla could take sixteen hundred bathers at a time; those of Diocletian held three thousand.

A bathing Roman sloshed and gasped his way through a series of variously heated pools – from the frigidarium at the cold end of the scale to the calidarium at the other. En route he or she would stop in the unctorium (or unctuarium) to be fragrantly oiled and then forwarded to the laconium, or steam room, where, after working up a good sweat, the oils were scraped off with an instrument called a strigil to remove dirt and other impurities. All this was done in a ritualistic order, though historians are not entirely agreed on what that order was, possibly because the specifics varied from place to place and time to time. There is quite a lot we don't know about Romans and their bathing habits – whether slaves bathed with free citizens, or how often or lengthily people bathed or with what degree of enthusiasm. Romans themselves sometimes expressed disquiet about the state of the water and what they found floating in it, which doesn't suggest that they were all necessarily as keen for a plunge as we generally suppose them to be.

It seems, however, that for much of the Roman era the baths were marked by a certain rigid decorum, which assured a healthy rectitude, but that as time went on life in the baths – as with life in Rome generally – grew increasingly frisky, and it became common for men and women to bathe together and, possibly but by no means certainly, for females to bathe with male slaves. No one really knows quite what the Romans got up to in there, but whatever it was it didn't sit well with the early Christians. They viewed Roman baths as licentious and depraved – morally unclean if not hygienically so.

Christianity was always curiously ill at ease with cleanliness anyway, and early on developed an odd tradition of equating holiness with dirtiness. When St Thomas à Becket died in 1170, those who laid him out noted approvingly that his undergarments were 'seething with lice'. Throughout the medieval period, an almost sure-fire way to earn lasting honour was to take a vow not to wash. Many people walked from England to the Holy Land, but when a monk named Godric did it without getting wet even once he became, all but inevitably, St Godric.

Then in the Middle Ages the spread of plague made people consider more closely their attitude to hygiene and what they might do to modify their own susceptibility to outbreaks. Unfortunately, people everywhere came to exactly the wrong conclusion. All the best minds agreed that bathing opened the epidermal pores and encouraged deathly vapours to invade the body. The best policy was to plug the pores with dirt. For the next six hundred years most people didn't wash, or even get wet, if they could help it – and in consequence they paid an uncomfortable price. Infections became part of everyday life. Boils grew commonplace. Rashes and blotches were routine. Nearly everyone itched nearly all the time. Discomfort was constant, serious illness accepted with resignation.

Devastating diseases arose, killed millions and then, often, mysteriously vanished. The most notorious was plague (which was really two diseases: bubonic plague, named for the swollen buboes that victims got in the neck, groin or armpit, and the even more lethal and infectious pneumonic plague, which overwhelmed the respiratory system), but there were many others. The English sweating sickness, a disease about which we still know almost nothing, had epidemics in 1485, 1508, 1517 and 1528, killing thousands as it went, before disappearing, never to return (or at least not yet). It was followed in the 1550s by another strange fever – 'the new sickness' – which 'raged horribly throughout the realm and killed an exceeding great number of all sorts of men, but especially gentlemen and men of great wealth', as one contemporary noted. In between and sometimes alongside were outbreaks of ergotism, which came from a fungal infection of rye grain. People who ingested poisoned grain suffered delirium, seizures, fever, loss of consciousness and eventually, in many cases, death. A curious aspect of ergotism is that it came with a cough very like a dog's bark, which is thought to be the source of the expression 'barking mad'.

The worst disease of all, because it was so prevalent and so devastating, was smallpox. Smallpox was of two principal types: ordinary and haemorrhagic. Both were bad, though haemorrhagic (which involved internal bleeding as well as skin pustules) was more painful and lethal, killing 90 per cent of its victims, nearly double the rate for ordinary smallpox. Until the eighteenth century when vaccination came in, smallpox killed 400,000 people a year in Europe west of Russia. No other disease came close to the totals smallpox achieved.

For survivors, smallpox was a cruelly fickle disease, leaving many of its survivors blinded or dreadfully scarred, but others unscathed. It had existed for millennia, but didn't become common in Europe until the early sixteenth century. Its first recorded appearance in England was 1518. A bout of smallpox began with the sudden onset of high fever, accompanied by aches, pains and powerful thirst. On about the third day, usually, pustules began to appear and to spread across the body in quantities that varied from victim to victim. The worst news was to learn that a loved one was 'exceeding full'. In the worst cases, the victim became essentially one large pustule. This stage was accompanied by more high fevers, and the pustules would break, releasing a foul-smelling pus. If the victim survived them she would generally survive the illness. But her problems were hardly ended. The pustules now scabbed over and began to itch in a most agonizing manner. Not until the scabs fell off did one know whether or how seriously one was scarred. As a young woman, Queen Elizabeth was nearly killed by smallpox, but recovered completely and without scars. Her friend Lady Mary Sidney, who nursed her, was not so lucky. 'I left her a full fair lady,' wrote her husband, '. . . and when I returned I found her as foul a lady as the smallpox could make her.' The Duchess of Richmond, who modelled for the figure of Britannia on the English penny, was similarly disfigured a century later.

Smallpox also had much to answer for regarding the treatment of other diseases. The release of pus led to the conviction that the body was trying to rid itself of poisons, so smallpox victims were vigorously bled, purged, lanced and sweated – remedies that were soon applied to all kinds of conditions and nearly always only made matters worse. Smallpox was so called to distinguish it from the great pox, or syphilis.

Clearly not all of these dreadful maladies were directly

related to washing, but people didn't necessarily know that or even care. Although everyone knew that syphilis was spread through sexual contact, which could of course take place anywhere, it became indelibly associated with bathhouses. Prostitutes generally were banned from coming within a hundred paces of a bathhouse and eventually Europe's bathhouses were closed altogether. With the bathhouses gone, most people got out of the habit of washing – not that many of them were entirely in it to begin with. Washing wasn't unknown, just a little selective. 'Wash your hands often, your feet seldom, and your head never' was a common English proverb. Queen Elizabeth, in a much-cited quote, faithfully bathed once a month 'whether she needs it or no'. In 1653, John Evelyn, the diarist, noted a tentative decision to wash his hair annually. Robert Hooke, the scientist, washed his feet often (because he found it soothing), but appears not to have spent much time damp above the ankles. Samuel Pepys mentions his wife's bathing only once in the diary he kept for nine and a half years. In France, King Louis XIII went unbathed until almost his seventh birthday, in 1608.

Water, when it was used at all, tended to be purely for medicinal purposes. By the 1570s Bath and Buxton were both popular spas, but even then people were dubious. 'Methinks it cannot be clean to go so many bodies together in the same water,' Pepys noted in the summer of 1668 when considering the spa experience. Still, he found he liked it and spent two hours in the water on his inaugural immersion, then paid someone to carry him back to his rooms wrapped in a sheet.

By the time Europeans began to visit the New World in large numbers they had grown so habitually malodorous that the Indians nearly always remarked at how bad they smelled. Nothing, however, bemused the Indians more than the European habit of blowing their noses into a fine handkerchief, folding it carefully and placing it back in their pockets as if it were a treasured memento.

There is no doubt that *some* standards of cleanliness were expected. When an observer of the court of King James I noted that the king never went near water except to daub his fingertips with a moist napkin, he was writing in a tone of disgust. And it is notable that people who were really grubby were generally famous for it, among whom we might include the eleventh Duke of Norfolk, who was so violently opposed to soap and water that his servants had to wait till he was dead drunk to scrub him clean; Thomas Paine, the pamphleteer, whose surface was an uninterrupted accretion of dirt; and even the refined James Boswell, whose body odour was a wonder to many in an age when that was assuredly saying something. But even Boswell was left in awe by his contemporary the Marquis d'Argens, who wore the same undershirt for so many years that when at last he was persuaded to take it off, it had so fixed itself upon him 'that pieces of his skin came away with it'. For some, however, filthiness became a kind of boast. The aristocratic Lady Mary Wortley Montagu, who was one of the first great female travellers, was so grubby that after shaking her hand a new acquaintance blurted out in amazement how dirty they were. 'What would you say if you saw my feet?' Lady Mary responded brightly. Many people grew so unused to being exposed to water in quantity that the very prospect of it left them genuinely fearful. When Henry Drinker, a prominent Philadelphian, installed a shower in his garden as late as 1798, his wife

Elizabeth put off trying it out for over a year, 'not having been wett all over at once, for 28 years past', she explained.

By the eighteenth century the most reliable way to get a bath was to be insane. Then they could hardly soak you enough. In 1701 Sir John Floyer began to make a case for cold bathing as a cure for any number of maladies. His theory was that plunging a body into chilly water produced a sensation of 'Terror and Surprize' which invigorated dulled and jaded senses.

Benjamin Franklin tried another tack. During his years in London, he developed the custom of taking 'air baths', basking naked in front of an open upstairs window. This can't have got him any cleaner, but it seems to have done him no harm and it must at least have given the neighbours something to talk about. Also strangely popular was 'dry washing' – rubbing oneself with a brush to open the pores and possibly dislodge lice. Many people believed that linen had special qualities that absorbed dirt from the skin. As Katherine Ashenburg has put it, 'they "washed" by changing their shirts'. Most, however, fought dirt and odour by either covering it with cosmetics and perfumes or just ignoring it. Where everyone stinks no one stinks.

But then suddenly water became fashionable, though still only in a medicinal sense. In 1702 Queen Anne went to Bath for treatment of her gout, which boosted its curative reputation and prestige very considerably, though Anne's problems really had nothing to do with water and everything to do with overeating. Soon spa towns were cropping up all over – Harrogate, Cheltenham, Llandrindod Wells in Wales. But coastal towns claimed that the really curative waters were those of the sea – though, curiously, only within the immediate vicinity of their own particular communities. Scarborough on the Yorkshire coast guaranteed that its waters provided a balm against 'Apoplexy, Epilepsie, Catalepsie, Vertigo, Jaunders, Hypochondriack Melancholy and Windiness'.

The most celebrated pioneer of water cures was Dr Richard Russell, who in 1750 wrote, in Latin, a book on the curative properties of seawater, translated four years later as *A Dissertation Concerning the Use of Sea-Water in Diseases of the Glands*. Russell's book recommended seawater as an efficacious treatment for any number of disorders, from gout and rheumatism to congestion of the brain. Sufferers had not only to immerse themselves in seawater but to drink it in copious volumes. Russell set up practice in the fishing village of Brighthelmstone on the Sussex coast and became so successful that the town grew and grew and transmogrified into Brighton, the most fashionable coastal resort in the world in its day. Russell has been called 'the inventor of the sea'.

Many in the early days bathed naked (and often caused much outrage among those inclined to take a good long look, sometimes with the aid of a telescope) while the more modest draped themselves liberally, and sometimes dangerously, in heavy robes. The real outrage came when the poorer elements started to turn up, and often stripped off on the beach 'in promiscuous numbers' and then shuffled into the water for what was, for most of them, effectively their one bath of the year. For purposes of modesty bathing machines were invented. These were simply wagons that could be wheeled into the water, with doors and steps that allowed the client to enter the water safely and discreetly. A big part of the beneficial effects of sea bathing wasn't the immersion so much as the vigorous rubbing down with dry flannels afterwards.

Brighton's future was permanently assured when in September 1783, just as the American revolution ended with the signing of the Treaty of Paris, the Prince of Wales visited the resort for the first time. He hoped to find some relief from swollen glands in his throat, and did. He liked it so much that he immediately built his exotic pavilion there. The prince installed a private bath that was filled with seawater, so that he didn't have to expose himself to the gaze of the common people when he took his treatments.

George III, similarly seeking privacy, went to Weymouth, a sleepy port further west in Dorset, but was dismayed to find thousands of well-wishers on the beach waiting to observe his first dip. When he entered the water, draped in a voluminous gown of blue serge, a band hidden in a neighbouring bathing machine struck up 'God Save the King'. Still, the king loved his trips to Weymouth and went almost annually until his growing madness made it impossible for him to submit his troubled brain to public gaze.

Tobias Smollett, the novelist and doctor, who suffered from chest problems, took the practice to the Mediterranean. He went swimming daily in Nice, to the astonishment of the locals. 'They thought it very strange, that a man seemingly consumptive should plunge into the sea, especially when the weather was so cold; and some of the doctors prognosticated immediate death,' one contemporary wrote. In fact, the practice caught on and Smollett's travel book, *Travels through France and Italy* (1766), did a great deal to create the Riviera.

It didn't take long for charlatans to realize that good

money could be made in the bathing game. One of the most successful was James Graham (1745–94). A self-proclaimed physician, unqualified by anything beyond his own bravura, Graham became hugely successful in Bath and London in the second half of the eighteenth century. He used magnets, batteries and other thrumming apparatus to cure patients of any number of disorders, but especially those responsible for sexual unhappiness, such as impotence and frigidity. He took medicinal bathing to a higher, enticingly erotic level, offering his clients milk baths, friction baths and mudbaths – or Earth Baths, as he called them – all provided in a theatrical setting involving music, classical statuary, perfumed air and scantily clad hostesses, one of whom was said to be Emma Lyon, the future Lady Hamilton and mistress of Lord Nelson. For those whose problems failed to respond to these enticing ministrations, Graham provided an enormous, powerfully electrified 'Celestial Bed' at a cost of £50 a night. The mattress was filled with rose leaves and spices.

Unfortunately Graham was carried away with his success and took to making boasts that even his most devoted adherents found insupportable. He titled one lecture 'How to Live for Many Weeks, Months or Years Without Eating Anything Whatever', and in another he guaranteed his listeners a healthful life to the age of 150. As his claims grew more preposterous, his business faltered and then went into steep decline. In 1782 his goods were seized to pay his debts and that was the end of James Graham.

Graham is always portrayed now as a ludicrous quack, and in large part of course he was, but it is also worth remembering that many of his beliefs – cold baths, plain food, hard beds, windows opened wide to fill bedrooms with healthful frosty air, and above all an abiding horror of masturbation – became cherished fixtures of English life that lasted well beyond his brief spell of celestial importance.

As people adjusted to the idea that they might now safely get wet from time to time, longstanding theories about personal hygiene were abruptly reversed. Now, instead of it being bad to have pink skin and open pores, the belief took hold that the skin was in fact a marvellous ventilator – that carbon dioxide and other toxic inhalations were expelled *through* the skin, and that if pores were blocked by dust and other ancient accretions natural toxins would become trapped within and would dangerously accumulate. That was why dirty people – the great unwashed of Thackeray – were so often sick. Their clogged pores were killing them. In one graphic demonstration, a doctor showed how a horse, painted all over in tar, grew swiftly enfeebled and piteously expired. (In fact, the problem for the horse wasn't to do with respiration, it was to do with temperature regulation, though the point was, from the horse's perspective, obviously academic.)

Washing for the sake merely of being clean and smelling nice was remarkably slow in coming, however. When John Wesley, the founder of Methodism, coined the phrase 'Cleanliness is next to Godliness' in a sermon in 1778, he meant clean clothes, not a clean body. With respect to bodily cleanliness, he recommended only 'frequent shaving and foot washing'. When the young Karl Marx went off to college in the 1830s, his fretting mother gave him strict instructions regarding hygiene and particularly enjoined him to have 'a weekly scrub with sponge and soap'. By the time of the Great Exhibition, things were clearly turning. The exhibition itself featured more than 700 soaps and perfumes, which must have reflected some level of demand, and two years later cleanliness received another timely boost when the government finally abolished the longstanding soap tax. Even so, as late as 1861 an English doctor could write a book called *Baths and How to Take Them*.

What really got the Victorians to turn to bathing, however, was the realization that it could be gloriously punishing. The Victorians had a kind of instinct for self-torment, and water became a perfect way to make that manifest. Many diaries record how people had to break the ice in their washbasins in order to ablute in the morning, and the Reverend Francis Kilvert noted with pleasure how jagged ice clung to the side of his bath and pricked his skin as he merrily bathed on Christmas morning in 1870. Showers, too, offered great scope for punishment, and were often designed to be as powerful as possible. One early type of shower was so ferocious that users had to don protective headgear before stepping in lest they be beaten senseless by their own plumbing.

II

Perhaps no word in English has undergone more transformations in its lifetime than 'toilet'. Originally, in about 1540, it was a kind of cloth, a diminutive form of 'toile', a word still used to describe a type of linen. Then it became a cloth for use on dressing tables. Then it became the items on the dressing table (whence 'toiletries'). Then it became the dressing table itself, then the act of dressing, then the act of receiving visitors while dressing, then the dressing room itself, then any kind of private room near a bedroom, then a room used lavatorially, and finally the lavatory itself. Which explains why 'toilet water' in English can describe something you would gladly daub on your face or, simultaneously, 'water in a toilet'.

Garderobe, a word now extinct, went through a similar but slightly more compacted transformation. A combination of 'guard' and 'robe', it first signified a storeroom, then any private room, then (briefly) a bedchamber and finally a privy. However, the last thing privies often were was private. The Romans were particularly attached to the combining of evacuation and conversation. Their public latrines generally had twenty seats or more in intimate proximity, and people used them as unselfconsciously as modern people ride a bus. (To answer an inevitable question, a channel of water ran across the floor in front of each row of seats; users dipped sponges attached to sticks into the water for purposes of wiping.) Being comfortable with strangers lasted far into modern times. Hampton Court contained a 'Great House of Ease', which could accommodate fourteen users at once. Charles II always took two attendants with him when he went into the lavatory. Mount Vernon, George Washington's home, has a lovingly preserved privy with two seats side by side.

The English for a long time were particularly noted for their unconcern about lavatorial privacy. Giacomo Casanova, the Italian adventurer, remarked on a visit to London how frequently he saw someone 'ease his sluices' in full public view along roadsides or against buildings. Pepys notes in his diary how his wife squatted in the road 'to do her business'.

'Water closet' dates from 1755 and originally signified the place where royal enemas were administered. The French from 1770 called an indoor toilet *'un lieu à l'anglaise'* or 'an English place', which would seem a potential explanation for where the English term 'loo' comes from. At Monticello, Thomas Jefferson installed three indoor privies – probably the first in America – which incorporated air vents to take the odour away. By Jeffersonian standards (or actually any standards) they weren't technologically advanced: the waste simply fell into a collecting pot, which was emptied by slaves. However, at the White House – or President's House, as it was then – Jefferson in 1801 installed three of the first flushing toilets to be found anywhere. They were powered by rainwater cisterns installed in the attic.

The Reverend Henry Moule, a vicar in Dorset, invented the earth closet in the mid-nineteenth century. The earth closet was essentially a commode that incorporated a storage tank filled with dry earth that, with the pull of a handle, released a measured dose of soil into the receptacle, masking the smell and sight of one's leavings. Earth closets were much appreciated for a time, particularly in rural areas, but were swiftly overtaken by flushing toilets, which didn't just cover one's waste but whisked it away in a torrent of water. Or at least they did when they worked well, which wasn't always, or even often, in the early days.

Most people continued to use chamber pots which they kept in a cupboard in their bedrooms or closet, and which were known (for entirely obscure reasons) as jordans. Foreign visitors were frequently appalled by the English habit of keeping chamber pots in cupboards or sideboards in the dining room, which the men would pull out and use as soon as the women had withdrawn. Some rooms came supplied with a 'necessary chair' in the corner as well. A French visitor to Philadelphia, Moreau de Saint-Méry, noted with astonishment how one man removed the flowers from a vase and peed in it. Another French visitor at about the same time reported asking for a chamber pot for his bedroom and being told just to go out the window like everyone else. When he insisted upon being provided with *some*thing in which to do his business, his bemused host brought him a kettle, but firmly reminded him that she would need it back in the morning in time for breakfast.

The most notable feature about anecdotes involving toilet practices is that they always – really, always – involve people from one country being appalled by the habits of those from another. There were as many complaints about the lavatorial customs of the French as the French made of others. One that had been around for centuries was that in France there was 'much pissing in chimnies' there. The French were also commonly accused of relieving themselves on staircases, 'a practice which was still to be found at Versailles in the eighteenth century', writes Mark Girouard in *Life in the French Country House*. It was the boast of Versailles that it had one hundred bathrooms and three hundred commodes, but they were oddly under-used, and in 1715 an edict reassured residents and visitors that henceforth the corridors would be cleared of faeces weekly.

Most sewage went into cesspits, but these were commonly neglected and the contents often seeped into neighbouring water supplies. In the worst cases they overflowed. Samuel Pepys recorded one such occasion in his diary: 'Going down into my cellar . . . I put my foot into a great heap of turds . . . by which I found that Mr Turner's house of office is full and comes into my cellar, which doth trouble me.'

The people who cleaned cesspits were known as nightsoil men, and if there has ever been a less enviable way to make a living I believe it has yet to be described. They worked in teams of three or four. One man – the most junior, we may assume – was lowered into the pit itself to scoop waste into buckets. A second stood by the pit to raise and lower the buckets, and the third and fourth carried the buckets to a waiting cart. Nightsoil work was dangerous as well as disagreeable. Workers ran the risk of asphyxiation and even of explosions since they worked by the light of a lantern in powerfully gaseous environments. The *Gentleman's Magazine* in 1753 related the case of one nightsoil man who went into a privy vault in a London tavern and was overcome almost at once by the foul air. 'He call'd out for help, and immediately fell down on his face,' one witness reported. A colleague who rushed to the man's aid was similarly overcome. Two more men went to the vault, but could not get in because of the foul air, though they did manage to open the door a little, releasing the worst of the gases. By the time rescuers were able to haul the two men out, one was dead and the other was beyond help.

Because nightsoil men charged hefty fees, cesspits in poorer districts were seldom emptied and frequently overflowed – not surprisingly given the pressures put on the average inner-city cesspit. Crowding in many London districts was almost unimaginable. In St Giles, the worst of London's rookeries – scene of Hogarth's *Gin Lane* – 54,000 people were crowded into just a few streets. By one count, eleven hundred people lived in twenty-seven houses along one alley; that is more than forty people per dwelling. In Spitalfields, further east, inspectors found sixty-three people living in a single house. The house had nine beds – one for every seven occupants. A new word, of unknown provenance, sprang into being to describe such neighbour-hoods: 'slums'. Charles Dickens was one of the first to use it, in a letter of 1851.

Such masses of humanity naturally produced enormous volumes of waste – far more than any system of cesspits could cope with. In one fairly typical report an inspector recorded visiting two houses in St Giles where the cellars were filled with human waste to a depth of three feet. Outside, the inspector continued, the yard was six inches deep in excrement. Bricks had been stacked like stepping stones to let the occupants cross the yard.

At Leeds in the 1830s, a survey of the poorer districts found that many streets were 'floating with sewage'; one street, housing 176 families, had not been cleaned for fifteen years. In Liverpool, as many as one-sixth of the populace lived in dark cellars, where wastes could all too easily seep in. And of course human waste was only a small part of the enormous heaps of filth that were generated in the crowded and rapidly industrializing cities. In London, the Thames absorbed anything that wasn't wanted: condemned meat, offal, dead cats and dogs, food waste, industrial waste, human faeces and much more.

Animals were marched daily to Smithfield Market to be turned into beefsteaks and mutton chops; they deposited 40,000 tons of dung en route in a typical year. That was, of course, on top of all the waste of dogs, horses, geese, ducks, chickens and rutting pigs that were kept domestically. Gluemakers, tanners, dyers, tallow chandlers, chemical enterprises of all sorts, all added their by-products to the sea of daily sludge. Much of this rotting detritus ultimately found its way into the Thames, where the hope was that the tide would carry it out to sea. But of course tides run in both directions, and the tide that carried waste out towards the sea brought a good deal of it back when it turned. The river was a perpetual 'flood of liquid manure', as one observer put it. Smollett, writing in *Humphry Clinker*, said that 'human excrement is the least offensive part', for the river also contained 'all the drugs, minerals and poisons, used in mechanics and manufacture, enriched with the putrefying carcases of beasts and men; and mixed with the scourings of all the wash-tubs, kennels, and common sewers'. The Thames grew so noxious that when a tunnel being dug at Rotherhithe sprang a leak the first matter through the breach was not river water but concentrated gases, which were ignited by the miners' lamps, putting them in the absurdly desperate position of trying to outrun incoming waters *and* clouds of burning air.

The streams that fed into the Thames were often even worse than the Thames itself. The River Fleet was in 1831 'almost motionless with solidifying filth'. Even the Serpentine in Hyde Park became so progressively putrid that park users stayed upwind of it. In the 1860s, a layer of sewage fifteen feet deep was dredged from the bottom.

Into this morass came something that proved, un-expectedly, to be a disaster: the flush toilet. Flush toilets of a type had been around for some time. The very first was built by John Harington, godson to Queen Elizabeth. When Harington demonstrated his invention to her in 1597, she expressed great delight and had it immediately installed in Richmond Palace. But it was a novelty well ahead of its time and almost two hundred years passed before Joseph Bramah, a cabinetmaker and locksmith, patented the first modern flush toilet in 1778. It caught on in a modest way. Many others followed. But early toilets often didn't work well. Sometimes they backfired, filling the room with even more of what the horrified owner had very much hoped to be rid of. Until the development of the U-bend and water trap – that little reservoir of water that returns to the bottom of the bowl after each flush – every toilet bowl acted as a conduit to the smells of cesspit and sewer. The backwaft of odours, particularly in hot weather, could be unbearable.

This problem was resolved by one of the great and surely most extraordinarily appropriate names in history, that of Thomas Crapper (1837–1910), who was born into a poor family in Yorkshire and reputedly walked to London at the age of eleven. There he became an apprentice plumber in Chelsea. Crapper invented the clas-sic and, in Britain, still familiar toilet with an elevated cistern activated by the pull of a chain. Called the Marlboro Silent Water Waste Preventer, it was clean, leak-proof, odour-free and wonderfully reliable, and their manufacture made Crapper very rich and so famous that it is often assumed that he gave his name to the slang term 'crap' and its many derivatives. In fact, 'crap' in the lavatorial sense is very ancient and 'crapper' for a toilet is an Americanism not recorded by the *Oxford English Dictionary* before 1922. Crapper's name, it seems, was just a happy accident.

The breakthrough event for flush toilets was the Great Exhibition, where they became one of the featured attractions. More than eight hundred thousand people patiently endured long queues to experience the flush toilets – a novelty for most of them – and were so enchanted by the noise and cleansing swirl of water that they rushed to have them installed in their own homes. Perhaps no expensive consumer item in history has taken off more quickly. By the mid-1850s, some two hundred thousand of them were working away in London.

The problem was that London's sewers were designed only to drain off rainwater and couldn't cope with a steady deluge of solid waste. The sewers filled up with a dense, gloopy sludge that wouldn't wash away. People known as flushermen were employed to find blockages and clear them. Other sewery professions included toshers and mudlarks who delved through muck, in sewers and along fetid riverbanks, for lost jewellery or the odd silver spoon. Toshers made a good living, all things considered, but it was dangerous. The air in the sewers could be lethal. Since the sewer network was vast and unrecorded, there were many reports of toshers getting lost and failing to find their way out. Many were at least rumoured to have been attacked and devoured by rats.

Murderous epidemics were routine in the lightly sanitized, pre-antibiotic world. The cholera invasion of 1832 left an estimated 60,000 Britons dead. It was followed by a devastating influenza epidemic in 1837–8 and further cholera outbreaks in 1848, 1854 and 1867. Between and amid these attacks on the nation's tranquillity came deadly bursts of typhoid fever, rheumatic fever, scarlet fever, diphtheria and smallpox, among many others. Typhoid fever alone killed 1,500 people or more a year from 1850 to 1870. Whooping cough killed about 10,000 children a year from 1840 to 1910. Measles killed even more. There were, in short, an awful lot of ways to die in the nineteenth century.

Cholera wasn't terribly feared at first, for the decidedly unworthy reason that it was thought primarily to affect poor people. It was accepted wisdom almost everywhere in the nineteenth century that the poor were poor because they were born to be. Although a few impoverished people might generously be described as undeserving, most were by nature 'improvident, reckless and intemperate, and with habitual avidity for sensual gratification', as one government report crisply summarized it. Even Friedrich Engels, a far more sympathetic observer than most, could write in *The Condition of the Working Class in England*: 'The facile character of the Irishman, his crudity, which places him but little above the savage, his contempt for all humane enjoyments, in which his very crudeness makes him incapable of sharing, his filth and poverty, all favour drunkenness.'

So when in 1832, people in the crowded inner cities began to drop in large numbers from a brand-new disease from India called cholera, it was generally viewed as just one of those unfortunate things that befell the poor from time to time. Cholera became known as 'the poor man's plague'. In New York City, more than 40 per cent of the victims were poor Irish immigrants. Blacks were disproportionately affected too. The state medical commission in New York actually declared that the disease was confined to the dissolute poor and 'arises entirely from their habits of life'.

But then cholera began to strike down people in well-to-do neighbourhoods too, and very quickly the terror became general. People had not been so unnerved by a disease since the Black Death. The distinguishing feature of cholera was its quickness. The symptoms – violent diarrhoea and vomiting, agonizing cramps, crushing headache – came on in an instant. The mortality rate was 50 per cent, and sometimes higher, but it was the swiftness of it – the fearful, headlong transition from complete wellness to sudden agony, delirium and death – that people found terrifying. To see a loved one well at breakfast and dead by suppertime was a horrifying experience.

Other diseases actually wrecked more lives. Those who survived cholera generally recovered completely, unlike scarlet fever victims who were often left deaf or brain-damaged, or smallpox sufferers who could be horribly disfigured. Yet it was cholera that became a national obsession. Between 1845 and 1856, over seven hundred books on cholera were published in English. What particularly troubled people was that they didn't know what caused it or how to escape it. 'What is cholera?' the *Lancet* asked in 1853. 'Is it a fungus, an insect, a miasma, an electrical disturbance, a deficiency of ozone, a morbid off-scouring of the intestinal canal? We know nothing.'

The most common belief was that cholera and other terrible diseases arose from impure air. Anything that was wasted or foul – sewage, corpses in graveyards, decomposing vegetation, human exhalations – was thought to be disease-producing and potentially lethal. 'Malarious aromata rampage invisible through every street,' wrote one chronicler, a touch colourfully, at mid-century. 'Atmospheric poison and pungent factor and gaseous filth cry aloud and spare not, and the wayfaring man inhales at every breath a pair of lungs full of vaporized decomposing gutter mud and rottenness.' Liverpool's chief medical officer in 1844 calculated with confident precision the actual extent of the damage, reporting to Parliament: 'By the mere action of the lungs of the inhabitants of Liverpool a stratum of air sufficient to cover the entire surface of the town to a depth of three feet is daily rendered unfit for the purposes of respiration.'

The most devoted and influential believer in miasma theory was Edwin Chadwick, a secretary of the Poor Law Commission and author of *A Report on the Sanitary Condition of the Labouring Population of Great Britain*, which became a somewhat improbable bestseller in 1842. Chadwick's fundamental belief was that if you got rid of smells, you got rid of disease. 'All smell is disease,' he explained to a parliamentary inquiry. His wish was to clean up poor neighbourhoods and the habitations within them, not to make conditions more agreeable for the inhabitants but simply to get rid of the smells.

Chadwick was an intense and cheerless figure, much given to petty jealousies and arguments over position. A lawyer by training, he spent most of his life working on various royal commissions: on making improvements to the poor laws, on conditions in factories, on levels of sanitation in cities, on preventing avoidable deaths, on reorganizing the registration of births, deaths and marriages. Almost no one liked him. His work on the poor law of 1834, which introduced a national system of work-houses that were almost penal in their nature, made him widely despised among working people – 'the most unpopular single individual in the whole United Kingdom', according to one biographer. Even his family seems not to have had any affection for him. Chadwick's mother had died when he was small, and his father re-married and started a second family in the west of England. Eventually, this second family emigrated to Brooklyn, and they appear to have had no more to do with each other. One of the children of the second marriage was Henry Chadwick, whose career path went in a different direction altogether. He became a sportswriter and an energetic early promoter of organized baseball. Indeed he is sometimes described as the father of the modern game. He devised the scorecard, box score, batting average, earned run average and many of the other statistical intricacies on which baseball enthusiasts dote. The reason that a baseball box score and cricket summary are so strik-ingly similar is that he modelled the former on the latter.*

The miasma theory had just one serious flaw: it was entirely without foundation. Unfortunately only one man saw this, and he couldn't get others to see it with him. His name was John Snow.

---

* There is slightly more to this. James Chadwick, the father of these two men, had earlier in his life been a teacher in Manchester, where he taught science to John Dalton, who is generally credited with the dis-covery of the atom. Then, as a radical journalist, he had gone to Paris where he had lived for a time with Thomas Paine. So although he was a man of no particular importance himself, he served as a direct link between Thomas Paine and the French Revolution, the discovery of the atom, the sewage of London and the beginnings of professional baseball.

Snow was born in York in 1813 in modest circumstances – his father was a common labourer – and however much that might have coloured his life socially, it served him well in terms of insightfulness and compassion, for almost uniquely among medical authorities he did not blame the poor for their own diseases but saw that their conditions of living left them vulnerable to influences beyond their control. No one had ever brought that kind of open-mindedness to the study of epidemiology before.

Snow studied medicine in Newcastle but settled in London. There he became one of the leading anaesthetists of his day, at a time when anaesthesia was still an un-nervingly unproven field. Rarely has the word 'practice' been more apposite with respect to a doctor's endeavours. Even now anaesthesia is a delicate business, but in the early days when dosages were based on little more than hunches and hopeful assumptions, coma, death and other dire consequences were all too common. In 1853 Snow was called in to administer chloroform to Queen Victoria as she underwent labour in her eighth pregnancy. The use of chloroform was highly unexpected because it was not only new – it had been discovered, by a doctor in Edinburgh, just six years before – but also decidedly dangerous. Many people had died under its application already. To use it merely to help the queen cope with the pain of childbirth would be, in the view of most medical men, wildly incautious. The *Lancet* reported the matter as a worrying rumour and professed itself astonished that any qualified medical man would take such risks with the royal personage in any circumstance less than a crisis. Yet Snow seems to have had no hesitation in applying chloroform then or later, even though he was vividly and continually reminded of the risks of anaesthetics in his practice. In April 1857, for instance, he killed a patient by experimenting on him with a new type of anaesthetic, amylene, and misguessing what was the tolerable dosage. Exactly one week later he was applying chloroform to the queen again.

When not helping people to lose consciousness before surgery, Snow spent a great deal of time trying to understand where diseases came from. He particularly wondered why cholera devastated some neighbourhoods while sparing others. In Southwark, the rate of cholera deaths was six times higher than in neighbouring Lambeth. If cholera was caused by bad airs, then why would people in neighbouring boroughs, breathing the same air, have such discrepant rates of infection? Besides, if cholera was spread by smell then those who dealt most directly with bad odours – toshers, flushermen, nightsoil handlers and others whose livelihood was human waste – ought to be the most frequent victims. But they weren't. After the 1848 outbreak, Snow couldn't find a single flusherman who had died.

Snow's lasting achievement was not just to understand the cause of cholera but to collect the evidence in a scientifically rigorous manner. He made the most careful maps showing the exact distributions of where cholera victims lived. These made intriguing patterns. For instance, Bethlehem Hospital, the famous lunatic asylum, had not a single victim, while people on facing streets in every direction were felled in alarming numbers. The difference was that the hospital had its own water supply, from a well in the grounds, while people outside took their water from public wells. In the same way, the people of Lambeth drank water that was piped in from clean sources outside the city, whereas those in neighbouring Southwark took their water directly from the polluted Thames.

Snow announced his findings in a pamphlet of 1849, *On the Mode of Communication of Cholera*, which demonstrated a clear link between cholera and water contaminated with human faeces. It is one of the most important documents in the history of statistics, public health, demographics and forensic science – one of the most important documents, in short, of the nineteenth century. No one listened and the epidemics kept coming.

In 1854, a particularly virulent outbreak hit Soho. In a single neighbourhood around Broad Street more than five hundred people died in ten days, making it, as Snow noted, probably the most devastating occurrence of sudden mortality in history, worse even than the great plague. The toll would have been higher except that so many people fled the district.

The patterns of deaths presented some puzzling anomalies. One of the victims died in Hampstead and another in Islington – both miles away. Snow hiked out to where the outlying victims had lived and interviewed relatives and neighbours. It turned out that the Hampstead victim was a fan of Broad Street water – she liked it so much that she had it delivered regularly to her house – and had taken a draught shortly before becoming ill. The Islington victim was her niece, who had come to visit and had drunk some water too.

Snow managed to persuade the parish council to remove the handle from a water pump on Broad Street, after which cholera deaths in the neighbourhood vanished – or so it is commonly reported. In fact, the epidemic was already subsiding by the time the handle was removed, largely because so many people had fled.

Despite the accumulated evidence, Snow's conclusions were still rejected. When Snow appeared before a parliamentary select committee, the chairman, Sir Benjamin Hall, found it impossible to credit his findings. In a dumbfounded tone Hall asked Snow: 'Are the Committee to understand, taking the case of bone-boilers, that no matter how offensive to the sense of smell of effluvia that comes from the bone-boiling establishments may be, yet you consider that it is not prejudicial in any way to the health of the inhabitants of the district?'

'That is my opinion,' replied Snow, but unfortunately his manner, always diffident, was less forthright than his conclusions, and authorities continued to reject them.

It is hard now to appreciate just how radical and unwelcome Snow's views were. Many authorities actively detested him for them. The *Lancet* concluded that he was in the pocket of business interests which wished to continue to fill the air with 'pestilent vapours, miasms and loathsome abominations of every kind' and make themselves rich by poisoning their neighbours. 'After careful enquiry,' the parliamentary inquiry concluded, 'we see no reason to adopt this belief.'

Finally the inevitable happened. In the summer of 1858 London suffered a combination of heatwave and drought in which waste accumulated and wasn't washed away. Temperatures soared into the nineties and stayed there – an unusual condition for London. The result was 'the Great Stink', as *The Times* dubbed it. The Thames grew so noxious that almost no one could bear to be near it. 'Whoso once inhales the stink can never forget it,' wrote one newspaper. The curtains of the new Houses of Parliament were drawn tight and doused in a solution of chloride of lime to mitigate the lethal smells, but the result was something like panic. Parliament had to be suspended. Some members, according to Stephen Halliday, tried to venture into the library, overlooking the river, 'but they were instantaneously driven to retreat, each man with a handkerchief to his nose'.

Snow never got to see this or any of his ideas vindicated. He died suddenly of a stroke in the midst of the Great Stink, not knowing that one day he would be considered a hero. He was just forty-five years old. At the time, his death was hardly noted.

Happily, another heroic figure was about to stride on to the scene – Joseph Bazalgette. By chance, Bazalgette worked in offices just around the corner from Snow, though the two men never met as far as is known. Bazalgette was a very small man, short and feather-light, but compensated for his jockey-like stature with a spectacularly bushy moustache that reached literally from ear to ear. Like that other great Victorian engineer Isambard Kingdom Brunel, his antecedents were French, though the family had been settled in England for thirty-five years by the time Joseph was born in 1819. His father was a Royal Naval commander and Bazalgette grew up in an atmosphere of privilege, educated by private tutors and given every advantage in life.

Disqualified from a military career by his elfin stature, he trained as a railway engineer, but in 1849, aged thirty, he joined the Metropolitan Commission of Sewers, where he soon rose to the position of chief engineer. Sanitation has never had a greater champion. Nothing concerning sewage and waste disposal escaped his scrutiny. Troubled that there were almost no public lavatories in London, he devised a plan to place public toilets at critical spots throughout the city. By collecting urine and selling it as an industrial product (stale urine was vital to the processing of alum, for one thing), he calculated that each urinal could produce £48 of income a year, a very handsome return. That plan was never adopted, but it did instil the general conviction that where sewers were concerned Joseph Bazalgette was the man to turn to.

After the Great Stink it became clear that London's sewerage system needed to be rebuilt, and Bazalgette was handed the job. The challenge was formidable. Bazalgette had to insert into an immensely busy city some 1,200 miles of tunnels, which would last indefinitely, carry away every particle of waste generated by three million people, and be able to handle future growth of unknowable dimensions. He would have to acquire land, negotiate rights of way, procure and distribute materials, and direct hordes of labourers. The scale of every aspect of the job was exhausting merely to contemplate. The tunnels required 318 million bricks, and necessitated the digging up and redistributing of 3.5 million cubic yards of earth. All this was to be done on a budget of just £3 million.

Bazalgette brilliantly exceeded every expectation. In the process of building the new sewer system he transformed three and a half miles of riverfront through the creation of the Chelsea, Albert and Victoria embankments (which is where a lot of that displaced earth went). These new embankments not only provided space for a mighty intercepting sewer – a kind of sewer superhighway – but also left ample room for a new Underground line and

Construction of a sewage tunnel near Old Ford, Bow, East London.

ducts for gas and other utilities below and a new relief road above. Altogether he reclaimed fifty-two acres of land, over which he scattered parks and promenades. An incidental feature of the embankments was that they narrowed the river and made it flow faster, improving its ability to cleanse itself. It would be hard to name an engineering project anywhere that offered a wider array of improvements – to public health, transportation, traffic management, recreation and river management. This is the system that still drains London. Outside of the city's parks, the embankments remain among the most agreeable environments in London.

Because of the limits on his funds, Bazalgette could afford to take the sewage only as far as the eastern edge of the metropolis, to a place called Barking Reach. There mighty outfall pipes disgorged 150 million gallons of raw, lumpy, potently malodorous sewage into the Thames each day. Barking was still twenty miles from the open sea, as the dismayed and unfortunate people all along those twenty miles never stopped pointing out, but the tides were vigorous enough to haul most of the discharge safely (if not always odourlessly) out to sea, and ensured that there were never again any sewage-related epidemics in London.

The new sewage outfalls did, however, have an unfortunate role in the greatest tragedy ever experienced on the Thames. In September 1878, a pleasure boat named the *Princess Alice*, packed to overflowing with day-trippers, was returning to London after a day at the seaside, when it collided with another ship at Barking at the very place and moment when the two giant outfall pipes surged into action. The *Princess Alice* sank in less than five

minutes. Nearly eight hundred people drowned in a choking sludge of raw sewage. Even those who could swim
found it nearly impossible to make headway through the
glutinous filth. For days afterwards bodies bobbed to the
surface. Many, *The Times* reported, were so bloated with
gaseous bacteria that they wouldn't fit into normal coffins.

In 1876, Robert Koch, then an unknown country doctor in
Germany, identified the microbe, *Bacillus anthracis*,
responsible for anthrax. Seven years later, he identified
Vibrio cholerae, another bacillus, as the cause of cholera. At
long last there was proof that individual micro-organisms
caused specific diseases. It is remarkable to think that we
have had electric lights and telephones for about as long as
we have known that germs kill people. Edwin Chadwick
never did believe that, and continued throughout his life
to suggest ways of eliminating odours in order to keep
people healthy. One of his last and more singular proposals was to build across London a series of towers
modelled on the new Eiffel Tower in Paris. In Chadwick's
vision, the towers would act as mighty ventilators, pulling
in fresh, healthful air from the heights and pumping it
back out at ground level. He went to his grave in the
summer of 1890 implacably convinced that the cause of
epidemics was atmospheric vapours.

Bazalgette, meanwhile, moved on to other projects. He
built some of London's handsomest bridges, at
Hammersmith, Battersea and Putney, and drove through
the heart of London several bold new streets designed to
alleviate congestion, including Charing Cross Road and
Shaftesbury Avenue. Late in life he was knighted, but he
never really received the fame he deserved. Sewer

engineers seldom do. He is commemorated with a modest statue on the Victoria Embankment beside the Thames. He died a few months after Chadwick.

III

In America, the situation was more complicated than in England. Travellers to North America were often struck by the fact that epidemics tended to be rarer and milder there. There was a good reason for this: American communities were generally cleaner. This was not so much because Americans were more fastidious in their habits as because their communities were more open and spacious, creating less chance for contamination and cross-infection. At the same time, however, people in the New World had several additional diseases to contend with, and some of them were completely mystifying. One such was 'the milk sick'. People who drank milk in America sometimes grew delirious and swiftly died – Abraham Lincoln's mother was one such victim – but infected milk tasted and smelled no different from ordinary milk, and no one knew what the infectious agent was. Not until well into the nineteenth century did anyone finally deduce that it came from cows grazing on a plant called white snakeroot, which was harmless to the cows but made their milk toxic to drink.

Even more lethal and widely feared was yellow fever. A viral disease, it was called yellow fever because the skin of victims often turned sallow. The real symptoms, however, were high fever and black vomit. Yellow fever came into

America aboard slave ships from Africa. The first case was in Barbados in 1647. It was a horrible disease. A doctor who got it said it felt 'as if three or four hooks were fastened on to the globe of each eye and some person, standing behind me, was dragging them forcibly from their orbits back into the head'. Nobody knew what its cause was, but there was a general feeling – more instinct than intellectual certainty – that putrid water was at the root of things.

In the 1790s, a heroic English immigrant named Benjamin Latrobe began a long campaign to clean up water supplies. Latrobe was only in America because of a personal misfortune. He was a successful architect and engineer in England when in 1793 his wife died in child-birth. Devastated, he decided to emigrate to America, his mother's native country, to try to rebuild his life. For a time he was the only formally trained architect and engineer in the country, and as such he landed many important com-missions, from the Bank of Pennsylvania building in Philadelphia to the new Capitol Building in Washington.

His principal preoccupation, however, was with the belief that dirty water was killing thousands of people unnecessarily. After a devastating outbreak of yellow fever in Philadelphia, he persuaded the authorities to fill in the city swamps and bring in clean, fresh water from outside the city boundaries. The changes had a miraculous effect and yellow fever never came back to Philadelphia with anything like the same force again. Latrobe took his efforts elsewhere and, ironically, while working in New Orleans in 1820, he contracted yellow fever himself and died.

Where cities failed to improve water supplies, heavy penalties were paid. Until about 1800, all Manhattan's fresh water came from a single filthy pool – little more than a 'common sewer', in the words of one contemporary – in lower Manhattan known as the Collect Pond. But matters grew much worse as the population soared after the building of the Erie Canal. By the 1830s, it was estimated that a hundred tons of excrement were added to the city's cesspits each day, often with contaminating effects on nearby wells. Water in New York was generally, and often visibly, polluted and undrinkable. New York in 1832 not only had a cholera epidemic but also one of yellow fever. Together they claimed more than four times as many victims as in Philadelphia with its cleaner supplies. The dual outbreak acted as a spur to New York in much the way the Great Stink motivated London, and in 1837 work started on the Croton Aqueduct, which when finished in 1842 finally began to deliver clean, safe water to the city.

But where America was really ahead of the rest of the world was in the provision of private bathrooms. Here the main driver was not homeowners but hotels. The very first hotel in the world to offer a bath for every bedroom was the Mount Vernon Hotel in the resort community of Cape May, New Jersey. This was in 1853 and was so far ahead of its time that over half a century passed before any other hotels offered such extravagance. Increasingly, however, bathrooms – albeit shared and down the corridor rather than private and in one's room – became standard in hotels, first in the United States and then increasingly in Europe, and hoteliers who failed to heed this trend paid a hefty price.

Nowhere was that more memorably demonstrated than at the vast and otherwise glorious Midland Hotel at St Pancras Station in London. Designed by the great

George Gilbert Scott, who was also responsible for the Albert Memorial, the Midland was intended to be the most magnificent hotel in the world when it opened in 1873. It cost the equivalent of £300 million in today's money and was a wonder in almost every way. Unfortunately – in fact, amazingly – Scott provided just four bathrooms to be shared among six hundred bedrooms. Almost from the day of its opening, the hotel was a failure.

In private homes the provision of bathrooms was more hit and miss. Until quite late in the nineteenth century many houses had plumbing to their kitchen and perhaps to a downstairs toilet, but lacked a proper bathroom because there wasn't enough pressure in the pipes to get water upstairs. In Europe, even when pressure allowed, the rich proved unexpectedly reluctant to bring bathrooms into their lives. 'Bathrooms are for servants,' sniffed one English aristocrat. Or as the Duc de Doudeauville in France responded loftily when asked if he would be putting in plumbing in his new house: 'I am not building a hotel.' Americans, by contrast, were much more attached to the satisfactions of hot water and flushing toilets. When the newspaper baron William Randolph Hearst bought St Donat's, a Welsh castle, the first thing he did was install thirty-two bathrooms.

Bathrooms were not at first decorated any more than you would decorate a boiler room, so they tended to be starkly utilitarian. In existing houses, baths had to be fitted in wherever they could. Usually they took the place of a bedroom, but sometimes were jemmied into alcoves or other odd corners. In the rectory at Whatfield in Suffolk the bath was simply put behind a screen in the downstairs front hall. Baths, toilets and basins tended to be of exceedingly variable sizes. A bath at Lanhydrock House in Cornwall was so big that a stepladder was needed to climb into it. Others, with showers built in, looked as if they were designed to wash a horse.

Technological problems slowed the take-up of bathrooms, too. Casting a one-piece bath that was neither too thick nor too heavy was a surprisingly challenging proposition. It was easier in some ways to build a cast-iron bridge than a cast-iron bath. There was also the problem of giving the bath a finish that wouldn't chip, stain, graze into hairline cracks or simply wear away. Hot water proved to be a formidably corrosive medium. Zinc, copper and cast-iron baths looked splendid when new but wouldn't keep a finish. It wasn't until the invention of porcelain enamels, about 1910, that baths became durable and attractive. The process involved spraying a mix of powder on to cast iron and baking it repeatedly till it acquired a porcelain-like gleam. Porcelain enamels are in fact neither porcelain nor enamel but a vitreous coating – in essence a type of glass. Enamel bath surfaces would be quite transparent if whiteners or other tints weren't added to the glazing compound.

At last the world had baths that looked good and stayed looking good for a long time. But they were still extremely expensive. A bath alone could easily cost $200 in 1910 – a price well beyond the range of most households. But as manufacturers improved the processes of mass manufacture, prices fell and by 1940 an American could buy an entire bath suite – sink, bath and toilet – for $70, a price nearly everyone could afford.

Elsewhere, however, baths remained luxuries. In Europe

a big part of the problem was a lack of space in which to put bathrooms. In 1954 just one French residence in ten had a shower or bath. In Britain the journalist Katharine Whitehorn has recalled that as recently as the late 1950s she and her colleagues on the magazine *Woman's Own* were not allowed to do features on bathrooms as not enough British homes had them, and such articles would only promote envy.

As for our old rectory, it had no bathroom in 1851, which is of course no surprise. However, the architect, the endlessly fascinating Edward Tull, did include a water closet – quite a novelty in 1851. Even more novel was where he elected to put it: on the landing of the main stair-case, behind a thin partition. Apart from the water closet being in an odd and rather inconvenient place, the partition would have had the effect of closing off the stair window, leaving the staircase veiled in permanent darkness.

The absence of any outlet pipes on the drawings of the house exterior suggests that Tull may not entirely have thought all this through. The point is, in any case, academic as the water closet was never built.

CHAPTER SEVENTEEN

The Dressing Room

I

TOWARDS THE END of September 1991, two German hikers, Helmut and Erika Simon of Nuremberg, were making their way along a glacier high in the South Tyrolean Alps, at a place called the Tisenjoch Pass, on the borders of Austria and Italy, when they happened upon a human body protruding from the ice at the glacier's edge. The body was leathery and severely emaciated but intact.

The Simons made a two-mile detour to a manned mountain hut at Similaun to report their discovery. Police were summoned, but when they arrived it quickly became apparent that this was not a matter for them but for pre-historians. With the body were personal effects – copper axe, flint knife, arrows and quiver – that connected him to a much earlier, more primitive age.

Subsequent radiocarbon dating showed that the man had died over five thousand years ago. He was quickly nicknamed Ötzi, after the nearest major valley, the Ötztal; others called him the Iceman. Ötzi had not only a full range of tools but also all his clothing. Nothing so complete and ancient had ever been found before.

Contrary to common assumption, bodies that fall into glaciers almost never pop out at the terminal end in an impeccably preserved state. Glaciers grind and churn with slow but brutal force, and any bodies within them are generally crushed to molecules. Very occasionally they are stretched to outlandish lengths, like characters flattened by a steamroller in a cartoon. If no oxygen gets to the body, it may undergo a process called saponification in which the flesh transmutes into a waxy, foul-smelling substance called adipocere. Such bodies look eerily as if they have been carved from soap and lose nearly all meaningful definition.

Ötzi's body was preserved as well as it was through a combination of unusually favourable circumstances. First, he died in the open on a day that was dry but with the temperature falling swiftly: effectively he was freeze-dried. Then he was covered by a series of dry, light snowfalls, and probably stayed in that perfectly frigid state for years before the glacier slowly claimed him. Even then he remained in an outlying eddy that saved him – and, no less importantly, his possessions – from being dispersed and crushed. Had Ötzi died a few steps closer to the glacier or a little lower down the slopes or in drizzle or sun, or in almost any other circumstances, he would not be with us now. However ordinary Ötzi may have been in life, in death he became the very rarest of corpses.

What made Ötzi uniquely exciting was that this was not a burial, with personal effects thoughtfully arranged about him, but a person found straight from life, with the day-to-day items he had on him when he died. Nothing like that had ever been found before, and it was almost wholly undone by four days of over-exuberant recovery efforts. Passers-by and sightseers were allowed to take turns hacking away at the ice that held the body. One well-meaning helper seized a stick and tried digging with it, but it snapped in two. 'The stick,' the *National Geographic* reported, 'turned out to be part of the hazel-wood and larch-wood frame of the Iceman's backpack.' The volunteers, in short, were trying to dig out the corpse using his own priceless artefacts.

The case was dealt with by Austrian police, and the body, once freed, was whisked away to a refrigerator in Innsbruck. But a subsequent GPS investigation showed that in fact Ötzi had been just inside Italian territory when found, and after some legal wrangling the Austrians were ordered to surrender their treasured body, and Ötzi was driven over the Brenner Pass to Italy.

Today Ötzi lies on a slab in a refrigerated room in the archaeological museum in Bolzano, a German-speaking city in the north of Italy. His skin has the colour and texture of fine leather, and is stretched tight across his bones. His face wears an expression that looks very like weary resignation. Since being hauled off the mountain nearly twenty years ago, Ötzi has become the most forensically studied human being in history. Scientists could determine many of the details of his life with startling precision. With electron microscopes they could see that on the day of his death he consumed ibex and deer meat, bread made from a type of wheat called spelt, and some unidentified vegetables. From pollen grains recovered from his colon and lungs they were able to deduce that he had died in the spring and had begun the day in the valley below. By studying isotopic trace elements in his teeth, they could even work out what he had eaten as a child and therefore where he had been raised, and concluded that he had grown up in the Eisack Valley, in what is now Italy, then moved to a valley called the Vinschgau further west near the modern border with Switzerland. The biggest surprise of all was how old he was: at least forty but possibly as much as fifty-three, making him exceedingly old for the period. But there was also much they couldn't explain, including how he had died, and what he was doing nearly two miles above sea level at the time of his death. His bow was unstrung and only half made, and the arrows mostly had no flights and so were useless, yet for some reason he took them with him.

Normally not many people stop at small archaeological museums in out-of-the-way provincial towns, but Bolzano's museum is thronged with visitors throughout the year and the gift shop does a brisk trade in Ötzi keepsakes. Visitors queue to peer at him through a small window. He lies naked on his back on a glass slab. His brown skin glistens from the mist that is perpetually sprayed over him as a preservative. In fact, there is nothing innately distinctive about Ötzi. He is a completely normal if unusually old and well-preserved human being. What is extraordinary are his many possessions. They are the material equivalent of time travel.

Ötzi had a lot of stuff – shoes, clothing, two birchbark canisters, sheath, axe, bowstave, quiver and arrows, miscellaneous small tools, some berries, a piece of ibex meat and two spherical lumps of birch fungus, each about the size of a large walnut and carefully threaded with sinew. One of the canisters had contained glowing embers wrapped in maple leaves, for starting fires. Such an assemblage of personal effects was unique. Some of the items were, as it were, really unique in that they had never been imagined, much less seen. The birch fungus was a particular mystery because it was obviously treasured, and yet birch fungus is not known to be good for anything.

His equipment employed eighteen different types of wood – a remarkable variety. The most surprising of all his tools was the axe. It was copper-bladed and of a type known as a Remedello axe, after a site in Italy where they were first found. But Ötzi's axe was hundreds of years older than the oldest Remedello axe. 'It was,' in the words of one observer, 'as if the tomb of a medieval warrior had yielded a modern rifle.' The axe changed the timeframe for the copper age in Europe by no less than a thousand years.

But the real revelation and excitement were the clothes. Before Ötzi we had no idea – or, to be more precise, nothing but ideas – of how stone age people dressed. Such materials as survived existed only as fragments. Here was a complete outfit and it was full of surprises. His clothes were made from the skins and furs of an impressive range of animals – red deer, bear, chamois, goat and cattle. He also had with him a woven grass rectangle that was three feet long. This might have been a kind of rain cape, but it might equally have been a sleeping mat. Again, nothing like it had ever been seen or imagined.

Ötzi wore fur leggings held up with leather strips attached to a waist strap that made them look uncannily – almost comically – like the kind of nylon stockings and garter sets that Hollywood pin-ups wore in the Second World War. Nobody had remotely foreseen such a get-up. He wore a loincloth of goatskin and a hat made from the fur of a brown bear – probably a kind of hunting trophy. It would have been very warm and covetably stylish. The rest of his outfit was mostly made from the skin and fur of red deer. Hardly any came from domesticated animals, the opposite of what was expected.

The boots were the greatest surprise of all. They looked like nothing so much as a pair of bird's nests sitting on soles of stiffened bear skin, and seemed hopelessly ill-designed and insubstantial. Intrigued, a Czech foot and shoe expert named Vaclav Patek carefully fashioned a replica pair, using exactly the same design and materials, then tried them on a mountain walk. They were, he reported in some astonishment, 'more comfortable and capable' than any modern boots he had ever worn. Their grip on slippery rock was better than modern rubber, and it was all but impossible to get blisters in them. They were, above all, exceedingly effective against cold.

Despite all the forensic probings, ten years passed before anyone noticed that embedded in Ötzi's left shoulder was an arrowhead. Closer inspection showed also that his clothes and weapons were speckled with the blood of four other people. Ötzi, it turned out, had been killed in a violent showdown of some kind. Why his murderers chased him up to a high mountain pass is a question that is not easily answered, even speculatively. Still more mysterious is why the murderers didn't help themselves to his possessions. Ötzi's personal items, particularly his axe, had real value. Yet having evidently stalked him for quite a distance and engaged in a remarkably bloody fight at close quarters – clearly it takes quite a lot of lashing out to draw the blood of four people – they left him where he fell, with his possessions undisturbed. It is of course lucky for us that they did, for his personal effects provide answers to all kinds of otherwise unanswerable questions, except the one that seems bound to tantalize for ever now – namely, what on earth was going on up there?

We are in the dressing room – or what at least was called the dressing room on Edward Tull's original plans. One of Tull's many architectural curiosities was that he didn't provide direct access between the dressing room and Mr Marsham's bedroom next door but had both decanting separately into the upstairs passage. So in order to dress or undress, Mr Marsham would have had to leave his bedroom and walk a few steps along the corridor to the dressing room – rather an odd way to go about things bearing in mind that just a few steps away was the 'Female Servant's Bedroom' – which is to say, that of the loyal spinster Miss Worm. Such an arrangement would almost certainly have guaranteed occasional encounters, which we may presume would tend to be awkward. But then again perhaps not. A separate oddity is how cosily proximate their bedrooms were considering how rigorously their domains were separated by day. It is certainly a hard household to figure.

In any case, Mr Marsham apparently had second thoughts because in the house as built the dressing room and bedroom are in fact connected. The dressing room is now, and probably has been for the better part of a century, a bathroom. We still do some of our dressing in there, however, which is as well because the long and really quite mysterious history of dressing is what we have come here to talk about.

*   *   *

How long people have been dressing themselves is a
question not at all easy to answer. All that can be said is
that about forty thousand years ago, after an immensely
long period in which humans didn't do much at all except
procreate and survive, there stepped from the shadows the
big-brained, behaviourally modern people commonly
known as Cro-Magnons (after a cave in the Dordogne
region of France where they were first found) and that
among these new people was some ingenious soul who
came up with one of the greatest, most underrated inventions in history: string. String is marvellously
elemental. It is simply two pieces of fibre placed side by
side and twisted together. That achieves two things: it
makes a cord that is strong and it allows long cords to be
built up from short fibres. Imagine where we would be
without it. There would be no cloth and clothing, fishing
lines, nets, snares, rope, leashes, tethers, slings, the bows in
bows and arrows, and a thousand useful things more.
Elizabeth Wayland Barber, a textile historian, was hardly
exaggerating when she called it the 'weapon that allowed
the human race to conquer the earth'.

Historically the two most common fibres were linen
and hemp. Linen was made from flax and was popular
because flax grows tall – up to a height of four feet – and
quickly. Flax can be sown one month and harvested the
next. The downside is that flax is tediously demanding in
its preparation. Some twenty different actions are required
to separate flax fibres from their woody stems and soften
them enough for spinning. These actions have arcane
names like braking, retting, swingling (or scutching)
and hackling or heckling, but essentially they involve

pounding, stripping, soaking and otherwise separating the pliant inner fibre, or bast, from its woodier stem. It is striking to think that when we heckle a speaker today we use a term that recalls the preparation of flax from the early Middle Ages.

The result of all that effort was a sturdy and adaptable fabric: linen. Although we tend to think of linen as snowy white, its natural hue is brown. To make it white, it had to be bleached in sunlight, a slow process that could take months to execute. The poorer stuff was left unbleached and made into canvas or sacking. The principal drawback of linen is that it doesn't take a dye well, so there isn't a great deal you can do with it to make it exciting.

Hemp was roughly similar to flax, but coarser and not so comfortable to wear, so it tended to be used for things like rope and sails. It did, however, have the evidently very considerable compensating advantage that you could smoke it and get high, which Barber believes accounts for its prevalence and rapid spread in antiquity. Not to put too fine a point on it, people throughout the ancient world were very, very fond of hemp, and grew more of it than they needed for ropes or sails.

But the primary clothing material of the Middle Ages was wool. Wool was a lot warmer and more hard-wearing than linen, but wool fibres are short and must have been difficult to work, especially as early sheep were surprisingly unwoolly creatures. Their wool, such as it was, originally was a downy undercoating beneath dreadlocks of tangled hair. To turn sheep into the blocks of fleeciness we know and value today took centuries of devoted breeding. Moreover, wool wasn't sheared originally. It was painfully plucked. It is little wonder that sheep are such skittish animals when humans are around.

Even once medieval people had a pile of wool in front of them, their work was really just beginning. To turn it into cloth required washing, combing, carding, teaseling, warping, sizing and fulling, among many other processes. Fulling consisted of beating and shrinking the cloth; sizing involved the application of a glaze. Combing the fibres flat created a hard-wearing but comparatively stiff fabric: a worsted. For softer wool, carding paddles were used to make the fibres fluffier. The hair of weasels, stoats and other animals was sometimes blended into the mix to make the finished cloth more lustrous.

The fourth principal fabric was silk. Silk was a rare luxury, literally worth its weight in gold. Accounts of crime in the eighteenth and nineteenth centuries nearly always dwell on the way criminals were imprisoned or trans-ported to Australia for the theft of a handkerchief or packet of lace or some other seeming trifle, but in fact these were often items of great value. A pair of silk stockings could cost £5 and a packet of lace could sell for £20 – enough to live on for a couple of years and an exceedingly serious loss to any shopkeeper. A silk cloak would cost £50 – well beyond the means of any but the highest nobility. Most people, if they had silk at all, had it in the form of ribbons or other trim. The Chinese ferociously guarded the secrets of silk production; the punishment for exporting a single mulberry seed was execution. At least as far as northern Europe was concerned they needn't have worried too much because mulberry trees were too sensitive to frost to thrive there. Britain tried hard for a hundred years to pro-duce silk, and sometimes got good results, but ultimately couldn't overcome the drawback of periodic harsh winters.

With these few materials, and some trimmings like feathers and ermine, people managed to make wondrous outfits – so much so that by the fourteenth century rulers felt it necessary to introduce what were known as sumptuary laws, to limit what people wore. Sumptuary laws laid down with fanatical precision what materials and colours of fabric a person could wear. In Shakespeare's day, someone with an income of £20 a year was permitted to wear a satin doublet but not a satin gown, while someone worth £100 a year had no restrictions on satin, but could wear velvet only on doublets and then so long as the velvet wasn't crimson or blue – colours reserved for people of still higher status. Restrictions existed too on the amount of fabric one could employ in a particular article of clothing, and whether it might be worn pleated or straight and so on. When Shakespeare and his fellow players were given royal patronage by King James I in 1603, one of the perks of the appointment was that they were given, and allowed to wear, four and a half yards of scarlet cloth – a considerable honour for someone in as louche a profession as acting.

Sumptuary laws were enacted partly to keep people within their class, but partly also for the good of domestic industries, since they were often designed to depress the importation of foreign materials. For the same reason for a time there was a Statute of Caps, aimed at helping national capmakers through a depression, which required people to wear caps instead of hats. For obscure reasons, Puritans resented the law and were often fined for flouting it. But on the whole sumptuary laws weren't much enforced. Various clothing restrictions were enshrined in statutes in 1337, 1363, 1463, 1483, 1510, 1533 and 1554, but records show they were never much enforced. They were repealed altogether in 1604.

For anyone of a rational disposition, fashion is often nearly impossible to fathom. Throughout many periods of history – perhaps most – it can seem as if the whole impulse of fashion has been to look maximally ridiculous. If one could be maximally uncomfortable as well, the triumph was all the greater.

Dressing impractically is a way of showing that one doesn't have to do physical work. Throughout history, and across many cultures, this has generally been far more important than comfort. In the sixteenth century, to take just one example, starch came into fashion. The result was the magnificent ruffs known as piccadills. Really enormous piccadills made eating almost impossible and necessitated the fashioning of special long-handled spoons, so that diners could get food to their lips. But there must have been a lot of dismaying dribbles and a general sense of hunger at mealtimes for many.

Even the simplest things had a glorious pointlessness to them. When buttons came in, about 1650, people couldn't get enough of them and arrayed them in decorative profusion on the backs and collars and sleeves of coats where they didn't actually do anything. One relic of this is the short row of pointless buttons that are still placed on the underside of jacket sleeves near the cuff. These have always been purely decorative and have never had a purpose, yet three hundred and fifty years on we continue to attach them as if they are the most earnest necessity.

Perhaps the most irrational fashion act of all was the

male habit for 150 years of wearing wigs. Samuel Pepys, as with so many things, was in the vanguard, noting with some apprehension the purchase of a wig in 1663 when they were not yet common. It was such a novelty that he feared people would laugh at him in church, and was greatly relieved, and a little proud, to find that they did not. He also worried, not unreasonably, that the hair of wigs might come from plague victims. Perhaps nothing says more about the power of fashion than that he continued wearing wigs even while wondering if they might kill him.

Wigs might be made of almost anything – human hair, horsehair, cotton thread, goat hair, silk. One maker advertised a model made of fine wire. They came in many styles – bag, bob, campaign, grizzle, Ramillies, cauliflower, brown tie, riding bob and more, all denoting some crucial difference in length of braid or bounciness of curl. A full wig could cost £50 and wigs were so valuable that they were left as bequests in wills. The more substantial the wig the higher up the social echelon one stood – one became literally a bigwig. Wigs were also one of the first things snatched by robbers. The ridiculousness of outsized hairpieces didn't escape comedic notice. Vanbrugh in *The Relapse* had one of his characters, a wigmaker, boast of a wig 'so long and full of hair that it may serve you for a hat and cloak in all weathers'.

All wigs tended to be scratchy, uncomfortable and hot, particularly in summer. To make them more bearable, many men shaved their heads, so we should be surprised to see many famous seventeenth- and eighteenth-century figures as their wives saw them first thing in the morning. It was an odd situation. For a century and a half men got rid of their own hair, which was perfectly comfortable, and instead covered their heads with something foreign and *un*comfortable. Very often it was actually their own hair made into a wig. People who couldn't afford wigs tried to make their hair *look* like a wig.

Wigs took a lot of maintenance. Once every week or so they had to be sent out to have their buckles (from the French *boucles*, meaning curls) reshaped on heated rollers, and possibly baked in an oven, a process known as fluxing. From about 1700, for reasons that had nothing to do with common sense or practicality, it became fashionably necessary to place on one's head a daily snowfall of white powder. The main powdering agent was simple flour. When wheat harvests failed in France in the 1770s, there were riots all over as starving people realized that diminished supplies of flour were not being baked into bread, but were being used to powder the privileged heads of aristocrats. By the late eighteenth century, hair powders were commonly coloured – blue and pink were especially popular – and scented, too.

Powdering could be done while the wig was on a wooden stand, but it was widely agreed that maximum stylishness was achieved by powdering the wig while it was on. The procedure required the owner to don his wig, cover his shoulders and upper body with a cloth and stick his face in a paper funnel (to avoid choking) while a servant or 'frisseur' armed with a bellows dispensed clouds of powder on to his head. A few more fastidious people took matters further. A certain Prince Raunitz employed four valets to puff out four clouds of powder, each dyed a different colour, through which the prince smartly strode in order to achieve exactly the right effect. Learning of this, Lord Effingham employed five French frisseurs just to look after his hair; Lord Scarborough hired six.

And then, pretty abruptly, wigs went out of fashion. Wigmakers, in desperation, petitioned George III to make wig-wearing by males compulsory, but the king declined. By the early 1800s nobody wanted them and old wigs were commonly used as dust mops. Today they survive only in certain courtrooms in Britain and the Commonwealth. Judicial wigs these days are made of horsehair and cost about £600, I'm told. To avoid a look of newness – which many lawyers fear might suggest in-experience – new wigs are customarily soaked in tea to give them a suitable air of age.

Women, meanwhile, took wig-wearing literally to another level – building their hair up on a wire scaffold known as a pallisade or commode. By mixing greased wool and horsehair with their own hair they could attain truly monumental heights. Female wigs sometimes rose as much as two and a half feet, making the average wearer roughly seven and a half feet tall. When travelling to engagements they often had to sit on the floor of their carriages or ride with their heads out the windows. At least two fatalities were attributed to women's hair catching fire after brushing against chandeliers.

Women's hair became so complicated that it took on a whole new vocabulary, and so ornate that individual curls or sections of curl had names – *frivolité, des migraines, l'insurgent, monte la haut, sorti, frelange, flandon, burgoigne, choux, crouche, berger, confident* and many more. ('Chignon', for a knot at the back of the head, is about the only word that survives from this once-extensive

Extreme hair: Miss Prattle consulting Doctor Double Fee about her Pantheon Head Dress.

THE DRESSING ROOM   543

vocabulary.) Because of the amount of work involved, it was not uncommon for women to leave their hair untouched for months on end, except to add a little paste from time to time to keep everything cemented in place. Many slept with their necks on special wooden blocks to keep their hairstyles elevated and undisturbed. One consequence of failing to wash was that their hair often swarmed with insects, particularly weevils. One woman reportedly miscarried when she discovered that mice were nesting in her upper decks.

The heyday of the towering hairstyles for women was the 1790s when men were already giving up wigs. Generally women's wigs were festooned with ribbons and feathers, but sometimes with even more elaborate devices. John Woodforde, in his history of vanity, mentions a woman who had a model ship, complete with sails and cannon, riding the waves of her headwear, as if protecting it from invasion.

In the same period it became fashionable to wear artificial moles, known as *mouches*. Gradually these artificial patches took on shapes, like stars or crescent moons, which were worn on the face, neck and shoulders. One lady is recorded as sporting a coach and six horses galloping across her cheeks. At the peak of the fashion, people wore a superabundance of *mouches* until they must have looked rather as if they were covered in flies. Patches were worn by men as well as women, and were said to reflect one's political leanings by whether they were worn on the right cheek (Whigs) or left cheek (Tories). Similarly, a heart on the right cheek signalled that the wearer was married, and on the left cheek that he or she was engaged. Patches became so complicated and various that they generated a whole vocabulary, too, so that a patch on the chin was known as a *silencieuse*, one on the nose was called *l'impudente* or *l'effrontée*, one in the middle of the forehead was a *majestueuse*, and so on all around the head. In the 1780s, just to show that creative ridiculousness really knew no bounds, it became briefly fashionable to wear fake eyebrows made of mouse skin.

Patches at least were not toxic, and as such were almost the only beauty aid in centuries that wasn't. There was in England a long tradition of poisoning oneself in the name of beauty. Pupils could also be attractively dilated with drops of belladonna, or deadly nightshade. Most dangerous of all was ceruse, a paste made of white lead and commonly known as 'paint'. Ceruse was very popular. For females with smallpox scars it was applied as a kind of grout, to fill in the divots, but even many women who were free of blemishes used it to give themselves a lovely ghostly pallor. Ceruse remained popular for a remarkably long time. The first reference to it as a cosmetic is in 1519 when it was recorded that women of fashion 'whyte their face, necke and pappis [which is to say breasts] with cerusse' and in 1754 the *Connoisseur*, a periodical, was still marvelling that 'every lady you meet is besmeared with unguent ceruss and plaister'. Ceruse had three principal drawbacks: it cracked when the wearer smiled or grimaced; after a few hours it turned grey; and if used long enough it could very well kill. At the very least, it could make eyes swell painfully and teeth loosen and fall out. At least two well-known beauties, the courtesan Kitty Fisher and the socialite Maria Gunning, Countess of Coventry, are said to have died from ceruse poisoning, both while only in their twenties, but no one can begin to guess how many others may have had their lives shortened or constitutions unsettled by their attachment to ceruse.

Toxic potions were popular too. Well into the nineteenth century, many women drank a concoction called Fowler's Solution, which was really just dilute arsenic, to improve their complexions. Dante Gabriel Rossetti's wife, Elizabeth Siddal (who is best remembered as the model for the drowned Ophelia in the painting by John Everett Millais), was a devoted swallower of the stuff and it almost certainly contributed to her early death in 1862.*

Men wore make-up too, and indeed for a century or so were inclined to display breathtaking effeminacy, sometimes in the most unexpected circumstances. Louis XIV's brother, the Duc d'Orléans, 'in spite of being one of history's most famous sodomites', in the startlingly forthright words of Nancy Mitford, was a brave soldier, but an unorthodox one. He would arrive at the battlefield 'painted, powdered, all his eyelashes stuck together, covered with ribbons and diamonds', she wrote in *The Sun King*. 'He would never wear a hat for fear of flattening his wig. Once in action he was as brave as a lion, only afraid of what the sun and dust might do to his complexion.' Men as well as women festooned their hair with plumes and feathers, and tied ribbons to each bouncing curl. Some men took to wearing high-heeled shoes – not clunky platform shoes but slender, spiky heels up to six inches high – and to carrying furry muffs to keep their hands

---

* Overcome with grief, her husband buried her with a sheaf of poems that he had failed to copy; seven years later he thought better of the gesture, had the grave dug up and retrieved the poems, which were published the following year.

warm. Some carried parasols in the summer. Nearly all drenched themselves in perfume. They became known as macaronis, from a dish they first encountered on Italian tours.

So it is curious that the people who actually brought some restraint to matters – namely the rival sartorial tribe the dandies – have become associated in the popular consciousness with overdress. Nothing, with respect to male attire, could be further from the truth, and the quint-essence of that muted splendour was George 'Beau' Brummell, who lived from 1778 to 1840. Brummell was not rich or talented or blessed with brains. He just dressed better than anyone ever had before. Not more colourfully or extravagantly, but simply with more care.

He was born in reasonably privileged circumstances on Downing Street, his father a trusted adviser to the prime minister, Lord North. Brummell went to Eton and, briefly, to Oxford, before taking up a position in the military in the Prince of Wales's regiment, the 10th Hussars. If he had any aptitude for command in battle, it was never tested; his function essentially was to look good in uniform and to act as a kind of companion and assistant to the prince at formal gatherings. In conse-quence, he and the prince became close friends.

Brummell lived in Mayfair and for some years his house was the epicentre of one of the more improbable rituals in London's history – that of a procession of grown men of great eminence arriving each afternoon to watch him dress. Among those regularly in attendance were the Prince of Wales, three dukes, a marquess, two earls and the playwright Richard Brinsley Sheridan. They would sit and watch in respectful silence as Brummell began the daily process of grooming with a bath. It was generally thought an amazement that he bathed every day – 'and every part of his body', as one witness added with special astonishment. Moreover he did it in *hot* water. Sometimes he added milk, which itself set a fashion, though not an entirely happy one. When word got out that the withered and miserly Marquess of Queensberry, who lived nearby, was also in the habit of taking milk baths, milk sales in the district plummeted because it was rumoured that he returned the milk for resale after he had immersed his crusty and decrepit skin in it.

The attire of dandies was studiously muted. Brummell's apparel was confined almost entirely to three plain colours: white, buff and blue-black. What distinguished dandies was not the richness of their plumage but the care with which they assembled themselves. It was all about getting a perfect line. They would spend hours making sure every crease and furl was perfect, unimprovable. A visitor, arriving at Brummell's to find the floor strewn with cravats, once asked Robinson, his long-suffering valet, what was going on. 'Those,' Robinson sighed, 'are our failures.' Dandies dressed and redressed endlessly. In a day they would typically get through at least three shirts and two pairs of trousers, four or five cravats, two waistcoats, several pairs of stockings and a small stack of handkerchiefs.

Some of the fashion was dictated by the ever-increasing stoutness of the Prince of Wales (or 'Prince of Whales', as he was snickeringly known behind his back). By the time he reached his thirties, the prince had taken on such a fleshy sprawl that he had to be forcibly strapped into a corset – a 'Bastille of Whalebone', in the words of one who was allowed to see it – which his attendants tactfully referred to as his 'belt'. All this pushed his upper body fat upwards through the neck hole, like toothpaste coming out of a tube, so the very high collars fashionable in his day were a kind of additional mini-corset, designed to hide an abundance of chins and the floppy wattle of his neck.

The one sartorial area in which dandies did stand out, as it were, was in their trousers. Pantaloons were often worn tight as paint and were not a great deal less revealing, particularly as they were worn without underwear. The night after seeing the Count d'Orsay, Jane Carlyle noted in her diary, perhaps just a touch breathlessly, that the count's pantaloons were 'skin-coloured and fitting like a glove'. The style was based on the riding trousers of Brummell's regiment. Jackets were tailored with tails at the back, but were cut away in front so that they perfectly framed the groin. It was the first time in history that men's apparel was consciously designed to be more sexy than ladies'.

It appears that Brummell could have had almost any lady he longed for, and many men, too, but whether he did or not is intriguingly uncertain. On the evidence, it appears that Brummell was asexual; we don't know of any relationship, male or female, he engaged in that involved intercourse other than aural. Curiously, for a man famed for his appearance, we don't know what he looked like. Four reputed likenesses of him exist, but they are all strikingly different from one another, and there is now no telling which, if any, is actually faithful.

Brummell's fall from grace was abrupt and irreversible. He and the Prince of Wales had a falling out and ceased speaking. At a social occasion, the prince pointedly ignored Brummell and instead spoke to his companion. As the prince withdrew, Brummell turned to the companion and made one of the most famously ill-advised remarks in social history. 'Who's your fat friend?' he asked.

Such an insult was social suicide. Shortly afterwards Brummell's debts caught up with him and he fled to France. He spent the last two and a half decades of his life living in poverty, mostly in Calais, growing slowly demented but always looking, in his restrained and careful way, sensational.

II

At just the time that Beau Brummell was dominating the sartorial scene in London and beyond, one other fabric was beginning to transform the world, and in particular the manufacturing world. I refer to cotton. Its place in history can hardly be overstated.

Cotton is such a commonplace material now that we forget that it was once extremely precious – more valuable than silk. But then in the seventeenth century, the East India Company began importing calicoes from India (from the city of Calicut, from which they take their name), and suddenly cotton became affordable. Calico was then essentially a collective term for chintzes, muslins, percales and other colourful fabrics, which caused unimaginable delight among western consumers because they were light and washable and the colours didn't run.

Although some cotton was grown in Egypt, India dominated the cotton trade, as we are reminded by the endless numbers of words that came into English by way of that trade: 'khaki', 'dungarees', 'gingham', 'muslin', 'pyjamas', 'shawl', 'seersucker' and so on.

The sudden surge of Indian cotton pleased consumers, but not manufacturers. Unable to compete with this wonder fabric, European textile workers bayed for protection almost everywhere, and almost everywhere they received it. The importation of finished cotton fabrics was banned in much of Europe throughout the eighteenth century.

Raw cotton could still be imported, which provided a powerful incentive to the British cloth industry to exploit it. The problem was that cotton was very hard to spin and weave, so people turned their attention to trying to solve these two problems. The solution they came up with is called the Industrial Revolution.

Turning bales of fluffy cotton into useful products like bedsheets and blue jeans involves two fundamental operations: spinning and weaving. Spinning is the process of turning short lengths of cotton fibre into long spools of thread by adding short fibres a little at a time and giving them a twist – the very process mentioned with string. Weaving is effected by interlacing two sets of strings or fibres at right angles to form a mesh. The machine for doing this is a loom. All that a loom does is hold one set of strings tight so that a second set can be fed through the first to make a weave. The tight set of strings is called the warp. The second, active set is called the weft – which is simply an old form of the verb 'weave'. By interlacing horizontal and vertical threads you form a fabric. Most everyday household cloths – sheets, handkerchiefs and the like – are still made from this basic, straightforward type of weave.

Spinning and weaving were cottage industries, and supported large numbers of people. Traditionally, spinning was the work of women and weaving the work of men. Spinning, however, took a lot longer than weaving, and the disparity grew even worse after 1733 when John Kay, a young man from Lancashire, invented the flying shuttle – the first of the breakthrough innovations that the industry required. Kay's mobile shuttle doubled the speed at which weaving could be performed. Spinners, already unable to keep up, fell ever more hopelessly behind, and so problems developed all along the supply line with enormous economic stresses for all concerned.

According to the story as traditionally recounted, weavers and spinners alike grew so furious with Kay that they attacked his home and he had to flee to France, where he died a pauper. The story is repeated in most histories even now with 'dogmatic fervour', in the words of the industrial historian Peter Willis, but in fact, Willis insists, there is no truth in it at all. Kay did die poor, but only because he didn't manage his life very well. He proposed to manufacture the machines himself and rent them out to mill owners, but he set the rental so high that no one would pay it. Instead his device was widely pirated, and he spent all his funds unsuccessfully fighting for compensation through the courts. Eventually he went to France, hoping – vainly – to find more success there. He lived almost another fifty years after his invention. He was never attacked or driven away.

*   *   *

A generation would pass before anyone could find a solution to the spinning problem, and it came from an unexpected quarter. In 1764, an illiterate weaver from Lancashire named James Hargreaves produced an ingeniously simple device known as the spinning jenny, which did the work of ten spinners by incorporating multiple spindles. Not much is known about Hargreaves beyond that he was born and grew up in Lancashire, married young and had twelve children. There is no known likeness. He was the poorest and unluckiest of all the major figures of the early Industrial Revolution. Unlike Kay, Hargreaves really *did* experience trouble. A mob of angry locals came to his house and burned twenty half-finished jennies and most of his tools – a cruel and desperate loss to a poor man – and so for a prudent period he stopped making jennies and went into bookkeeping. The jenny, incidentally, was not named after his daughter, as is often stated; 'jenny' was a northern word for an engine.

Hargreaves's machine doesn't look much in illustrations – it was essentially just ten bobbins on a frame, with a wheel to make them rotate – but it transformed Britain's industrial prospects. Less happily, it also hastened the introduction of child labour because children, nimbler and smaller than adults, were better able to make running repairs to broken threads and the like in the jenny's more inaccessible extremities.

Before his invention, homeworkers spun 500,000 pounds of cotton in England every year by hand. By 1785, thanks to Hargreaves's machine and the refined versions that followed, that figure had leapt to 16 million pounds. Hargreaves, however, didn't share in the prosperity that his machines created, thanks in large part to the machinations of Richard Arkwright, the least attractive, least inventive but most successful of all the figures of the early Industrial Revolution.

Like Kay and Hargreaves, Arkwright was a Lancashire man – where would the Industrial Revolution have been without Lancashire men? – born in Preston in 1732, which made him eleven years younger than Hargreaves and nearly thirty years younger than Kay. (It is as well to remember that the Industrial Revolution wasn't a sudden explosive event, but more a gradual unfolding of improvements over many lifetimes and in lots of different fields.) Before he became a man of industry Arkwright was a publican, a wigmaker, and a barber-surgeon with a speciality in pulling teeth and bleeding those who were unwell. He seems to have got interested in cloth production through a friendship with another John Kay – this one a clockmaker who was no relation to the John Kay of the flying shuttle – and with his help began to pull together all the machinery and components necessary to bring the whole of mechanical cloth production under one roof. Arkwright was not a man troubled by a lot of scruples. He stole the rudiments of the spinning jenny from Hargreaves without hesitation or remorse (let alone compensation), wriggled out of business deals and abandoned friends and partners whenever it became safe or profitable to do so.

He did have a genuine knack for making mechanical improvements, but his real genius was in turning possibilities into realities. He was an organizer – a hustler really – but a very, very good one. Through a combination of hard work, luck, opportunism and icy ruthlessness, he built up, for a short but extremely lucrative time, a virtual monopoly on the cotton business in England.

The people displaced by Arkwright's machinery weren't merely inconvenienced; they were often reduced to the basest desperation. Arkwright evidently saw this coming because he built his first factory like a fortress in a remote corner of Derbyshire – already a remote county – and fortified it with cannons and even a supply of five hundred spears. He cornered the market in the mechanical production of cloth, and in consequence grew fabulously rich, if not loved or especially happy. At his death in 1792, he employed five thousand workers and was worth half a million pounds – a fabulous sum for any man, but particularly for someone who had spent much of his life as a wigmaker and barber-surgeon.

In fact, the Industrial Revolution hadn't become truly industrial yet. The man who made it so was the most un-expectedly pivotal figure of his or almost any other age: the Reverend Edmund Cartwright (1743–1823). Cartwright came from a well-heeled and locally important Nottinghamshire family and had aspirations to be a poet, but went into the Church and was appointed to a rector-ship in Leicestershire. A chance conversation with a cloth manufacturer led him to design – absolutely from out of nowhere – the power loom in 1785. Cartwright's looms transformed the world economy and made Britain truly rich. By the time of the Great Exhibition in 1851, a quarter of a million power looms were in operation in England, and the number grew by an average of 100,000 per decade before peaking at 805,000 in 1913, by which time nearly three million were in operation throughout the world.

Had Cartwright been compensated to anything like the degree his inventions merited, he would have been the richest man of his age – as rich as John D. Rockefeller or Bill Gates in theirs – but in fact he earned nothing directly from his invention at all, and actually became indebted through trying to protect and enforce his patents. In 1809, Parliament awarded him a lump payment of £10,000, almost nothing compared with Arkwright's £500,000 but enough to let him live out his final days in comfort. Meanwhile, he had developed an appetite for invention, and came up with rope-making and wool-combing machines, both very successful, as well as novel types of printing presses, steam engines, roof tiles and bricks. His last invention, patented shortly before his death in 1823, was for a hand-cranked carriage 'to go without horses', which his patent application confidently declared would allow two men, cranking steadily but without undue exertion, to cover up to 27 miles of ground in a day over even the steepest terrain.

With power looms humming, the cotton industry was ready to take off, but the mills needed far more cotton than existing sources could supply. The obvious place to grow it was the American South. The climate, too hot and dry for many crops, was perfect for cotton. Unfortunately, the only variety that would grow well in most southern soils was a difficult type known as short staple cotton. This was impossible to harvest profitably because each boll was packed with sticky seeds – three pounds of them for every pound of cotton fibre – and these had to be plucked out by hand one by one. Separating seeds from fibre was such a labour-intensive operation that even with slave labour it could not be done economically. The costs of feeding and clothing the slaves were far greater than the amount of usable cotton that even the most diligent hand-plucking could produce.

The man who solved the problem grew up a long way from any plantations. His name was Eli Whitney, he came from Westborough, Massachusetts, and, if all the elements of the story are true (which, as we are about to see, they may well not be), it was the luckiest of chances that allowed him to make his name immortal.

The story as conventionally told is this: after graduating from Yale in 1793, Whitney accepted a job as a tutor to a family in South Carolina, but upon arriving discovered that the promised salary was to be halved. Offended, he refused the position, which satisfied honour but left him fundless and a long way from home.

While sailing south he had met a vivacious young widow named Catharine Greene, wife of the late General Nathanael Greene, a hero of the American revolution. A grateful nation had awarded Greene a plantation in Georgia for his support of George Washington through the darkest hours of the war. Unfortunately, Greene, a New Englander, was unused to Georgian heat, and on his first summer there fatally keeled over from sunstroke. It was to Greene's widow that Whitney turned now.

Mrs Greene was by this time cohabiting enthusiastically and fairly openly with another Yale man named Phineas Miller, her plantation manager, and they welcomed Whitney into their household. There Whitney was introduced to the cotton seed problem. Examining a boll he at once thought he could see a solution, retired to the plantation workshop and devised a simple rotating drum that used nails to snag cotton fibre as it turned, leaving the seeds behind. His new device was so efficient that it could do the work of fifty slaves. Whitney patented his 'gin' (a shortened form of 'engine') and prepared to become stupendously wealthy.

That is the story as conventionally told. It appears, however, that a good deal of it may not actually be quite true. The suggestion now is that Whitney already knew Miller – their Yale connection does seem improbably co-incidental otherwise – that he was equally acquainted with the problems of growing cotton on American soil, and that he travelled south, probably at Miller's behest, knowing that he would try to invent a gin. Moreover, it appears that the work may not have been done in a couple of hours on the plantation, but over weeks or months in a workshop back in Westborough. Whatever the actuality of its invention, the gin truly was a marvel. Whitney and Miller formed a partnership with every expectation of getting rich, but they were disastrous businessmen. For the use of their machine, they demanded a one-third share of any harvest – a proportion that plantation owners and southern legislators alike saw as frankly rapacious. That Whitney and Miller were both Yankees didn't help sentiment either. Stubbornly they refused to modify their demands, convinced that southern growers could not hold out in the face of such a transforming piece of technology. They were right about the irresistibility, but failed to note that the gin was also easily pirated. Any halfway decent carpenter could knock one out in a couple of hours. Soon plantation owners across the south were harvesting cotton with home-made gins. Whitney and Miller filed sixty suits in Georgia and many others elsewhere, but found little sympathy in southern courts. By 1800 – just seven years after the gin's invention – Miller and Catharine Greene were in such desperate straits that they had to sell the plantation.

The South, however, was growing very rich. Cotton was soon the most traded commodity in the world and two-thirds of all that cotton came from there. American cotton exports went from almost nothing before the invention of the cotton gin to a staggering two billion pounds by the outbreak of the Civil War. At its peak, Britain took 84 per cent of it all.

Before cotton, slavery had been in decline, but now there was a great need for labour because picking cotton, as opposed to processing it, was extremely labour-intensive. At the time of Whitney's invention slavery existed in just six US states; by the outbreak of the Civil War it was legal in fifteen. Worse, the northern slave states like Virginia and Maryland, where cotton couldn't be successfully grown, turned to exporting slaves to their southern neighbours, thus breaking up families and intensifying the suffering for tens of thousands. Between 1793 and the outbreak of the Civil War, over 800,000 slaves were shipped south.

At the same time, the booming cotton mills of England needed huge numbers of workers – more than population increase alone could easily provide – so increasingly they turned to child labour. Children were malleable, cheap and generally quicker at darting about among machinery and dealing with snags, breakages and the like. Even the most enlightened mill owners used children freely. They couldn't afford not to.

So Whitney's gin not only helped to make many people rich on both sides of the Atlantic, but also re-invigorated slavery, turned child labour into a necessity and paved the way for the American Civil War. Perhaps never has anyone with a simple, well-meaning invention generated more general prosperity, personal disappointment and inadvertent suffering than Eli Whitney with his gin. That is quite a lot of consequence for a simple rotating drum.

Eventually some southern states did agree to pay Whitney a little. Altogether he made about $90,000 from the gin – just enough to cover his costs. Returning north, he settled in New Haven, Connecticut, and there hit on the idea that would finally make him rich. In 1798, he landed a contract to make ten thousand muskets for the federal government. The guns were to be manufactured by a new method, which came to be known as the Whitney system or American system. The idea was to build machines that would create an endless supply of matching parts, which could then be assembled into completed products. No worker would need any particular skills. The skills would all be in the machines. It was a brilliant concept. Daniel J. Boorstin has called it the innovation that made America rich.

The guns were urgently needed because at the time America seemed on the brink of going to war with France. The contract was for $134,000 – the largest government contract ever signed in America at that time – and was given to Whitney even though he had no machines and no experience of making guns, but in 1801, in a moment treasured by generations of history books, Whitney demonstrated to President John Adams and President-elect Thomas Jefferson how a tableful of random parts could be assembled into a complete gun. In fact, behind the scenes Whitney was having all kinds of problems getting the system to work. The guns were delivered more than eight years late, long after the crisis that had prompted their manufacture had abated. Moreover, a twentieth-century analysis of the surviving guns showed that they weren't actually made by the Whitney system at all, but incorporated parts that had been hand-crafted in the factory. The famous demonstration for the presidents was done with bogus parts. Whitney, it turns out, spent most of the eight years not working on the musket order at all, but using the money from the contract to further his efforts to gain compensation for the cotton gin.

III

Compared with anything that had gone before, cotton was a wonderfully light and cool material, yet it did almost nothing to stifle the impulse to dress ridiculously, particularly where women were concerned. As the nineteenth century progressed women became increasingly embedded in attire. By the 1840s a woman might carry beneath her dress a knee-length chemise, a camisole, up to half a dozen petticoats, a corset and drawers. The idea, as one historian has noted, was 'to eliminate, as far as possible, any impression of shape'. All of this sartorial infrastructure could be dauntingly weighty. A woman could easily go about her daily business under 40 pounds of clothing. How they managed to deal with urinary needs is a question that seems to have escaped historical enquiry. Crinolines, or hoopskirts, made of whalebone or steel were introduced as a way of giving shape without requiring so much underclothing, but while the load was fractionally lightened the scope for clumsiness was greatly increased. As Liza Picard has put it: 'One wonders how, or whether, Victorian ladies managed to traverse a properly equipped drawing room in a full crinoline without sweeping several small tables clear.' Getting into a carriage required consideration and cunning, as one fascinated correspondent indicated in a letter home: 'Miss Clara turned round and round like a peacock, undecided which way to make the attempt. At last she chose a bold sideways dash, and entered with a squeeze of the petticoat, which suddenly expanded to its original size, but when her sisters had followed her there was no room for the Major' (or indeed anyone else).

Crinolines also lifted slightly when the wearer bent – when leaning to strike a croquet ball, for instance – offering an electrifying glimpse of frilly leggings to any man wise enough to say, 'After you.' When strained, crinolines had a dismaying tendency to invert and fly upwards, like a stressed umbrella. Stories abounded of women left trapped and staggering inside misbehaving hoops. Lady Eleanor Stanley recorded in her diary how the Duchess of Manchester tripped going over a stile – why she decided to attempt to negotiate a stile in a hoopskirt is a separate imponderable – and ended up exposing her tartan knickerbockers 'to the view of all the world in general and the Duc de Malakoff in particular'. High winds were a special source of disorder, and stairs a positive danger. The greatest risk of all, however, was fire. 'Many wearers of crinolines were burnt to death by inadvertently approaching a fire,' C. Willett and Phillis Cunnington note in their unexpectedly solemn *History of Underclothes*. One manufacturer advertised proudly, if unnervingly, that its crinolines 'do not cause accidents, do not appear at inquests'.

The golden age of crinolines was 1857–66, by which point they were largely being abandoned, not because they were dangerous and preposterous, but because they were increasingly being worn by the lower orders, destroying their exclusivity. 'Your lady's maid must now have her crinoline,' tutted one magazine, 'and it has even become essential to factory girls.' The danger of crinolines among the grinding cogs and whirring belts of factory machinery is easy enough to imagine.

The abandonment of crinolines didn't mean that the age of pointless discomfort was at last coming to an end. Far from it, for crinolines gave way to corsets, and corsets became the most punishing form of apparel in centuries. A few authorities found this strangely heartening, on the apparent grounds that it somehow denoted sacrifice and chastity. The *Englishwoman's Domestic Magazine*, the Beetons' popular periodical, approvingly noted in 1866 how the boarders at one girls' school were strapped into their corsets on a Monday morning and left constrained until Saturday, when they were allowed to ease the stays for an hour 'for purposes of ablution'. Such a regime, the magazine noted, allowed the average girl to reduce her waist size from twenty-three inches to thirteen in just two years.

The quest to reduce circumference at almost any cost to comfort was real enough, but the enduring belief that some women had ribs surgically removed to make their midsections even more compressible is, happily, a myth. Valerie Steele, in the engagingly precise and academic *The Corset: A Cultural History*, could find no evidence that even one such operation had ever been undertaken. For one thing, nineteenth-century surgical techniques were simply not up to it.

For medical experts tight corsets became something of an obsession in the second half of the nineteenth century. There wasn't a functioning system within the body, it appeared, that wasn't gravely susceptible to suffering and breakdown from the constricting effects of lace and whalebone. Corsets kept the heart from beating freely, which made the blood grow congested. Sluggish blood in turn led to almost a hundred recorded afflictions – incontinence, dyspepsia, liver failure, 'congestive hypertrophy of the uterus' and loss of mental faculties, to name a notable few. The *Lancet* regularly investigated the dangers of tight corsets and concluded that in at least one case the victim's heartbeats were so impeded that she died. Some doctors additionally believed that tightly laced undergarments gave women a greater susceptibility to tuberculosis.

Inevitably, a sexual dimension became attached to corset-wearing. The tone of anti-corset literature for women was strikingly similar to the tone of anti-masturbation literature for men. By restricting blood flow and compressing organs in the vicinity of the reproductive zone, corsets, it was feared, could lead to a tragic increase in 'amative desires' and possibly even induce involuntary 'voluptuous spasms'. Gradually clothing fears extended to every part of the body where clothes were worn snugly. Even tight-fitting shoes, it was suggested, could engender some dangerous tingling, if not a full-throttled, table-rattling spasm. In the worst cases, women could actually be unhinged by their clothing. Orson Fowler, author of an attack tantalizingly entitled *Tight-Lacing, Founded on Physiology and Phrenology; or, the Evils Inflicted on the Mind and Body by Compressing the Organs of Animal Life, Thereby Retarding and Enfeebling the Vital Functions*, propounded the theory that the unnatural distortion of circulation pushed extra blood to the woman's brain which had the capacity to cause a permanent and disturbing change in personality.

The one place where there really was danger from tight corsets was in the development of babies. Many women wore corsets perilously deep into pregnancy, even pulling them tighter to hide for as long as possible the indelicate evidence that they had been party to an unseemly burst of voluptuous spasms.

Victorian rigidities were such that ladies were not even allowed to blow out candles in mixed company, as that required them to pucker their lips suggestively. They could not say that they were going 'to bed' – that planted too stimulating an image – but merely that they were 'retiring'. It became effectively impossible to discuss clothing in even a clinical sense without resort to euphemisms. Trousers became 'nether integuments' or simply 'inexpressibles' and underwear was 'linen'. Women could refer among themselves to petticoats or, in hushed tones, stockings, but could mention almost nothing else that brushed bare flesh.

Behind the scenes, however, things were a little spicier than we are sometimes led to suppose. Chemical dyes – some of them quite rich and colourful – became available in mid-century and one of the first places they appeared was on underclothes, a matter that scandalized many since it raised the obvious question of for whose delight all that colour was intended. The embroidery of underwear became similarly popular and identically scandalous. In the very year that it was praising an English girls' school for keeping the young ladies murderously strapped into corsets for a week at a time, the *Englishwoman's Domestic Magazine* was also railing that 'the amount of embroidery put upon underclothing nowadays is sinful; a young lady spent a month in hemstitching and embroidering a garment which it was scarcely possible that any other human being, except her laundress, would ever see'.

One thing they didn't have were brassieres. Corsets pushed up from below, which held breasts in place, but for true comfort (I am told) breasts are better held up by slings. The first person to see this was a lingerie manufacturer named Luman Chapman, of Camden, New Jersey, who secured a patent in 1863 for 'breast puffs' – a kind of early halter top. Between 1863 and 1969, exactly 1,230 patents on bras were taken out in the United States. The word 'brassiere', from a French word meaning 'upper arm', was first used in 1904 by the Charles R. DeBevoise Company.

One small but tenacious myth may be demolished here. It has been sometimes written that the bra was the invention of one Otto Titzling. In fact, if such a person ever existed, he played no part in the invention of foundation garments. And on that slightly disappointing note, we may move on to the nursery.

CHAPTER EIGHTEEN

The Nursery

I

IN THE EARLY 1960S, in a hugely influential book called *Centuries of Childhood*, a French author named Philippe Ariès made a startling claim. He declared that before the sixteenth century, at the very earliest, there was no such thing as childhood. There were small human beings, of course, but nothing in their lives made them meaningfully distinguishable from adults. 'The idea of childhood did not exist,' he pronounced with a certain finality. It was essentially a Victorian invention.

Ariès was not a specialist in the field, and his ideas were based almost entirely on indirect evidence, much of it now held to be a little doubtful, but his views struck a chord and were widely taken up. Soon other historians were declaring that children before the modern period were not just ignored but actually weren't much liked. 'In traditional society, mothers viewed the development and happiness of infants younger than two with indifference,' declared Edward Shorter in *The Making of the Modern*

Family (1976). The reason for this was high infant mortality. 'You couldn't permit yourself to become attached to an infant that you knew death might whisk away,' he explained. These views were almost exactly echoed by Barbara Tuchman in the best-selling *A Distant Mirror* two years later. 'Of all the characteristics in which the medieval age differs from the modern,' she wrote, 'none is so striking as the comparative absence of interest in children.' Investing love in young children was so risky – 'so unrewarding' was her curious phrase – that everywhere it was suppressed as a pointless waste of energy. Emotion didn't come into it at all. Children were merely 'a product', in her chilling view. 'A child was born and died and another took its place.' Or as Ariès himself explained, 'The general feeling was, and for a long time remained, that one had several children in order to keep just a few.' These views became so standard among historians of childhood that twenty years would pass before anyone questioned whether they might represent a serious misreading of human nature, not to mention the known facts of history.

There is no doubt that children once died in great numbers and that parents had to adjust their expectations accordingly. The world before the modern era was over-whelmingly a place of tiny coffins. The figures usually cited are that one-third of children died in their first year of life and half failed to reach their fifth birthdays. Even in the best homes death was a regular visitor. Stephen Inwood notes that the future historian Edward Gibbon, growing up rich in healthy Putney, lost all six of his siblings in early childhood. But that isn't to say that parents were any less devastated by a loss than we would be today. The diarist John Evelyn and his wife had eight children and lost six of them in childhood, and were clearly heartbroken each time. 'Here ends the joy of my life,' Evelyn wrote simply after his oldest child died three days after his fifth birthday in 1658. The writer William Brownlow lost a child each year for four years, a chain of misfortune that 'hast broken me asunder and shaken me to pieces', he wrote, but in fact he and his wife had still more to endure: the tragic pattern of annual deaths continued for three years more until they had no children left to yield.

No one expressed parental loss better (as no one expressed most things better) than William Shakespeare. These lines are from *King John*, written soon after his son Hamnet died at the age of eleven in 1596:

> Grief fills the room up of my absent child
> Lies in his bed, walks up and down with me,
> Puts on his pretty looks, repeats his words,
> Remembers me of all his gracious parts,
> Stuffs out his vacant garments with his form.

These are not the words of someone for whom children are a product, and there is no reason to suppose – no evidence anywhere, including that of common sense – that parents were ever, at any point in the past, commonly indifferent to the happiness and well-being of their children. One clue lies in the name of the room in which we are now.* 'Nursery' is first recorded in English in

* We can't be sure that this room ever actually was a nursery. It is another of the afterthought rooms not included on Edward Tull's original plans, so there are no blueprint labels to guide us. But its modest dimensions and position next door to the main bedroom strongly suggest that it was intended as a nursery rather than just an additional

1330 and has been in continuous use ever since. A room exclusively dedicated to the needs and comforts of children would hardly seem consistent with the belief that children were of no consequence within the household. No less significant is the word 'childhood' itself. It has existed in English for over a thousand years (the first recorded use is in the Lindisfarne Gospels circa AD 950), so whatever it may have meant emotionally to people, as a state of being, a condition of separate existence, it is indubitably ancient. To suggest that children were objects of indifference or barely existed as separate beings would appear to be a simplification at best.

That isn't to say that childhood in the past was the long, carefree gambol we like to think it now. It was anything but. Life was full of perils from the moment of conception. For mother and child both, the most dangerous milestone was birth itself. When things went wrong, there was little any midwife or physician could do. Doctors, when called at all, frequently resorted to treatments that only increased the distress and danger, draining the exhausted mother of blood (on the grounds that it would relax her – then seeing loss of consciousness as proof of success), padding her with blistering poultices or otherwise straining her dwindling reserves of energy and hope.

Not infrequently babies became stuck. In such an eventuality, labour could go on for three weeks or more, until baby or mother or both were spent beyond recovery. If a baby died within the womb, the procedures for getting

bedroom, which raises yet another intriguing and unanswerable question about the bachelor Mr Marsham's hopes and intentions.

A woman giving birth in the eighteenth century. (Note the way modesty is preserved by the sheet pulled around the doctor's neck.)

it out are really too horrible to describe. Suffice it to say that they involved hooks and bringing the baby out in pieces. Such procedures not only brought unspeakable suffering to the mother, but also much risk of damage to her uterus and even graver risk of infection. Considering the conditions, it is amazing to report that only between one and two mothers in a hundred died in childbirth. However, because most women bore children repeatedly (seven to nine times on average) the odds of death at some point in a woman's childbearing experience rose dramatically, to about one in eight.

For children, birth was just the beginning. The first years of life weren't so much a time of adventure as of mis-adventure, it seems. In addition to the endless waves of illness and epidemic that punctuated every existence, accidental death was far more common – breathtakingly so, in fact. Coroners' rolls for London in the thirteenth and fourteenth centuries include such abrupt childhood terminations as 'drowned in a pit', 'bitten by sow', 'fell into pan of hot water', 'hit by cart-wheel', 'fell into tin of hot mash', 'trampled in crowd' and many more in similarly disturbing vein. Emily Cockayne relates the sad case of a little boy who lay down in the road and covered himself with straw to amuse his friends. A passing cart squashed him.

Ariès and his adherents took such deaths as proof of parental carelessness and lack of interest in children's well-being, but this is to impose modern standards on historic behaviour. A more generous reading would bear in mind that every waking moment of a medieval mother's life was full of distractions. She might have been nursing a sick or dying child, racked with fever herself, struggling to start a fire (or put one out) or any of a thousand other things. If children aren't bitten by sows today, it is not because they are better supervised. It is because we don't keep sows in the kitchen.

A good many modern conclusions are based on mortality rates from the past that are not actually all that certain. The first person to look carefully into the matter was, a little unexpectedly, the astronomer Edmond Halley, who is of course principally remembered now for the comet named for him (though in fact he didn't discover it, but merely recognized it as the same comet that had been noticed by others on three previous visits; it didn't become known as Halley's comet until 1758, long after he died). Halley was a tireless investigator into scientific phenomena of all kinds, and produced papers on everything from magnetism to the soporific effects of opium. In 1693, he came across figures for annual births and deaths in Breslau, Silesia (now Poland), which fascinated him because they were so unusually complete. He realized that from them he could construct charts from which it was possible to work out the life expectancy of any person at any point in his existence. He could say that for someone aged twenty-five the chances of dying in the next year were 80 to 1 against, that someone who reached thirty could reasonably expect to live another twenty-seven years, that the chances of a man of forty living another seven years were 5.5 to 1 in favour, and so on. These were the first actuarial tables, and, apart from anything else, they made the life insurance industry possible.

Halley's findings were reported in the *Philosophical Transactions of the Royal Society*, a scientific journal, and for that reason seem to have escaped the full attention of social historians, which is unfortunate because there is much of interest in them. Halley's figures showed, for instance, that in Breslau there were seven thousand women of child-bearing age, yet only twelve hundred children were born each year – 'little more than a sixth part', as he noted. Clearly the great majority of women at any time were taking careful steps to avoid pregnancy. So childbirth, in Breslau anyway, wasn't some inescapable burden to which women had to submit, but a largely voluntary act.

Halley's figures also showed that infant mortality was not quite as bad as the figures now generally cited would encourage us to suppose. In Breslau, slightly over a quarter of babies died in their first year, and 44 per cent were dead by their seventh birthday. These are bad numbers, to be sure, but appreciably better than the comparable figures of one-third and one-half usually cited. Not until seventeen years had passed did the proportion of deaths among the young of Breslau reach 50 per cent. That was actually worse than Halley had expected and he used his report to make the point that people should not expect to live long lives, but rather should steel themselves for the possibility of dying before their time. 'How unjustly we repine at the shortness of our Lives,' he wrote, 'and think our selves wronged if we attain not Old Age; where it appears hereby, that the one half of those that are born are dead in Seventeen years . . . [So] instead of murmuring at what we call an untimely Death, we ought with Patience and unconcern to submit to that Dissolution which is the necessary Condition of our perishable Materials.' Clearly expectations concerning death were much more complicated than a simple appraisal of the numbers might lead us to conclude.

A further complication of the figures – and a sound reason for women limiting their pregnancies – was that just at this time women across Europe were dying in droves from a mysterious new disease that doctors were powerless to defeat or understand. Called puerperal (from the Latin term for 'child') fever, it was first recorded in Leipzig in 1652. For the next two hundred and fifty years doctors would be helpless in the face of it. Puerperal fever was particularly dreaded because it came on suddenly, often several days after a successful birth when the mother was completely well. Within hours the victim would be severely fevered and delirious, and would remain in that state for about a week until she either recovered or expired. More often than not she expired. In the worst outbreaks, 90 per cent of victims died. Until late in the nineteenth century most doctors attributed puerperal fever either to bad air or lax morals, when in fact it was their own grubby fingers transferring microbes from one tender uterus to another. As early as 1847, a doctor in Vienna, Ignaz Semmelweis, realized that if hospital staff washed their hands in mildly chlorinated water deaths of all types declined sharply, but hardly anyone paid any attention to him, and decades more would pass before antiseptic practices became general.

For a lucky few women, there was at least some promise of greater safety with the arrival of obstetrical forceps, which allowed babies to be repositioned mechanically. Unfortunately their inventor, Peter Chamberlen, chose not to share his invention with the world, but kept it secret for the sake of his own practice, and his heirs maintained this lamentable tradition for a hundred years more until forceps were independently devised by others. In the meantime, untold thousands of women died in unnecessary agony. Forceps were not without risks of their own, it must be said. Unsterilized and clearly invasive, they could easily damage both baby and mother if not wielded with the utmost delicacy. For this reason, many medical men were reluctant to deploy them. In the most celebrated case, Princess Charlotte, heir presumptive to the British throne, died giving birth to her first child in 1817 because the presiding physician, Sir Richard Croft, would not allow his colleagues to use forceps to try to relieve her suffering. In consequence, after more than fifty hours of exhausting and unproductive contractions, both baby and mother died. Charlotte's death changed the course of British history. Had she lived, there would have been no Victorian period because no Queen Victoria. The nation was shocked and unforgiving. Stunned and despondent over how universally he was reviled, Croft retired to his chambers and put a bullet through his head.

For most human beings, children and adults both, the dominant consideration in life until modern times was purely, unrelievedly economic. In poorer households – and that is what most homes were, of course – every person was, from the earliest possible moment, a unit of production. John Locke, in a paper for the Board of Trade in 1697, suggested that the children of the poor should be put to work from the age of three, and no one thought that unrealistic or unkind. The Little Boy Blue of the nursery rhyme – the one who failed to keep the sheep from the meadow and the cows from the corn – is unlikely to have been more than about four years old; older hands were needed for more robust work.

In the worst circumstances, children were sometimes given the most back-breaking of jobs. Those as young as six, of both sexes, were put to work in mines, where their small frames allowed them access to tight spaces. Because of the heat and to save their clothes, they often worked naked. (Grown men also traditionally worked naked; women usually worked naked to the waist.) For much of the year those who worked in mines never saw sunlight, which left many stunted and weak from Vitamin D deficiencies. Even comparatively light labour was often dangerous. Children in the ceramics factories of the Potteries in the Midlands cleaned out pots containing residues of lead and arsenic, inducing a slow poisoning that condemned many to eventual paralysis, palsies and seizures.

The least envied child workers of all were the chimney sweeps, or 'climbing boys' as they were also known. They started earlier, worked harder, died sooner than any other group. Most began their short careers at about the age of five, though the records show one boy articled into the profession at three and a half, an age at which even the simplest tasks must have been confusing and frightening. Little boys were needed because flues were tight and often wildly convoluted. 'Some,' writes John Waller, 'turned at right angles, ran horizontally or diagonally, even zig-zagged or plunged downwards before rising up towards the stack. One London chimney switched direction an amazing fourteen times.' It was brutal work. One method of encouraging the boys not to slack was to light a pile of straw in the grate to send a blast of heat up the chimney after them. Many climbing boys ended their short careers stooped and ruined by the age of eleven or twelve. Cancer of the scrotum seems to have been a particular occupational hazard.

In such a harsh and hopeless world, the case of Isaac Ware stands out as a happy miracle. Ware's is a name that crops up regularly in architectural histories of the eighteenth century, for he was the leading building critic of the age and his opinions carried a great deal of weight. (It was he, you may remember from our visit to the cellar, who helped to make red brick unfashionable in the mid-eighteenth century by pronouncing it 'fiery and disagreeable to the eye'.) But Ware was not born to a life of eminence. He started, in fact, as a street urchin and chimney sweep, and owed his polish and success to a single extraordinary act of kindness. In about 1712 an anonymous gentleman – never formally identified but more or less universally assumed to be the third Earl of Burlington, the builder of Chiswick House and one of the tastemakers of the age – was walking up Whitehall in London when he spotted a young sweep on the pavement making a sketch of the Banqueting House with a piece of charcoal. The drawing showed such extraordinary talent that Burlington was drawn to examine it, but the boy, thinking he was in trouble, burst into tears and tried to rub it out. The gentleman calmed him and engaged him in conversation, and became so impressed with the boy's natural brightness that he purchased his freedom from his employer, took him into his own household, and began the long process of turning him into a gentleman. He sent him on a grand tour of Europe and had him trained in all the refinements of life.

Under this tutelage Ware became an accomplished if not brilliant architect, but his real gift was as an arbiter and thinker. His several important books included a respected translation of Palladio's *I Quattro Libri*, and *The Complete Body of Architecture*, which became a kind of bible of taste and discernment for professionals and amateurs both. Yet he never entirely shed his humble origins. When he died in 1766, his skin, it was said, still bore the indelible sooty stains of the chimney sweep.

Ware was, needless to say, an exception. Most children were wholly at the mercy of their employers, and were sometimes treated in the most shocking manner. In one briefly notorious case, a farmer at Malmesbury, Wiltshire, hit on the idea of castrating two of his young apprentices and selling them to an opera company as singers. He was thwarted in the second part of his ambition, but unfortunately not before he had successfully snipped his way to the first.

Until well into the nineteenth century children received almost nothing in the way of legal protection. Before 1814 no law forbade the theft of a child, for instance. In Middlesex in 1802 a woman named Elizabeth Salmon, after abducting a child named Elizabeth Impey, was charged with stealing her cap and gown because that was the only part of the offence that was illegal. Because abduction carried so little risk, it was widely believed that gypsies stole children and sold them on, and there appears to have been some truth in that. A celebrated case was that of a Mary Davis, a woman of good background, who in 1812 found her lost son sweeping a chimney at an inn at which by chance she was staying.

The Industrial Revolution only made matters worse, at least at first. Before the 1844 Factory Act reduced the work day for children, most worked twelve- to fourteen-hour days, six days a week. Some worked even longer, particularly during busy periods when it was necessary to meet large orders. Apprentices at one mill in 1810 were discovered to be at their machines from ten to six in the morning till after nine at night, with a single meal break of thirty to forty-five minutes for dinner, and that was sometimes taken while standing at machines. In many factories, discomfort was considerable. Some materials, like flax, had to be kept moist as they were being worked, so workers were permanently drenched by spray off the machines. In winter it must have been unbearable. Nearly all industrial machinery was dangerous, but especially when those working around it were starved and exhausted. Some children reportedly were so tired that they hadn't the energy to eat, and fell asleep with food in their mouths.

At least they had steady work. For those dependent on casual labour, existence was an endless lottery. One-third of the inhabitants of central London were estimated in 1750 to go to bed each night 'almost Pennyless', and the proportion only worsened as time went on. Casual labourers seldom knew when they woke in the morning whether they would earn enough that day to eat. So comprehensively dire were conditions for many that Henry Mayhew devoted a whole volume of his four-volume *London Labour and the London Poor* to the lowest of the low, scavengers, whose desperation led them to find value in almost anything that was dropped by the roadside. As he wrote:

> Many a thing which in a country town is kicked by
> the penniless out of their path . . . will in London be

snatched up as a prize; it is money's worth. A crushed
and torn bonnet, for instance, or, better still, an old
hat, napless, shapeless, crownless, and brimless, will
be picked up in the street, and carefully placed in a
bag . . .

The conditions in which they lived were sometimes so
squalid as to shock even the most hardened investigators.
One housing inspector in the 1830s reported: 'I found
[one room] occupied by one man, two women, and two
children, and in it was the dead body of a poor girl who
had died in childbirth a few days before.' Poor parents
habitually produced large broods, as a sort of pension
policy, hoping that enough offspring would survive to
support them in their dotage. By the second half of the
nineteenth century, one-third of families in England had
eight or more children, another third had five to seven,
and a final third (the wealthier third overwhelmingly) had
four or fewer. In poorer districts it was a rare household
that could adequately feed everyone, so malnutrition at
some level was more or less endemic. At least 15 per cent
of children, it is thought, had the bowed legs and pelvic
distortions of rickets, and these unfortunates were overwhelmingly found among the poorest of the poor. One
doctor in mid-Victorian London published a list of the
things he had seen tiny infants fed – jellied calves-feet,
hard muffins soaked in oil, gristly meat they could not
chew. Toddlers sometimes survived on what fell on the
floor or they could otherwise scavenge. By the time they
were seven or eight, many children were sent out on to the
streets to fend for themselves. By the 1860s, London had
an estimated one hundred thousand 'street Arabs' who

had no education, no skills, no purpose and no future. 'Their very number makes one stand aghast,' one contemporary recorded.

Yet the idea of educating them was treated almost universally with abhorrence. The fear was that educating the poor would fill them with aspirations to which they were neither suited nor, frankly, entitled. Sir Charles Adderley, who was in charge of government education policy in the late 1850s, stated flatly: 'It is clearly wrong to keep ordinary children of the working-class at school after the age at which their proper work begins.' To do so 'would be as arbitrary and improper as it would be to keep the boys at Eton and Harrow at spade labour'.

No one better represented the harsh side of beliefs than the Reverend Thomas Robert Malthus (1766–1834), whose *Essay on the Principle of Population as It Affects the Future Improvements of Society* was published anonymously in 1798 and became immediately and resoundingly influential. Malthus blamed the poor for their own hardships and opposed the idea of relief for the masses on the grounds that it simply increased their tendency to idleness. 'Even when they have an opportunity of saving,' he wrote, 'they seldom exercise it for all that is beyond their present necessities goes, generally speaking, to the alehouse. The poor-laws of England may therefore be said to diminish both the power and the will to save among the common people, and thus to weaken one of the strongest incentives to sobriety and industry, and consequently to happiness.' He was particularly troubled by the Irish, and believed, as he wrote to a friend in 1817, that 'a great part of the population should be swept from the soil'. This was not a man with a lot of Christian charity in his heart.

In consequence of the unrelentingly dire conditions, mortality figures soared wherever the poor congregated. In Dudley, in the Midlands, the average life expectancy at birth at mid-century had sunk to just 18.5 years, a lifespan not seen in Britain since the Bronze Age. In even the healthiest cities, the average life expectancy was twenty-six to twenty-eight, and nowhere in urban Britain did it exceed thirty.

As ever, those who suffered most were the youngest, yet their welfare and safety excited remarkably scant attention. There can be few more telling facts about life in nineteenth-century Britain than that the founding of the Society for the Prevention of Cruelty to Animals preceded by sixty years the founding of a similar organization for the protection of children. It is perhaps no less notable that the first named was made *Royal* Society for the Prevention of Cruelty to Animals in 1840, a little more than a decade and a half after its founding. The National Society for the Prevention of Cruelty to Children remains to this day regally unblessed.

II

Just when it must have seemed to the poor of England that life couldn't get much worse, life got worse. The cause of the blow was the introduction and strict implementation of new poor relief laws starting in 1834. Poor relief had always been a sensitive issue. What particularly exercised many better-off Victorians was not the sad plight of the poor, but the cost. Poor laws had been around since Elizabethan times, but it was left to each parish to decide how to administer them. Some were reasonably generous, but others were so cheap that they were known to carry sick people or women in labour into another parish so that they became another jurisdiction's responsibility. Illegitimate births were a particular source of official irritation, and making sure that malfeasants were both suitably punished and made to shoulder the responsibility for what they had done was an almost obsessive preoccupation for local authorities. A typical decree from a court in Lancashire – this one in the late 1600s – reads:

> Jane Sotworth of Wrightington, spinster, swears that Richard Garstange of Fazerkerley, husbandman, is the father of Alice, her bastard daughter. She is to have charge of the child for two years, provided she does not beg, and Richard is then to take charge until it is twelve years old. He shall give Jane a cow and 6 shillings in money. Both he and she shall this day be whipped in Ormeskirke.

By the early nineteenth century, the problem of poor relief had become a national crisis. The costs of the Napoleonic wars had severely strained the national exchequer, and matters only worsened with the coming of peace as some three hundred thousand soldiers and sailors returned to civilian life and began looking for work in an already depressed economy.

The solution, almost everyone agreed, was to set up a national network of workhouses where rules would be enforced consistently to a single national standard. A commission, whose secretary was the indefatigable Edwin Chadwick, considered the matter with the thoroughness typical of the age (and of Chadwick) and at length produced a thirteen-volume report. The one point on which there was a consensus was that the new workhouses should be made as disagreeable as possible, to keep them from becoming attractive to the poor. One of those providing testimony offered a cautionary tale so symptomatic of prevailing thought that it is worth giving here in full:

> I remember the case of a family named Wintle, consisting of a man, his wife, and five children. About two years ago, the father, mother and two children, were very ill, and reduced to great distress, being obliged to sell all their little furniture for their subsistence; they were settled with us; and as we heard of their extreme distress, I went to them to offer relief; they, however, strenuously refused the aid. I reported this to the churchwarden, who determined to accompany me, and together we again pressed on the family the necessity of receiving relief; but still they refused, and we could not prevail upon them to accept our offer. We felt so much interested in the case, however, that we sent them 4 shillings in a parcel with a letter, desiring them to apply for more, if they continued ill; this they did, and from that time to this (now more than two years) I do not believe that they have been for three weeks off our books, although there has been little or no ill health in the family. Thus we effectually spoiled the habits

> acquired by their previous industry; and I have no
> hesitation in saying, that, in nine cases out of ten,
> such is the constant effect of having tasted of parish
> bounty.

The commissioners' report piously thundered against those 'who value parish support as their privilege, and demand it as their right'. Poor relief had become so generously available, the commissioners believed, that 'it appears to the pauper that the Government has undertaken to repeal, in his favour, the ordinary laws of nature; to enact that the children shall not suffer for the misconduct of their parents – the wife for that of the husband, or the husband for that of the wife; that no one shall lose the means of comfortable subsistence, whatever be his indolence, prodigality or vice.' With a zeal that came perilously close to paranoia, the report went on to suggest that a poor working man might wilfully choose to 'revenge himself on the parish' by marrying and producing children to 'increase that local overpopulation which is gradually eating away the fund out of which he and all the other labourers of the parish are to be maintained'. He had nothing to lose from such a strategy, after all, for his children could be put to work at home and 'become a source of profit to the parents if the trade is good, and, if it should fail, they are maintained by the parish'.

To make sure that the poor were never rewarded for their idleness, the new workhouses were made as strict and joyless as possible. Husbands were separated from wives, children from their parents. At some workhouses inmates were required to wear prison-style uniforms. Food was calculatedly grim. ('On no account must the diet be superior or equal to the ordinary mode of subsistence of the labouring classes of the neighbourhood,' decreed the commissioners.) Conversation in dining halls and during hours of work was forbidden. All hope of happiness was ruthlessly banished.

Inmates had to perform hours of daily work to earn their meals and shelter. One common task was picking oakum. Oakum was old rope that had been heavily coated in tar to make it usable for ships' caulking. To pick it was simply to disentangle strands so that they could be reused. It was hard and unpleasant work – the stiff fibres could inflict painful cuts – and agonizingly slow. At Poplar Workhouse in east London male inmates were required to pick five and a half pounds of oakum per day – a quota nearly twice that imposed on prison convicts. Those who failed to achieve their targets were put on a reduced diet of bread and water. By 1873, two-thirds of the inmates at Poplar were on short rations. At Andover Workhouse in Hampshire, where inmates were made to crush bones for fertilizer, they were said to be so permanently famished that they sucked the bones to get at the marrow.

Medical care almost everywhere was scant and reluctantly granted. Workhouse patients commonly underwent surgery without anaesthetics to keep down costs. Disease was endemic. Tuberculosis of two types – phthisis (or consumption) and scrofula, which affected bones, muscle and skin – was notoriously rife, and typhus was a constant fear. Because children were so weakened generally, diseases that are now minor inconveniences were then devastating. Measles killed more children in the nineteenth century than any other illness. Whooping cough and croup killed tens of thousands more, and no place was more conducive to their spread than a stale and crowded workhouse.

Some workhouses were so bad that they generated their own diseases. One vague and chronic malady – now thought to have been a combination of skin infections – was simply called 'the itch'. It was almost certainly due to lack of hygiene, though poor diet would have contributed too. Dietary insufficiencies and poor hygiene made threadworms, tapeworms and other sinuous invaders more or less universal. A patent medicine company in Manchester produced a purgative which was guaranteed to expel, faithfully and perhaps just a touch explosively, every last unwelcome parasite in the intestinal tract. One user proudly testified that he had brought forth three hundred worms, 'some of them of Uncommon Thickness'. People in workhouses could only dream of such salvation, however.

Ringworm and other fungoid infections were endemic too. Lice were a constant problem. One treatment was to soak bedlinen in a solution of mercuric chloride and chloride of lime, which made the sheets poisonous not only to the lice but to the unfortunates who slept on them. Inmates were also often roughly sanitized upon arrival. At one workhouse in the Midlands, a boy named Henry Cartwright was deemed so malodorous that the matron ordered him to be thrust into a solution of sulphuret of potash in an attempt to eliminate his body odour. Instead she merely eliminated the poor boy. By the time he was hauled out, he had suffocated. Authorities weren't entirely indifferent to such abuses. At Brentwood, Essex, when a nurse named Elizabeth Gillespie threw a girl down a flight of stairs to her death, she was brought to trial and sentenced to five years in prison. Even so, physical and sexual abuse, particularly of the young, was widespread.

In practice, the workhouses could only hold so many people – no more than about a fifth of England's paupers at any one time. The rest of the nation's indigent survived on 'outdoor relief' – small sums to help with rent and food. Collecting these sums was sometimes made almost impossibly difficult. C. S. Peel notes the case of an unemployed shepherd in Kent – 'an honest and industrious man, out of work through no fault of his own' – who was required to make a round trip of twenty-six miles on foot each day to collect paltry relief of one shilling and sixpence for himself, his wife and five children. The shepherd made the trudge daily for nine weeks before eventually collapsing from weakness and hunger. In London, a woman named Annie Kaplan, left to bring up six children after her husband died, was told that she could not support six children on the meagre sum she was to receive and was instructed to nominate two children to send to an orphanage. Kaplan refused. 'If four'll starve, six'll starve,' she declared. 'If I have a piece of bread for four, I'll have a piece of bread for six . . . I'm not giving anybody away.' The authorities entreated her to reconsider, but she would not, so they gave her nothing. What became of her and her children is unknown.

One of the few figures who actively sympathized with the plight of the poor was also one of the most interestingly improbable. Friedrich Engels came to England at the age of just twenty-one in 1842 to help run his father's textile factory in Manchester. The firm, Ermen & Engels, manufactured sewing thread. Although young Engels was a faithful son and a reasonably conscientious businessman – eventually he became a partner – he also spent a good deal of his time modestly but persistently embezzling funds to support his friend and collaborator Karl Marx in London.

It would be hard to imagine two more improbable founders for a movement as ascetic as Communism. While earnestly desiring the downfall of capitalism, Engels made himself rich and comfortable from all its benefits. He kept a stable of fine horses, rode to hounds at weekends, enjoyed the best wines, maintained a mistress, hobnobbed with the elite of Manchester at the fashionable Albert Club – in short, did everything one would expect of a successful member of the gentry. Marx, meanwhile, constantly denounced the bourgeoisie but lived as bourgeois a life as he could manage, sending his daughters to private schools and boasting at every opportunity of his wife's aristocratic background.

Engels's patient support for Marx was little short of wondrous. In that milestone year of 1851, Marx accepted a job as a foreign correspondent for the *New York Daily Tribune*, but with no intention of actually writing any articles. His English wasn't good enough, for one thing. His idea was that Engels would write them for him and he would collect the fee, and that is precisely what happened. Even then, the income wasn't enough to support his carelessly extravagant lifestyle, so he had Engels embezzle money for him from his father's firm. Engels did so for years, at considerable risk to himself.

In between running a factory and supporting Marx, Engels took a genuine interest in the plight of the poor in Manchester. He wasn't always terribly open-minded. As we saw in the previous chapter, he didn't think much of the Irish and was always prepared to believe that the poor were responsible for their own sad fate. Yet no one wrote with more feeling about life in Victorian slums. In *The Condition of the Working Class in England* he described people living in 'measureless filth and stench' amid 'masses of refuse, offal and sickening filth'. He related the case of one woman whose two little boys, freezing and on the brink of starvation, had been caught stealing food. When a policeman took the boys home, he found the mother with six other children 'literally huddled in a little back room, with no furniture but two old rush-bottomed chairs with the seats gone, a small table with two legs broken, a broken cup and a small dish. On the hearth was scarcely a spark of fire, and in one corner lay as many old rags as would fill a woman's apron, which served the whole family as a bed.'

Engels's descriptions were unquestionably touching and are often quoted now, but what is frequently forgotten is that his book was published only in German in 1845 and not translated into English for thirty-two years. As a reformer of British institutions, Engels had no influence at all until long after the reforms had begun.

Elsewhere, however, the conditions of the poor were beginning to attract attention. In the 1860s a fashion arose among journalists to disguise themselves as tramps and enter casual workhouses – what we would now call shelters – to investigate and report on the conditions within, allowing readers the safely vicarious thrill of experiencing the horrifying conditions without leaving the comforts of home. Readers learned how inmates at Lambeth Workhouse were required to strip naked and step into a murky bath, 'the colour of weak mutton broth', which was filled with the sloughed and scummy leavings of earlier bathers. Beyond were grim dormitories where men and boys, 'all perfectly naked', were crowded together on beds that were little more than pallets. 'Youths lay in the arms of men, men were enfolded in each other's embrace; there was neither fire, nor light nor supervision, and the weak and feeble were at the complete mercy of the strong and ruffianly. The air was laden with a pestilential stench.'

Stirred by these reports, a new breed of benefactors began to found an extraordinary range of organizations – a Committee for Promoting the Establishment of Baths and Wash Houses for the Labouring Classes, a Society for the Suppression of Juvenile Vagrancy, a Society for Promoting Window Gardening Amongst the Working Classes of Westminster, even a Society for the Rescue of Boys Not Yet Convicted of Any Criminal Offence – nearly always with the hope of helping the poor to remain or become sober, Christian, industrious, hygienic, law-abiding, parentally responsible or otherwise virtuous. Still others strived to improve housing conditions for the poor. One of the most generous was George Peabody, an American businessman who settled in England in 1837 (he it was, you may remember, who provided the emergency funding that allowed the American displays to be installed at the Great Exhibition) and spent much of his vast fortune building apartment blocks for the poor all over London. Peabody estates housed almost fifteen thousand people in clean, comparatively roomy flats, though the heavy hand of paternalism was still painfully evident. Tenants were not allowed to apply paint or wallpaper, install curtains or otherwise significantly personalize their homes. In consequence, they were not much cheerier than prison cells.

But the real change was the sudden growth of domestic missionary work, reflected most particularly in the endeavours of one man who did more to help impoverished children (often whether they wanted it or not) than anyone before him. His name was Thomas Barnardo. He was a young Irishman who came to London in the early 1860s and was so horrified by conditions faced by helpless youths that he set up an organization formally called the National Incorporated Association for the Reclamation of Destitute Waif Children, though everyone came to know it as Dr Barnardo's.

Barnardo came from an exotic background. His family originated as Sephardic Jews in Spain, but moved first to Germany and then to Ireland. By the time Thomas came along in 1845, the family's religious affiliation had switched to the more ferocious end of Protestantism. Barnardo himself came under the sway of the fundamentalist Plymouth Brethren, which is what brought him to London in the early 1860s with the intention to qualify as a doctor and undertake missionary work in China. He never got to China. In fact, he never qualified as a doctor. Instead he began to take a missionary interest in homeless young boys (and eventually girls as well). With borrowed money, he opened his first home in Stepney, in east London.

Barnardo was a brilliant publicist and developed an immensely successful campaign based around striking before-and-after photographs of the children he rescued. The 'before' photos showed grubby (and often scantily clad) waifs of sullen mien, while the 'after' photographs showed them scrubbed, alert and radiant with the joy of Christian salvation. The campaigns were so successful that soon Barnardo was expanding his interests in many directions, opening infirmaries, homes for deaf and dumb children, homes for homeless bootblacks, and much more. The slogan emblazoned along the façade of the Stepney home was 'No Destitute Child Ever Refused Admission'. It was an unusually noble sentiment, and many people hated Barnardo for it. The problem was that taking in boys unconditionally was an affront to the principles of the 1834 New Poor Law.

Barnardo's boundless ambition brought him into conflict with a fellow missionary, Frederick Charrington. The scion of an immensely wealthy brewing family based in the East End, Charrington had come into missionary work abruptly when one day he saw a drunken man beating his wife outside a Charrington pub from which he had just emerged, as his wife begged him for money to feed their hungry children. From that moment Charrington embraced temperance, renounced his inheritance and began working among the poor. He saw the Mile End Road as his personal fiefdom, so when Barnardo announced his intention to open a temperance café there, Charrington took umbrage and embarked on a relentless campaign of character assassination. Assisted by an itinerant preacher named George Reynolds (who had until lately been a railway porter) he spread rumours that Barnardo had lied about his background, misrun his homes, slept with his landlady and deceived the public through false advertising. Barnardo's homes, he additionally hinted, were outposts of sodomy, drunkenness, blackmail and other vices of the most depraved sort.

Unfortunately for Barnardo, an uncomfortably large proportion of this was true. Barnardo was something of a liar and made matters worse by responding with clumsy lies now. When it was alleged that he was misrepresenting himself as a doctor – a fairly serious offence under the Medical Act of 1858 – Barnardo produced a diploma from a German university, but it was shown almost at once to be a poor forgery. It was also proven that he had faked many before-and-after photographs of children he had rescued, making them look much more destitute than in fact they were. Many of the staged photographs depicted the children in artfully torn clothing that exposed alluring quantities of flesh, which many now interpreted as basely appealing to prurient interests. Even Barnardo's most faithful supporters found their loyalties strained. Apart from concerns about his character and probity, many worried about his levels of debt. One of the bedrock principles of the Plymouth Brethren was a devotion to thrift, yet Barnardo borrowed freely and repeatedly in order to keep opening more missions.

In the end, Barnardo was found guilty of faking photographs and of claiming wrongly to be a doctor, but exonerated on all the more serious charges. Ironically, life in a Barnardo home was scarcely more attractive than life in the dreaded workhouses. Inmates were roused from bed at 5.30 a.m. and required to work until 6.30 in the evening, with short breaks for meals, prayers and a little schooling. Evenings were devoted to military drills, classes and more prayers. Any boy caught trying to escape was placed in solitary confinement. Barnardo didn't merely recruit children, but snatched them off the streets in a spirit of 'philanthropic abduction'. Every year about fifteen hundred of these boys were summarily shipped off to Canada to make room in the homes for more boys.

By the time of his death in 1905, Barnardo had taken in 250,000 children. He left the organization indebted to the tune of £250,000 – a colossal sum.

III

We have spoken so far only of poor children, but well-to-do children had torments of their own to endure. These were torments of the sort that many of the starving poor would have been glad to get, to be sure, but they were torments none the less. Mostly they involved emotional adjustments and learning to live in a world that was shorn of affection. Almost from the moment of emerging from the womb, middle- and upper-class children in Victorian Britain were expected to be obedient, dutiful, honest, hard-working, stiff-upper-lipped and emotionally self-contained. An occasional handshake was about as much physical warmth as one could expect after infancy. The typical home of the prosperous classes in Victorian Britain was, in the words of one contemporary, an outpost of 'cold, harsh and emphatically inhuman reserve which cuts off anything like that friendly, considerate, sympathetic intercourse which ought to mark every family relation'.

Well-off children often had to endure the hardships of character building. Isabella Beeton's brother-in-law, Willy Smiles, had eleven children but only set out breakfast for ten, to discourage slowness in arriving at the table. Gwen

Raverat, daughter of a Cambridge academic, recalled in later life how she was required to sprinkle her daily porridge with salt, instead of the glistening heaps of sugar her parents enjoyed, and forbidden jam with her bread on the grounds that anything so flavoursome would wreak havoc upon her moral fibre. A contemporary, of similar background, recorded wistfully of the food served to her and her sister through childhood: 'We had oranges at Christmas. Marmalade we never saw.'

With the crushing of taste buds came also a curious respect for the character-building powers of fearfulness and dread. Extremely popular were books that prepared young readers for the possibility that death could take them at any moment, and if it didn't get them it would almost certainly get their mama, papa or favourite sibling. Such books always stressed how wonderful heaven was (though it seemed also to be a place without jam). The intention ostensibly was to help children not to be frightened of dying, though the effect was almost certainly the opposite.

Other literary works were designed to make sure children understood what a foolish and unforgivable offence it was to disobey an adult. A popular poem, 'The Dreadful Story of Pauline and the Matches', recounted the tale of a little girl who failed to heed her mother's gentle invocation not to play with matches. As the poem put it:

> *But Pauline would not take advice,*
> *She lit a match, it was so nice!*
> *It crackled so, it burned so clear, –*
> *Exactly like the picture here*
> *She jumped for joy and ran about,*
> *And was too pleased to put it out.*

Now see! Oh see! What a dreadful thing
The fire has caught her apron-string;
Her apron burns, her arms, her hair;
She burns all over, everywhere.

To make sure there was no possibility of misinterpretation, the poem carried a vivid illustration showing a
young girl engulfed in a ball of flame, on her face a look
of profoundest consternation. The poem concludes:

So she was burnt with all her clothes
And arms and hands, and eyes and nose;
Till she had nothing more to lose
Except her little scarlet shoes;
And nothing else but these was found
Among her ashes on the ground.

'The Dreadful Story of Pauline and the Matches' was
one of a series of poems by a German doctor named
Heinrich Hoffmann, who wrote them originally as a way
of encouraging his own children to follow lives of rigid
circumspection. Hoffmann's books were highly popular
and went through many translations (including one by
Mark Twain). All followed the same pattern, which was to
present children with a temptation difficult to refuse, then
show them how irreversibly painful were the consequences of succumbing. Almost no childhood activity
escaped the possibility of corrective brutality in
Hoffmann's hands. In another of his poems, 'The Story of
Little Suck-a-Thumb', a boy named Conrad is warned not
to suck his thumbs because it will attract the attention of

a ghoulish figure known as the great tall tailor who always
comes

> To little boys that suck their thumbs.
> And ere they dream what he's about
> He takes his great sharp scissors out.
> And cuts their thumbs clean off – and then
> You know, they never grow again.

Alas, little Suck-a-Thumb ignores the advice and dis-
covers that punishment in Hoffmann's world is swift and
irreversible:

> The door flew open, in he ran,
> The great red-legged scissor-man.
> Oh! children, see! the tailor's come
> And caught our little Suck-a-Thumb.

> Snip! Snap! Snip! the scissors go;
> And Conrad cries out – Oh! Oh! Oh!
> Snip! Snap! Snip! They go so fast;
> That both his thumbs are off at last.

> Mamma comes home; there Conrad stands,
> And looks quite sad, and shows his hands.
> 'Ah!' said Mamma, 'I knew he'd come
> To naughty little Suck-a-Thumb.'

For older children such poems may have been
amusing, but for smaller children they must often have
been – as they were intended to be – terrifying, particularly
as they were always accompanied by graphic illustrations

showing dismayed youngsters irreversibly in flame or spouting blood where useful parts of their body used to be.

Wealthier children were also often left to the mercy of servants and their private, peculiar whims. The future Lord Curzon, growing up as the son of a rector in Derbyshire, was terrorized for years by a semi-psychotic governess who tied him in a chair or locked him in a cupboard for hours at a time, ate the desserts from his dinner tray, compelled him to write letters confessing to crimes that he hadn't committed, and paraded him through the local village wearing a ridiculous smock and a placard around his neck announcing him as a 'LIAR', 'THIEF' or some other shameful condition that he had usually done nothing to merit. The experiences left him so traumatized that he couldn't bring himself to tell anyone about them until he was grown up. Rather milder, but nonetheless dismaying, was the experience of the future sixth Earl Beauchamp, who was left in the clutches of a governess who was a religious fanatic; she required him to attend seven church services every Sunday and to fill the time between by writing essays about the goodness of God.

For many the ordeals of early childhood were a modest warm-up for the stress of life in public schools. Rarely can hardship have been embraced with greater enthusiasm than in the English public school in the nineteenth century. From the moment of arrival pupils were treated to harsh regimens involving cold baths, frequent canings and the withholding from the diet of anything that could be remotely described as appetizing. Boys at Radley College, near Oxford, were so systematically starved that they were reduced to digging up flower bulbs from the school gardens and toasting them over candles in their rooms. At other schools where bulbs were not available, the boys simply ate the candles. The novelist Alec Waugh, brother of Evelyn, attended a prep school called Fernden that seemed to be singularly devoted to the ideals of sadism. On his first day there, his fingers were thrust into a pot of sulphuric acid to discourage him from biting his nails, and soon afterwards he was required to eat the contents of a bowl of semolina pudding into which he had just vomited, an experience that understandably dimmed his enthusiasm for semolina for the rest of his life.

Living conditions at private schools were always grim. Illustrations of school dormitories from the nineteenth century show them as being all but indistinguishable from the equivalent spaces in prisons and workhouses. Dormitories were often so cold that water froze overnight in jugs and bowls. Beds were little more than wooden platforms, often with nothing more for warmth and padding than a couple of rough blankets. Every night at Westminster and Eton some fifty boys were locked in together in vast halls and left without supervision till morning, so that the weakest were at the mercy of the strongest. Junior boys sometimes had to rise in the middle of the night to begin polishing boots, drawing water and engaging in all the other chores required of them before breakfast. It is little wonder that Lewis Carroll said in later life of his schooldays that nothing on earth would induce him to repeat that experience.

Many boys were flogged daily, some twice a day. Not being flogged at all was a cause for celebration. 'This week

I did much better at arithmetic and didn't have the birch once,' one boy wrote home happily from Winchester in the early 1800s. Floggings generally consisted of three to six strokes delivered on the run with a whip-like birch, but occasionally greater violence was done. In 1682, a headmaster at Eton had to resign after killing a boy. A remarkable number of young men developed a taste for the whistle and sting of a spanking – so much so that whipping for pleasure became known as 'le vice anglais'. At least two nineteenth-century prime ministers, Melbourne and Gladstone, were devoted flagellants, and a Mrs Collet in Covent Garden ran a brothel that specialized in providing sex with a smack.

Above all, offspring were expected to do as they were told, and to continue doing so long after they had reached their majority. Parents reserved to themselves the right to select marriage partners, careers, modes of living, political affiliations, style of dress and almost any other consideration that could be dictated, and frequently reacted with financial violence when their commands were disregarded. Henry Mayhew, the social reformer, was cut off when he declined to submit to his father's instructions to become a lawyer. So too, one after another, were six of his seven brothers. Only the seventh was keen to be a lawyer (or perhaps just keen to have the estate); he dutifully qualified and so inherited the lot. The poet Elizabeth Barrett was disinherited for marrying Robert Browning, who was not only a penniless poet but – the horror of it – the grandson of a publican. Similarly, the horrified parents of Alice Roberts disinherited her when she could not be dissuaded from marrying the indigent son of a Roman Catholic piano tuner. Fortunately for Miss Roberts the man was the future composer Edward Elgar, and he made her rich anyway.

Sometimes disinheritance was provoked by rather more trivial considerations. The second Lord Townshend, after years of being annoyed by his son's effeminacy, abruptly struck the hapless fellow from the will when he wandered into the room one day wearing pink ribbons on his shoes. Also much spoken of was the case of the sixth Duke of Somerset, known as 'the Proud Duke', who required his daughters always to stand in his presence and reportedly disinherited one of them when he awoke from a nap and caught the ungrateful wretch sitting.

What is often striking – and indeed depressing – is how swiftly parents withdrew not just funds but affections. Elizabeth Barrett and her father were intensely close, but when she declared her intention to marry Robert Browning, Mr Barrett immediately terminated all contact. He never spoke or wrote to his daughter again even though her marriage was to a man who was gifted and respectable, and based on the deepest bonds of love. In the mystifying world that was Victorian parenthood, obedience took precedence over all considerations of affection and happiness, and that odd, painful conviction remained the case in most well-heeled homes up until at least the time of the First World War.

So on the face of it, it would seem that Victorians didn't so much invent childhood as *dis*invent it. In fact, however, it was more complicated than that. By withholding affection to children when they were young but also then endeavouring to control their behaviour well into adulthood, Victorians were in the very odd position of simultaneously trying to suppress childhood *and* make it last for ever. It is perhaps little wonder that the end of Victorianism almost exactly coincided with the invention of psychoanalysis.

Defying a parent was so profoundly unacceptable that most children, even in adulthood, would simply not engage in it. A perfect illustration of this is Charles Darwin. When as a young man Darwin was offered the chance to join the voyage of HMS *Beagle* he wrote a touching letter to his father explaining precisely why and how desperately he wished to go, but took pains to assure his father that he would withdraw his name from consideration at once if the idea made his father even briefly 'uncomfortable'. Mr Darwin considered the matter and declared that the idea *did* make him uncomfortable, so Charles, without a peep of protest, withdrew his name. The idea of Charles Darwin not going on the *Beagle* voyage is to us unimaginable now. To Darwin what was unimaginable was disobeying his father.

Of course Darwin did get to go in the end, and a big part of the reason his father relented was an odd but crucial factor in the lives of many upper-class people: marriage within the family. Marrying cousins was astoundingly common into the nineteenth century, and nowhere is this better illustrated than with the Darwins and their cousins the Wedgwoods (of pottery fame). Charles married his first cousin Emma Wedgwood, daughter of his beloved Uncle Josiah. Darwin's sister Caroline, meanwhile, married Josiah Wedgwood III, Emma's brother and the Darwin siblings' joint first cousin. Another of Emma's brothers, Henry, married not a Darwin but a first cousin from another branch of his own Wedgwood family,

adding another strand to the family's wondrously convoluted genetics. Finally, Charles Langton, who was not
related to either family, first married Charlotte Wedgwood,
another daughter of Josiah and cousin of Charles, and
then upon Charlotte's death married Darwin's sister Emily,
thus becoming, it seems, his sister-in-law's sister-in-law's
husband and raising the possibility that any children of
the union would be their own first cousins. What all this
meant in terms of relationships between nephews, nieces
and the next generation of cousins is very nearly beyond
computing.

What it produced, rather unexpectedly, is one of the
happiest family groupings of the nineteenth century.
Nearly all the Darwins and Wedgwoods seem to have been
genuinely fond of each other, which is a very good thing
for us because when Darwin's father expressed misgivings
about the *Beagle* voyage, Darwin's Uncle Josiah was happy
to intercede on his behalf and to have a word with
Charles's father, his cousin Robert. What's more, Robert
was willing to be persuaded to change his mind because of
his respect and affection for Josiah.

So, thanks to his uncle and a tradition of keeping
genes within the family, Charles Darwin did go to sea for
the next five years, and gathered the facts that allowed him
to change the world. And that takes us conveniently, if a
little unexpectedly, to the top of the house and the last
space we will pass through.

CHAPTER NINETEEN

The Attic

I

IN THE EVENTFUL SUMMER of 1851, while crowds flocked to the Great Exhibition in London and Thomas Marsham settled into his new property in Norfolk, Charles Darwin delivered to his publishers a hefty manuscript, the result of eight years of devoted enquiry into the nature and habits of barnacles. Called *A Monograph of the Fossil Lepadidae, or, Pedunculated Cirripedes of Great Britain*, it doesn't sound like the most diverting of works, and wasn't, but it secured his reputation as a naturalist, and gave him, in the words of one biographer, 'the authority to speak, when the time was ripe, on variability and transmutation' – on evolution, in other words. Remarkably, Darwin hadn't finished with barnacles yet. Three years later he produced a 684-page study of sessile cirripedes and a more modest companion work on the barnacle fossils not mentioned in the first work. 'I hate a barnacle as no man ever did before,' he declared upon the conclusion of the work, and it is hard not to sympathize.

Fossil Lepadidae was not a huge seller, but it did no worse than another book published in 1851 – a strange, mystically rambling parable on whale hunting, called simply *The Whale*. This was a timely book since whales everywhere were being hunted to extinction, but the critics and buying public failed to warm to it, or even understand it. It was too dense and puzzling, too packed with introspection and hard facts. A month later the book came out in America with a different title: *Moby-Dick*. It did no better there. The book's failure was a surprise because the author, thirty-two-year-old Herman Melville, had enjoyed great success with two earlier tales of adventure at sea, *Typee* and *Omoo*. *Moby-Dick*, however, never took off in his lifetime. Nor did anything else he wrote. He died all but forgotten in 1891. His last book, *Billy Budd*, didn't find a publisher until more than thirty years after his death.

Although it is unlikely that Mr Marsham was acquainted with either *Moby-Dick* or *Fossil Lepadidae*, both reflected a fundamental change that had lately overtaken the thinking world: an almost obsessive urge to pin down every stray morsel of discernible fact and give it permanent recognition in print. Fieldwork was now all the rage among gentlemen of a scientific bent. Some went in for geology and the natural sciences. Others became antiquaries. The most adventurous of all sacrificed homely comforts and often years of their lives to explore distant corners of the world. They became – a new word, coined in 1834 – *scientists*.

Their curiosity and devotion were inexhaustible. No place was too remote or inconvenient, no object unworthy of consideration. This was the era in which the plant hunter Robert Fortune travelled across China disguised as a native gathering information on the growing and pro-cessing of tea, when David Livingstone pushed up the Zambezi and into the darkest corners of Africa, when botanical adventurers combed the interiors of North and South America looking for interesting and novel speci-mens, and when Charles Darwin, just twenty-two years old, set forth as a naturalist on the epic voyage that would change his life, and ours, in ways that no one could then begin to imagine.

Almost nothing Darwin encountered during the five years of the voyage failed to excite his attention. He recorded so many facts and acquired such a wealth of specimens that it took him a decade and a half just to get through the barnacles. Among much else, he collected hundreds of new species of plant, made many important fossil and geological discoveries, developed a widely admired hypothesis to explain the formation of coral atolls, and acquired the materials and insights necessary to create a revolutionary theory of life – not bad going for a young man who, had his father had his way, would instead now be a country parson like our own Mr Marsham, a prospect Darwin dreaded.

One of the ironies of the *Beagle* voyage was that Darwin was engaged by Captain Robert FitzRoy because he had a background in theology and was expected to find evidence to support a biblical interpretation of history. In persuading Robert Darwin to let Charles go, Josiah Wedgwood had been at pains to stress that 'the pursuit of natural history . . . is very suitable to a Clergyman'. In the event, the more Darwin saw of the world, the more convinced he became that Earth's history and dynamics were vastly more protracted and complicated than conventional thinking allowed. His coral atolls theory, for one, required a passage of time far beyond any allowed by biblical timescales, a fact that infuriated the devout and volatile Captain FitzRoy.

Eventually, of course, Darwin devised a theory – survival of the fittest, as we commonly know it; descent with modification, as he called it – that explained the wondrous complexity of living things in a way that didn't require the intervention of a deity at all. In 1842, six years after the end of his voyage, he sketched out a 230-page summary outlining the theory's principal elements. Then he did an extraordinary thing: he locked it away in a drawer, and kept it there for the next sixteen years. The subject, he felt, was too hot for public discussion.

Long before Darwin came along, however, people were already finding things that didn't accord with orthodox beliefs. One of the first such finds, in fact, was just a few miles down the road from the Old Rectory in the village of Hoxne, where in the late 1790s a wealthy landowner and antiquary named John Frere discovered a cache of flint tools lying alongside the bones of long-extinct animals, suggesting a coexistence that wasn't supposed to happen. In a letter to the Society of Antiquaries in London, he reported that the tools were made by people who 'had not the use of metals . . . [which] may tempt us to refer them to a very remote period indeed'. This was an exceedingly keen insight for the time – too keen, in fact, and it was almost completely ignored. The secretary of the society thanked him for his 'curious and most interesting communication', and, for the next forty years or so, that was the end of the matter.*

But then others began finding tools and ancient bones in puzzling proximity. In a cave near Torquay in Devon, Father John MacEnery, a Catholic priest and amateur excavator, uncovered more or less incontrovertible evidence that humans had hunted mammoths and other creatures now extinct. MacEnery found this idea so uncomfortably at odds with biblical precepts that he kept his findings to himself. Then a French customs officer named Jacques Boucher de Perthes found bones and tools together on the Somme plain and wrote a long and influential work, *Celtic and Antediluvian Antiquities*, which attracted international attention. At much the same time, William Pengelly, an English headmaster, re-examined MacEnery's cave and another in nearby Brixham and announced the findings that MacEnery was too distraught to share. So by mid-century it was becoming increasingly evident that Earth possessed not just a lot of history, but what would come to be known as prehistory, though that word wouldn't be coined until 1871. It is telling that these ideas were so radical that there weren't yet even words for them.

Then in the early summer of 1858, from Asia, Alfred Russel Wallace famously dropped a bombshell into Darwin's lap. He sent him the draft of an essay, 'On the Tendency of Varieties to Depart Indefinitely from the Original Type'. It was Darwin's own theory, innocently and independently arrived at. 'I never saw a more striking co-incidence,' Darwin wrote. 'If Wallace had my manuscript

---

* A hundred years later when the significance of the find was finally realized, a geological period was named the Hoxnian after the village where Frere made his discovery.

sketch written out in 1842, he could not have made a better short abstract.'

Protocol required Darwin to step aside and allow Wallace full credit for the theory, but Darwin couldn't bring himself to make such a noble gesture. The theory meant too much to him. A complicating factor at this time was that his son Charles, aged eighteen months, was gravely ill with scarlet fever. Despite this, Darwin found time to dash off letters to his most eminent scientific friends, and they helped him to contrive a solution. It was agreed that Joseph Hooker and Charles Lyell would present summaries of both papers to a meeting of the Linnean Society in London, giving Darwin and Wallace joint priority for the new theory. This they duly did on 1 July 1858. Wallace, far away in Asia, knew nothing of these machinations. Darwin didn't attend because on that day he and his wife were burying their son.

Darwin immediately set to work expanding his sketch into a full-length book, and in November 1859 it was published as *On the Origin of Species by Means of Natural Selection, or the Preservation of Favoured Races in the Struggle for Life*. It was an immediate bestseller. It is almost impossible now to imagine how much Darwin's theory unsettled the intellectual world, or how desperately many people wished it not to be correct. Darwin himself remarked to a friend that writing his book felt 'like confessing to a murder'.

Many devout people simply couldn't accept that the Earth was as ancient and randomly enlivened as all the new ideas indicated. One leading naturalist, Philip Henry Gosse, produced a somewhat desperate alternative theory called 'prochronism' in which he suggested that

God had merely made the Earth look old, to give people of inquisitive minds more interesting things to wonder over. Even fossils, Gosse insisted, had been planted in the rocks by God during his busy week of Creation.

Gradually, however, educated people came to accept that the world was not just older than biblically supposed, but much more complicated, imperfect and confused. Naturally, all this undermined the confident basis on which clergymen like Mr Marsham operated. In terms of their pre-eminence, it was the beginning of the end.

In their enthusiasm to unearth treasures, many of the new breed of investigators perpetrated some fairly appalling damage. Artefacts were dug from the soil 'like potatoes', in the words of one alarmed observer. In Norfolk, members of the new Norfolk and Norwich Archaeological Society – founded shortly before Mr Marsham took up his position in our parish – stripped well over a hundred burial mounds, a good portion of the county total, without leaving any record of what they had found or how it was arrayed, to the despair of later generations of scholars.

There is a certain obvious and painful irony in the thought that just as Britons were discovering their past, they were simultaneously destroying a good part of it. Perhaps no one better exemplified this new breed of rapacious collector than William Greenwell (1820–1918), canon of Durham Cathedral, whom we met much earlier as the inventor of Greenwell's glory, the celebrated (among those who celebrate such things) trout fly. In the course of a long career, Greenwell built up an extraordinary assemblage of artefacts 'by gift, by purchase and by felony', in the words of one historian. He single-handedly excavated – though 'devoured' might be the better word – 443 burial mounds all across England. His methods could be described as keen but slapdash. He left virtually no notes or records, so it is often all but impossible to know what came from where.

Greenwell's one compensating virtue was that he introduced the resplendently named Augustus Henry Lane Fox Pitt Rivers to the magic of archaeology. Pitt Rivers is memorable for two things: as one of the most important of early archaeologists and the nastiest of men. We have met him in passing already in this volume. He was the formidable figure who insisted his wife should be cremated. ('Damn it, woman, you shall burn' was his cheery catchphrase.) He came from an interesting family, some of whose members we have also encountered before, notably two great-aunts of his who could fairly be described as firecrackers. The first, Penelope, married Viscount Ligonier of Clonmell. It was she, you may recall, who had an affair with an Italian count, then ran off with her footman. The second was the young woman who married Peter Beckford, but fell disastrously in love with his cousin William, builder of Fonthill Abbey. Both were the daughters of George Pitt, first Baron Rivers, from whom our Pitt Rivers took both halves of his name.

Augustus Pitt Rivers was a large and intimidating figure with a fiery temper at the end of a very short fuse who presided imperiously over an estate of 27,000 acres called Rushmore, near Salisbury. He was notoriously meanspirited. Once his wife invited local villagers to Rushmore for a Christmas party, and was heartbroken when no one turned up. What she didn't know was that her husband, learning of her plans, had sent a servant to padlock the estate gates.

He was capable of the most sudden and disproportionate violence. After banishing one of his sons from the estate for some untold infraction, he forbade his other children to have any contact with him. But one daughter, Alice, took pity on her brother and met him at the estate edge to pass him some money. Learning of this, Pitt Rivers intercepted Alice as she returned to the house and beat her to the ground with her own riding crop.

Pitt Rivers's particular speciality – a kind of hobby, it would seem – was evicting aged tenants. On one occasion he served notice on a man and his crippled wife, both in their eighties. When they begged him to reconsider as they had no living relatives and nowhere to go, he responded briskly: 'I was extremely sorry to get your letter & to see how much you disliked leaving Hinton. To be brief I feel my duties to the property necessitate my occupying the house as soon as possible.' The couple were forthwith ejected, though in fact Pitt Rivers never moved in and, according to his biographer, Mark Bowden, almost certainly never intended to.*

For all his personal shortcomings, Pitt Rivers was an

---

* Pitt Rivers's eldest son, Alexander, seems to have inherited his father's affection for tormenting tenants. One, a man of previously mild character, was so driven to despair by young Alexander that he wrote 'BLACKGUARD LANDLORD' with weedkiller in large letters across the Rushmore lawn. Alexander sued for libel and was awarded token damages of one shilling, but rejoiced in the fact that the trial costs had reduced the tenant to destitution. Pitt Rivers's other eight children seem mostly to have been pretty decent. George – the one banished from the estate and thus the inadvertent cause of his sister's beating – became a successful inventor with a particular interest in electric lighting. He demonstrated an incandescent bulb at the Paris Exhibition of 1881 that was deemed the equal of anything produced by Edison or Swan.

outstanding archaeologist – indeed, was one of the fathers of modern archaeology. He brought method and rigour to the field. He carefully labelled shards of pottery and other fragments at a time when that was not routinely done. The idea of organizing archaeological finds into a systematic sequence – a process known as typology – was his invention. Unusually, he was less interested in glittering treasure than in the objects of everyday life – beakers, combs, decorative beads and the like – which had mostly gone undervalued theretofore. He also brought to archaeology a devotion to precision. He invented a device called a craniometer, which could make very exact measurements of human skulls. After his death, his collection of artefacts formed the foundation of the great Pitt Rivers Museum in Oxford.

Thanks in large part to Pitt Rivers's exacting methodology, by the second half of the nineteenth century archaeology was becoming more like a science and less like a treasure hunt, and the more careless excesses of the early antiquaries were becoming a thing of the past. In the wider world, however, destruction was getting worse. Practically all the ancient monuments in Britain were in private hands and no law compelled owners to look after them. Stories abounded of people destroying artefacts, either because they found them a nuisance or failed to appreciate their rarity. In Orkney, a farmer at Stenness, not far from Skara Brae, demolished a prehistoric megalith known as the Stone of Odin because it was in his way when he ploughed, and was about to start on the now-famous Stones of Stenness when horrified islanders persuaded him to desist.

Even something as peerless as Stonehenge was

astoundingly insecure. Visitors commonly carved their names in the stones or chipped off pieces to take away as souvenirs. One man was found banging away on a sarsen with a sledgehammer. In the early 1870s, the London and South-Western Railway announced plans to run a line right through the heart of the Stonehenge site. When people complained, a railway official countered that Stonehenge was 'entirely out of repair, and not the slightest use to anyone now'.

Clearly, Britain's ancient heritage needed a saviour. Enter one of the most extraordinary fellows of that extraordinary age. His name was John Lubbock and it is remarkable that he is not better known. It would be hard to name any figure who did more useful things in more fields and won less lasting fame for it.

The son of a wealthy banker, Lubbock grew up as a neighbour of Charles Darwin in Kent. He played with Darwin's children and was constantly in and out of the Darwin house. He had a gift for natural history, which endeared him to the great man. The two spent many hours together in Darwin's study looking at specimens in matching microscopes. At one point when Darwin was depressed, young Lubbock was the only visitor he would receive.

Upon reaching adulthood, Lubbock followed his father into banking, but his heart was in science. He was a tireless, if slightly eccentric, experimenter. Once he spent three months trying to teach his dog to read. Developing an interest in archaeology, he learned Danish because Denmark was then the world leader in the field. He had a particular interest in insects, and kept a colony of bees in his sitting room, the better to study their habits. In 1886 he

SIR JOHN LUBBOCK, M.P., F.R.S.

How doth the Banking Busy Bee
Improve his shining Hours
By studying on Bank Holidays
Strange Insects and Wild Flowers!

*Punch cartoon of John Lubbock, architect of the Bank Holidays Act
and the Ancient Monuments Protection Act.*

discovered the pauropods – one of the family of tiny, and previously unsuspected, mites mentioned in our earlier discussion of household creatures. Since, as we have seen, many mites weren't noticed by science at all until the middle of the twentieth century, to identify a family of them in 1886 was a signal achievement, particularly for a banker whose scientific pursuits were limited to evenings and weekends. No less significant was his study of the variability of nervous systems in insects, which lent important support to Darwin and his idea of descent with modification just at a time when Darwin really needed it.

As well as being a banker and keen entomologist, Lubbock was also a distinguished archaeologist, trustee of the British Museum, Member of Parliament, vice-chancellor (or head) of London University, and author of popular books, among rather a lot else. As an archaeologist, he coined the terms 'palaeolithic', 'mesolithic' and 'neolithic', and was one of the first to use the handy new word 'prehistoric'. As a politician and Member of Parliament for the Liberal Party, he became a champion of the working man. He introduced legislation to limit the hours worked in shops to ten hours a day, and in 1871 he pushed through – virtually single-handedly – the Bank Holidays Act, which introduced the breathtakingly radical idea of a paid secular holiday for workers.* It is almost impossible now to imagine what excitement this caused. Before Lubbock's new law, most employees were excused from work on Good Friday,

* The name 'bank holiday' was an odd one, and Lubbock never really explained why he elected to call it that instead of 'national holiday' or 'workers' holiday' or something similarly descriptive. It is sometimes suggested that he meant the holiday only for bank workers, but that is not so. It was always intended for all.

Christmas Day or Boxing Day (but not generally both) and
Sundays, and that was it. The idea of having a bonus day
off – and in summer at that – was almost too thrilling to
bear. Lubbock was widely agreed to be the most popular
man in England and bank holidays for a long time were
affectionately known as 'St Lubbock's days'. No one in his
age would ever have supposed that his name would one
day be forgotten.

But it is for one other innovation that Lubbock is of
importance to us here: the preservation of ancient monuments. In 1872 Lubbock learned from a rector in rural
Wiltshire that a big chunk of Avebury, an ancient circle of
stones considerably larger than Stonehenge (though not
so picturesquely composed), was about to be cleared away
for new housing. Lubbock bought the threatened land,
along with two other ancient monuments nearby, West
Kennet Long Barrow and Silbury Hill (an enormous manmade mound – the largest in Europe), but clearly he
couldn't protect every worthy thing that grew threatened,
so he began to press for legislation to safeguard historic
treasures. Achieving this ambition was not nearly as
straightforward as common sense would suggest it ought
to be because the ruling Tories under Benjamin Disraeli
saw it as an egregious assault on property rights. The idea
of giving a government functionary the right to come on
to the land of a person of superior caste and start telling
him how to manage his estate was preposterous – out-
rageous. Lubbock persevered, however, and in 1882, under
the new Liberal government of William Ewart Gladstone,
he managed to push through Parliament the Ancient
Monuments Protection Act – a landmark piece of
legislation if ever there was one.

Because the protection of monuments was such a sensitive issue, it was agreed that the first Inspector of Ancient Monuments should be someone landowners could respect, ideally a large landowner himself. It so happened that Lubbock knew just the person – the man who was about to become his new father-in-law, none other than Augustus Henry Lane Fox Pitt Rivers.

Their relationship through marriage must have been as surprising to them as it is to us. For one thing, the two men were nearly the same age. It just happened that the recently widowed Lubbock met Pitt Rivers's daughter Alice on a weekend stay at Castle Howard in the early 1880s. Lubbock was nearly fifty, Alice just eighteen. What caused a spark between them is beyond plausible guessing, but they were married soon afterwards. It wasn't an outstandingly happy marriage. She was younger than some of his children, which made for awkward relationships, and appears to have had little interest in his work, but the one certainty is that life with Lubbock was better than being beaten to the ground with a riding crop.

Whether Lubbock was unaware of Pitt Rivers's brutality to Alice or was simply prepared to overlook it – and little says more of the age than that either was possible – he and Pitt Rivers had a happy working relationship, no doubt because they had so many interests in common. As Inspector of Ancient Monuments, Pitt Rivers's powers were not spectacular. His brief was to identify important monuments that might be endangered, and to offer to take them into state care if the owner wished. Although this would relieve owners of the cost of maintaining sites, most baulked because it was such an unprecedented step to cede control of any part of one's estate. Even Lubbock hesitated before relinquishing Silbury Hill. The act carefully excluded houses, castles and ecclesiastical structures. All that left was prehistoric monuments. The Office of Works provided Pitt Rivers with almost no money – half of his budget one year was spent on putting a low fence around a single burial mound – and in 1890 it removed his salary altogether, thereafter merely covering his expenses. Even then it asked him to stop 'touting' for more monuments.

Pitt Rivers died in 1900. In eighteen years, he managed to list (or 'schedule', as the parlance has it) just forty-three monuments, barely over two a year. (The number of scheduled ancient monuments today is over 19,000.) But he had helped to set two immeasurably important precedents – that ancient things are precious enough to protect and that owners of ancient monuments have a duty to look after them. These policies weren't always enforced with much rigour in his day, but the principles embedded in them were crucial, and they inspired others to take additional protective actions. The Society for the Protection of Ancient Buildings, led by the designer William Morris, was founded in 1877, and the National Trust followed in 1895. At last British monuments began to enjoy some measure of formal protection.

Risks continued, however. Stonehenge remained in private hands, and the owner, Sir Edmund Antrobus, refused to listen to government advice or even have inspectors on his land. Around the turn of the century it was reported that an anonymous buyer was interested in shipping the stones to America to re-erect as a tourist attraction somewhere out west. Had Antrobus accepted such an offer, there was nothing in law anyone could do to stop him. Nor indeed for many years was there anyone willing to try. For ten years after Pitt Rivers's death, the position of Inspector of Ancient Monuments was left vacant to save funds.

II

Even as all this was unfolding, life in the British countryside was being severely reshaped by an event that is little remembered now, but was one of the most economically catastrophic in modern British history: the agricultural depression of the 1870s, when harvests were abysmal in seven years out of ten. This time, however, farmers and landowners couldn't compensate by raising prices, as they always had in the past, because now they faced vigorous competition from overseas. America in particular had become a vast agricultural machine. Thanks to the McCormick reaper and other large, clattery implements, America's prairies had become devastatingly productive. Between 1872 and 1902, American wheat production increased by 700 per cent. In the same period, British wheat production fell by more than 40 per cent.

Prices collapsed too. Wheat, barley, oats, bacon, pork, mutton and lamb all roughly halved in value during the last quarter of the nineteenth century. Wool dropped from 28 shillings per fourteen-pound bundle to just 12. Thousands of tenant farmers were ruined. More than one hundred thousand farmers and farmworkers left the land. Fields stood idle. Rents went unpaid. Nowhere was there any prospect of relief. Country churches became conspicuously empty as parish rolls shrank. Those worshippers who remained were poorer than ever. It wasn't a great time to be a country clergyman. It never would be again.

At the height of the agricultural crisis, the British government under the Liberals did an odd thing. It invented a tax designed to punish a class of people who were already suffering severely and had done nothing in particular to cause the current troubles. The class was large landowners. The tax was death duties. Life was about to change utterly for thousands of people, including our own Mr Marsham.

The designer of the new tax was Sir William George Granville Venables Vernon Harcourt, the chancellor of the exchequer, a man who seems not to have been liked much by anyone at any point in his life, including his own family. Known familiarly, if not altogether affectionately, as 'Jumbo' because of his magnificent rotundity, Harcourt was an unlikely persecutor of the landed classes since he was one of them himself. The Harcourt family home was Nuneham Park in Oxfordshire, which we have visited in this book already. Nuneham, you may remember, was where an earlier Harcourt reconfigured the estate but failed to recollect where the old village well had been, fell into it and drowned. For as long as there had been Tories, the Harcourts had numbered themselves among them, so William's joining of the Liberals was seen within his family as the darkest treachery. Even Liberals were startled by his tax. Lord Rosebery, the prime minister (who was himself a big landowner), wondered if some relief should at least be granted in those cases where two inheritors died in quick succession. It would be harsh, Rosebery thought, to tax an estate a second time before the legatee had had a chance to rebuild the family finances. Harcourt, however, refused all appeals for concessions.

That Harcourt stood almost no chance of inheriting his own family property no doubt coloured his principles. In fact, to his presumed surprise, he *did* inherit it when his elder brother's son died suddenly, but heirlessly, in the spring of 1904. Harcourt didn't get to enjoy his good fortune long, however. He expired six months later himself, which meant that his heirs were among the first to be taxed twice over in exactly the way that Rosebery had feared and he had dismissed. Life doesn't often get much neater than that.

Death duties in Harcourt's time were a comparatively modest 8 per cent on estates valued at £1 million or more, but they proved to be such a reliable source of revenue, and so popular with the millions who didn't have to pay them, that they were raised again and again until by the eve of the Second World War they stood at 60 per cent – a level that would make even the richest eyes water. At the same time, income taxes were raised repeatedly and other new taxes invented – an Undeveloped Land Duty, an Incremental Value Duty, a Super Tax – all of which fell disproportionately on those with a lot of land and plummy accents. For the upper classes the twentieth century became, in the words of David Cannadine, a time 'of encircling gloom'.

Most lived within a semi-permanent state of crisis. When things got really bad – when a roof needed replacing or a tax demand hit the mat – disaster could generally be staved off by selling heirlooms. Paintings, tapestries, jewels, books, porcelain, silver plate, rare stamps, whatever would attract a reasonable price poured out of English stately homes and into museums or the hands of foreigners. This was the age in which Henry Clay Folger bought every Shakespeare First Folio he could lay hands on and George Washington Vanderbilt bought treasures enough to fill his 250-room Biltmore mansion, when men like Andrew Mellon, Henry Clay Frick and J. P. Morgan acquired Old Masters by the wagonload, and William Randolph Hearst acquired almost anything else that was going.

There was hardly a great house in Britain that didn't yield something at some point. The Howards at Castle Howard relinquished 110 Old Masters and more than a thousand rare books. At Blenheim Palace, the dukes of Marlborough sold stacks of paintings, including eighteen works by Rubens and more than a dozen by Van Dyck, before belatedly discovering the financial attractiveness of marrying rich Americans. The fabulously rich Duke of Hamilton sold nearly £400,000 worth of glittery oddments in 1882, then returned a few years later to sell some £250,000 more. For many, the great auction houses of London assumed something of the qualities of pawn shops.

When the owners had sold everything of value from walls and floors, they sometimes sold the walls and floors, too. A room with all its fittings was extracted from Wingerworth Hall in Derbyshire and inserted into the St Louis Art Museum. A Grinling Gibbons staircase was removed from Cassiobury Park in Hertfordshire and re-erected in the Metropolitan Museum of Art in New York. Sometimes entire houses went, as with Agecroft Hall, a handsome Tudor manor in Lancashire, which was taken to pieces, packed into numbered crates and shipped to

Richmond, Virginia, where it was reassembled and still proudly stands.

Very occasionally there was some good in all the hardship. The heirs of Sir Edmund Antrobus, unable to maintain his estate, put it on the market in 1915. A local businessman and racehorse breeder named Sir Cecil Chubb bought Stonehenge for £6,600 – roughly £300,000 in today's money, so not a trifling sum – and very generously gave it to the nation, making it safe at last.

Such happy outcomes were exceptional, however. For many hundreds of country houses there was no salvation, and the sad fate was decline and eventual demolition. Almost all the losses were unfortunate. Some were little short of scandalous. Streatlam Castle, once one of the finest homes in County Durham, was given to the Territorial Army, which used it, amazingly, for target practice. Aston Clinton, a nineteenth-century house of vast and exuberant charm once owned by the Rothschilds, was bought by Buckinghamshire County Council and torn down to make way for a soulless vocational training centre. So low did the fortunes of stately homes sink that one in Lincolnshire reportedly was bought by a film company just so that it could burn it down for the climactic scene of a movie.

Nowhere was entirely safe, it seems. Even Chiswick House, a landmark building by any measure, was nearly lost. For a time it was a lunatic asylum, but by the 1950s it was empty and listed for demolition. Fortunately, enough sense prevailed to save it, and it is now in the safe care of English Heritage, a public body. The National Trust rescued some two hundred other houses over the course of the century, and a few survived by turning themselves into tourist attractions – not always entirely smoothly at first.

A grandmother at one stately home, Simon Jenkins relates, refused to leave one of the rooms whenever there was horse-racing on the television. 'She was voted the best exhibit,' Jenkins adds. Many other large houses found new lives as schools, clinics or other institutions. Sir William Harcourt's Nuneham Park spent much of the twentieth century as a training centre for the Royal Air Force. (It is now a religious retreat.)

Hundreds more, however, were unceremoniously whisked away. By the 1950s, the peak period of destruction, stately homes were disappearing at the rate of about two a week. Exactly how many great houses went altogether is unknown. In 1974, the Victoria & Albert Museum in London staged a celebrated exhibition, 'The Destruction of the Country House', in which it surveyed the enormous loss of stately homes in the previous century. Altogether the curators, Marcus Binney and John Harris, counted 1,116 great houses lost, but further research raised that number to 1,600 even before the exhibition was over, and the figure now is generally put at about 2,000 – a painfully substantial number bearing in mind that these were some of the handsomest, jauntiest, most striking, ambitious, influential and patently cherishable residences ever erected on the planet.

III

So that was the situation for Mr Marsham and his century as they headed jointly towards their closing years. From the perspective of domesticity, there has never been a more interesting or eventful time. Private life was completely transformed in the nineteenth century – socially, intellectually, technologically, hygienically, sartorially, sexually and in almost any other respect that could be made into an adverb. Mr Marsham was born (in 1822) into a world that was still essentially medieval – a place of candlelight, medicinal leeches, travel at walking pace, news from afar that was always weeks or months old – and lived to see the introduction of one marvel after another: steamships and speeding trains, telegraphy, photography, anaesthesia, indoor plumbing, gas lighting, antisepsis in medicine, refrigeration, telephones, electric lights, recorded music, cars and planes, skyscrapers, motion pictures, radio, and literally tens of thousands of tiny things more, from mass-produced bars of soap to push-along lawnmowers.

It is almost impossible to conceive just how much radical day-to-day change people were exposed to in the nineteenth century, particularly in the second half. Even something as elemental as the weekend was brand new. The term is not recorded in English before 1879, when it appears in the magazine *Notes & Queries* in the sentence: 'In Staffordshire, if a person leaves home at the end of his week's work on the Saturday afternoon to spend the evening of Saturday and the following Sunday with friends at a distance, he is said to be spending his *weekend* at So-and-so.' Even then, clearly, it only signified Saturday afternoon and Sunday, and then only for certain people. Not until the 1890s did it become universally understood, if not yet universally enjoyed, but an entitlement to relaxation was unquestionably on its way.

The irony in all this is that just as the world was getting more agreeable for most people – more brilliantly lit, more reliably plumbed, more leisured and pampered and gaudily entertaining – it was quietly falling apart for the likes of Mr Marsham. The agricultural crisis that began in the 1870s and ran on almost indefinitely was as palpably challenging to country parsons as it was to the wealthy landowners on whom they depended, and it was doubly difficult for those whose family wealth was tied to the land, as Mr Marsham's was.

By 1900, a parson's earnings were much less than half in real terms what they had been fifty years before. *Crockford's Clerical Directory* of 1903 bleakly recorded that a 'considerable section' of the clergy now lived at a level of 'bare subsistence'. A Reverend F. J. Bleasby, it further noted, had made 470 unsuccessful applications for a curacy, and finally, in humbling defeat, had entered a workhouse. The well-off parson was resoundingly and irremediably a thing of the past.

The rambling parsonages that had once made the life of a country clergyman commodious and agreeable were now for many just vast and leaky burdens. Many twentieth-century clergy, coming from more modest backgrounds and struggling on much reduced incomes, couldn't afford to maintain such spacious properties. A Mrs Lucy Burnett, wife of a country vicar in Yorkshire, plaintively explained to a church commission in 1933 just how big was the vicarage that she had to manage: 'If you played a brass band in my kitchen I don't think you could hear it in the drawing room,' she said. The responsibility for interior improvements fell to the incumbents, but increasingly they were too impoverished to effect any.

'Many a parsonage has passed twenty, thirty, even fifty years without any redecoration at all,' Alan Savidge wrote in a history of parsonages in 1964.

The simplest solution for the Church was to sell off the troublesome parsonages, and to build something smaller nearby. The Church of England Commissioners, the officials in charge of these disposals, were not always the most astute of businesspeople, it must be said. Anthony Jennings, in *The Old Rectory* (2009), notes how in 1983 they sold just over three hundred parsonages at an average price of £64,000, but spent an average of £76,000 on building much inferior replacements.

Of the 13,000 parsonages that existed in 1900, just 900 are still in Church of England ownership today. Our rectory was sold into private hands in 1978. (I don't know for how much.) Its history as a rectory lasted 127 years, during which time it was home to eight clergy. Curiously, all seven later rectors stayed longer in the house than the shadowy figure who built it. Thomas Marsham departed in 1861, after just ten years, to take up a new post as rector of Saxlingham, a position of almost exactly equal obscurity in a village twenty miles to the north, near the sea.

Why he built himself such a substantial house is a question that can now never be answered. Perhaps he hoped to impress some delightful young woman of his acquaintance, but she declined him and married another. Perhaps she did choose him, but died before they could wed. Both outcomes were common enough in the mid-nineteenth century and either would explain some of the rectory's design mysteries, such as the presence of a nursery and the vague femininity of the plum room, though nothing we can suggest can now ever be more than a guess. All that can be said is that whatever happiness he found in life it was not within the bounds of marriage.

We may at least hope that his relationship with his devoted housekeeper Miss Worm had some measure of warmth and affection, however awkwardly expressed. It was almost certainly the longest relationship of either of their lives. When Miss Worm died in 1899 at the age of seventy-six she had been his housekeeper for over half a century. In that same year the Marsham family estate at Stratton Strawless was sold in fifteen lots, presumably because no one could be found to buy it whole. The sale marked the end of four hundred years of prominence for the Marsham family in the county. Today all that remains as a reminder of that is a pub called the Marsham Arms in the nearby village of Hevingham.

Mr Marsham lived on for not quite six years more. He died in a retirement home in a nearby village in 1905. He was eighty-three years old and, apart from time away for schooling, had lived the whole of his life on Norfolk soil, within an area just slightly more than twenty miles across.

IV

We started here in the attic – a long time ago now, it seems – when I clambered up through the loft hatch to look for the source of a leak. (It turned out to be a slipped tile that was allowing rain through.) There, you may recall, I discovered a door that led out on to a space on the roof giving a view of the countryside. The other day, I hauled myself back up there for the first time since I began work on the book. I wondered vaguely if I would see the world differently now that I know a little about Mr Marsham and the circumstances in which he lived.

In fact, no. What was surprising to me was not how much the world below had changed since Mr Marsham's day but how little. A resurrected Mr Marsham obviously would be struck by some novelties – cars speeding along a road in the middle distance, a helicopter passing noisily overhead – but mostly he would gaze upon a landscape that was seemingly timeless and utterly familiar.

That air of permanence is of course a deception. It isn't that the landscape isn't changing, but just changing too slowly to be noticed, even over the course of 160 years or so. Go back far enough and you would see plenty of change. Travel five hundred years backwards and there would be almost nothing familiar except the church, a few hedgerows and field shapes and the dawdling line of some of the roads. Go a bit further than that and you might see the Roman fellow who dropped the phallic pendant with which we began the book. Go way back – to 400,000 years ago, say – and you would find lions, elephants and other exotic fauna grazing on arid plains. These were the creatures that left the bones that so fascinated early antiquaries like John Frere at nearby Hoxne. The site of his find is too distant to be seen from our roof, but the bones he collected could easily have come from animals that once grazed on our land.

Remarkably, what brought those animals to this part of the world was a climate just three degrees centigrade or so warmer than today. There are people alive now who will live in a Britain that warm again. Whether it will be a parched Serengeti or a verdant paradise of home-grown wines and year-round fruit is beyond the scope of this book to guess. What is certain is that it will be a very different place, and one to which future humans will have to adjust at something much faster than a geological pace.

One of the things not visible from our rooftop is how much energy and other inputs we require now to provide us with the ease and convenience that we have all come to expect in our lives. It's a lot – a shocking amount. Of the total energy produced on Earth since the Industrial Revolution began, half has been consumed in the last twenty years. Disproportionately it was consumed by us in the rich world; we are an exceedingly privileged fraction.

Today it takes the average citizen of Tanzania almost a year to produce the same volume of carbon emissions as is effortlessly generated every two and a half days by a European, or every twenty-eight hours by an American. We are, in short, able to live as we do because we use resources at hundreds of times the rate of most of the planet's other citizens. One day – and don't expect it to be a distant day – many of those six billion or so less well off people are bound to demand to have what we have, and to get it as easily as we got it, and that will require more resources than this planet can easily, or even conceivably, yield.

The greatest possible irony would be if in our endless quest to fill our lives with comfort and happiness we created a world that had neither. But that of course would be another book.

Bibliography

Abse, Joan, *John Ruskin: The Passionate Moralist*. London: Quartet Books, 1980.

Ackroyd, Peter, *Albion: The Origins of the English Imagination*. London: Chatto & Windus, 2002.

Acton, Liza, *Modern Cookery for Private Families*. London: Longman, Brown, Green and Longmans, 1858.

Adams, William Howard (ed.), *The Eye of Thomas Jefferson*. Washington: National Gallery of Art, 1976.

Addison, Sir William, *Farmhouses in the English Landscape*. London: Robert Hale, 1986.

Alcabes, Philip, *Dread: How Fear and Fantasy Have Fueled Epidemics from the Black Death to Avian Flu*. New York: Public Affairs, 2009.

Alexander, Boyd, *England's Wealthiest Son: A Study of William Beckford*. London: Centaur Press, 1962.

Allen, Edward, *How Buildings Work: The Natural Order of Architecture*. New York: Oxford University Press, 1980.

Amato, Ivan, *Stuff: The Materials the World Is Made Of*. New York: Basic Books, 1997.

Andrade, E. N. da C., *A Brief History of the Royal Society*. London: Royal Society, 1960.

Ariès, Philippe, *Centuries of Childhood: A Social History of Family Life*. London: Jonathan Cape, 1962.

Arnstein, Walter L., *Britain Yesterday and Today: 1830 to the Present*. Lexington, Mass.: D. C. Heath and Co., 1971.

Ashenburg, Katherine, *The Dirt on Clean: An Unsanitized History*. New York: North Point Press/Farrar, Straus and Giroux, 2007.

Ashton, Rosemary, *Thomas and Jane Carlyle: Portrait of a Marriage*. London: Chatto & Windus, 2001.

Aslet, Clive, *The American Country House*. New Haven: Yale University Press, 1990.

Ayres, James, *Domestic Interiors: The British Tradition 1500–1850*. New Haven: Yale University Press, 2003.

Baer, N. S., and R. Snethlage (eds), *Saving Our Architectural Heritage: The Conservation of Historic Stone Structures*. Chichester: John Wiley & Sons, 1997.

Baird, Rosemary, *Mistress of the House: Great Ladies and Grand Houses 1670–1830*. London: Weidenfeld & Nicolson, 2003.

Bakalar, Nicholas, *Where the Germs Are: A Scientific Safari*. New York: John Wiley & Sons, 2003.

Baker, Hollis S., *Furniture in the Ancient World: Origins and Evolution 3100–475 BC*. New York: Macmillan, 1966.

Baldon, Cleo, and I. B. Melchior, *Steps and Stairways*. New York: Rizzoli International, 1989.

Ball, Philip, *Bright Earth: The Invention of Colour*. London: Viking, 2001.

Balter, Michael, *The Goddess and the Bull: Çatalhöyük: An Archaeological Journey to the Dawn of Civilization*. New York: Free Press, 2005.

Barber, E. J. W., *Prehistoric Textiles: The Development of Cloth in the Neolithic and Bronze Ages, with Special Reference to the Aegean*. Princeton, N.J.: Princeton University Press, 1991.

——, *Women's Work: The First 20,000 Years; Women, Cloth and Society in Early Times*. New York: W. W. Norton, 1994.

Barker, Graeme, *The Agricultural Revolution in Prehistory: Why Did Foragers Become Farmers?* Oxford: Oxford University Press, 2006.

Barr, Andrew, *Drink: A Social History of America*. New York: Carroll & Graf, 1999.

Bascomb, Neal, *Higher: A Historic Race to the Sky and the Making of a City*. New York: Broadway Books, 2003.

Bates, Elizabeth Bidwell, and Jonathan L. Fairbanks, *American Furniture 1620 to the Present*. New York: Richard Marek Publishers, 1981.

Baugh, Albert C., and Thomas Cable, *A History of the English Language* (5th edn). Upper Saddle River, N.J.: Prentice Hall, 2002.

Bax, B. Anthony, *The English Parsonage*. London: John Murray, 1964.

Beard, Geoffrey, *The Work of Robert Adam*. Edinburgh: John Bartholomew & Son, 1978.

Beauchamp, K. G., *Exhibiting Electricity*. London: The Institution of Electrical Engineers, 1997.

Beckford, William (translated and edited by Boyd Alexander), *Life at Fonthill, 1807–1822: With Interludes in Paris and London*. London: R. Hart-Davis, 1957.

Beebe, Lucius, *The Big Spenders*. Garden City, New York: Doubleday, 1966.

Beeton, Mrs Isabella, *The Book of Household Management*. London: S. O. Beeton, 1861.

Belanger, Terry, *Lunacy and the Arrangement of Books*. New Castle, Delaware: Oak Knoll Press, 2003.

Bentley, Peter J., *The Undercover Scientist: Investigating the Mishaps of Everyday Life*. London: Random House, 2008.

Berenbaum, May R., *Bugs in the System: Insects and Their Impact on Human Affairs*. Reading, Mass.: Helix Books, 1995.

Beresford, John (ed.), *The Diary of a Country Parson: The Reverend James Woodforde* (5 vols). Oxford: Clarendon Press, 1924.

Bernstein, William, *A Splendid Exchange: How Trade Shaped the World*. London: Atlantic Books, 2008.

Berry, R. J. (ed.), *Biology of the House Mouse*. London: Zoological Society of London, 1981.

Best, Gary Dean, *The Dollar Decade: Mammon and the Machine in 1920s America*. Westport, Conn.: Praeger Publishers, 2003.

Binney, Marcus, *SAVE Britain's Heritage, 1975–2005: Thirty Years of Campaigning*. London: Scala Publishers, 2005.

Boardman, Barrington, *From Harding to Hiroshima*. New York: Dembner Books, 1985.

Bodanis, David, *The Secret Garden*. New York: Simon & Schuster, 1992.

——, *Electric Universe: The Shocking True Story of Electricity*. New York: Crown Publishers, 2005.

Boorstin, Daniel J., *The Americans: The National Experience*. New York: Random House, 1965.

——, *The Discoverers*. London: Penguin, 1983.

Boucher, Bruce, *Palladio: The Architect in His Time*. New York: Abbeville Press, 1994.

Bourke, Joanna, *Fear: A Cultural History*. London: Virago Press, 2005.

Bourne, Jonathan, and Vanessa Brett, *Lighting in the Domestic Interior: Renaissance to Art Nouveau*. London: Sotheby's, 1991.

Bourne, Russell, *Cradle of Violence: How Boston's Waterfront Mobs Ignited the American Revolution*. Hoboken, N.J.: John Wiley & Sons, 2006.

Bowden, Mark, *Pitt Rivers: The Life and Archaeological Work of Lieutenant-General August Henry Lane Fox Pitt Rivers, DCL, FRS, FSA*. Cambridge: Cambridge University Press, 1991.

Bowers, Brian, *A History of Electric Light and Power*. London: Science Museum, 1982.

Brady, Patricia, *Martha Washington: An American Life*. New York: Viking, 2005.

Brand, Stewart, *How Buildings Learn: What Happens After They're Built*. New York: Viking, 1994.

Brands, H. W., *The First American: The Life and Times of Benjamin Franklin*. London: Doubleday, 2000.

Breen, T. H., *The Marketplace of Revolution: How Consumer Politics*

Shaped American Independence. Oxford: Oxford University Press, 2004.

Brett, Gerard, *Dinner Is Served: A History of Dining in England, 1400–1900*. London: Rupert Hart-Davis, 1968.

Bridenbaugh, Carl, *Early Americans*. New York: Oxford University Press, 1981.

Briggs, Asa, *Victorian People: Some Reassessments of People, Institutions, Ideas and Events, 1851–1867*. London: Odhams Press, 1954.

Brimblecombe, Peter, *The Big Smoke: A History of Air Pollution in London Since Medieval Times*. London: Methuen, 1987.

Brittain-Catlin, Timothy, *The English Parsonage in the Early Nineteenth Century*. Reading: Spire Books, 2008.

Brodie, Fawn M., *Thomas Jefferson: An Intimate History*. New York: W. W. Norton, 1974.

Brooke, Iris, *English Costume of the Seventeenth Century*. London: Adam & Charles Black, 1934.

Brooks, John, *Once in Golconda: A True Drama of Wall Street 1920–1938*. New York: Harper & Row, 1969.

Brothwell, Don and Patricia, *Food in Antiquity: A Survey of the Diet of Early Peoples*. Baltimore: Johns Hopkins University Press, 1969.

Brown, Kevin, *The Pox: The Life and Near Death of a Very Social Disease*. Stroud, Gloucestershire: Sutton Publishing, 2006.

Bruce, Robert V., *Bell: Alexander Graham Bell and the Conquest of Solitude*. London: Victor Gollancz, 1973.

Brunskill, Ian, and Andrew Sanders, *Great Victorian Lives: An Era in Obituaries*. London: Times Books, 2007.

Brunskill, Ronald, *Brick Building in Britain*. London: Victor Gollancz, 1990.

——, and Alec Clifton-Taylor, *English Brickwork*. London: Hyperion/Ward Lock, 1977.

Burchard, John, and Albert Bush-Brown, *The Architecture of America: A Social and Cultural History*. Boston: Little, Brown, 1961.

Burkhardt, Frederick, and Sydney Smith (eds), *The Correspondence of Charles Darwin, 1821–1836*. Cambridge: Cambridge University Press, 1985.

Burns, Ric, and James Sanders, *New York: An Illustrated History*. New York: Knopf, 1999.

Burrows, Edwin G., and Mike Wallace, *Gotham: A History of New York City to 1898*. New York: Oxford University Press, 1999.

Bushman, Richard L., *The Refinement of America: Persons, Houses, Cities*. New York: Vintage Books, 1992.

Busvine, James R., *Insects and Hygiene: The Biology and Control of Insect Pests of Medical and Domestic Importance in Britain*. London: Methuen, 1951.

Byles, Jeff, *Rubble: Unearthing the History of Demolition*. New York: Harmony Books, 2005.

Cadbury, Deborah, *Seven Wonders of the Industrial World*. London: Harper Perennial, 2004.

Calman, Sir Kenneth C., *Medical Education: Past, Present and Future*. Edinburgh: Churchill Livingstone, 2007.

Campbell, James, Eric John and Patrick Wormald, *The Anglo-Saxons*. Oxford: Phaidon, 1982.

Cannadine, David, *The Pleasures of the Past*. London: Collins, 1989.

——, *Aspects of Aristocracy: Grandeur and Decline in Modern Britain*. New Haven: Yale University Press, 1994.

——, *The Decline and Fall of the British Aristocracy*. London: Penguin, 2005.

Carlyle, Thomas and Jane (Charles R. Sanders, ed.), *The Collected Letters of Thomas Jane Welsh Carlyle* (37 volumes). Durham, North Carolina: Duke University Press, 1970–2009.

Carpenter, Kenneth J., *The History of Scurvy and Vitamin C*. Cambridge: Cambridge University Press, 1986.

Carson, Gerald, *The Polite Americans*. New York: William Morrow, 1966.

Carter, Gwendolen M., *The Government of the United Kingdom*. New York: Harcourt Brace Jovanovich, 1972.

Carter, W. Hodding, *Flushed: How the Plumber Saved Civilization*. New York: Atria Books, 2006.

Carver, Martin, *Sutton Hoo: Burial Ground of Kings*. London: British Museum Press, 1998.

Caspall, John, *Fire and Light in the Home pre-1820*. Woodbridge, Suffolk: Antique Collectors Club, 1987.

Cassidy, Tina, *Birth: A History*. London: Chatto & Windus, 2007.

Catchpole, Antonia, David Clark and Robert Peberdy, *Burford: Buildings and People in a Cotswold Town*. London: Phillimore, 2008.

Catling, Harold, *The Spinning Mule*. Newton Abbot: David & Charles, 1970.

Chadwick, Edwin, *Report from His Majesty's Commissioners for Inquiring into the Administration and Practical Operation of the Poor Laws*. London: B. Fellowes, 1834.

Chadwick, George F., *The Works of Sir Joseph Paxton*. London: Architectural Press, 1961.

Chadwick, Owen, *The Victorian Church*. London: Adam & Charles Black, 1970.

Chandos, John, *Boys Together: English Public Schools 1800–1864*. London: Hutchinson, 1984.

Chisholm, Kate, *Fanny Burney: Her Life, 1752–1840*. London: Chatto & Windus, 1998.

Churchill, Allen, *The Splendor Seekers*. New York: Grosset & Dunlap, 1974.

Cieraad, Irene (ed.), *At Home: An Anthropology of Domestic Space*. Syracuse, New York: Syracuse University Press, 1999.

Clark, H. F., *The English Landscape Garden*. London: Pleiades Books, 1948.

Cleland, Liza, Mary Harlow and Lloyd Llewellyn-Jones (eds), *The Clothed Body in the Ancient World*. London: Oxbow Books, 2005.

Clifton-Taylor, Alec, *The Pattern of English Building*. London: Faber and Faber, 1987.

Cloudsley-Thompson, J. L., *Spiders, Scorpions, Centipedes and Mites*. London: Pergamon Press, 1968.

Cockayne, Emily, *Hubbub: Filth, Noise and Stench in England 1600–1770*. New Haven: Yale University Press, 2007.

Cohen, Deborah, *Household Gods: The British and Their Possessions*. New Haven: Yale University Press, 2006.

Coleridge, Anthony, *Chippendale Furniture, Circa 1745–1765*. New York: Clarkson N. Potter, 1968.

Colley, Linda, *Britons: Forging the Nation 1707–1837*. London: Pimlico, 1992.

Collingwood, W. G., *The Life of John Ruskin*. London: Methuen and Co., 1900.

Collins, Irene, *Jane Austen: The Parson's Daughter*. London: Hambledon Press, 1998.

Colquhoun, Kate, *A Thing in Disguise: The Visionary Life of Joseph Paxton*. London: Harper Perennial, 2004.

——, *Taste: The Story of Britain Through Its Cooking*. London: Bloomsbury, 2007.

Corson, Richard, *Fashions in Hair: The First Five Thousand Years*. London: Peter Owen, 1965.

——, *Fashions in Makeup from Ancient to Modern Times*. London: Peter Owen, 2003.

Cossons, Neil (ed.), *The Making of the Modern World: Milestones of Science and Technology*. London: John Murray, 1992.

Cowan, Henry J., *The Master Builders: A History of Structural and Environmental Design from Ancient Egypt to the Nineteenth Century*. New York: John Wiley & Sons, 1977.

Cowan, Ruth Schwartz, *More Work for Mother: The Ironies of Household Technology from the Open Hearth to the Microwave*. New York: Basic Books, 1983.

Coward, Barry, *The Stuart Age: England, 1603–1714* (2nd edn). London: Longman, 1980.

Cox, Margaret, *Life and Death in Spitalfields, 1700 to 1850*. York: Council for British Archaeology, 1996.

Crinson, Mark, and Jules Lubbock, *Architecture, Art or Profession?*

Three Hundred Years of Architectural Education in Britain. Manchester: Prince of Wales Institute of Architecture, 1994.

Crompton, Frank, *Workhouse Children*. London: Sutton Publishing, 1997.

Crossley, Fred H., *Timber Building in England: From Early Times to the End of the Seventeenth Century*. London: B. T. Batsford, 1951.

Crowfoot, Elisabeth, Frances Pritchard and Kay Staniland, *Textiles and Clothing c. 1150–c. 1450*. London: HMSO, 1992.

Cruickshank, Dan, *The Story of Britain's Best Buildings*. London: BBC, 2002.

Crystal, David, *The Stories of English*. London: Allen Lane, 2004.

Cullwick, Hannah, *The Diaries of Hannah Cullwick, Victorian Maidservant*. London: Virago, 1984.

Cummings, Richard Osborn, *The American and His Food: A History of Food Habits in the United States*. Chicago: University of Chicago Press, 1970.

Cunningham, Hugh, *The Children of the Poor: Representations of Childhood Since the Seventeenth Century*. Oxford: Blackwell, 1991.

Cunnington, C. Willett, and Phillis Cunnington, *The History of Underclothes*. London: Faber and Faber, 1951.

Curl, James Stevens, *The Victorian Celebration of Death*. London: Sutton Publishing, 2000.

Dale, Antony, *James Wyatt: Architect, 1746–1813*. Oxford: Basil Blackwell, 1936.

Dalzell, Robert F., and Lee Baldwin Dalzell, *George Washington's Mount Vernon: At Home in Revolutionary America*. Oxford: Oxford University Press, 1998.

Daniels, Jonathan, *The Time Between the Wars: Armistice to Pearl Harbor*. New York: Doubleday, 1966.

Daumas, Maurice (ed.), *A History of Technology and Invention: Progress Through the Ages* (3 vols). New York: Crown Publishing, 1979.

642   AT HOME

David, Saul, *The Indian Mutiny: 1857*. London: Viking, 2002.

Davidson, Marshall B., *The American Heritage History of Colonial America*. Boston: American Heritage, 1967.

Davies, Norman, *The Isles: A History*. London: Macmillan, 1999.

Davies, Stevie, *A Century of Troubles: England 1600–1700*. London: Pan Macmillan/Channel 4, 2001.

Davin, Anna, *Growing Up Poor: Home, School and Street Life in London, 1870–1914*. London: Rivers Oram Press, 1996.

Davis, Dorothy, *A History of Shopping*. London: Routledge & Kegan Paul, 1966.

Davis, Pearce, *The Development of the American Glass Industry*. Cambridge, Mass.: Harvard University Press, 1949.

De Botton, Alain, *The Architecture of Happiness*. New York: Pantheon, 2006.

Deetz, James, *In Small Things Forgotten: The Archaeology of Early American Life*. New York: Doubleday, 1977.

DeLaine, J., and D. E. Johnston (eds), *Roman Baths and Bathing*. Portsmouth, Rhode Island: Journal of Roman Archaeology, 1999.

Desmond, Adrian, and James Moore, *Darwin*. London: Michael Joseph, 1991.

de Sola Pool, Ithiel, *Forecasting the Telephone: A Retrospective Technology Assessment*. Norwood, N. J.: Ablex Publishing, 1983.

Díaz-Andreu, Margarita, *A World History of Nineteenth-Century Archaeology: Nationalism, Colonialism, and the Past*. Oxford: Oxford University Press, 2007.

Dillon, Francis, *The Pilgrims*. Garden City, N.Y.: Doubleday, 1975.

Dirks, Nicholas B., *The Scandal of Empire: India and the Creation of Imperial Britain*. Cambridge, Mass.: Belknap Press, 2006.

Dolin, Eric J., *Leviathan: The History of Whaling in America*. New York: W. W. Norton, 2007.

Douglas, Ann, *Terrible Honesty: Mongrel Manhattan in the 1920s*. New York: Noonday Press/Farrar, Straus and Giroux, 1995.

Downes, Kerry, *Sir John Vanbrugh: A Biography*. London: Sidgwick & Jackson, 1987.

Dutton, Ralph, *The English Country House*. London: B. T. Batsford, 1935.

Dyer, Christopher, *Making a Living in the Middle Ages: The People of Britain 850–1520*. New Haven: Yale University Press, 2002.

Ede, Janet, and Norma Virgoe, *Religious Worship in Norfolk: The 1851 Census of Accommodation and Attendance at Worship*. Norwich: Norfolk Record Society, 1998.

Eden, Mary, and Richard Carrington, *The Philosophy of the Bed*. London: Hutchinson, 1961.

Ekirch, A. Roger, *At Day's Close: A History of Nighttime*. London: Phoenix, 2006.

Elliott, Charles, *The Transplanted Gardener*. New York: Lyons & Burford, 1995.

Emsley, John, *The Elements of Murder: A History of Poison*. Oxford: Oxford University Press, 2005.

Evans, G. Blakemore (ed.), *The Riverside Shakespeare*. Boston: Houghton Mifflin Co., 1974.

Evenson, A. Edward, *The Telephone Patent Conspiracy of 1876: The Elisha Gray–Alexander Bell Controversy and Its Many Players*. Jefferson, N.C.: McFarland and Co., 2000.

Fagan, Brian, *The Long Summer: How Climate Changed Civilization*. London: Granta, 2004.

Farrell-Beck, Jane, and Colleen Gau, *Uplift: The Bra in America*. Philadelphia: University of Pennsylvania Press, 2002.

Felstead, Alison, Jonathan Franklin and L. Pinfield, *Directory of British Architects, 1834–1900*. London: Mansell, 1993.

Fernández-Armesto, Felipe, *Food: A History*. London: Pan, 2001.

Filby, Frederick A., *A History of Food Adulteration and Analysis*. London: George Allen & Unwin, 1934.

Flanders, Judith, *The Victorian House: Domestic Life from Childbirth to Deathbed*. London: HarperCollins, 2003.

——, *Consuming Passions: Leisure and Pleasure in Victorian Britain*. London: Harper Perennial, 2007.

Flannery, Tim, *The Weather Makers: The History and Future Impact of Climate Change*. Melbourne: Text Publishing, 2005.

Fletcher, Anthony, *Growing Up in England: The Experience of Childhood, 1600–1914*. New Haven: Yale University Press, 2008.

Forbes, Esther, *Paul Revere and the World He Lived In*. Boston: Houghton Mifflin, 1942.

Fort, Tom, *The Grass Is Greener: Our Love Affair with the Lawn*. London: HarperCollins, 2000.

Fortey, Adrian, *Objects of Desire: Design and Society Since 1750*. London: Thames & Hudson, 1995.

Foss, Michael, *The Age of Patronage: The Arts in Society 1660–1750*. London: Hamish Hamilton, 1971.

Fowler, Brenda, *Iceman: Uncovering the Life and Times of a Prehistoric Man Found in an Alpine Glacier*. London: Macmillan, 2001.

Fraser, Antonia, *King Charles II*. London: Weidenfeld & Nicolson, 1979.

——, *The Weaker Vessel: Woman's Lot in Seventeenth-Century England*. London: Phoenix Press, 1984.

Freedman, Paul, *Out of the East: Spices and the Medieval Imagination*. New Haven: Yale University Press, 2008.

Gardiner, Juliet, *Wartime: Britain 1939–1945*. London: Headline, 2004.

Garrett, Elisabeth Donaghy, *At Home: The American Family 1750–1870*. New York: Henry N. Abrams, 1990.

Garrett, Laurie, *The Coming Plague: Newly Emerging Diseases in a World Out of Balance*. New York: Farrar, Straus and Giroux, 1994.

Gascoigne, John, *Joseph Banks and the English Enlightenment:*

Useful Knowledge and Polite Culture. Cambridge: Cambridge University Press, 1994.

Gayle, Margot, and Carol Gayle, *Cast-Iron Architecture in America: The Significance of James Bogardus.* New York: W. W. Norton & Co., 1998.

Gelis, Jacques, *History of Childbirth: Fertility, Pregnancy and Birth in Early Modern Europe.* Boston: Northeastern University Press, 1991.

George, Wilma, *Biologist Philosopher: A Study of the Life and Writings of Alfred Russel Wallace.* London: Abelard-Schuman, 1964.

Gerin, Winifred, *Charlotte Brontë: The Evolution of Genius.* Oxford: Clarendon Press, 1967.

Gilbert, Christopher, *The Life and Works of Thomas Chippendale.* London: Christie's, 1978.

Girouard, Mark, *Life in the English Country House: A Social and Architectural History.* New Haven: Yale University Press, 1978.

——, *The Victorian Country House.* New Haven: Yale University Press, 1979.

——, *Life in the French Country House.* New York: Alfred A. Knopf, 2000.

Gloag, John, *English Furniture.* London: Adam & Charles Black, 1952.

Gloag, John, and Derek Bridgwater, *A History of Cast Iron in Architecture.* London: George Allen & Unwin, 1948.

Glynn, Ian, and Jennifer Glynn, *The Life and Death of Smallpox.* London: Profile Books, 2004.

Godfrey, Eleanor S., *The Development of English Glassmaking 1560–1640.* Oxford: Clarendon Press, 1975.

Goodman, Dena, and Kathryn Norberg, *Furnishing the Eighteenth Century: What Furniture Can Tell Us About the European and American Past.* London: Routledge, 2007.

Goodwin, Lorine Swainston, *The Pure Food, Drink, and Drug Crusaders, 1879–1914.* Jefferson, N. C.: McFarland & Co., 1999.

Gordon, John Steele, *An Empire of Wealth: The Epic History of American Economic Power*. New York: Harper Perennial, 2005.

Gosnell, Mariana, *Ice: The Nature, the History, and the Uses of an Astonishing Science*. New York: Alfred A. Knopf, 2005.

Gotch, J. Alfred, *The Growth of the English House: From Early Feudal Times to the Close of the Eighteenth Century* (2nd edn). London: Batsford, 1909.

Gray, Charlotte, *Reluctant Genius: Alexander Graham Bell and the Passion for Invention*. New York: Arcade Publishing, 2006.

Green, Charles, *Sutton Hoo: The Excavation of a Royal Ship-Burial*. London: Merlin Press, 1963.

Green, Harvey, *The Light of the Home: An Intimate View of the Lives of Women in Victorian America*. New York: Pantheon, 1983.

Green, Sally, *Prehistorian: A Biography of Vere Gordon Childe*. Bradford-on-Avon, Wiltshire: Moonraker Press, 1981.

Grenville, Jane, *Medieval Housing*. London: Leicester University Press, 1997.

Grohskopf, Bernice, *The Treasure of Sutton Hoo: Ship-Burial for an Anglo-Saxon King*. London: Robert Hale, 1971.

Grosvenor, Edwin S., and Morgan Wesson, *Alexander Graham Bell: The Life and Times of the Man Who Invented the Telephone*. New York: Harry N. Abrams, 1997.

Guinness, Desmond, and Julius Trousdale Sadler, Jr, *The Palladian Style in England, Ireland and America*. London: Thames & Hudson, 1976.

Halliday, Stephen, *The Great Stink of London: Sir Joseph Bazalgete and the Cleansing of the Victorian Capital*. Stroud, Gloucesstershire: Sutton Publishing, 1999.

Halperin, John, *The Life of Jane Austen*. Baltimore: Johns Hopkins University Press, 1984.

Hanson, Neil, *The Dreadful Judgement: The True Story of the Great Fire of London, 1666*. London: Doubleday, 2001.

——, *The Confident Hope of a Miracle: The True History of the Spanish Armada*. London: Doubleday, 2003.

Hardyment, Christina, *From Mangle to Microwave: The Mechanization of Household Work*. Cambridge: Polity Press, 1985.

——, *Home Comfort: A History of Domestic Arrangements*. London: Viking, 1992.

Harris, Eileen, *Going to Bed*. London: HMSO, 1981.

——, *Keeping Warm*. London: Victoria & Albert Museum, 1982.

——, *The Genius of Robert Adam: His Interiors*. New Haven: Yale University Press, 2001.

Hart-Davis, Adam, *What the Tudors and Stuarts Did for Us*. London: Boxtree/Pan Macmillan, 2002.

Hartley, Sir Harold, *The Royal Society: Its Origins and Founders*. London: Royal Society, 1960.

Harvey, John, *English Medieval Architects: A Biographical Dictionary Down to 1550*. London: B. T. Batsford, 1954.

Headley, Gwyn, and Wim Meulenkamp, *Follies: A National Trust Guide*. London: Jonathan Cape, 1986.

Heaton, Trevor (ed.), *Norfolk Century*. Norwich: Eastern Daily Press, 1999.

Heffer, Simon, *Moral Desperado: A Life of Thomas Carlyle*. London: Weidenfeld & Nicolson, 1995.

Hemlow, Joyce (ed.), *The Journals and Letters of Fanny Burney (Madame d'Arblay)*, vol.6. Oxford: Clarendon Press, 1975.

Henderson, W. O., *The Life of Friedrich Engels*. London: Frank Cass, 1976.

Herbert, Victor, *Nutrition Cultism: Facts and Fictions*. Philadelphia: George F. Sticley Co., 1980.

Hibbert, Christopher, *London: The Biography of a City*. New York: William Morrow & Co., 1969.

——, *The Court at Windsor: A Domestic History*. London: Penguin, 1982.

——, *Redcoats and Rebels: The War for America, 1770–1781*. London: Grafton Books, 1990.

——, *Queen Victoria: A Personal History*. London: HarperCollins, 2000.

——, *Elizabeth I: A Personal History of the Virgin Queen*. London: Penguin, 2001.

Hill, Rosemary, *Stonehenge*. London: Profile Books, 2008.

——, *God's Architect: Pugin and the Building of Romantic Britain*. London: Penguin, 2008.

Hirst, Francis W., *Life and Letters of Thomas Jefferson*. London: Macmillan, 1926.

Hix, John, *The Glass House*. London: Phaidon, 1974.

Hobsbawm, E. J., *Industry and Empire*. London: Penguin, 1968.

Hodder, Ian, *The Leopard's Tale: Revealing the Mysteries of Çatalhöyük*. London: Thames & Hudson, 2006.

Holderness, B. A., *Pre-Industrial England: Economy and Society from 1500 to 1750*. London: J. M. Dent & Sons, 1976.

Holme, Thea, *The Carlyles at Home*. London: Persephone, 2002.

Horn, Pamela, *The Rise and Fall of the Victorian Servant*. Dublin: Gill and Macmillan, 1975.

——, *Pleasures and Pastimes in Victorian Britain*. Stroud, Gloucestershire: Sutton Publishing, 1999.

Howarth, Patrick, *The Year Is 1851*. London: William Collins Publishers, 1951.

Hoyt, William G., and Walter B Langbein, *Floods*. Princeton, N.J.: Princeton University Press, 1955.

Hughes, Kathryn, *The Short Life and Long Times of Mrs Beeton*. London: Fourth Estate, 2005.

Hunt, Tristram, *Building Jerusalem: The Rise and Fall of the Victorian City*. London: Phoenix, 2005.

Hutchinson, Horace G., *Life of Sir John Lubbock, Lord Avebury*. London: Macmillan, 1914.

Hyam, Ronald, *Britain's Imperial Century, 1815–1914: A Study of Empire and Expansion*. Basingstoke: Palgrave/Macmillan, 2002.

Inwood, Stephen, *A History of London*. London: Macmillan, 1998.

——, *City of Cities: The Birth of Modern London*. London: Macmillan, 2005.

Israel, Paul, *Edison: A Life of Invention*. New York: John Wiley & Sons, 1998.

Jackson-Stops, Gervase, *The Country House in Perspective*. London: Pavilion, 1990.

Jacobs, Jane, *The Economy of Cities*. London: Jonathan Cape, 1970.

Jenkins, David (ed.), *The Cambridge History of Western Textiles* (2 vols). Cambridge: Cambridge University Press, 2003.

Jenkins, Simon, *England's Thousand Best Houses*. London: Penguin, 2004.

Jennings, Anthony, *The Old Rectory: The Story of the English Parsonage*. London: Continuum, 2009.

Jespersen, Otto, *Growth and Structure of the English Language* (9th edn). Garden City, N.Y: Doubleday, 1956.

John, Eric, *Reassessing Anglo-Saxon England*. Manchester: Manchester University Press, 1996.

Johnson, Malcolm, *St Martin-in-the-Fields*. Chichester, West Sussex: Phillimore & Co., 2005.

Johnson, Matthew, *Housing Culture: Traditional Architecture in an English Landscape*. London: UCL, 1993.

Johnston, Shirley, *Palm Beach Houses*. New York: Rizzoli International, 1991.

Jokilehto, Jukka, *A History of Architectural Conservation*. Oxford: Butterworth-Heinemann, 1999.

Jones, Maldwyn Allen, *American Immigration*. Chicago: University of Chicago Press, 1960.

Joy, Edward T., *Getting Dressed*. London: Victoria and Albert Museum, 1981.

Jupp, Peter C., and Clare Gittings, *Death in England*. Manchester: Manchester University Press, 1999.

Kay, Jane Holtz, *Lost Boston*. Boston: Houghton-Mifflin, 1980.

Keay, John, *The Spice Route: A History*. London: John Murray, 2005.

Kelly, Alison, *The Book of English Fireplaces*. London: Country Life Books, 1968.

——, *Mrs Coade's Stone*. Upton-upon-Severn: Self-Publishing Association/Georgian Group, 1999.

Kelly, Ian, *Beau Brummell: The Ultimate Dandy*. London: Hodder & Stoughton, 2005.

Keneally, Thomas, *The Great Shame and the Triumph of the Irish in the English-Speaking World*. New York: Nan Talese/Doubleday, 1999.

King, Ross, *The Judgment of Paris: The Revolutionary Decade That Gave the World Impressionism*. New York: Walker & Co., 2006.

Kipple, Kenneth F., and K. C. Ornelas (eds), *The Cambridge World History of Food*. Cambridge: Cambridge University Press, 2000.

Kisseloff, Jeff, *You Must Remember This: An Oral History of Manhattan from the 1890s to World War II*. New York: Harcourt Brace Jovanovich, 1989.

Kostof, Spiro, *America by Design*. New York: Oxford University Press, 1987.

Koven, Seth, *Slumming: Sexual and Social Politics in Victorian London*. Princeton, N.J.: Princeton University Press, 2004.

Kronenberger, Louis (ed.), *Atlantic Brief Lives: A Biographical Companion to the Arts*. Boston: Atlantic Monthly Press, 1965.

Kurlansky, Mark, *Salt: A World History*. London: Vintage, 2003.

——, *The Big Oyster: New York in the World, a Molluscular History*. London: Jonathan Cape, 2006.

Kyvig, David E., *Daily Life in the United States, 1920–1939*. Westport, Conn.: Greenwood Press, 2002.

Lacey, Robert, *Sir Walter Ralegh*. London: History Book Club, 1973.

——, and Danny Danziger, *The Year 1000: What Life Was Like at the Turn of the First Millennium*. London: Abacus, 2003.

Laing, Alastair, *Lighting: The Arts and Living*. London: Victoria & Albert Museum, 1982.

Laing, Lloyd, *The Archaeology of Late Celtic Britain and Ireland, c. 400–1200 AD*. London: Methuen, 1975.

Lamb, H. H., *Historic Storms of the North Sea, British Isles and Northwest Europe*. Cambridge: Cambridge University Press, 1991.

Lambton, Lucinda, *Vanishing Victoriana*. London: Elsevier/Phaidon, 1976.

——, *Lucinda Lambton's A to Z of Britain*. London: HarperCollins, 1996.

Lancaster, John, *Engineering Catastrophes: Causes and Effects of Major Accidents*. Cambridge: Abington Publishing, 1997.

Larwood, Jacob, *The Story of London's Parks*. London: Chatto & Windus, 1881.

Lasdun, Susan, *The English Park: Royal, Private and Public*. London: Andre Deutsch, 1991.

Laslett, Peter, *The World We Have Lost: England Before the Industrial Age* (2nd edn). New York: Scribner, 1993.

Leahy, Kevin, *Anglo-Saxon Crafts*. London: Tempus, 2003.

Leapman, Michael, *The World for a Shilling: How the Great Exhibition of 1851 Shaped a Nation*. London: Headline, 2001.

——, *Inigo: The Troubled Life of Inigo Jones, Architect of the English Renaissance*. London: Headline, 2003.

Lees-Milne, James, *Earls of Creation: Five Great Patrons of Eighteenth-Century Art*. London: Hamish Hamilton, 1962.

Lehmann, Gilly, *The British Housewife: Cookery-Books, Cooking and Society in Eighteenth-Century Britain*. Totnes: Prospect Books, 2003.

Levi, Peter, *The Life and Times of William Shakespeare*. London: Macmillan, 1998.

Lewis, R. A., *Edwin Chadwick and the Public Health Movement, 1832–1854*. London: Longmans, Green and Co., 1952.

Lind, Carla, *The Lost Buildings of Frank Lloyd Wright*. London: Thames & Hudson, 1996.

Lindsay, Jack, *1764: The Hurlyburly of Daily Life Exemplified in One Year of the Eighteenth Century*. London: Frederick Muller, 1959.

Lingeman, Richard, *Small Town America: A Narrative History 1620–The Present*. New York: G. P. Putnam's Sons, 1980.

Little, Lester D. (ed.), *Plague and the End of Antiquity: The Plague of 541–750*. Cambridge: Cambridge University Press, 2007.

Littlejohn, David, *The Fate of the English Country House*. Oxford: Oxford University Press, 1997.

Lofts, Norah, *Domestic Life in England*. London: Weidenfeld & Nicolson, 1976.

Longford, Elizabeth, *Wellington: A New Biography*. Stroud, Gloucestershire: Sutton Publishing, 2001.

Loudon, Mrs, *Practical Instructions in Gardening for Ladies*. London: John Murray, 1841.

Lovill, Justin (ed.), *Ringing Church Bells to Ward Off Thunderstorms and Other Curiosities from the Original Notes and Queries*. London: Bunbury Press, 2009.

Lubbock, Jules, *The Tyranny of Taste: The Politics of Architecture and Design in Britain 1550–1960*. New Haven: Yale University Press, 1995.

Lucie-Smith, Edward, *Furniture: A Concise History*. New York: Oxford University Press, 1979.

Luyrette, Henri, *Gustave Eiffel*. New York: Rizzoli International, 1985.

Lynes, Russell, *The Domesticated Americans*. New York: Harper & Row, 1963.

Macinnis, Peter, *The Killer Beans of Calabar and Other Stories*. Sydney: Allen & Unwin, 2004.

Mackay, James A., *Sounds Out of Silence: A Life of Alexander Graham Bell*. Edinburgh: Mainstream Publishing, 1997.

Maher, James T., *The Twilight of Splendor: Chronicles of the Age of American Palaces*. Boston: Little, Brown, 1975.

Mann, Charles C., *1491: New Revelations of the Americas Before Columbus*. New York: Vintage, 2005.

Margetson, Stella, *The Long Party: High Society in the Twenties and*

Thirties. Farnborough: D. C. Heath, 1974.

Mark, Robert, *Light, Wind and Structure: The Mystery of the Master Builders*. Cambridge, Mass.: MIT Press, 1990.

Markham, Violet R., *Paxton and the Bachelor Duke*. London: Hodder & Stoughton, 1935.

Marsden, Christopher, *The English at the Seaside*. London: Collins, 1947.

Marston, Maurice, *Sir Edwin Chadwick*. London: Leonard Parsons, 1925.

Mathias, Peter, *The First Industrial Nation: An Economic History of Britain, 1700–1914* (2nd edn). London: Methuen, 1983.

Matthews, Leonard H. (ed.), *The Whale*. London: George Allen & Unwin, 1968.

McCurdy, Howard E., *Space and the American Imagination*. Washington: Smithsonian Institution Press, 1997.

McCusker, John J., and Russell R. Menard, *The Economy of British America, 1607–1789*. Chapel Hill: University of North Carolina Press, 1985.

McEwen, Indra Kagis, *Vitruvius: Writing the Body of Architecture*. Cambridge, Massachusetts: MIT Press, 2003.

McGee, Harold, *On Food and Cooking: The Science and Lore of the Kitchen*. London: Unwin Hyman, 1986.

McLaughlin, Jack, *Jefferson and Monticello: The Biography of a Builder*. New York: Henry Holt, 1988.

McPhee, John, *In Suspect Terrain*. New York: Noonday Press/Farrar, Straus & Giroux, 1987.

McWilliams, James E., *A Revolution in Eating: How the Quest for Food Shaped America*. New York: Columbia University Press, 2005.

Meacham, Standish, *Life Apart: The English Working Class 1880–1914*. London: Thames & Hudson, 1977.

Melosi, Martin V., *Garbage in the Cities: Refuse, Reform and the Environment 1880–1980*. College Station: Texas A&M University Press, 1981.

——, *The Sanitary City: Urban Infrastructure in America from Colonial Times to the Present*. Baltimore: Johns Hopkins University Press, 2000.

Mennim, Michael, *Hall Houses*. York: William Sessions, 2005.

Mercer, David, *The Telephone: The Life Story of a Technology*. Westport, Conn.: Greenwood Press, 2006.

Mercer, Eric, *Furniture 700–1700*. London: Weidenfeld & Nicolson, 1969.

Miles, David, *The Tribes of Britain*. London: Weidenfield & Nicolson, 2005.

Miller, Ross, *American Apocalypse: The Great Fire and the Myth of Chicago*. Chicago: University of Chicago Press, 1990.

Mingay, G. E. (ed.), *The Agricultural Revolution: Changes in Agriculture 1650–1880*. London: Adam & Charles Black, 1997.

Mitchell, James K., and Kenichi Soga, *Fundamentals of Soil Behavior*. New York: John Wiley & Sons, 2005.

Mitford, Nancy, *The Sun King: Louis XIV at Versailles*. London: Sphere, 1969.

Moran, Joe, *Queuing for Beginners: The Story of Daily Life from Breakfast to Bedtime*. London: Profile Books, 2007.

Mordaunt Crook, J., *The Rise of the Nouveaux Riches: Style and Status in Victorian and Edwardian Architecture*. London: John Murray, 1999.

Morley, John, *Death, Heaven and the Victorians*. London: Studio Vista, 1971.

Morris, Richard, *Churches in the Landscape*. London: J. M. Dent & Sons, 1989.

Mowl, Timothy, *William Beckford: Composing for Mozart*. London: John Murray, 1998.

Moxham, Roy, *Tea: Addiction, Exploitation, and Empire*. London: Constable, 2003.

Mumford, Lewis, *The City in History: Its Transformations and its Prospects*. London: Sector & Warburg, 1961.

Murphy, Shirley Forster, *Our Homes, and How to Make Them Healthy*. London: Cassell, 1883.

Nasaw, David, *Going Out: The Rise and Fall of Public Amusements*. New York: Basic Books, 1993.

Newman, Lucile F. (ed.), *Hunger in History: Food Shortage, Poverty and Deprivation*. Oxford: Basil Blackwell, 1990.

Newton, Norman T., *Design on the Land: The Development of Landscape Architecture*. Cambridge, Mass.: Belknap Press, 1971.

Oakley, J. Ronald, *God's Country: America in the Fifties*. New York: Dembner Books, 1986.

Oliphant, Margaret, *The Curate in Charge* (2nd edn). London: Macmillan, 1876.

Olmsted, Frederick Law, *Walks and Talks of an American Farmer in England*. London: David Bogue, 1852.

Olson, Sherry H., *Baltimore: The Building of an American City*. Baltimore: Johns Hopkins University Press, 1980.

Ordish, George, *The Great Wine Blight*. London: Sidgwick & Jackson, 1987.

Owen, David, *The Walls Around Us: The Thinking Person's Guide to How a House Works*. New York: Villard, 1992.

——, *Sheetrock & Shellac: A Thinking Person's Guide to the Art and Science of Home Improvement*. New York: Simon & Schuster, 2006.

Owen-Crocker, Gale R., *Dress in Anglo-Saxon England*. London: Boydell Press, 1986.

Palladio, Andrea, *The Four Books of Architecture* (facsimile edn). London: Isaac Ware, 1738.

Palmer, Arlene, *Glass in Early America*. New York: W. W. Norton, 1993.

Parissien, Steven, *Adam Style*. London: Phaidon, 1992.

——, *Palladian Style*. London: Phaidon, 1994.

——, *The Georgian House*. London: Aurum Press, 1995.

Paston-Williams, Sara, *The Art of Dining: A History of Cooking and Eating*. London: National Trust, 1993.

Patton, Mark, *Science, Politics and Business in the Work of Sir John Lubbock: A Man of Universal Mind*. Aldershot: Ashgate, 2007.

Peatross, C. Ford (ed.), *Historic America: Buildings, Structures and Sites*. Washington, D.C.: Library of Congress, 1983.

Petersen, Christian, *Bread and the British Economy, circa 1770–1870*. Aldershot: Scolar Press, 1995.

Petroski, Henry, *The Evolution of Useful Things*. New York: Vintage Books, 1994.

Pettigrew, Jane, *Tea: A Social History*. London: National Trust, 2001.

Picard, Liza, *Elizabeth's London: Everyday Life in Elizabethan London*. London: Orion Books, 2003.

——, *Restoration London*. London: Weidenfeld & Nicolson, 1997.

——, *Dr Johnson's London: Life in London, 1740–1770*. London: Weidenfeld & Nicolson, 2000.

——, *Victorian London: The Life of a City 1840–1870*. London: Phoenix, 2005.

Piponnier, Françoise, and Perrine Mane, *Dress in the Middle Ages*. New Haven: Yale University Press, 1997.

Planel, Philippe, *Locks and Lavatories: The Architecture of Privacy*. London: English Heritage, 2000.

Platt, Colin, *The Architecture of Medieval Britain: A Social History*. New Haven: Yale University Press, 1990.

Plumridge, Andrew, and Wim Meulenkamp, *Brickwork: Architecture and Design*. New York: Harry N. Abrams, 1993.

Pollan, Michael, *The Omnivore's Dilemma: A Natural History of Four Meals*. London: Penguin Books, 2007.

Pollard, Justin, *Seven Ages of Britain*. London: Hodder & Stoughton, 2003.

Porter, Roy, *Flesh in the Age of Reason*. London: Allen Lane, 2003.

Postgate, Raymond, *Story of a Year: 1848*. London: Jonathan Cape, 1955.

Pryce, Will, *Buildings in Wood: The History and Traditions of Architecture's Oldest Building Material*. New York: Rizzoli International, 2005.

Pullar, Philippa, *Consuming Passions: A History of English Food and Appetite*. London: Book Club Associates, 1977.

Quiney, Anthony, *Town Houses of Medieval Britain*. New Haven: Yale University Press, 2003.

Raby, Peter, *Alfred Russel Wallace: A Life*. London: Chatto & Windus, 2001.

Rackham, Oliver, *The History of the Countryside*. London: J. M. Dent & Sons, 1986.

Rapport, Mike, *1848: Year of Revolution*. New York: Basic Books, 2008.

Rathje, William, and Cullen Murphy, *Rubbish! The Archaeology of Garbage*. Tucson: University of Arizona Press, 2001.

Reader, John, *Cities*. London: William Heinemann, 2004.

——, *Propitious Esculent: The Potato in World History*. London: William Heinemann, 2008.

Renfrew, Colin, *The Prehistory of Orkney*. Edinburgh: Edinburgh University Press, 1985.

Reynolds, Andrew, *Later Anglo-Saxon England: Life and Landscape*. Stroud, Gloucestershire: Sutton Publishing, 1999.

Reynolds, Reginald, *Beds, With Many Noteworthy Instances of Lying On, Under or About Them*. London: Andre Deutsch, 1952.

Ribeiro, Aileen, *Dress in Eighteenth-Century Europe, 1715–1789*. London: B. T. Batsford, 1984.

Richardson, Tim, *The Arcadian Friends: Inventing the English Landscape*. London: Bantam Press, 2007.

Riis, Jacob A., *How the Other Half Lives: Studies Among the Poor*. London: Sampson Low, Marston, Searle & Rivington, 1891.

Ritchie, Graham and Anna, *Scotland: Archaeology and Early History*. London: Thames and Hudson, 1981.

Ritchie, Anna, *Prehistoric Orkney*. London: Batsford, 1995.

Rivers, Tony, Dan Cruickshank, Gillian Darley and Martin Pawley, *The Name of the Room: A History of the British House and Home*. London: BBC, 1992.

Roach, Mary, *Bonk: The Curious Coupling of Sex and Science*. New York: W. W. Norton & Co., 2008.

Romer, John, *The History of Archaeology*. New York: Facts on File, 2001.

Root, Waverley, and Richard de Rochemont, *Eating in America: A History*. New York: William Morrow, 1976.

Rose, Michael, *The English Poor Law 1780–1930*. Newton Abbot: David & Charles, 1971.

Rosenthal, Joel T. (ed.), *Essays on Medieval Childhood: Responses to Recent Debates*. Donington, Lincolnshire: Shaun Tyas, 2007.

Roth, Leland M., *American Architecture: A History*. Boulder, Colorado: Westview Press, 2001.

Roueché, Berton, *Curiosities of Medicine: An Assembly of Medical Diversions 1552–1962*. London: Victor Gollancz, 1963.

Russell, E. John, *A History of Agricultural Science in Great Britain: 1620–1954*. London: George Allen & Unwin, 1966.

Rybczynski, Witold, *Home: A Short History of an Idea*. London: Pocket Books, 1987.

——, *Waiting for the Weekend*. New York: Viking, 1991.

——, *City Life: Urban Expectations in a New World*. London: Scribner, 1995.

——, *A Clearing in the Distance: Frederick Law Olmsted and America in the Nineteenth Century*. New York: Scribner, 1999.

——, *The Look of Architecture*. New York: Oxford University Press, 2001.

——, *The Perfect House: A Journey with the Renaissance Master Andrea Palladio*. New York: Scribner, 2002.

Salmon, Frank, *Building on Ruins: The Rediscovery of Rome and English Architecture*. Aldershot: Ashgate Press, 2000.

Salvadori, Mario, *Why Buildings Stand Up: The Strength of Architecture*. New York: W. W. Norton, 1980.

——, and Matthys Levy, *Structural Design in Architecture*. Englewood Cliffs, N.J.: Prentice-Hall, 1967.

Sambrook, Pamela A., *The Country House Servant*. Stroud,

Gloucestershire: Sutton Publishing/National Trust, 2004.

Savidge, Alan, *The Parsonage in England: Its History and Architecture*. London: SPCK, 1964.

Scheller, William G., *Barons of Business: Their Lives and Lifestyles*. Los Angeles: Beaux Arts Editions, 2002.

Schlereth, Thomas J., *Victorian America: Transformations in Everyday Life, 1876–1915*. New York: HarperCollins, 1991.

Schneer, Jonathan, *The Thames: England's River*. London: Little, Brown, 2005.

Schofield, John, *Medieval London Houses* (2nd edn). New Haven: Yale University Press, 2003.

Scott, Geoff, *Building Disasters and Failures: A Practical Report*. London: The Construction Press Ltd, 1976.

Scott, George Ryley, *The Story of Baths and Bathing*. London: T. Werner Laurie Ltd, 1939.

Selinus, Olle, *Essentials of Medical Geology: Impacts of the Natural Environment on Public Health*. Amsterdam: Elsevier, 2005.

Shapiro, Laura, *Something from the Oven: Reinventing Dinner in 1950s America*. New York: Viking, 2004.

Shorter, Edward, *The Making of the Modern Family*. London: Collins, 1976.

Simmons, I. G., *An Environmental History of Great Britain from 10,000 Years Ago to the Present*. Edinburgh: Edinburgh University Press, 2001.

——, *Global Environmental History: 10,000 BC to AD 2000*. Edinburgh: Edinburgh University Press, 2008.

Simo, Melanie L., *Loudon and the Landscape: From Country Seat to Metropolis*. New Haven: Yale University Press, 1988.

Simon, Linda: *Dark Light: Electricity and Anxiety from the Telegraph to the X-Ray*. Orland: Harvest/Harcourt, 2004.

Sinclair, David, *The Pound: A Biography*. London: Century, 2000.

Skaggs, Jimmy M., *The Great Guano Rush: Entrepreneurs and American Overseas Expansion*. New York: St Martin's Press, 1994.

Smith, Anthony, *The Body*. London: George Allen & Unwin, 1968.

Smith, Bernard J., and Patricia A. Warke (eds), *Processes of Urban Stone Decay*. London: Donhead, 1995.

Smollett, Tobias, *The Expedition of Humphry Clinker*. Athens, Georgia: University of Georgia Press, 1990.

Sokolov, Raymond, *Why We Eat What We Eat*. New York: Summit Books, 1991.

Solnit, Rebecca, *Wanderlust: A History of Walking*. London: Verso, 2002.

Southern, R. W., *The Making of the Middle Ages*. London: Hutchinson's University Library, 1953.

Spann, Edward K., *The New Metropolis: New York City, 1840–1857*. New York: Columbia University Press, 1981.

Sproule, Anna, *Lost Houses of Britain*. Newton Abbot: David & Charles, 1982.

Standage, Tom, *A History of the World in Six Glasses*. New York: Walker & Co., 2005.

Starkey, David, *Elizabeth: The Struggle for the Throne*. London: HarperCollins, 2001.

Steele, Valerie, *Fashion and Eroticism: Ideals of Feminine Beauty from the Victorian Era to the Jazz Age*. New York: Oxford University Press, 1985.

——, *The Corset: A Cultural History*. New Haven: Yale University Press, 2001.

Steinbach, Susie, *Women in England, 1760–1914: A Social History*. London: Weidenfeld & Nicolson, 2004.

Steingarten, Jeffrey, *The Man Who Ate Everything: And Other Gastronomic Feats, Disputes, and Pleasurable Pursuits*. New York: Alfred A. Knopf, 1998.

Stenton, F. M., *Anglo-Saxon England*. Oxford: Clarendon Press, 1971.

Stern, Robert A. M., *Pride of Place: Building the American Dream*. Boston: Houghton-Mifflin, 1986.

Stewart, Amy, *The Earth Moved: On the Remarkable Achievements of Earthworms*. London: Frances Lincoln, 2004.

Stewart, Rachel, *The Town House in Georgian London*. New Haven: Yale University Press, 2009.

Strasser, Susan, *Never Done: A History of American Housework*. New York: Pantheon, 1982.

Stringer, Chris, *Homo Britannicus: The Incredible Story of Human Life in Britain*. London: Allen Lane, 2006.

Strong, Roy, *Tudor and Jacobean Portraits*. London: HMSO, 1960.

——, *A Little History of the English Country Church*. London: Vintage Books, 2008.

Stroud, Dorothy, *Capability Brown*. London: Faber and Faber, 1999.

Sullivan, Robert, *Rats: A Year with New York's Most Unwanted Inhabitants*. London: Granta, 2005.

Summerson, John, *Architecture in Britain 1530 to 1830*. London: Penguin, 1963.

——, *The Unromantic Castle and Other Essays*. London: Thames & Hudson, 1990.

——, *The Life and Work of John Nash, Architect*. London: Allen & Unwin, 1980.

Sutherland, Daniel E., *The Expansion of Everyday Life, 1860–1876*. New York: Harper & Row, 1986.

Sweet, Rosemary, *Antiquaries: The Discovery of the Past in Eighteenth-Century Britain*. London: Hambledon, 2004.

Tannahill, Reay, *Food in History*. London: Eyre Methuen, 1973.

——, *Sex in History*. London: Abacus, 1981.

Taylor, Christopher, *Village and Farmstead: A History of Rural Settlement in England*. London: George Philip & Son, 1983.

Taylor, Derek, *Ritzy: British Hotels 1837–1987*. London: Milman Press, 2003.

Templer, John A., *The Staircase: Studies of Hazards, Falls and Safer Design*. Cambridge, Mass.: MIT Press, 1992.

Thane, Elswyth, *Potomac Squire*. New York: Duell, Sloan and Pearce, 1963.

Thomas, Charles, *Celtic Britain*. London: Thames & Hudson, 1936.

Thompson, E. P., *The Making of the English Working Class*. London: Penguin, 1968.

Thompson, F. M. C. (ed.), *The Cambridge Social History of Britain 1750–1950* (vol. 2). Cambridge: Cambridge University Press, 1990.

Thompson, M. W., *General Pitt-Rivers: Evolution and Archaeology in the Nineteenth Century*. Bradford-on-Avon: Moonraker Press, 1977.

Thornton, Peter, *Seventeenth-Century Interior Decoration in England, France and Holland*. New Haven: Yale University Press, 1979.

Thurber, James, *The Years with Ross*. New York: Ballantine Books, 1972.

Thurley, Simon, *Hampton Court: A Social and Architectural History*. New Haven: Yale University Press, 2003.

——, *Lost Buildings of Britain*. London: Viking, 2004.

Tinniswood, Adrian, *The Polite Tourist: A History of Country House Visiting*. London: National Trust, 1989.

Tipper, Jess, *The Grubenhaus in Anglo-Saxon England: An Analysis and Interpretation of the Evidence from a Most Distinctive Building Type*. Yedingham, North Yorkshire: Landscape Research Centre, 2004.

Tomalin, Claire, *Samuel Pepys: The Unequalled Self*. London: Viking, 2002.

Traill, David A., *Schliemann of Troy: Treasure and Deceit*. London: John Murray, 1995.

Trevelyan, G. M., *Illustrated English Social History, Volume 3: The Eighteenth Century*. London: Penguin, 1966.

Trigger, Bruce G., *Gordon Childe: Revolutions in Archaeology*. London: Thames & Hudson, 1980.

Trollope, Frances, *Domestic Manners of the Americans*. New York: Alfred A. Knopf, 1949.

Tuchman, Barbara, *A Distant Mirror: The Calamitous Fourteenth*

Century. New York: Knopf, 1978.

Tunis, Edwin, *Colonial Living*. Cleveland, Ohio: World Publishing, 1957.

Turner, Jack, *Spice: The History of a Temptation*. London: Vintage, 2005.

Turner, Roger, *Capability Brown and the Eighteenth-Century English Landscape*. London: Phillimore, 1999.

Uglow, Jenny, *A Little History of British Gardening*. London: Chatto & Windus, 2004.

Upton, Dell, and John Michael Vlatch (eds), *Common Places: Readings in American Vernacular Architecture*. Athens, Georgia: University of Georgia Press, 1986.

Vanderbilt II, Arthur, *Fortune's Children: The Fall of the House of Vanderbilt*. London: Michael Joseph, 1990.

Van Dulken, Stephen, *Inventing the Nineteenth Century: The Great Age of Victorian Inventions*. London: British Library, 2001.

Vidal, Gore, *The Last Empire: Essays 1992–2000*. New York: Doubleday, 2001.

Vinten-Johansen, Peter, Howard Brody, Nigel Paneth, Stephen Rachman and Michael Rip, *Cholera, Chloroform, and the Science of Medicine: A Life of John Snow*. Oxford: Oxford University Press, 2003.

Vitruvius (translated by Morris Hicky Morgan), *The Ten Books of Architecture*. Cambridge, Mass.: Harvard University Press, 1914.

Wagner, Gillian, *Barnardo*. London: Weidenfeld & Nicolson, 1979.

Waller, John, *The Real Oliver Twist: Robert Blincoe: A Life That Illuminates an Age*. Cambridge: Icon Books, 2005.

Walvin, James, *Beside the Seaside: A Social History of the Popular Seaside Holiday*. London: Allen Lane, 1978.

Ware, Susan (ed.), *Forgotten Heroes*. New York: Free Press, 1998.

Warner, Jessica, *Craze: Gin and Debauchery in an Age of Reason*. New York: Four Walls Eight Windows, 2002.

Watkin, David, *Regency: A Guide and Gazetteer*. London: Barrie & Jenkins, 1982.

Watts, Sheldon, *Epidemics and History: Disease, Power and Imperialism*. New Haven: Yale University Press, 1997.

Waugh, Alexander, *Fathers and Sons*. London: Review Books, 2004.

Webster, Robin G. M. (ed.), *Stone Cleaning and the Nature, Soiling and Decay Mechanisms of Stone*. London: Donhead, 1992.

Weightman, Gavin, *The Frozen-Water Trade: A True Story*. New York: Hyperion, 2003.

——, *The Industrial Revolutionaries: The Creation of the Modern World, 1776–1914*. London: Atlantic Books, 2007.

Weinreb, Ben, and Christopher Hibbert, *The London Encyclopaedia*. London: Macmillan, 1985.

Weisman, Alan, *The World Without Us*. London: Virgin Books, 2007.

West, Anthony James, *The Shakespeare First Folio: The History of the Book* (2 vols). Oxford: Oxford University Press, 2001.

Wharton, Edith, and Ogden Codman, Jr, *The Decoration of Houses*. New York: W. W. Norton, 1998.

Wheen, Francis, *Karl Marx*. London: Fourth Estate, 1999.

White, Gilbert, *The Natural History of Selborne*. London: Penguin, 1977.

Wilbur, Marguerite Eyer, *The East India Company and the British Empire in the Far East*. New York: Richard R. Smith, 1945.

Wilkinson, Philip, *The Shock of the Old: A Guide to British Buildings*. London: Channel 4 Books, 2001.

Willes, Margaret, *Reading Matters: Five Centuries of Discovering Books*. New Haven: Yale University Press, 2008.

Wilson, Bee, *Swindled: From Poison Sweets to Counterfeit Coffee – the Dark History of the Food Cheats*. London: John Murray, 2008.

Winkle, Kenneth J., *The Young Eagle: The Rise of Abraham Lincoln*.

Dallas: Taylor Trade Publishing, 2001.

Wise, Sarah, *The Italian Boy: Murder and Grave-Robbery in 1830s London*. London: Jonathan Cape, 2004.

Wolmar, Christian, *Fire and Steam: How the Railways Transformed Britain*. London: Atlantic Books, 2007.

Wood, Margaret, *The English Medieval House*. London: Bracken Books, 1983.

Wood, Peter, *Poverty and the Workhouse in Victorian Britain*. Stroud, Gloucestershire: Sutton Publishing, 1991.

Woodforde, John, *The History of Vanity*. London: St Martin's Press, 1992.

Woolf, Virginia, *The London Scene*. London: Snow Books, 1975.

Worsley, Giles, *England's Lost Houses from the Archives of Country Life*. London: Aurum Press, 2002.

Wright, Lawrence, *Warm and Snug: The History of the Bed*. London: Routledge & Kegan Paul, 1962.

——, *Clean and Decent: The Fascinating History of the Bathroom and the Water-Closet*. London: Penguin, 2000.

Wright, Ronald, *A Short History of Progress*. Toronto: Anansi Press, 2004.

Yafa, Stephen, *Cotton: The Biography of a Revolutionary Fiber*. New York: Penguin, 2006.

Yarwood, Doreen, *The Architecture of England: From Prehistoric Times to the Present Day*. London: B. T. Batsford, 1963.

Yergin, Daniel, *The Prize: The Epic Quest for Oil, Money, and Power*. New York: Simon & Schuster, 1991.

Youings, Joyce, *Sixteenth Century England*. London: Penguin, 1984.

For Notes and Sources please go to
www.billbryson.co.uk/at home

Acknowledgements

As ever, I am much indebted to many people for expert help and guidance in the preparation of this book, in particular the following:

In England: Professors Tim Burt, Maurice Tucker and Mark White of Durham University; the Reverend Nicholas Holtam of St Martin-in-the-Fields Church, London; the Very Reverend Michael Sadgrove of Durham Cathedral; Keith Blackmore of *The Times*; Beth McHattie and Philip Davies of English Heritage; Aosaf Afzal, Dominic Reid and Keith Moore of the Royal Society; and the staff of the London Library and Durham University Library.

In the United States: Elizabeth Chew, Bob Self, Susan Stein, Richard Gilder and Bill Beiswanger of Monticello; Dennis Pogue of Mount Vernon; Jan Dempsey of the Wenham Public Library in Massachusetts; and the staff of the Lauinger Library at Georgetown University and Drake University Library in Des Moines.

I am also indebted in ways too numerous to cite to Carol Heaton, Fred Morris, Gerry Howard, Marianne

Velmans, Deborah Adams, Sheila Lee, Dan McLean, Alison Barrow, Larry Finlay, Andrew Orme, Daniel Wiles, and Tom and Nancy Jones. I must express particular thanks to my children Catherine and Sam for much heroic and good-natured assistance. Above all, and as always, my greatest thanks is to my dear and infinitely patient wife, Cynthia.

List of Illustrations

or Octagon, Fonthill Abbey, engraving after George Cattermole, 1823: © Historical Picture Archive/ Corbis.

p. 273   'Table glass including decanters, claret jugs and a carafe', from *The Book of Household Management* by Isabella Mary Beeton, 1892: © 2009 The British Library.

p. 298   'Over London by Rail', engraving by Gustave Doré from *London: a Pilgrimage* by Gustave Doré and Blanchard Jerrold, 1872.

p. 308   Eiffel Tower under construction at 110 metres high, Paris, 1888: Topfoto/Roger-Viollet.

p. 342   Patent for the 'Little Nipper' mousetrap invented by James Henry Atkinson, filed 27 June 1899 and published as GB 13277/1899: courtesy British Library.

p. 367   *The Rake's Levée*, plate II from 'A Rake's Progress' by William Hogarth, 1735: © Mary Evans Picture Library/Alamy.

p. 415   Sketch of the Villa Rotonda, Vicenza, by Sir Charles Barry, 1820: RIBA Library Drawings Collection; and nineteenth-century engraving of Monticello, Virginia.

p. 438   'Perspective of a staircase' from *A compleat treatise on perspective* by Thomas Malton, 1779: RIBA Library Photographs Collection.

p. 463   'Four-Pointed Urethral Ring' from *On the Pathology and Treatment of Spermatorrhoea* by John Laws Milton, 1887: Wellcome Library, London.

p. 518   Construction of the great sewage tunnels near Old Ford, Bow, 1859–65, wood engraving: Wellcome Library, London.

Index

The Life and Times of the Thunderbolt Kid
Travels round my childhood
Bill Bryson

---

*'Is this the most cheerful book I've ever read? . . .
Hilarious . . . A lovely happy book'*
EVENING STANDARD

BILL BRYSON'S first travel book opened with the immortal line, 'I come from Des Moines. Somebody had to.' In this deeply funny new book, he travels back in time to explore the ordinary kid he once was, in the curious world of 1950s America. It was a happy time, when almost everything was good for you, including DDT, cigarettes and nuclear fallout. This is a book about one boy's growing up. But in Bryson's hands, it becomes everyone's story, one that will speak volumes – especially to anyone who has ever been young.

*'Bryson at his best: Laugh out loud . . . Rollicking good
stories laced with a savagery that his nice-guy voice makes
both funny and affectionate'*
OBSERVER

*'Funny, effortlessly readable . . . Always manages to slam on the
brakes with a good joke just when things might get sentimental'*
DAILY MAIL

*'Wittily incisive . . . Like Alan Bennett, Bryson can play the
teddy-bear and then deliver a sudden, grizzly-style swipe . . .
Might tell us as much about the oddities of the American way
as a dozen think-tanks'*
INDEPENDENT

*'His greatest gift is as a humorist, so it is the snickers, the
guffaws and the undignified belly laughs he delivers on almost
every page that make it worth buying'*
SYDNEY MORNING HERALD

9780552772549

A Short History of Nearly Everything

Bill Bryson

'It deserves to sell as many copies as there are protons in the full stop that ends this review (at least 500,000,000,000).
MAIL ON SUNDAY

'The very book I have been looking for most of my life . . . trunkloads of information, amazing stories and extraordinary personalities'
DAILY MAIL

BILL BRYSON describes himself as a reluctant traveller, but even when he stays safely at home he can't contain his curiosity about the world around him. *A Short History of Nearly Everything* is his quest to understand everything that has happened from the Big Bang to the rise of civilization – how we got from there, being nothing at all, to here, being us. The ultimate eye-opening journey through time and space, revealing the world in a way most of us have never seen it before.

'Brims with strange and amazing facts . . . Destined to become a modern classic of science writing'
NEW YORK TIMES BOOK REVIEW

'The amount of ground covered is truly impressive . . . It's hard to imagine a better rough guide to science'
GUARDIAN

'A thoroughly enjoyable, as well as educational, experience. Nobody who reads it will ever look at the world around them in the same way again'
DAILY EXPRESS

'A travelogue of science, with a witty, engaging, and well-informed guide who loves his patch and is desperate to share its delights with us'
THE TIMES

9780552997041

Icons of England

Edited by Bill Bryson

Foreword by HRH The Prince of Wales

A salute to the English countryside

*'There are particular places in England that come as close to
perfection as you're ever likely to find on this planet'*
Bill Bryson

Bill Bryson invited over ninety of our best-loved writers, broad-
casters and commentators to pick their 'icons of England'. The
resulting celebration of the English countryside is an idiosyncratic and personal collection that ranges across landscape,
history, cherished memories and that most English of subjects,
the weather.

Contributions from, among others:
Kate Adie   Antony Beevor   Alan Titchmarsh
Sebastian Faulks   Michael Palin   Andrew Marr   Rick Stein
Jo Brand   Sister Wendy Beckett   Jonathan Dimbleby
Wendy Cope   Joan Bakewell   Dick Francis
Robert Macfarlane   Melvyn Bragg   Zac Goldsmith
Simon Jenkins   Eric Clapton   John Sergeant   Kevin Spacey
Gavin Pretor-Pinney   Libby Purves   Alexei Sayle
John Sergeant   Jon Snow   Kevin Spacey   Francis Wheen
Benjamin Zephaniah   Adrian Chiles   Trisha Goddard
Simon Barnes   Anthony Sher   Ronald Blythe

9780552776356

Down Under

Bill Bryson

IT IS THE DRIEST, flattest, hottest, most desiccated, infertile and climatically aggressive of all the inhabited continents and still Australia teems with life – a large portion of it quite deadly. In fact, Australia has more things that can kill you in a very nasty way than anywhere else.

Ignoring such dangers – and yet curiously obsessed by them Bill Bryson journeyed to Australia and promptly fell in love with the country. And who can blame him? The people are cheerful, extrovert, quick-witted and unfailingly obliging: their cities are safe and clean and nearly always built on water; the food is excellent; the beer is cold and the sun nearly always shines. Life doesn't get much better than this . . .

9780552997034